BTEC Level 2 Firsts in
SPORT

Second Edition

Darrel Barsby, Rob Commons, Gez Rizzo, Michala Swales, Ian Wood and Ray Barker

OXFORD
UNIVERSITY PRESS

OXFORD
UNIVERSITY PRESS

Great Clarendon Street, Oxford OX2 6DP

Oxford University Press is a department of the University of Oxford.

It furthers the University's objective of excellence in research, scholarship, and education by publishing worldwide in

Oxford   New York   Auckland   Cape Town   Dar es Salaam   Hong Kong
Karachi   Kuala Lumpur   Madrid   Melbourne   Mexico City   Nairobi
New Delhi   Shanghai   Taipei   Toronto

With offices in

Argentina   Austria   Brazil   Chile   Czech Republic   France   Greece
Guatemala   Hungary   Italy   Japan   Poland   Portugal   Singapore
South Korea   Switzerland   Thailand   Turkey   Ukraine   Vietnam

Oxford is a registered trade mark of Oxford University Press
in the UK and in certain other countries

© Oxford University Press 2013

The moral rights of the author have been asserted

Database right Oxford University Press (maker)

First published 2013

British Library Cataloguing in Publication Data

Data available

978 019 912991 1

10 9 8 7 6 5 4

Printed in Malaysia by Vivar Printing Sdn. Bhd.

Paper used in the production of this book is a natural, recyclable product made from wood grown in sustainable forests. The manufacturing process conforms to the environmental regulations of the country of origin.

Acknowledgements

The publishers would like to thank the following for permission to reproduce photographs: **p.4:** Nick Potts/PA Archive/Press Association Images; **p.4:** Jaggat/Shutterstock.com; **p.5:** Sipa Press/Rex Features; **p.5:** Wayne Drought/Associated Press; **p.5:** Xinhua/Landov; **p.4:** Jeff Lewis/Associated Press; **p.6:** Press Association Images; **p.6:** Nick Ansell/PA Archive/Press Association Images; **p.7:** PA Wire/PA Archive/Press Association Images; **p.7:** Matt Dunham/Associated Press; **p.12:** Press Association Images; **p.13:** Erik Isakson/Corbis; **p.13:** iStockphoto; **p.14:** Shutterstock.com; **p.15:** Dick Makin Imaging; **p.15:** Brass Ring Fitness; **p.16:** Press Association Images; **p.17:** Lynne Sladky/Associated Press; **p.17:** EMPICS/PA Images; **p.18:** PA/PA Photos; **p.27:** BSIP, MAY/Science Photo Library; **p.28:** Brian McEntire/iStockphoto; **p.30:** Pavel Rahman/Associated Press; **p.30:** Getty Images; **p.32:** Associated Press; **p.34:** Press Association Images; **p.34:** Photographers Direct; **p.34:** Press Association Images; **p.35:** Shutterstock.com; **p.35:** ABACA; **p.35:** Press Association Images; **p.35:** Associated Press; **p.35:** Istock; **p.36:** Press Association Images; **p.36:** Shutterstock.com; **p.36:** Fotolia; **p.37:** Press Association Images; **p.41:** Dartfish UK; **p.33:** Alessandra Tarantino/AP/Press Association Images; **p.38:** IMAGEMORE Co., Ltd./Alamy; **p.38:** Fernando Vergara/AP/Press Association Images; **p.38:** Christian Liewig/TempSport/Corbis; **p.45:** Newspix/Rex Features; **p.46:** Popperfoto/Getty Images; **p.47:** Arsenal FC via Getty Images; **p.50:** David Davies/PA Archive/Press Association Images; **p.52:** Dave Thompson/PA Archive/Press Association Images; **p.54:** Hannah Johnston/Getty Images; **p.56:** ARND WIEGMANN/Reuters/Corbis; **p.57:** Dave Hunt/EPA; **p.61:** Phil Oldham/Colorsport/Corbis; **p.70:** Press Association Images; **p.77:** Press Association Images; **p.77:** Tim Clayton/Corbis; **p.77:** Press Association Images; **p.79:** AFP/Getty Images; **p.79:** Pete Niesen/Shutterstock.com; **p.80–81:** PA/Press Association Images; **p.82:** A Woodman; **p.90:** Eliza Snow/iStockphoto; **p.90:** Imaj/iStockphoto; **p.90:** PetrePlesea/iStockphoto; **p.90:** MoniqueRodriguez/iStockphoto; **p.93:** EMPICS Sport/PA Photos; **p.100:** Keith Morris/Alamy; **p.100:** Amana Images inc./Alamy; **p.103:** Van Hilversum/Alamy; **p.104:** Matt Dunham/Associated Press; **p.104:** PA/PA Photos; **p.110:** Dick Makin/Dick Makin Imaging; **p.111:** Jeff Morgan/Alamy; **p.103:** Clarissa Leahy; **p.104:** asiseeit/Istock; **p.107:** Adam Davy/EMPICS Sport; **p.112:** © Michael DeYoung/Corbis; **p.113:** Stephen Finn/Shutterstock; **p.118:** Diane Diederich/iStockphoto; **p.126:** Hannes Eichinger/Shutterstock; **p.120:** Kirk Strickland/Istock; **p.120:** Pete Saloutos/Shutterstock; **p.120:** CHEN WS/Shutterstock; **p.121:** Johnny Green/PA Archive/Press Association Images; **p.121:** indykb/iStockphoto.com; **p.121:** indykb/iStockphoto.com; **p.122:** Susannah Ireland/Rex Features; **p.123:** Xinhua/Landov; **p.124:** Lehtikuva OY/Rex Features; **p.129:** John Walton/EMPICS Sport/Press Association Images; **p.129:** ABACA; **p.129:** Fuse/Getty Images; **p.129:** Sylvaine Thomas/Fotolia; **p.129:** LANDOV/Press Association Images; **p.129:** David J. Phillip/Associated Press; **p.132:** Corbis; **p.134:** STEVE GSCHMEISSNER/Science Photo Library; **p.139:** 3D4MEDICAL.COM/Science Photo Library; **p.140:** Getty Images; **p.142:** David Davies/PA Archive/Press Association Images; **p.142:** Getty Images for adidas/Getty Images Publicity/Getty Images; **p.143:** Cathy Yeulet/123rf; **p.143:** Scott Heavey/Getty Images Sport/Getty Images; **p.143:** Aleksandar Hubenov/123rf; **p.144:** Bryn Lennon/Getty Images Sport/Getty Images; Matthew Lewis/Getty Images Sport/Getty Images; **p.145:** Glasgow 2014 Commonwealth Games; **p.145:** Dan Kitwood/Getty Images Sport/Getty Images; **p.147:** Jon Kopaloff/FilmMagic/Getty Images; **p.147:** Getty Images for Speedo/Getty Images Publicity/Getty Images; **p.147:** ANDREW YATES/AFP/Getty Images; **p.148:** AISPIX by Image Source/Shutterstock; **p.148:** Christopher Lee/Getty Images Entertainment/Getty Images; **p.149:** Laszlo Szirtesi/Shutterstock.com; **p.151:** Copyright Crown; **p.153:** Pukka Pies Ltd; **p.153:** Mike Ehrmann/Getty Images; **p.153:** Stuart Franklin/Getty Images Sport/Getty Images; **p.153:** Ian Walton/Getty Images Sport/Getty Images; **p.154:** Copyright UK Sport; **p.154:** Fei Maohua/Xinhua Press/Corbis; **p.156:** Tony Bowler/Shutterstock.com; **p.157:** Walter Arce/Action Sports Photography/Dreamstime; **p.157:** Copyright Advertising Standards Authority Limited; **p.157:** jaggat/Shutterstock.com; **p.160:** David W. Leindecker/Shutterstock.com; **p.168:** Evabattrick/dreamstime; **p.168:** Dotshock/Shutterstock; **p.168:** Tbradford/iStockphoto; **p.171:** Monkey Business Images/Shutterstock; **p.173:** Nigel Paul Monckton/Shutterstock; **p.173:** Morgan Lane Photography/Shutterstock; **p.173:** Kostas Tsipos/Shutterstock; **p.173:** Monkey Business Images/Shutterstock; **p.173:** Fotolia; **p.174:** Liv friis-larsen/Shutterstock; **p.174:** Adisa/Shutterstock; **p.174:** Matthewennisphotography/iStockphoto; **p.175:** Copyright Crown; **p.177 & 181:** Crown copyright material is reproduced with the permission of the Controller Office of Public Sector Information (OPSI); **p.184:** Rex Features; **p.186:** Garo/Phanie/Rex Features; **p.186–188:** Copyright Drinkaware; **p.189:** Randy Platt/iStockphoto; **p.189:** Roger Bamber/Alamy; **p.191:** Four Oaks/Shutterstock; **p.192:** Ahmed Maher/Shutterstock.com; **p.192:** Cheryl Ann Quigley/Shutterstock.com; **p.192:** Nick R./istockphoto; **p.192:** Diego Barbieri/Shutterstock.com; **p.192:** Csakisti/Dreamstime; **p.194:** Alexander Raths/123rf; **p.197:** Offside/Rex Features; **p.199:** Paul Morton/iStockphoto; **p.200:** HSE Books; **p.201:** EMPICS Sports Photo Agency/PA Images; **p.204:** Patsy Michaud/Shutterstock; **p.205:** © DIEGO AZUBEL/epa/Corbis; **p.207:** YAKOBCHUK VASYL/Shutterstock; **p.209:** Stu Forster/Getty Images Sport/Getty Images; **p.209:** Julien Behal/PA Images; **p.209:** Imaga/Icon SMI; **p.209:** EMPICS Sport/PA Photos; **p.209:** Rebecca Naden/PA Archive Press/Press Association Images; **p.211:** Laurence Griffiths/Getty Images Sport/Getty Images; **p.212:** Bob Winsett; **p.213:** Alison Bowden/Fotolia; **p.209:** Julien Behal/PA Images; **p.219:** Vince Bucci/Stringer; **p.215:** Mölnlycke Health Care; **p.222:** Bradley Mason/iStockphoto; **p.222:** Rob Friedman/iStockphoto; **p.222:** Yui Mok/PS Archive/PA Images; **p.222:** Press Association Images; **p.230–231:** Dick Makin/Dick Makin Imaging; **p.232:** PA/Press Association Images; **p.235:** Yuri Arcurs/Fotolia; **p.233:** Hybrid Images/cultura/Corbis; **p.241:** © Adrian Sherratt/Alamy; **p.241:** John Lumb/Shutterstock; **p.242:** Getty Images; **p.244:** Michael DeYoung/Corbis; **p.245:** Oliver Self/Justin Deeny; **p.245:** Natthawat Wongrat/Shutterstock; **p.245:** BUCS/Careers-in-Sport.co.uk; **p.247:** StockLite/Shutterstock; **p.249:** Supri Suharjoto/Shutterstock; **p.250:** Robert Kneschke/Shutterstock; **p.251:** Greg Epperson/Shutterstock; **p.252:** Press Association Images; **p.253:** Elenaphotos21/Shutterstock.com; **p.253:** Maxisport/Shutterstock.com; **p.254:** StfW/Alamy; **p.254:** Hawkeye; **p.258:** Stephane Reix/For Picture/Corbis; **p.259:** Shakh Aivazov/Associated Press; **p.260:** SAURABH DAS/Associated Press; **p.263:** Pete Saloutos/CORBIS; **p.264:** Fabrice Coffrini/AFP/GettyImages; **p.266:** Scott Barbour/Getty Images Sport/Getty Images; **p.266:** Jackson Laizure/Getty Images Sport/Getty Images; **p.268:** Paul Chiasson/Assciated Press; **p.268:** Patrick Tuohy/Shutterstock.com; **p.269:** Firstsignal/istockphoto.com; **p.269:** Scott Heavey/Getty Images Sport/Getty Images; **p.270:** Photosport Int/Rex Features; **p.270:** Neale Cousland/Shutterstock.com; **p.273:** Duif du Toit/Gallo Images/Getty Images Sport/Getty Images; **p.280:** 3drenderings/Shutterstock..

Artwork by Q2A

Cover photo by Peter Bernik/Shutterstock.

The authors and publisher are grateful to the following for permission to reprint copyright material:

p.145 *XX Commonwealth Games* 'Mission, Vision and Values' statement from the official website at http://www.glasgow2014.com, and the Glasgow 2014 Logo, copyright © Glasgow 2014 Ltd, reproduced by permission of Glasgow 2014 Ltd.

p.245 *Careers in Sport* web page: 'Football Development Manager' from www.careers-in-sport.co.uk reproduced by permission of Sport IQ Publications Ltd.

Every effort has been made to contact copyright holders of material reproduced in this book. If notified, the publishers will be pleased to rectify any errors or omissions at the earliest opportunity.

Contents

Unit 1: Fitness for Sport and Exercise

Components of fitness

A person is considered to be physically fit if they are able to carry out all of their daily tasks easily and without becoming fatigued. However, being 'fit for sport' requires a much higher level of fitness than that needed for activities such as walking the dog or gardening.

Fitness for sport can be broken down into eleven individual components, grouped under two main headings: physical fitness and skill-related fitness. A good level of both physical fitness and skill-related fitness is needed to be successful in most sports, but the relative importance of each component is dependent upon the sport chosen. A component that may be vitally important for one sport may be much less important for another. Elite athletes need a thorough understanding of all the components in order to be successful, so that training sessions can be tailored to their individual needs.

Physical fitness

Aerobic endurance: This is a measure of how efficiently you are able to keep your muscles supplied with nutrients and oxygen while you are exercising. Aerobic endurance is sometimes called cardiorespiratory endurance, aerobic fitness or cardiorespiratory fitness.

The cardiorespiratory system is made up of:

- The cardiovascular system: This is responsible for transporting oxygen and nutrients to all the tissues in the body and removing waste products, such as carbon dioxide, from them. The three main components of this circulatory system are the heart, the blood and the blood vessels.
- The respiratory system: This is responsible for bringing oxygen into the body. It has two main components: the lungs and the airways.

Marathon runners and distance cyclists require a high level of aerobic endurance to be able to keep working over a long period of time in a race.

Your aerobic endurance can be improved by taking part in aerobic training.

Muscular endurance: You have a good level of muscular endurance if your muscles can keep exerting force for a long time. This can mean that they are able to contract many times, for example, when running a marathon, or it can mean that they can sustain one contraction for a long period of time, for example, when pulling in a tug of war. Muscles need a good supply of oxygen (see aerobic endurance) and a good supply of energy in the form of glycogen, a type of sugar that is broken down to release energy.

Professional footballers need a high level of muscular endurance to keep them moving around the pitch for 90 minutes.

Muscular endurance can be improved by taking part in weight-training activities, by running or by regularly performing exercises such as sit-ups and press-ups.

> **Physical fitness**

Body composition: This is a measure of how much of your body is made up of fat-free mass, of vital organs, and how much is made up of fat. It is important to have a good balance of the two but sports players usually have a greater proportion of muscle.

Some sports performers, such as rowers, require a large muscle mass to give them lots of power and strength, but others, such as marathon runners, require a lower muscle mass so that they don't have to carry 'extra' body mass as they are running. Some sports performers, such as sumo wrestlers, even require quite a large mass of body fat to be successful.

Everyone is born with a predisposition to a particular body composition, although small changes can be made by varying your diet and the amount/type of exercise that you take part in. The important thing is to have the correct body composition for your sport.

Flexibility: This is the ability to move all your joints through their full range of movements smoothly. Flexibility is determined by how elastic the ligaments and tendons are at a joint, how strong the muscles are that pull against the joint, and the shape of the bones that form the joint. Most joints are designed to give either strength or flexibility, so the shape of the bones is usually the most important factor in determining flexibility. For example, the shoulder joint is made up of a ball-shaped bone (the end of the humerus) and a cup-shaped bone (the end of the scapula), allowing lots of movement in many directions.

Gymnasts have to be flexible so that they can twist their bodies into different shapes when performing routines or vaults.

Flexibility can be improved by taking part in lots of stretching exercises on a regular basis.

Speed: This is how long it takes for an individual or an object to travel a certain distance, and the faster something moves, the greater its speed.

$$\text{Speed} = \frac{\text{Distance}}{\text{Time}}$$

Speed is measured in metres per second (m/s).

For example, when Usain Bolt runs 100 metres in 9.58 seconds, he is running at a speed of:

$$\frac{100}{9.58} = 10.44 \text{ m/s}$$

The three main types of speed are:

- Accelerative speed, the speed with which you start moving faster, which is seen in sprints of up to 30 metres.
- Pure speed, your maximum speed, which is seen in sprints of up to 60 metres.
- Speed endurance, being able to maintain your maximum speed or near your maximum speed for a period of time, which is seen during sprints with short recovery periods in between.

Speed is important in many team sports to help players beat their opponents. For example, netballers need speed so that they can get into spaces more quickly than their opponents and rugby players need speed to be able to beat their opponents to the try-line.

Speed is often said to be something that we are born with, although some improvements can be made by taking part in strength training and sprint training.

Muscular strength: This is the amount of force, measured in kilograms (kg) or Newtons (N), that can be generated by a muscle when it is contracting. There are lots of different types of strength but the main two are:

- Explosive strength, the amount of force that can be exerted in one quick, powerful contraction, which is useful in sports such as the javelin and the high jump. It is closely linked to power.
- Dynamic strength, the amount of force that can be exerted repeatedly by a muscle, which is useful when completing sit-ups or when cycling. It is closely linked to muscular endurance.

Strength can be increased by taking part in weight training. Smaller weights are lifted many times to improve dynamic strength and heavier weights are lifted fewer times to improve explosive strength.

BRONZE

1. Choose five sports and, for each one, describe the three most important components of physical fitness.

SILVER

2. Choose five sports and, for each one, explain the three most important components of physical fitness.

3. Rank the components of physical fitness, in order, from the most important to the least important, for each of the following sports performers: a footballer, a cyclist taking part in the Tour de France, and a swimmer in the 50-metre freestyle. Give reasons to justify your rankings.

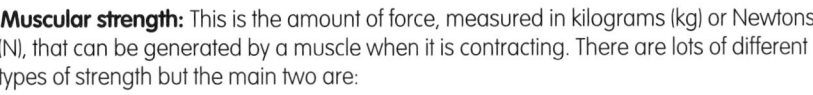

Skill-related fitness

Agility: Is the ability of a sports player to move and change direction quickly, precisely and under control. For example, a basketball player has to change direction quickly when dribbling and driving towards the basket. Training has little or no effect on improving agility.

Balance: Is the ability to keep the body stable, when still or moving, by keeping the centre of gravity over the base of support. There are two types of balance:

- A static balance is performed when little or no movement takes place – for example, during a headstand.
- A dynamic balance is performed when movement takes place during a balance – for example, during a cartwheel.

An individual's overall level of balance is not really something that can be trained, although the ability to perform a particular type of balance, such as a headstand, can be improved through practice.

Skill-related fitness

Coordination: Is the ability to move two or more parts of the body at the same time efficiently and accurately, while ensuring a smooth flow of movement. Even simple acts, such as walking, require a degree of coordination, but a much higher level of coordination is required when playing a tennis shot. Again, an individual's level of coordination cannot be improved through training, although the ability to perform a particular task can be improved through practice.

Power: Is the ability to combine strength with speed and is expressed as the time it takes to perform a task. Power is very closely linked to explosive strength. Power is needed in most sports, although it is more obvious in some. For example, boxers need power to be able to punch hard and fast, while golfers need power in order to hit the ball over a greater distance.

Reaction time: This is the time it takes to respond to a stimulus, such as a ball coming towards you when fielding in cricket. The shorter the amount of time it takes to respond, the quicker the reactions of the performer. Reaction time is incredibly important in events such as the 100 metres because the sprinter who responds fastest to the sound of the gun has a better chance of winning the race. Reaction time cannot be improved through training, although the time taken to respond to a simple stimulus, like the starting gun, can be improved through practice. It is likely, though, that this is more about anticipating the gun than responding to it.

BRONZE

4. For each component of skill-related fitness, name one sport that requires a high level of that component and one sport that requires a low level of that component. For example, reaction time is very important in sprint events but not very important for those competing in a marathon.

SILVER

5. Choose one sport and rank the components of skill-related fitness, in order, from the most important to the least important. Give an example, from your chosen sport, of each component in action. For example, rowers require a low level of agility because they do not have to change direction very often, other than to move forwards and backwards in a rhythm.

6. Rank the components of skill-related fitness, in order, from the most important to the least important, for each of the following sports performers: a footballer, a cyclist taking part in the Tour de France, and a swimmer in the 50-metre freestyle. Give reasons to justify your rankings.

Determining exercise intensity

In order for training to be effective, it has to be designed so that it is specific to each individual. And, as such, the intensity of the exercises should differ from person to person. What represents considerable aerobic stress for an untrained person will fall well below an elite athlete's requirements. The simplest method for calculating exercise intensity is to use a performer's working heart rate.

Maximum Heart Rate (MHR)

Before calculating a working heart rate, it is necessary to first calculate a performer's MHR, which can be defined as 'the maximum number of times a person's heart can contract in one minute'. This is done using the following equation:

$$MHR = 220 - age$$

Therefore a 20-year-old's MHR $= 220 - 20 = 200$ beats per minute (bpm)

Once we have calculated a person's MHR, we can then use the training pyramid to calculate their working heart rate.

The training pyramid

The training pyramid is a way of calculating how hard you need to train and how long each training session should be. Each section of the pyramid represents a different training zone and the higher the zone, the harder you need to work. The width of the zone represents the amount of time that you need to train in that zone. So, if you are working in the aerobic training zone, you would work for longer and have longer but fewer rest periods than you would if you were working in the speed zone, because the aerobic zone takes up a wider section of the pyramid.

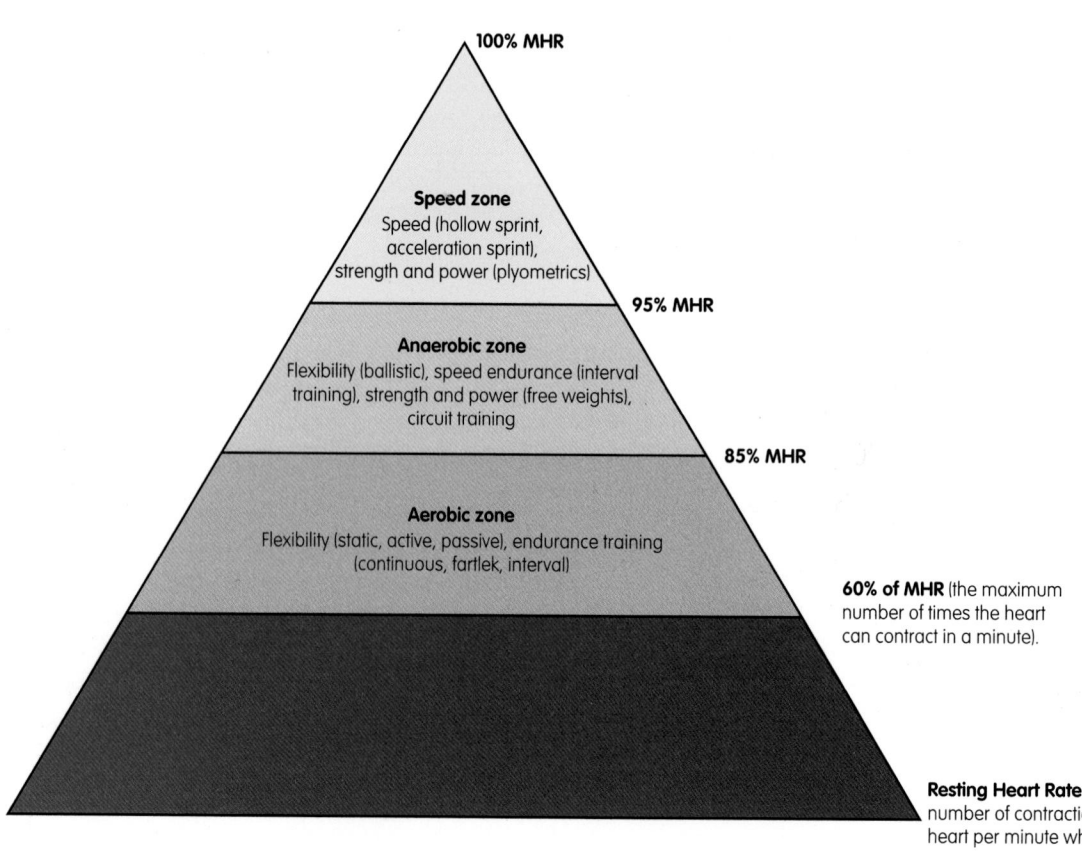

100% MHR

Speed zone
Speed (hollow sprint, acceleration sprint), strength and power (plyometrics)

95% MHR

Anaerobic zone
Flexibility (ballistic), speed endurance (interval training), strength and power (free weights), circuit training

85% MHR

Aerobic zone
Flexibility (static, active, passive), endurance training (continuous, fartlek, interval)

60% of MHR (the maximum number of times the heart can contract in a minute).

Resting Heart Rate (RHR, the number of contractions of the heart per minute when resting).

If a 20-year-old's MHR $= 220 - 20 = 200$bpm, then his training zones can be calculated as follows:

- The aerobic zone $= 60{-}85\%$ of 200bpm $= 120{-}170$bpm
- The anaerobic zone $= 85{-}95\%$ of 200bpm $= 170{-}190$bpm
- The speed zone $= 95{-}100\%$ of 200bpm $= 190{-}200$bpm

Therefore, a 20-year-old who wishes to undertake continuous training to improve his cardiovascular health and fitness should work hard enough to make his heart contract between 120bpm and 170bpm in order to train in the aerobic zone. Slower than 120bpm would have little or no training effect and above 170bpm would cause the performer to become fatigued too quickly.

The Borg Rating of Perceived Exertion Scale

In sports and exercise testing, the Borg Rating of Perceived Exertion Scale, or 'Borg RPE', is used to measure exercise intensity by asking a performer to rate their perceived level of exertion. Borg found that there is a direct relationship between how the performer feels, and their heart rate, breathing rate and working oxygen levels. Doctors use the scale to document a patient's exertion during health tests. Sports coaches use it to assess the intensity at which athletes work during training and competition.

There are a number of Borg RPE scales in existence but the most common is the Fifteen Point Scale.

6	20% effort
7	30% effort: very, very light intensity
8	40% effort
9	50% effort: very light intensity
10	55% effort
11	60% effort: fairly light intensity
12	65% effort
13	70% effort: somewhat hard intensity
14	75% effort
15	80% effort: hard intensity
16	85% effort
17	90% effort: very hard intensity
18	95% effort
19	100% effort: very, very hard intensity
20	Exhaustion

The Borg Rating of Perceived Exertion (RPE) Fifteen Point Scale.

Borg suggested that there was a direct relationship between a person's perceived exertion level and their heart rate so that:

RPE (Rating of Perceived Exertion) $\times$ 10 $=$ Heart Rate (HR)

Therefore, a person who perceives themselves to be working at around level 15 on the Borg RPE Fifteen Point Scale is likely to have a heart rate of around 150bpm at the time.

BRONZE

1. Suggest a suitable training zone for a 25-year-old javelin thrower.

2. Suggest a suitable training zone for a 25-year-old marathon runner.

SILVER

3. Apart from the difference in heart rates, what other differences would there be in the training schedules of the javelin thrower and the marathon runner? Why?

BRONZE

4. Using the BORG RPE Fifteen Point Scale, rate your perceived exertion for every sporting activity you perform over the period of one week.

SILVER

5. Look at the ratings you recorded for Activity 4 and justify each score.

Principles of training

Improving a performer's fitness levels requires training that adheres to the principles of training. The principles of training can be remembered using the acronym 'FITT for SPORT followed by some R&R'.

Frequency

Frequency refers to the number of times exercise is undertaken each week.

It is recommended that each of us should take part in a minimum of 30 minutes of physical activity three times each week, to achieve the minimal level of fitness required to live a healthy life. A top-class sportsperson will have to train a lot more than this to achieve success in their chosen sport.

Intensity

Intensity is how hard the exercise is.

While it is important for us to exercise at least three times a week, another important factor is the intensity at which we work. It is recommended that – to stay healthy – we

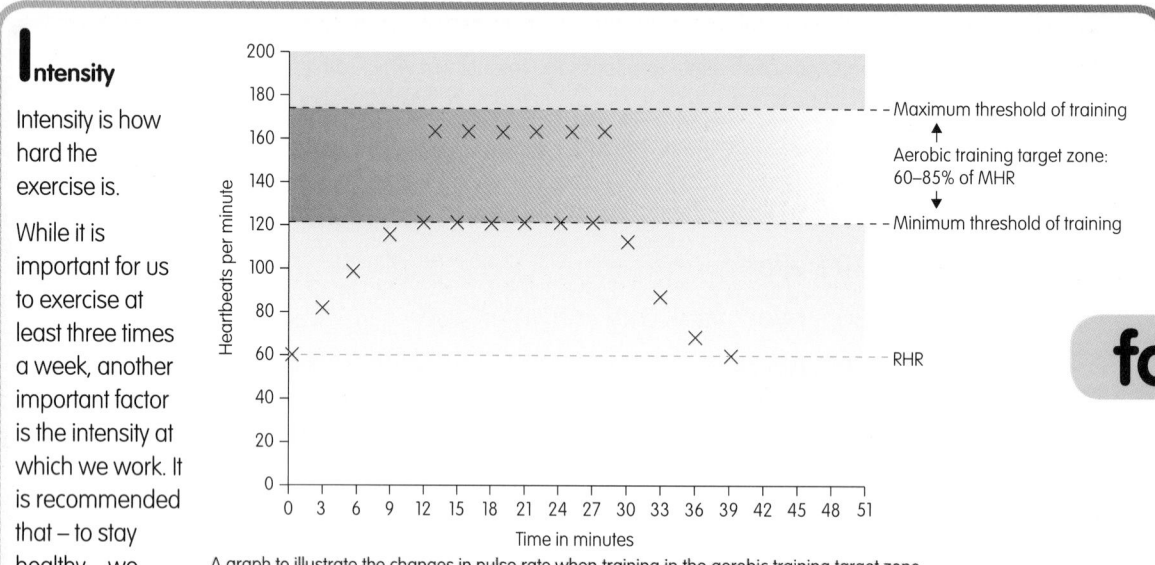

A graph to illustrate the changes in pulse rate when training in the aerobic training target zone.

must work in our target zone for at least 20 minutes of our minimum 30-minute sessions. When training for cardiovascular fitness our target zone is between 60 to 85 per cent of our MHR, and it is important that we train at this intensity because this is where our fitness will increase. When training for strength our target zone is between 60 to 85 per cent of the maximum weight we can lift.

Time

Time refers to how long each exercise session lasts.

It is important that we remain in the target zone for a minimum of 20 minutes to see improvements.

Type

Type refers to the nature of the exercise that the performer completes.

In order to keep training interesting and the performer motivated, it is essential that the type of training is varied, so that the performer does not complete the same activities every training session. For example, a long-distance runner may train on a track, run up and down hills, or train on the road.

for

BRONZE

1. List three ways that the intensity of exercise can be increased.

2. Write a paragraph to explain how fitness levels can be improved using FITT.

SILVER

3. Write a one-week training programme for a long-distance runner, using the FITT principles as the basis for your plan.

Specificity, and individual differences and needs

Specificity, and individual differences and needs means focusing training on activities relevant to an individual's sporting goals and needs.

To train for a particular sport or event, it is important that we apply appropriate training methods because each sport has its own specific requirements. Training programmes should include all the specific actions and skills that are used in the sport or event, and it is important that they are performed at game or event speed during training. Gymnasts and swimmers need to train differently, as do players of the same sport if they play in different positions.

When we plan a personal exercise programme, it is essential that we take the individual needs of the performer into account, so that they are appropriately challenged. A first-time marathon runner would not benefit from using a training plan designed for an elite marathon runner, for example, because their fitness levels would not be high enough. The less-experienced runner would find the programme too difficult and would risk injuring themselves.

Progressive overload

Progressive overload is about training at an appropriate intensity and gradually increasing the amount of stress we place on our bodies in order for fitness gains to occur. It means working above our minimum threshold of training (the minimum amount required to make fitness gains) and below our maximum threshold of training, in order to make fitness gains without risking injury. It does not mean training too hard or too much.

For example, a sportsperson looking to improve their muscular strength would need to gradually increase the amount of weight they lift in order to encourage the muscles to adapt to lifting heavier weights, therefore, increasing muscle growth.

adaptatiOn

By ensuring that you progressively overload your body during training you are encouraging it to adapt to the new stresses being placed upon it and it becomes stronger or faster than it was as a result. Adaptation occurs in the recovery period after a training session.

Reversibility

Our bodies need to be placed under stress in order to improve. If our bodies are not challenged, any strength, tone, or skill gains that have previously been made will be reversed.

Our bodies lose any gains made as a result of training three times faster than the gains were made. It really is 'use it or lose it', so it is important not to get injured or become demotivated.

variaTion

It is really important to vary a training programme so that you don't get bored and you continue to enjoy your exercise sessions.

followed by some

Rest & Recovery

Overtraining occurs when the intensity of exercise exceeds the body's ability to recover. A performer who has overtrained will cease to make progress, and can even begin to lose strength and fitness. Overtraining is a common problem in weight training, but runners and other athletes also experience it. It is important to remember that our bodies require time to rest and recover after exercise, so there is time for adaptation to take place. Even top-class athletes need to build rest and recovery time into their training programmes!

BRONZE

4. There are potential dangers with regards to overtraining, and not giving yourself rest and recovery time between training sessions. Write down as many reasons why overtraining can have a negative effect on our fitness as you can think of.

5. Different players in the same team sometimes have different fitness requirements. How many sports, other than football, can you think of where two team members have different training needs? How do their training needs differ and why?

SILVER

6. Develop a training programme for an elite marathon runner and a first-time marathon runner, taking their different training needs into account.

Fitness training methods

Fitness training is much more technical than simply going for a jog each day. Each of the components of fitness has to be trained in a different way and different training methods will develop some components more than others. Because all sports require a mixture of the components of fitness and everyone has different needs, participants should take part in a range of training methods.

Preparation for training

Before undertaking any form of training, it is important to consider the safety aspects of the session. This includes being aware of:

- The safe and correct use of any equipment used.
- The safe and correct application of training techniques.
- Undertaking a warm-up before beginning training.
- Performing an appropriate cool-down after training to aid recovery.
- Applying the FITT principles correctly for each training method.
- Ensuring that the method of training is appropriate for the component of fitness you are trying to develop (that you are following the principle of Specificity).

Warming up

Warming up properly improves performance because it prepares the mind and body for the main activity.

There are three phases to a warm-up.

1. **Pulse raising:** This aims to gradually raise the heart rate and warm up the largest muscle groups to the working rate. More oxygen is also made available to the working muscles, which will improve performance. Activities often include jogging, sidestepping and skipping.
2. **Stretching:** This aims to lengthen the specific muscles used in the main activity, helping to prevent injury. Most of this should be active stretching, which involves stretching the joints while moving.
3. **Joint mobilization:** This aims to move the joints into positions appropriate to the main activity, again helping to prevent injury. Activities often include rotation exercises, such as shoulder rotation, when the joint is moved carefully through its full range of movement.

A warm-up should take place before any form of physical activity.

Cooling down

Cooling down after a performance is just as important as warming up, although it is often overlooked by amateur performers. It returns the body to its pre-exercise state.

There are three phases to a cool-down:

1. **Pulse lowering:** This is a gentle activity that aims to gradually return the pulse rate to its resting rate. Typical activities include gentle jogging or cycling.
2. **Static stretching:** This aims to remove any lactic acid build-up in the working muscles to prevent stiffness or soreness after exercise.
3. **Developmental stretching:** Developmental stretches encourage the muscles to lengthen, increasing their flexibility. They can be static stretches or Proprioceptive Neuromuscular Facilitation (PNF) stretches and should be held for at least 30 seconds.

Flexibility training

Flexibility is the range of movement at a joint. Good flexibility and, therefore, a good range of movement at the joints can help prevent muscle injury, especially when it comes to activities that require explosive work, so it is important to all athletes, but some more than others. There are three training methods that improve flexibility: static stretching, ballistic stretching, and PNF stretching.

Static stretching

There are two main types of static stretching: active stretching and passive stretching. Active stretching is the name given to stretches where the performer applies the force that lengthens and stretches the muscle. Passive stretches, which are also referred to as assisted stretches, involve a partner, wall, barre, or other object assisting the performer with the stretch.

It is important that the muscles that will be used most by the performer are stretched. For example, an outfield player in a hockey team might focus their time stretching their hamstrings, quadriceps, and gastrocnemii, whereas the goalkeeper in the same team might spend more time stretching their deltoids and each latissimus dorsi. This is because the different positions place demands on different muscles.

A selection of the most commonly performed active static stretches. Each stretch is held for between 10 and 15 seconds.

Ballistic stretching

Ballistic stretching uses the momentum of moving limbs to force muscles beyond their normal range of motion. The fast, jerky movements should be performed on warm muscles, not cold muscles, to reduce the risk of injury. Martial artists will often perform ballistic stretching because the movements mimic the explosive nature of the sport.

A ballet dancer uses the barre to help stretch her hamstrings using a passive static stretch.

PNF stretching

With PNF stretching the performer has help from a partner or uses an immovable object to provide resistance, to push the limb to stretch the joint further than the performer can stretch it on their own. The muscle is held in an isometric contraction, where the length of the muscle doesn't change during the contraction, for six to ten seconds. The muscle is then relaxed before the partner stretches the muscle further using a passive static stretch. PNF stretches are often used in rehabilitation programmes.

A coach helping one of her clients with a PNF stretch.

BRONZE

3. a) Choose your favourite sport or activity. Fold a piece of A4 paper in half three times to create eight small boxes. In each box draw a diagram of a stretch that is suitable for your chosen sport or activity. Start with the upper body and finish with the lower body.

b) Describe each stretch making sure that your description includes the name(s) of the muscle(s) being stretched.

SILVER

4. On the reverse of your piece of A4 paper, write a brief explanation as to why you selected the stretches you did for Activity 3.

Strength, muscular endurance, and power training

Free weights

An effective way to improve strength and muscular endurance is to use free weights. Performers wanting to develop strength and power usually prefer free weights, dumbbells and barbells, to resistance machines because they encourage the body to develop its core strength, as the weight load is not as stable or controlled as it is with resistance machines. However, this means good technique is vital, as poor technique often leads to injury. All free-weight exercises should be performed carefully and the body should be worked through a full range of motion in order to develop muscles appropriately. It is often necessary for a 'spotter' to be used in order to ensure that no harm comes to the performer lifting the weight.

Each time a performer completes a lifting or moving action they are working against resistance, the amount of force or weight that must be lifted or moved. Each lift is known as one repetition or 'rep', and 'one repetition maximum' or '1RM' is the maximum weight a person can lift in a single repetition of an exercise. The number of repetitions a performer completes without a rest is called a 'set' and there should be a rest period of one to two minutes between each set. Usually, three sets of each exercise are performed.

Free weights are often preferred to resistance machines when trying to develop strength and power.

Varying the resistance, or load, and the number of reps provides different results:

- People who are training to improve their maximum strength should follow a programme that uses low reps and high loads: 90% 1RM (or 90% of the maximum weight they can lift) for one to six reps. They are producing a single movement against a high resistance.
- People who are training to improve their muscular endurance should use high reps and low loads: 50–60% 1RM for up to 20 reps. They are performing repetitive movements of a muscle or muscle group.
- People who are training to improve their elastic strength should use medium reps and medium loads: 75% 1RM for 12 reps. They are performing movements in very close succession, useful in sports such as gymnastics.

It is important to consider the order of the exercises in an exercise routine. People who wish to develop their strength should focus on exercises that develop their core muscles first, to stabilize the spine and pelvis, and then move on to assistance exercises, working muscles they need to use in their sport or focusing on one body part per training session if they are not training for a specific sport. It is important not to train the same body part in consecutive training sessions. In contrast, people who use free weights as part of a less specific programme, should alternate between upper and lower body exercises, and between push and pull exercises to prevent becoming tired too quickly.

It is very important that performers who use free-weight training rest after each session to give their bodies time to recover. Two days of rest is recommended between sessions in order for the muscles to fully recover, energy reserves to be topped up, and muscle tissue to be regenerated.

Circuit training

Circuit training consists of a series of exercises arranged in order and designed to develop general fitness, physical fitness, and/or skill-related fitness specific to a particular sport, depending on the exercises chosen.

The great advantage of circuit training is that, depending on the exercises chosen, it can be used to develop strength, power, muscular endurance, agility, aerobic endurance, and anaerobic endurance (the ability to work without burning oxygen for an extended period of time; top-class 800-metre runners can work anaerobically for approximately 90 seconds) in a limited time. It can also involve large numbers of participants in a relatively small space, and participants of different fitness levels can train together.

Circuit training involves six to ten different exercises, called stations, which are completed one after another. You perform each exercise for a set period of time before moving on to the next exercise after a brief, timed rest. When you have finished all the exercises you have completed one circuit and there is usually a slightly longer rest period between each circuit. The total number of circuits performed during a training session usually varies from two to six depending on your level of experience and/or your training goals.

To improve a component of fitness it is necessary to 'overload', to work harder than your body is used to working normally. Overload is achieved in circuit training by:

* Reducing target times (the time taken to complete a given number of repetitions).
* Reducing rest times (the time between each exercise).
* Increasing exercise resistance (increasing the difficulty of the exercise).
* Increasing repetitions (increasing the number of times the exercise is repeated, possibly in a given time).
* Increasing stations (increasing the number of exercises).
* Increasing circuits (increasing the number of times the circuit is completed).

The key thing to remember when designing a circuit is that the same body part should not be exercised consecutively to avoid fatigue and reduce the risk of injury. For this reason, it is important to alternate between exercises designed to work the upper body and exercises designed to work the lower body.

Circuit training can be easily adapted to suit the specific requirements of the performer.

Plyometrics

This is designed to improve strength and explosive power. It involves the performer jumping down off a box and then immediately back up onto another box, or something similar. On hitting the ground, the quadriceps muscle lengthens in an eccentric action to act as a brake. By immediately jumping back upwards, the quadriceps is forced to shorten quickly in a concentric action, thereby producing more power. You can see how this works by stretching an elastic band between your fingers. You will find that the further you stretch the elastic band, the more powerfully it contracts back.

Plyometrics is a training method used by performers who want to jump higher, run faster, throw further, or hit harder, such as sprinters and hurdlers, netball, volleyball and basketball players.

Plyometric exercises can easily be added to a circuit training session. Stations could include barrier hopping and jumping, skipping, drop jumps, lunging, bouncing, and incline press-ups. They need to be performed carefully, however, as they can cause muscle soreness.

A basketball player can use plyometric exercises, such as barrier hopping, to increase the height of his/her jump. The performer jumps up onto a box from the floor, completing three sets of 10–15 repetitions.

Aerobic endurance training

Aerobic endurance training requires the sports performer to work for an extended period of time, often longer than the actual event for which he or she is training. For example, Paula Radcliffe will often train upwards of four hours at a time, even though her event (the marathon) is usually over in less than two-and-a-half hours. Endurance training should take place largely in the aerobic training zone of the training pyramid and the work-to-rest ratio should be in the region of 3:1. This means that if you work for 30 minutes you should follow it with a ten-minute rest, and then repeat the session again. There are four types of endurance training:

- Continuous training
- Interval training
- Fartlek training
- Circuit training

Continuous training

Continuous training involves performing an activity – such as jogging, swimming, cycling, walking, or rowing – for an extended period of time (usually longer than 30 minutes) without rest. To improve aerobic fitness you should complete three to four sessions of continuous training per week.

Fartlek training

Fartlek training, also known as 'speed play', is a form of road running or cross-country running in which the runner, usually running alone, varies their pace significantly during the run. It is usually regarded as an advanced training technique for an experienced runner who has been using interval training to develop speed and to raise their anaerobic threshold. However, the 'average' runner can also benefit from a simplified form of fartlek training, to develop self-awareness and to introduce variety into their training programme.

Short, fast runs are alternated with recovery periods of slow running or jogging. The training is continuous with no rest periods. The vast majority of the running takes place in the aerobic zone but the short, fast sprints push the performer to work anaerobically for short periods at a time. Fartlek training takes place on the road or in a park and there is no predetermined schedule to follow. Instead the athlete sets the length of the intervals and their pace in response to how they are feeling. An advantage of fartlek training is that the athlete concentrates on feeling the pace and their physical response to it, thereby, developing self-awareness and pace-judgement skills. Also, the athlete is free to experiment with changes of pace and endurance as well as intensity by running with weights, a weighted backpack, or a harness, making it an excellent component of a distance runner's training programme. However, it is primarily a technique for advanced runners because it requires honesty to ensure a demanding workload, and maturity to avoid overdoing the pace or length of the intervals.

Interval training

Interval training consists of alternating intervals of running over a specific distance in a set time (in other words, fast running for anywhere between 30 seconds to five minutes), with recovery periods that are specified in terms of duration, distance, or both and which can consist of complete rest, walking, or light running. Interval training can improve anaerobic endurance when the work period is longer than 20 minutes and the rest period is one third of the work period. The appropriate work period is around 60 per cent of a person's maximum oxygen uptake – or VO_2 max – which is the volume of oxygen a person consumes while exercising at their maximum capacity. Decreasing the recovery periods and increasing the intensity of the work periods further develops anaerobic endurance. Training sessions will focus on specific race demands.

Interval training is similar to fartlek training, except that it is much more rigid. You decide before you start how long to run for, at what speed, and how long and often your rest periods will be. It is more suitable for the inexperienced athlete, as it does not require the same level of honesty and decision-making as fartlek training.

This type of training is a component of a balanced training programme that will include recovery days and a range of other running activities, depending on the goals of the individual. Mixing interval training with running a range of distances and different types of running (such as cross-country running and hill running) can contribute to overall fitness and the capacity to engage in successful competitive running.

Endurance training is crucial to the success of athletes such as Paula Radcliffe.

BRONZE

8. Try to perform each type of aerobic endurance training to see how it feels. Then, suggest a sports performer that would benefit from each type of training and a sports performer who would gain little or no benefit from each type of training.

9. a) Design a training session for a distance runner.

b) Based on the performer's ability, suggest ways of changing the session if they were running at school, county, regional, national, and international level.

10. List the benefits of fartlek training for an elite international athlete.

Speed training

Speed training is a way of developing a performer's speed over short distances. This is useful in almost all sports because speed can often be the difference between winning and losing. For example, footballers need to be able to cover a distance quickly to beat an opponent to the ball and tennis players need to be quick to reach the ball during a rally. Speed training should always be carried out in the speed zone of the training pyramid. It is of a very high intensity, so work periods should be short and frequent, and interspersed with lots of short rest periods. This makes speed training a type of interval training. It is generally accepted that a work-to-rest ratio of 1:6 is desirable. This means that a performer should work at a maximum level for a very short period, usually up to about 15 seconds, and then follow this with a rest period that is six times longer, repeating the sequence several times. There are three types of speed training:

- Hollow sprints
- Acceleration sprints
- Interval training

Hollow sprints
These are similar to interval training, in that a period of work is broken up by a 'hollow' period of either rest or lower-level work. A typical hollow sprint session would look something like this:

50m	Sprint	(6–7 seconds)
50m	Jog	(25 seconds)
50m	Sprint	(6–7 seconds)
50m	Walk	(30 seconds)
50m	Sprint	(6–7 seconds)
150m	Walk	(90 seconds)

This is repeated five times before a longer, ten-minute rest period.

Acceleration sprints
Acceleration sprints are a form of anaerobic training where the running speed is increased from jogging to striding and finally to sprinting at maximum pace. Each change of pace usually takes place after 50 metres, and rest periods of jogging or walking take place between each sprint.

As the name suggests, the aim here is to improve acceleration from a static, rolling, or sport-specific starting position. For example, rugby players may start the sprint by lying on the ground to simulate a ruck, whereas footballers may start with their back to the direction of the sprint to simulate turning away from a defender and sprinting into a space. The progressive nature of acceleration sprinting reduces the risk of muscle injury.

American sprinter Tyson Gray works on improving his speed in training.

Interval training
Interval training can be used to develop speed. The intervals should be shorter and performed at a higher intensity, as close to maximum intensity as possible, than they are if interval training is being used to develop aerobic endurance. The number of recovery periods and the length of the recovery periods should also be increased to compensate for the shorter and higher intensity intervals.

BRONZE

11. Try to perform each type of speed training to see how it feels. Then, suggest a sports performer who would benefit from each type of training and a sports performer who would gain little or no benefit from each type of training.

Speed training for footballers often involves turning away from a defender.

SPOTLIGHT on fitness training methods

BRONZE

1. Create a poster that can be placed in one of your school's sports facilities, which highlights health and safety issues relating to the use of specific equipment in that area.

2. Write a paragraph describing the most appropriate method of training for a sport of your choice.

SILVER

3. Create a table with the methods of training in the left-hand column and the principles of training in the top row.

Fill in each box stating how each principle of training can be applied to each method of training. The table below should start you off.

	Frequency	Intensity	Time
Circuit training	Increase the number of times you train each week.	Work within your target Heart Rate Zone.	Train for one hour per session.
Plyometrics			

GOLD

4. Choose one fitness training method and write a training guide for a friend or family member.

Conducting fitness tests

Sports participants should regularly undertake fitness testing so that the effects of their training can be evaluated. After all, there's no point in continuing with a training schedule that is no longer working! But, before carrying out fitness testing, there are a number of pre-test procedures that should be considered.

1 Checking the equipment

It is important to check the equipment to make sure that it is safe and working properly. This includes calibrating machines and, where necessary, checking that they are recording data accurately.

2 Informed consent

It is extremely important to ensure that you have informed consent from all participants who are going to take a test. No one should be asked to undertake a fitness test without first completing a consent form.

3 Choosing the fitness tests

Different sports place different emphasis on each component of fitness, with a component that is vitally important for one sport being much less important for another. It is, therefore, important to establish which components of fitness are most important for a performer and what the purpose of each fitness test is in order to carry out the appropriate fitness tests.

When deciding which fitness test to perform you should also consider the practicality as well as the advantages and disadvantages of each test. Some fitness tests, such as Bioelectrical Impedance Analysis (BIA), require expensive equipment that you might not have access to. In this case, it might be more appropriate to measure body composition using Body Mass Index (BMI).

4 Carrying out the fitness tests

You need to know the standard, published, method for completing each test and have the necessary equipment to hand. The results of each test must be accurately measured and recorded. A performer's results should then be compared against normative published data, data collected from peers, and against their own previously collected data, and the information analysed and evaluated and used to draw conclusions about the performer's strengths and weaknesses.

5 Reliability and validity of fitness tests

Reliability and validity are two of the major problems with using fitness tests. Reliability refers to the degree to which repeated measurements give the same result, and validity refers to the honesty of the test or – to put it another way – the degree to which the assessment method measures what it is intended to measure.

The reliability of a test is often called into question because the same person gets different results each time they complete it. This can be for a number of reasons:

- Is the test being conducted properly?
- Has the person suffered an injury since they last took the test?
- Is the equipment damaged in any way?
- Is the person using the same amount of effort each time? (Something that it is very difficult to determine.)

The results of a fitness test are more likely to be valid if the test uses expensive, specialized equipment, which has been designed specifically for the purpose of carrying out the test. If the test uses cheaper, everyday items, such as a stopwatch and a ruler, it is likely to be less valid.

The validity of a test is much more certain – either the test measures what it is supposed to measure or it doesn't. Perhaps the best example of a test providing results that are not valid is the multistage fitness test. This test has been designed to measure cardiovascular endurance (the ability to use oxygen effectively over a period of time). According to the rules of the test, the higher the level of the test reached, the higher the level of cardiovascular endurance. However, there are two serious flaws with this method:

- The test is supposed to measure cardiovascular endurance but a high degree of agility (to turn quickly each time), power (to push off each time), and speed (to maintain the required pace between bleeps) are also required. For this reason, a swimmer may have a very high level of cardiovascular endurance but not return good results because they aren't a very good runner. The test might, therefore, give invalid results.
- Towards the higher levels of the test, the performer may well be working anaerobically (without oxygen) and, as a result, would get a very high score even though their cardiovascular endurance was surpassed before the end of the test. In this case, the results would again be invalid.

This is not to say that the test should not be used. It does give a good **indication** of an individual's cardiovascular fitness. It is also cheap to carry out and can be administered to lots of participants at the same time. The key with any fitness test is to understand how useful the results are going to be and to make sure that it is carried out properly, according to the protocols (rules) of the test, to ensure that the results are reliable and valid.

The fitness tests

Over the next few pages you will see a range of tests that can be used to measure an individual's level of fitness. There are also suggested 'normal' or 'normative' results that you would expect from various levels of performer. It should be remembered that these are only some examples of fitness tests and that there are several others that can be used as well. It should also be stressed that the expected results are given only as a guide.

It is important to conduct fitness tests before starting a fitness-training programme. It is also important to use the results to design a suitable programme and have them as baseline data, which can be used to monitor and improve performance. A performer's results can be compared against normative published data, data collected from peers (from people of a similar age with similar abilities), and against their own previously collected data. The information can be analysed and evaluated – and used to draw conclusions about the performer's strengths and weaknesses. This knowledge can be used to justify recommendations to a performer about how they can improve their fitness to meet their long-term goals. The results from fitness tests can also be very useful as part of the medium-term goal-setting process, lending the weight of authority to suggestions about which fitness training methods are most appropriate.

BRONZE

1. Undertake each of the following fitness tests, recording the results accurately.

SILVER

2. Accurately administer each fitness test for your peer group.

GOLD

3. Comment on the reliability and validity of each fitness test that you have undertaken.

Flexibility

Sit and reach test

What do you need?
A box and a measuring tape or a sit and reach table

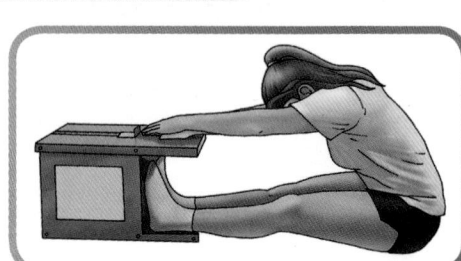

How do you do the test?
- Sit comfortably on the floor with your legs straight out in front of you.
- Place the measuring tape, with 0cm level with your feet, parallel with your legs. If you are using a sit and reach table, the measurements are already marked.
- Put the soles of your feet, shoulder width apart, against the box/table.
- Make sure your knees are locked/straight, as this is what determines hamstring flexibility. If your knees bend during the test, the results will be inaccurate.
- With your hands stretched towards your feet, lean forward and reach as far as possible with your fingertips. If possible, reach beyond the end of your toes and over the top of the box. You must make sure, however, that there are no jerky movements while doing this and that you are able to hold the reach for at least two seconds.
- You get three chances to stretch forward and then the fourth is measured.
- The distance that your fingers touch on the measuring tape/sit and reach table will be your score. If you don't make it to your toes then you will get a negative score, showing the distance you were from 0cm.

The sit and reach test can be measured in centimetres or inches.

Expected level	Male footballer	Male gymnast		Male	Female
Regional	7–10cm	10–12cm	Average 16–19-year-old	7–10cm	7–11cm
National	9–13cm	13–17cm			
International/professional	>15cm	>18cm			

(Source: Davis, B. et al. *Physical Education and the Study of Sport*, Mosby Publishing, 2000)

Advantages of the sit and reach test:
- It is a well-known test.
- It is quick and easy to perform.
- There is a lot of normative data to use for comparison.

Disadvantages of the sit and reach test:
- Variations in length of individuals' arms, legs, and trunk can make comparisons between people misleading.
- The test focuses specifically on the flexibility of the lower back and hamstrings, so does not measure the flexibility of other parts of the body.

Strength

Grip dynamometer

What do you need?

A grip dynamometer

How do you do the test?

- Use a grip dynamometer to measure grip strength.
- Record the maximum reading from three attempts using the dominant hand. Allow a one-minute recovery between each attempt.
- Grip strength can be measured in Kg or KgW, depending on the grip dynamometer used.

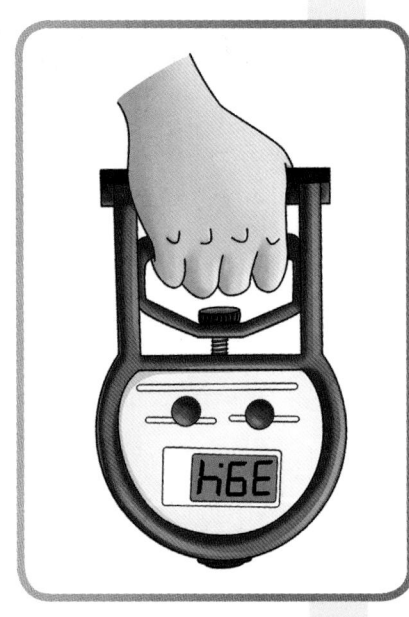

Expected level	Male footballer	Female footballer
Regional	> 40kg	> 28kg
National	> 45kg	> 32kg
International/professional	> 50kg	> 36kg

	Male	Female
Average 16–19-year-old	30–35kg	22–26kg

Advantages of the grip dynamometer:

- This is a simple test, which is easy to conduct.
- There is a lot of normative data to use for comparison.

Disadvantages of the grip dynamometer:

- The dynamometer must be adjusted for hand size. How well this is done has an effect on the accuracy of the measurement.

Aerobic endurance

VO_2 maximum – or, 'VO_2 max' – is a measurement of aerobic endurance. It describes the maximum amount of oxygen that the body can use in one minute per kilogram of body weight. It is measured in millilitres per kilogram per minute or ml/kg/min. Fitter people have a higher VO_2 max and can therefore exercise more intensely than people who aren't as fit.

Multistage fitness test, also known as the 'bleep test'

What do you need?

- Multistage fitness test CD
- CD player
- Cones
- 15–20-metre marked area

How do you do the test?

- The test involves continuous running between two lines, 15–20m apart, between recorded bleeps (played from the CD). The time between the bleeps decreases each minute or level. There are several versions of the test but one commonly used version has an initial running velocity of 8.5km per hour, which increases by 0.5km per hour each minute.
- You must always ensure that you have one foot on or beyond the 15–20-metre marker at the end of each shuttle run.
- If you reach the marker before the next beep, you should wait there until you hear it before resuming running.
- If you do not manage to reach the end of the shuttle run before the beep sounds then you are given two or three more attempts to catch up with the pace before being stopped.

Expected level	Female footballer	Female gymnast
Regional	Level 9	Level 8
National	Level 10	Level 9
International/professional	Level 12+	Level 10

21

Advantages of the multistage fitness test:

- Large groups can perform this test simultaneously.
- The test measures up to maximum capacity, unlike many other tests, which measure endurance.

Disadvantages of the multistage fitness test:

- Practice, motivation, and state of mind can massively influence the score attained.
- The scoring can be subjective.
- If the test is conducted outside, environmental conditions could affect the results.

Forestry step test

This is a variation of a stepping-type fitness test, which is used in the USA.

What do you need?

- Step (40cm for males, 33cm for females)
- Heart-rate monitor
- Metronome
- Published table for calculating maximal aerobic power

A person doing the step test.

How do you do the test?

- Record your body weight in the clothing you will be wearing for the test.
- Set the metronome at 90 beats per minute, to mark out a stepping rate of 22.5 steps per minute.
- Following the stepping rate set by the metronome, step up with the right leg and down with the right leg, then up with the left leg and down with the left leg. This is one step. Continue stepping for five minutes.
- After five minutes of stepping, sit down and measure your heart rate.
- Use your age, post-exercise heart rate, and body weight to calculate the maximal aerobic power using a published table.

	Fitness category						
	Superior	**Excellent**	**Very good**	**Good**	**Fair**	**Poor**	**Very poor**
Age and gender	Maximum oxygen consumption (ml/kg/min)						
15-year-old male	57+	56–52	51–47	46–42	41–37	36–32	<32
15-year-old female	54+	53–49	48–44	43–39	38–34	33–29	<29
20-year-old male	56+	55–51	50–46	45–41	40–36	35–31	<31
20-year-old female	53+	52–45	47–43	42–38	37–33	32–28	<28

Advantages of the forestry step test:

- This simple test requires minimal equipment and is therefore cheap to perform.
- It can be performed inside or outside.
- It is possible to self-administer this test.

Disadvantages of the forestry step test:

- Some people may not have the fitness level or coordination to maintain the required stepping rate.

Speed

35-metre sprint

The objective of this test is to monitor the athlete's level of sprint fatigue.

What do you need?
- 35-metre marked section in a straight line, preferably on a running track
- Starting blocks
- Stopwatch
- Assistant

How do you do the test?
- Sprint 35 metres from a standing start/sprint start using the blocks.
- Allow a 30-second recovery while walking back to the start.
- Repeat the sprint five times, completing a total of six sprints.
- Record the time for each sprint, which is usually measured in seconds (s).

At the present time, there is no data on expected levels available for this test, although it is generally accepted that a difference of less than 0.8 seconds between the first sprint and the last sprint represents excellent performance.

Advantages of the 35-metre sprint:
- This simple test requires minimal equipment and is therefore cheap to perform.
- It can be performed inside or outside.

Disadvantages of the 35-metre sprint:
- Human error in timekeeping can lead to incorrect or misleading results.

Speed and agility

Illinois agility run test

What do you need?
- Flat, non-slip surface
- 8 cones
- Stopwatch
- Assistant

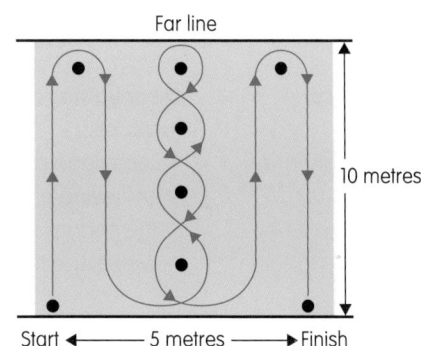

Far line

10 metres

Start ◄——— 5 metres ———► Finish

How do you do the test?
- Set up the course, as shown in the diagram.
- Warm up before beginning the test.
- Lie face down on the floor at the 'Start' cone.
- When your assistant gives the command 'Go' and starts the stopwatch, jump to your feet and run around the cones in the correct order to the finish.
- Your assistant should stop the stopwatch and record your time when you pass the 'Finish' cone.

The following are the national norms for 16 to 19-year-olds:

	Excellent	Above average	Average	Below average	Poor
Male	< 15.2 seconds	15.2–16.1 seconds	16.2–18.1 seconds	18.2–19.3 seconds	> 19.3 seconds
Female	< 17.0 secondss	17.0–17.9 seconds	18.0–21.7 seconds	21.8–23.0 seconds	> 23.0 seconds

(Source: Davis, B. et al., *Physical Education and the Study of Sport*, Mosby Publishing, 2000)

Advantages of the Illinois agility run test:
- It is cheap and easy to conduct.

Disadvantages of the Illinois agility run test:
- Human error can lead to inaccuracies in timing.
- Weather conditions and the surface can affect the results.

Anaerobic power

Vertical jump test

What do you need?
- Wall
- Measuring tape
- Chalk
- Partner
- Weighing scales

How do you do the test?
- Stand side-on to a wall and reach up with the hand closest to the wall. Keeping your feet flat on the ground, the point of the fingertips is marked or recorded by a partner. This is called the standing reach.
- Stand away from the wall and jump vertically as high as possible using both your arms and your legs to help you project your body upwards. Touch the wall at the highest point of the jump and have this marked or recorded.
- The difference in distance between the standing reach height and the jump height is the score. The best of three attempts is plotted on the Lewis nomogram on line 'D'.
- Weigh yourself and record your weight in kilograms on the nomogram on line 'Wt'.
- Use a ruler and a sharp pencil to join up the two plots. The line you have drawn will cross the power line ('P') on the nomogram. Read your power in kilograms per second (kgm/s).

	Males	Females
Above average	105+kgm/s	90+kgm/s
Average	95kgm/s	80kgm/s
Below average	<85kgm/s	<70kgm/s

Advantages of the vertical jump test:
- It is quick and easy to perform.

Disadvantages of the vertical jump test:
- Technique plays a big part in achieving a good score because the performer must mark the wall at the top of the jump.

D (cm)	P (kgm/s)	Wt (kg)
80	200	
70	180	100
60	150	90
	140	
	130	
50	120	80
40	100	
	90	70
30	80	
	70	60
	60	
20	50	50
	40	45
15	30	40
10	25	36

The Lewis nomogram. (From: E L Fox and D K Mathews: *Interval Training: Conditioning for sports and general fitness* (Saunders, 1974))

Muscular endurance

One-minute press-up test

What do you need?
- Stopwatch
- Partner

How do you do the test?
- Take up the starting position, with your arms straight, elbows locked, body straight, hands placed slightly wider than shoulder-width apart (with fingers pointing forward), and both feet on the floor.
- From the starting position, on the command 'Go', start the press-up by bending your elbows and lowering your body until the shoulders drop below the level of the elbows. Then return to the starting position. Pausing to rest is permitted only in the starting position.
- Your partner should count how many full press-ups are completed in one minute or up to the point where the performer retires from the test.

Expected level	Male footballer	Male swimmer
Regional	45 reps per minute	50 reps per minute
National	55 reps per minute	55 reps per minute
International/professional	65+ reps per minute	60 reps per minute

Advantages of the one-minute press-up test:
- It is quick and easy to set up.
- No specialist equipment is required.

Disadvantages of the one-minute press-up test:
- The press-up must be technically correct for it to count, and what makes a technically correct press-up is open to interpretation. This can lead to disputes about the total number.
- The performer will get tired if they stay in the ready position for too long. This can make testing many people simultaneously, difficult.

One-minute sit-up test

What do you need?
- Stopwatch
- Partner

How do you do the test?
- Lie on a carpeted or cushioned floor with your knees bent at approximately right angles and your feet flat on the ground. Your hands should be resting on your thighs.
- Squeeze your stomach, push your lower back flat, and raise your upper body high enough for your hands to slide along your thighs to touch the tops of your knees. Don't pull with your neck or head, and keep your lower back on the floor. Then return to the starting position.
- Your partner should count how many full sit-ups are completed in one minute or up to the point where the performer retires from the test.

Expected level	Female rower	Female gymnast
Regional	40 reps per minute	30 reps per minute
National	45 reps per minute	35 reps per minute
International/ professional	50 reps per minute	40 reps per minute

	Male	Female
Average 16–19-year-old	20–25 reps per minute	15–20 reps per minute

(Source: Davis, B. et al., *Physical Education and the Study of Sport,* Mosby Publishing, 2000)

Advantages of the one-minute sit-up test:
- The test is simple to perform.
- It requires minimal equipment.
- Large groups may be tested at once.

Disadvantages of the one-minute sit-up test:
- It is difficult to determine when a correct sit-up has been performed so there may be a dispute about the total number.

Body composition

Jackson-Pollock nomogram method for prediction of percent body fat

There is a layer of fat beneath the skin, which is called subcutaneous fat, and the percentage of total body fat can be estimated by taking a measure of the 'skinfold' at selected points on the body with a pair of callipers.

What do you need?

- Skinfold callipers
- Partner

How do you do the test?

- Measurements should be taken on dry skin on the right side of the body and the subject should stay relaxed during the test.
- Mark the mid point of each skinfold site with a pen.
- Grasp the skinfold firmly between your thumb and index finger and pull away from the body. The skinfold should be gripped about one centimetre away from the mid point.
- Maintaining your grip, place the callipers midway between the base and tip of the skinfold with the dial facing upwards and allow the callipers to release fully so that full tension is placed on the skinfold.
- Read the dial of the skinfold callipers to the nearest 0.5mm shortly after you have released the callipers. Continue to grasp the skinfold throughout testing.
- Take a minimum of two measurements at each site and calculate the average of the two readings.
- Add up the results for each of your three skinfold measurements and work out your percentage body fat result by plotting your age in years and the sum of the three skinfolds on the nomogram.
- Use a ruler and sharp pencil to join up the two plots. The line you have drawn will cross the percent body fat scale. Read your percent body fat result to the closest 0.5% according to your gender.

Chest: A diagonal fold, which is one half of the distance between the anterior auxiliary line and the nipple.

Abdominal: A vertical fold, which is 2cm to the right side of the belly button.

Thigh: A vertical fold, on the front of the thigh, halfway between the hip joint and the middle of the knee cap. The leg needs to be straight and relaxed.

The Jackson-Pollock nomogram skinfold sites for males.

Triceps: This is a vertical fold on the back midline of the upper arm, over the triceps muscle.

Suprailiac: A diagonal fold just above the hip bone and 2–3cm forward.

Thigh: A vertical fold, on the front of the thigh, halfway between the hip joint and the middle of the knee cap. The leg needs to be straight and relaxed.

The Jackson-Pollock nomogram skinfold sites for females.

Rating	Males per cent body fat (16–29 years)	Females per cent body fat (16–29 years)
Very low fat	<7	<13
Slim	7–12	13–20
Ideal	13–17	21–25
Overweight	18–28	26–32
Obese	29+	33+

Jackson-Pollock nomogram. (From: A S Jackson and M L Pollock: 'Generalized equations for predicting body density', 40 *British Journal of Nutrition* 497–504 (1978))

Advantages of the Jackson-Pollock nomogram method for prediction of percent body fat:
- It provides an accurate score for your body fat percentage.

Disadvantages of the Jackson-Pollock nomogram method for prediction of percent body fat:
- It is complicated and will require specialist help.
- It requires specialist equipment.
- Some people may feel uncomfortable stripping down in front of the tester.
- It can be difficult to ensure that the results are valid and reliable if the tester is inexperienced.

Body Mass Index (BMI)

Your BMI provides a way of calculating whether or not your body is of an ideal weight. A BMI test is designed for men and women over the age of 18, and although people under the age of 18 can use it, their results should not be taken to have any significant meaning.

What do you need?
- Weighing scales marked in kilograms
- Measuring tape
- Calculator
- Partner

How do you do the test?
- Measure your weight in kilograms.
- Measure your height in metres (so 182cm is actually 1.82m).
- Calculate your BMI using this formula below:

$$BMI = \frac{\text{weight (kg)}}{\text{height (m)} \times \text{height (m)}}$$

NHS Direct (UK) provides the following assessment of BMI measurements. If your BMI is:
- Less than 18.5kg/m^2 you are underweight for your height.
- 18.5 to 24.9kg/m^2 you are an ideal weight for your height.
- 25 to 29.9kg/m^2 you are over the ideal weight for your height.
- 30 to 39.9kg/m^2 you are obese.
- Over 39.9kg/m^2 you are very obese.

Measuring body fat using an Omron BF 302 body fat monitor.

Advantages of BMI:
- It involves a simple calculation using standard measurements.

Disadvantages of BMI:
- Muscle weighs more than fat, so bodybuilders and trained athletes will often have a BMI in excess of 25kg/m^2 without being overweight.

Bioelectrical Impedance Analysis (BIA)

Another way to measure body fat is to use BIA, where electrodes are attached to the wrist and the ankle, and an electrical current is passed from one to the other. Body fat restricts the flow of the electric current, so the more current that is needed, the greater the percentage of body fat the person has.

Advantages of BIA:
- The test accurately measures what percentage of your total body weight is made up of bone, muscle, fat, and water.
- It is quick and gives instant results.
- The test can be administered repeatedly over time without adverse effects.

Disadvantages of BIA:
- It requires expensive equipment and technical knowledge.

External Exam Practice

Tackling the exam

You can decide to take the exam when you are ready. It will be completed on a computer and will last for one hour. There are a total of 50 marks available and the number of marks for each question is shown in brackets. Depending on the number of marks you get, you will receive one of the following grades for the unit:

- Distinction at Level 2   • Merit at Level 2   • Pass at Level 2   • Level 1   • Unclassified.

The exam contains different types of questions, and some sample questions for you to practise are provided below.

1 Which of the following is the definition of muscular endurance? (1)

A The ability of the muscular system to work efficiently over a period of time. ◯

B The maximum force that can be generated by a group of muscles. ◯

C The ability of the cardiorespiratory system to work efficiently. ◯

D The ability of a performer to run for a long period of time. ◯

2 Power is a combination of two components of fitness. Which is the correct pairing? (1)

A Aerobic endurance and flexibility ◯

B Speed and body composition ◯

C Strength and speed ◯

D Strength and aerobic endurance ◯

3 The FITT principle has four elements. Link the element with its description. (4)

Frequency	How hard you train
Intensity	How long you train for
Type	How often you train
Time	What you train

4 Laura and her trainer are discussing how critical the components of fitness are to her successful participation as a gymnast.

Laura tells her trainer that she thinks that good physical and skill-related fitness help her to meet the demands her sport places on her, and help her to reach her optimal performance.

Explain how flexibility is important for Laura as a gymnast. (2)

5 (a) Steven is 20 years old. What is his Maximum Heart Rate? (1)

(b) What is Steven's Training Zone? (2)

You **must** show your calculations.

6 Below are incomplete definitions of some of the principles of training. Complete the sentences by entering the principle of training. (6)

(a) _____ training should consider the individual's sport or activity.

(b) _____ is how the body reacts when training loads are increased.

(c) _____ happens if training stops or the intensity of training is reduced.

(d) _____ is important to keep training fresh and exciting.

(e) Adaptation occurs during _____.

(f) _____ is about keeping training demanding enough to cause the body to adapt.

7 Link each component of fitness with an appropriate fitness test. (8)

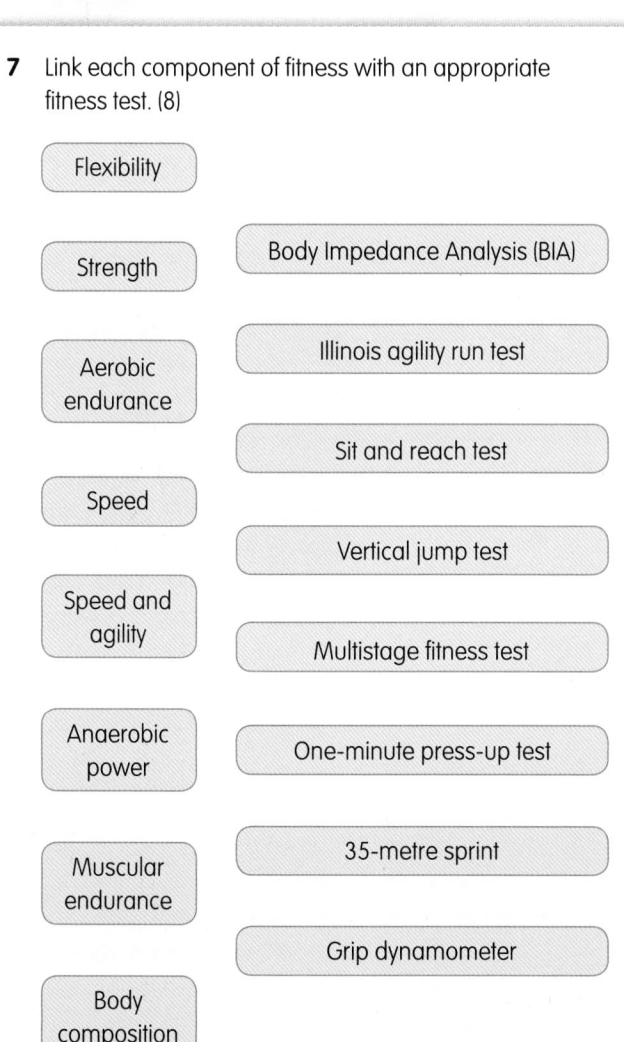

Flexibility	
Strength	Body Impedance Analysis (BIA)
	Illinois agility run test
Aerobic endurance	Sit and reach test
Speed	Vertical jump test
Speed and agility	Multistage fitness test
Anaerobic power	One-minute press-up test
Muscular endurance	35-metre sprint
	Grip dynamometer
Body composition	

8 (a) What type of training session is show in this photograph? (1)

   A Hollow sprints

   B Circuit training

   C Plyometrics

   D Interval training

(b) Describe how this method of training helps to improve fitness. (3)

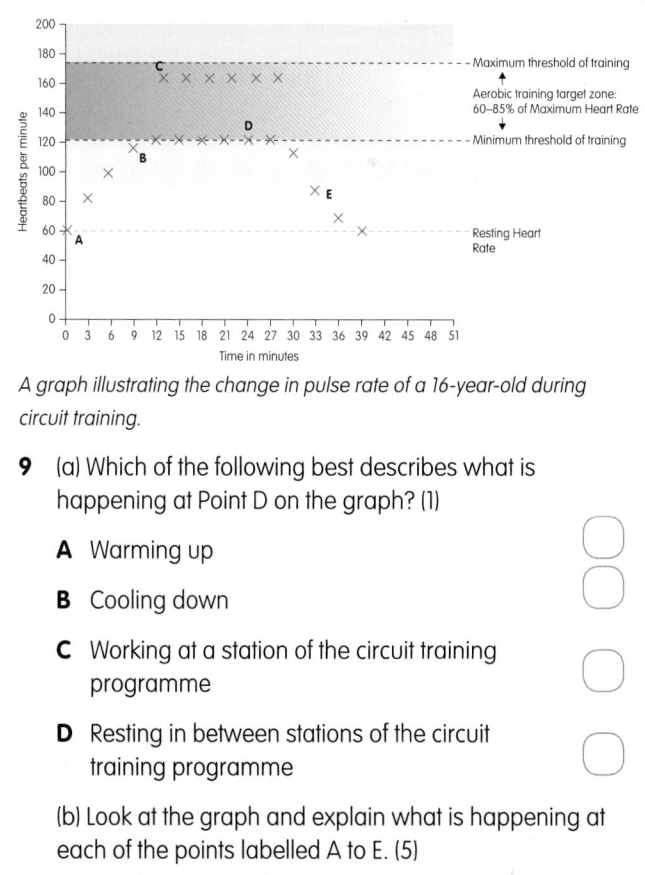

A graph illustrating the change in pulse rate of a 16-year-old during circuit training.

9 (a) Which of the following best describes what is happening at Point D on the graph? (1)

   A Warming up

   B Cooling down

   C Working at a station of the circuit training programme

   D Resting in between stations of the circuit training programme

(b) Look at the graph and explain what is happening at each of the points labelled A to E. (5)

10 A person's working heart rate will always be below their Maximum Heart Rate. Explain this statement. (2)

Unit 2: Practical Sports Performance

Rules, regulations, scoring systems, and officials

Understanding the rules, regulations, and scoring systems of the sports you participate in, as well as the roles and responsibilities of the officials involved, will help make you a more competent performer.

Rules, regulations, and scoring systems

Each sport generally has a national or international governing body that sets out specific rules or laws to ensure that a sport is played fairly by all competitors. For example, FIFA (Fédération Internationale de Football Association) governs football, the IRB (International Rugby Board) governs rugby, the BWF (Badminton World Federation) governs badminton and the IOF (International Orienteering Federation) governs orienteering.

Umpire Aleem Dar signals the fall of a wicket.

These rules will cover everything from how a game will be started to when a free kick may be awarded in a rugby game, for example. Each sport also has a set of regulations. These generally control how the sport will be played or conducted, including what surface it will be played on, what safety standards need to be met in order to help prevent injuries, and what equipment must be used.

Each sport has its own scoring system, from scoring three points in basketball for a shot outside the three-point arc to winning a point in badminton. Each sport also has its own methods or requirements for victory. Scoring systems form part of the rules that govern how a sport is played.

The roles and responsibilities of officials in sport

Every sport has one or more officials to oversee the running of a game, match, or competition to ensure that all rules and regulations are followed by competitors and that the scoring systems are applied correctly. If sports did not have officials it would be difficult to ensure that rules and regulations were applied fairly, and competitions would descend into chaos with opposing teams arguing. A good official will communicate well with players, managers, and spectators, by use of voice, whistle, and signals to ensure that everyone understands the decisions being made.

Some sports, such as cricket, Association Football, American football, and rugby union, have an official whose responsibility it is to analyse video footage of the game to help the primary officials make the right decision.

BRONZE

1. Research the rules, regulations, and scoring systems for one of your chosen sports.

2. Understanding the roles and responsibilities of the officials involved in the sports you have chosen will help you to improve as a sportsperson. Complete the table below for one of your chosen sports, listing all the officials involved along with their roles and responsibilities. Don't forget to include officials who aren't on the pitch or court throughout the match or game; some officials are out of sight but still have an important role to play.

GOLD

3. Make a list of any rules that frustrate you or you think need to be improved in your favourite sport.

Draft a letter to the national governing body for your chosen sport outlining why you think these rules need improvement, how they should be changed, and how you think these changes will benefit the game.

Official's role (for example, their title)	Official's responsibilities	Training or qualification required	Level of fitness required	Age restrictions

Unit 2 assignment, part one

Background

Your school or college has decided to hold an open evening to celebrate its success. It has invited local primary school students to take part in some of the different activities that are available. You have been asked to help plan and lead this event, and to ensure that all visiting students leave the open evening with some information about the different sports on offer and how they are officiated and regulated.

Task

Produce an information leaflet or an information video for visiting students that will cover two sports. Your leaflet or video should:

Grading criteria to be assessed
1A.1, 1A.2, 1A.3
2A.P1, 2A.P2, 2A.P3
2A.M1
2A.D1

- Describe the rules, regulations and scoring systems of a selected sport. (1A.1)
- Apply the rules of a selected sport in two given situations. (1A.2)
- Describe the roles of officials from a selected sport. (1A.3)

- Describe the rules, regulations and scoring systems of two selected sports. (2A.P1)
- Apply the rules of a selected sport in four specific situations. (2A.P2)
- Describe the roles and responsibilities of officials from two selected sports. (2A.P3)

- For each of two selected sports, explain the role and responsibilities of officials and the application of rules, regulations and scoring systems. (2A.M1)

- Compare and contrast the roles and responsibilities of officials from two selected sports, suggesting valid recommendations for improvement to the application of rules, regulations and scoring systems for each sport. (2A.D1)

Tackling the assignment

To meet the criteria for a Level 2 Pass you need to choose two sports and describe the rules, regulations, scoring systems, and the roles and responsibilities of officials within those sports. When you **describe** something you draw a picture of it in words for your audience. You also need to **apply** the rules of one of your chosen sports in four situations. This means you must describe each situation and state how the rules of the game come into play in that situation.

To achieve a Merit you need to explain the roles and responsibilities of officials and the way in which the rules,

regulations, and scoring systems are applied. To **explain** something you need to provide lots of examples to illustrate your description.

If you are aiming for a Distinction, you need to compare and contrast the roles and responsibilities of two officials, examining the similarities and differences between their roles and responsibilities. You then need to suggest valid recommendations in which the rules, regulations, and scoring systems of the sports you have been discussing could be improved.

Meeting the Level 2 Pass criteria

BTEC Level 2 Firsts in Sport

Unit 2, assignment one   Jodie Meehan

Badminton

Rules, regulations, and scoring

For singles matches, the rules include:

- A match consists of the best of three games.
- The player that first scores 21 points wins.
- The player that wins a rally adds one point to their score.
- If a score becomes 20–20, the player who scores two consecutive points shall win that game.

Referee and officials' participation

The referee is in overall charge of the tournament. The umpire is in charge of the match. The umpire supports the referee while the service judge calls service faults if they occur. There is also a line judge who indicates whether the shuttle has landed in or out of the court. The officials' decisions are final.

An umpire shall:

- Call a fault or let if either occur.
- Give a decision on any appeal regarding a point of dispute, if made before the next service is delivered.
- Ensure players and spectators are kept informed of the progress of the match.
- Record and report to the referee all matters in relation to continuous play, misconduct, and penalties.

> Jodie's presentation gives a clear explanation of the new scoring system in badminton and how it is used in singles and doubles play. If Jodie can produce a similar piece of work for her second sport she will meet the criteria for 2A.P1 and 2A.P3.

> To fully meet the criteria for a Level 2 Pass, Jodie also needs to describe four situations in which the rules of badminton are applied.

Meeting the Level 2 Merit criteria

BTEC Level 2 Firsts in Sport

Unit 2 assignment, part one   **Spencer Smith**

Leicester Tigers' number 8 came from an off-side position around the ruck and interfered with the play. Because the Tigers gained an advantage from this action, the referee blew the whistle and awarded a penalty kick to the opposition.

The laws of rugby state very clearly that the off-side line is directly through the ball, parallel to the try lines. It also states that when a player enters a ruck they must do so from behind the 'hindmost foot'. It was very clear in this incident that the number 8 had not come from behind the 'hindmost foot' of the ruck and, therefore, the referee was correct in awarding a penalty kick.

> This piece of work begins to meet the Merit criteria. Spencer has applied his knowledge of the rules and regulations of rugby to a specific example within a real game setting. He has explained the role of the referee in rugby and illustrated why the referee made his decision.

> To fully meet the Merit criteria, Spencer needs to do the same for the other officials involved with a rugby match and then produce material to the same standard for a second sport.

BTEC Level 2 Firsts in Sport

Unit 2 assignment, part one   **Michelle Gradage**

Compare and contrast the roles and responsibilities of officials from two sports

The roles and responsibilities of officials in football and badminton have some similarities and some differences. The officials in both sports are responsible for keeping the score, ensuring the rules are followed, and making sure that all of the players adhere to the code of conduct for fair play. However, although these responsibilities are fundamentally the same, they are also very different.

The scoring systems of both sports are very different. In badminton for instance, the score along with who won the previous rally, will affect who serves and which side they serve from. The official is also responsible for deciding whether or not the shuttle landed in or out. In contrast, in football keeping the score is much more straightforward as there are not normally as many goals scored as there are points won in a badminton match. The referee is given assistance on deciding who touched the ball last and therefore who restarts the game with a throw-in, corner, or goal kick.

Fair play, or unfair play, is a bigger difference between the two sports as football players often try to cheat the referee and this is not commonplace in the sport of badminton. Officials in badminton only have a maximum of four players to contend with, whereas in football the referee has to manage twenty-two outfield players as well as the managers and bench, who can sometimes be more of a handful than the players.

Michelle has made a good start comparing and contrasting the roles and responsibilities of the officials in both football and badminton. She has highlighted some of the key differences between the two sports and if she continues in this way and adds valid recommendations for improving each sport – including a section on improving the way roles are applied, a section on improving regulations, and a section on improving the scoring systems – she will meet the criteria for a Distinction.

Types of sports

Sports can be broadly grouped into two categories: team sports and individual sports.

Team sports

Invasion
Sports in which you invade the other team's territory and attempt to outwit them so that you can score goals or points, including Association Football, basketball, hockey, lacrosse, netball, rugby union, and rugby league.

Water
Team sports that take place in or on water, including water polo and synchronized swimming.

Adapted team sports
Team sports that have been adapted so they can be played by people with specific disabilities, including wheelchair basketball, goal ball, and football for the blind or partially sighted.

Team sports

Striking and fielding
Sports where players strike a ball to deceive or avoid the fielders and then run between wickets or around bases to score runs/points. These include cricket, rounders, and softball.

Net/wall
Sports in which one team tries to ensure a ball or other object lands in a target area that the opposing team is defending, including volleyball, badminton, and tennis.

Individual sports

Water
Individual sports that take place in or on water, including swimming, canoeing, and sailing.

Martial arts
Forms of unarmed combat or self-defence performed as a sport, including karate, judo, and tae kwon do.

Target
Sports where you aim an object at a target, including golf, archery, fencing, darts, shooting, and boccia.

Individual sports

Athletics
Sports in which you improve your personal best in relation to speed, height, distance, and accuracy, including running at all distances, hurdles, javelin, shot-put, hammer, discus, high jump, triple jump, cross-country running, and pole vault.

Net/wall
Sports in which a competitor tries to ensure a ball or other object lands in a target area that their opponent is defending, including tennis, table tennis, badminton, and squash.

Adventurous activities
Sports such as orienteering, skiing, and mountain biking, which test the performer's ability to compete against others in challenging situations, to finish a course first, or in the fastest time.

Aesthetic activities
Sports, such as trampolining and gymnastics, where the aim of the sport is to replicate movements to a high degree of accuracy and to perform a predetermined sequence.

BRONZE

1. To meet the criteria for this unit you must complete a series of practical sessions for at least two sports. The sessions must be led by a qualified instructor. Find out which sports you can take part in locally – at school, college, or at local clubs – and choose at least two to follow.

Skills, techniques, and tactics

All sports have a range of skills, techniques, and tactics that need to be developed in order for participants to be successful.

What is a skill?

A skill is something that often requires practice in order for someone to become proficient in it or able to carry it out consistently, again and again.

For example, when you learn to play badminton, one of the first, and most important, skills you learn is the serve. As you practise the serve over and over again, you become comfortable with the racket, your delivery is likely to become more effective, and you may find that you do not have to think about it as much as you did when you first started. When you watch professional badminton players you can see that the years of practice really do make a difference, because they rarely fail to place the serve almost exactly where they want it to go.

Some skills are sport-specific but many can be transferred from one sport to another. For example, the skill of passing a ball by throwing it between members of the same team is used in basketball, netball, and rugby.

Skills can be classified in one of three ways:

Discrete skills:
These are skills that have a definite beginning and a definite end, and which happen only once. A good example is the golf swing. It begins with the player addressing the ball, and ends at the point where the club is pointing behind the player (i.e. after the follow through phase). To perform the skill again, the player must make a conscious effort to return to the starting position.

Continuous skills:
These are skills that **do not** have a definite beginning and end, but which appear to be the same technique repeated over and over again. A good example is the leg action in cycling. Once the rider is moving, it is impossible to determine where one rotation ends and the next one begins, but it is clearly the same skill performed repeatedly.

BRONZE

1. List three discrete skills, three continuous skills, and three serial skills.

2. Break the serial skills you listed into their component parts. For example, the serial skill of the triple jump can be broken down into the hop, the skip, and the jump.

Serial skills:
These are a series of discrete skills performed in sequence. Perhaps the most recognizable example is the triple jump. Here, there are three discrete phases – the hop, the skip, and the jump – which are performed in sequence and are specific to this activity.

What is a technique?

A technique is the way in which you perform a particular skill. There are many different parts to a badminton serve and when you put all the parts together you are performing a skill; the way in which you put them together is your technique. Two people might be able to perform a skill equally effectively but one might have a much better technique than the other.

These images show a student completing four of the seven stages that make up a successful badminton serve.

What are tactics?

Tactics can be thought of as the plan of action set to outwit your opponent and gain an advantage. A coach may work with a badminton player during practice sessions to put together a game plan or series of tactics for the next game. The coach may point out weaknesses that are known about the opponent and how certain shots may be used to take control of the court as a result.

It is important to remember that tactics can be changed throughout a game, if things are not going as planned. For example, you often see coaches and managers shouting instructions, making substitutions, and changing the formation being used during football matches.

When devising tactics, they can be considered as a whole-team approach, an attacking approach, or a defending approach. Whichever method is used, tactics involve a working knowledge of:

- **Positioning:** This can be the position of the whole team (such as a zone defence in basketball), the position of an individual (such as playing from the baseline in tennis), or the positioning of small groups of players within a team (such as the positioning of the back row in rugby union). Usually, positioning will be considered in two basic situations: positioning when in attack and positioning when in defence. However, at the top level, teams will often use a combination of all these components of positioning.
- **Decision-making:** Knowledge of which skill to use in which situation is vital if you are going to beat an opponent. Usually, the decisions are made during the game or match, but in some cases prior knowledge of a team-mate's or an opponent's ability will cause a player to use a specific stroke or shot. For example, football teams who have a tall centre forward will often play high balls into the box, knowing that they have an increased chance of winning the ball in the air.
- **Variation:** Using the same tactics over and over again is rarely successful, particularly in professional sport. Opposing coaches, managers, teams, and players will quickly work out what is happening, and adjust their own tactics to cope. For example, if a team regularly plays high balls into the box because they have a tall centre forward, the defending team will quickly change their own tactics in an attempt to stop their opponents delivering the high balls. They may do this by shutting down wide players early or by moving their defence higher up the pitch and forcing the centre forward into an offside position. The attacking team then have to vary their tactics in order to be successful.
- **Conditions:** The weather can have a major impact on the tactics employed by a team or player. In high winds, golfers will try to keep the ball low to reduce the likelihood of a ball veering off target. In bright sunshine, rugby teams will kick the ball high towards their opponents so it is difficult for them to see, which increases the chances of a knock-on occurring. The importance of a game or the size of the crowd can also have a major effect on tactics. A tennis player, playing on centre court at Wimbledon for the first time, is likely to play to their own strengths and will rarely try to implement new tactics or play unusual strokes.
- **Use of space:** The most common tactic is to create space when attacking and to close down available space when defending. Players who are able to create space also create the time needed to make a decision, which in turn allows them to choose the most appropriate course of action (to decide whether to shoot, pass, or dribble in basketball, for example). A player who is denied time and space is much more likely to make a mistake.

BRONZE

3. Thinking about one of your chosen sports, create a large concept map identifying all the skills and techniques required for this sport.

4. Choose three attacking strategies used by a team or player in a sport of your choice, and describe ways that an opposing team or player could counteract them.

5. Plan a way of gathering evidence of the different skills, techniques, and tactics that you will develop in your chosen sports. You could keep a diary, a logbook or a portfolio; a record of witness testimonies, feedback sheets, or an observation record; and use audio or video equipment.

Developing skills, techniques, and tactics in training

It is essential that skills, techniques, and tactics are demonstrated during training in order for athletes to develop a thorough understanding of what is required and be able to perform effectively during competition. All demonstrations should take place within a safe, controlled environment. This means that athletes should stop and watch the demonstration rather than it taking place during competition, set plays, or drills.

There are three types of practice for developing skills, techniques, and tactics:

Isolated practice

During isolated practice, individual skills and techniques can be rehearsed over and over again, independently and without pressure from other players. Isolated practice allows an athlete to learn to successfully complete a specific skill or technique without fault.

Successful isolated practice will lead to accurate replication of skills in competitive situations.

Conditioned practice

A conditioned practice is similar to a full game, but conditions are applied to the game to force players to reproduce a certain skill, technique, or tactic. For example; a conditioned football match could have a limit on the number of touches a player can have before passing the ball therefore developing their ability to pass and move. Another way of developing this skill would be to insist on a certain number of passes between the team before someone can shoot at the goal.

Players work on their passing and moving in conditioned practices so that they perform this way come game day.

Competitive situations

Once skills and techniques have been thoroughly practised through isolated practice and skills, techniques, and tactics have been honed through conditioned practice, it is important to use them in competitive situations. There is no point being able to perform a perfect layup in basketball with your team-mates, if the speed of a competitive game and the pressure of a crowd causes you to make mistakes. A fully competitive situation will include teams fielding full sides, an appropriate opposition and the appropriate officials. These can take place in PE lessons, but are more commonly experienced during inter-school, club, and county fixtures.

Players use all the skills and techniques practised in training to outwit their opponents and try to win the game.

BRONZE

6. Prepare a training session for a sport of your choice that includes safe and appropriate participation in isolated practices and conditioned practices.

Unit 2 assignment, part two

Background

Your school is creating a 'Leadership Academy' for students. The academy is looking for energetic, well-motivated, and able students to work alongside staff from the sports development team to plan and lead a variety of sports festivals and competitions for primary school children. You have decided to apply to become a member of the Leadership Academy and need to prepare for the interview. You have been asked to bring along something to demonstrate your knowledge and understanding of sports activities.

Task

Collect and then present evidence that you regularly take part in different physical activities. Your presentation, which should last about 10–15 minutes, needs to:

Grading criteria to be assessed
1B.4, 1B.5
2B.P4, 2B.P5
2B.M2

 **LEVEL 1**

- Describe the technical demands of two selected sports. (1B.4)
- Use relevant skills and techniques effectively, in two selected sports, in isolated practices. (1B.5)

 **LEVEL 2 PASS**

- Describe the technical and tactical demands of two selected sports. (2B.P4)
- Use relevant skills, techniques and tactics effectively, in two selected sports, in conditioned practices. (2B.P5)

 **LEVEL 2 MERIT**

- Use relevant skills, techniques and tactics effectively, in two selected sports, in competitive situations. (2B.M2)

Tackling the assignment

There are a number of different ways that you could approach this assignment but a good one is to produce a video interview demonstrating your knowledge of the skills, techniques, and tactics that you have learned and use regularly in training and competitive situations for two of your chosen sports.

Reviewing sports performances

When we watch sports performers we often comment on how well they have performed skills and executed techniques. Understanding how to make accurate observations and constructively review sports performances – your own, your team's, and your opponent's – will help you become a better sportsperson. There are four stages to reviewing a sports performance.

Observation

A lot of information can be obtained about a performer's skills and techniques, and how well their tactics are working, by observing practical performances. Observations can be live, when the performance is happening and being observed in real-time, or recorded, when the performance has been filmed and is observed later. The latter method is favoured by most coaches and managers because the footage can be played back to different performers as many times as is necessary and, therefore, helps performers analyse their own performance.

An observation checklist is a very useful tool that helps an observer to focus on important aspects of a performance and to communicate their observations to the performer. An observation checklist will be specific to a particular sport and, to compile one, you need to think about:

- The skills and techniques the performer should be demonstrating.
- The tactics the performer should be demonstrating.

- The data to be collected. This could include information about points scored and conceded; times, distances, or heights achieved; passes, interceptions, and tackles; or penalties given away and other infringements of the rules.
- The level the performer is at. An observation checklist aimed at performers at club level will be different from one aimed at international performers, because international performers are at a higher level and will therefore be more likely to be working on fine-tuning their skills, techniques, and tactics.
- How you are going to record your observations during the performance. Are you going to tick boxes, make notes, or score performers against criteria?

Analysis and evaluation

When you have observed a performer you are ready to analyse and evaluate their performance. This involves looking carefully at your observations and highlighting the performer's strengths and areas for improvement.

Having a good understanding of the sport you are reviewing is vital if you are going to carry out an effective analysis of a performer. It is important to understand the skills and techniques of the sport, and how these can be applied tactically in different situations, so that the feedback you give to the performer about their strengths and weaknesses is appropriate.

When you are observing, analysing, and evaluating a performer, you should also look beyond the performance itself to consider the performer's strengths and weaknesses in other areas that aren't sport specific but that could have an impact on performance, including:

- **Application of and respect for the rules and regulations:** Performers who are very knowledgeable about their sport, or understand the rules and regulations and how they can be used to improve their performance, are often successful.
- **General fitness:** The ability of the individual to participate in their sport to a good standard without them getting tired and their performance deteriorating should be considered as much as their technical ability.

- **Teamwork:** For team sports, how well a performer works with other members of the team is just as important as, if not more important than, their individual skills and techniques. A coach or manager sometimes needs to decide whether a player with outstanding skills should be replaced by someone who has weaker skills but is more of a team player.
- **Discipline:** Good discipline in sport is essential, especially when you are competing at a high level. Good discipline will help keep a sports performer at the peak of their fitness both in terms of general fitness and also sport-specific fitness. An elite sports performer will need to keep up with their training schedule, even when times get tough or the weather is quite challenging.
- **Preparation:** All performers need to adequately prepare for an event, be it a 'friendly' game or part of a competition. An observer can quickly determine how well a performer understands the benefits of preparation and what impact it might have on their performance.
- **Effective decision-making:** A performer's ability to make decisions based on the flow of the game, race, or competition is very important. This highlights not only their technical ability but also their tactical sense of the game. Making good decisions at the right time, often makes the difference between winning and losing.
- **Health and safety:** A performer's knowledge of health and safety, and how they apply this knowledge to a competitive setting (to ensure they don't pose a risk to themselves or others), is very important.

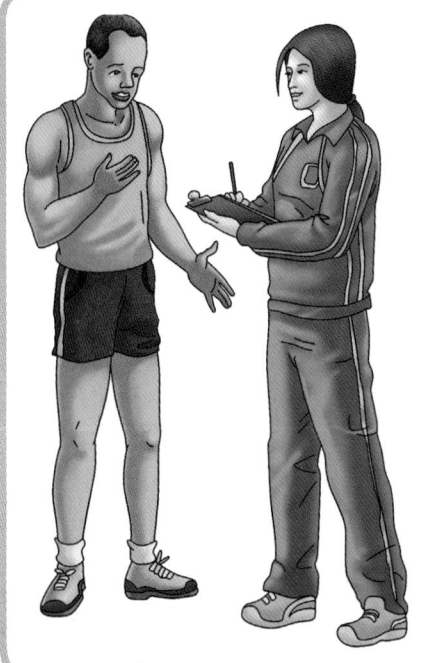

Review

When you have analysed and evaluated a performance and identified a performer's strengths and areas for improvement, you need to communicate your findings to the performer. It is important that you make sure your feedback is constructive and positive and, above all, that it motivates the performer.

One successful model for constructive feedback works like this:
- Ask the performer how they feel it went.
- Tell the performer how you think it went.
- Ask the performer what they think they did well.
- Tell the performer what you think they did well, using specific examples from your observation, analysis, and evaluation.
- Ask the performer what they think they could do differently or better.
- Tell the performer what you think they could do differently or better, using specific examples from your observation, analysis, and evaluation.
- Agree the next steps together. These could be short-term, medium-term, or long-term goals, and could focus on anything from individual skills, techniques, or tactics to teamwork or fitness.

Implementation

The next stage is to implement the changes required in order to improve performance. This can be done by:
- Working with coaches, teachers, and personal trainers or alone to create and stick to a personal training programme.
- Attending a course run by fully qualified coaches.
- Observing an elite performer in action, including professional players, world record holders, national competitors, and Olympic champions. The advantage of observing elite performers is that they will almost always display a technically perfect model. For example, Roger Federer's service shows the perfect model for each of the three phases: preparation, execution, and recovery. Watching his serve allows young players to compare their own performance with one that is accepted as perfect. It is even possible with modern technology to record your own performance of a skill and then overlay it on a recording of a professional performing the same skill, so that you can compare their body shape and positioning with your own.
- Seeking help or advice from a coach, a manager, or team-mates, or by approaching national government bodies for support and guidance if the help and advice needed isn't available within your school, college, or club.

This may sound straightforward but when a performer who has done something in a certain way for a long time is then asked to modify their practice, there can be difficulties. Sometimes, performers take a step backwards before making improvements. Their coach or manager needs to be aware of this and encourage them, giving praise when it is deserved and constantly motivating the performer to work hard.

Using video analysis software such as Dartfish™ can make implementing required changes easier. Here, the focus is a long jump.

Unit 2 assignment, part three

Background

As part of your ongoing development in your chosen sports, it is important that you are able to review your own performance. This helps you to understand how it feels to have your performance reviewed, which will make you better at reviewing the performances of others. Identifying your strengths and areas for improvement, and implementing the changes needed to improve your performance, will also make you a better athlete.

Task

Using yourself as a case study, create a presentation that illustrates how you can use an observation checklist to analyse performance and how the findings can be used to identify areas for improvement. You should:

Grading criteria to be assessed
1C.6, 1C.7
2C.P6, 2C.P7
2C.M3
2C.D2

- Produce, with guidance, an observation checklist that can be used effectively to review own performance in two selected sports. (1C.6)
- Review own performance in two selected sports, identifying strengths and areas for improvement. (1C.7)

- Independently produce an observation checklist that can be used effectively to review own performance in two selected sports. (2C.P6)
- Review own performance in two selected sports, describing strengths and areas for improvement. (2C.P7)

- Explain strengths and areas for improvement in two selected sports, recommending activities to improve own performance. (2C.M3)

- Analyse strengths and areas for improvement in two selected sports, justifying recommended activities to improve own performance. (2C.D2)

Tackling the assignment

When planning the checklist, you need to think carefully about what it is you are trying to find out. Most people can observe a performance and comment on something that is good or not so good, but your observation and analysis needs to be more detailed than this. Essentially, you need to look at each part of your performance: the individual skills used, how successfully the skills are applied, and your knowledge and understanding of the rules and regulations. Try to break down the information you want to find out; you may find producing a concept map is a useful starting point. Then, once you have a list of ideas, you can begin to group them together to form your checklist.

There are a number of different ways you can tackle the rest of the assignment but a good one is to produce a DVD showing you in action in your chosen sports. The DVD could demonstrate the skills, techniques, and tactics that you use regularly in game situations. You can then use your observation checklist to observe your performance, and your findings to review your performance.

Remember:

If you are aiming for a Level 2 Pass then it is important that you produce your observation checklist without support from your teacher or tutor.

Meeting the Level 2 Pass, Merit, and Distinction criteria

BTEC Level 2 Firsts in Sport

Unit 2 assignment, part three   Abi Edward
Observation checklist

Observation grade	Total observation grade	Player's overall performance
5 = Excellent	15–25	Poor
4 = Very good	26–36	Not very good
3 = Good	37–50	Good
2 = Not very good	51–65	Very good
1 = Poor	66–75	Excellent

Place the grade you think the player is performing at next to each skill in the table below.

Player's name: Abi Edwards	Sport: Badminton

	Observation grade
Physical abilities	
Has the player got good balance?	3
Is the player physically fit?	3
Mental abilities	
Is the player always concentrating?	3
Has the player got the determination to win or come back from behind?	2
Footwork/positioning	
Is the player in the centre of the court when attacking?	3
Does the player stand in a side-on position?	4
Ability to attack	
Does the player use a range of attacking shots?	3
Does the player place the shuttlecock where it's hard for the opponent to hit it?	4
Ability to defend	
Does the player use a range of defensive shots?	3
Does the player drive the opposition into a defensive position?	2
Shot selection	
Does the player perform the correct shots at the right time?	3
Does the player serve correctly depending on where the opposition is situated in the service box?	3
Tactical awareness	
Do the strokes played make the opposition move to the front and back of the court?	3
Application of skill	
Can the player perform a range of different shots?	4
Is the player comfortable playing difficult shots, such as the backhand drop shot?	2

Strengths	Areas to develop
On the whole, I play at a good standard, have a consistent game, and am generally successful in both attacking and defending situations. I am able to select and apply appropriate shots with success for the majority of the time.	More work needs to be done on driving the opposition into defensive positions, such as moving the opponent to the back of the court or forcing the opponent to play a backhand shot.

This observation checklist clearly shows that different areas of the performance are being observed. The framework allows skills and other factors, such as physical and psychological factors, to be observed. If the checklist was produced with some tutor support, Abi will achieve 1C.6. If it was produced without tutor support, she will achieve 2C.P6.

As it stands, this piece or work would achieve 2C.P7 because the performance has been reviewed and strengths and areas for improvement have been described.

To achieve 2C.M7, Abi would need to explain the strengths and areas for improvement, and not just describe them. To do this, she would need to make links between the observation grades and her analysis, and recommend things that the observed player could do to improve.

To achieve 2C.D2, Abi needs to go a step further and write about her own strengths and areas for improvement in her two selected sports in more detail and not just describe them. This means that she needs to write down what her areas for improvement are and say why they are important in her two sports, and then recommend activities that could help to improve her performance. Finally, she needs to write about why she has selected these particular activities and how she thinks they will help her improve her performance.

Unit 3: The Mind and Sports Performance

Personality and sports performance

Psychologist Raymond B Cattel defined personality as 'that which permits a prediction of what a person will do in a given situation'. An individual's personality is unique. It is based on a series of traits or characteristics that are exclusive to that person and these can have an impact on their sports performance.

Although someone's personality does not predict excellence in sport, psychologists believe that athletes who perform well often display positive mental characteristics or traits. They indicate that successful sports performers are often less anxious, less depressed, and less confused.

The structure of personality

Sports psychologist Rainer Martens believes that the structure of someone's personality depends on a series of factors, which can be presented visually.

Theories of personality

There are three main theories of personality: the trait approach, the situational approach, and the interactional approach.

The trait approach to personality

The trait approach to personality, based on the work of sports psychologist Matt Jarvis, states that personality traits are developed when we are very young and do not change as we grow older.

External / **Changing**

Role-related behaviours
The way in which a person behaves often depends on the circumstances they find themselves in or the role they take on at a particular time. For example, a person may be involved in a competitive basketball game at the weekend where they interact with their team-mates and show lots of communication skills, but when they are at home during the week they may enjoy spending time alone, not communicating with anyone other than family members.

Typical responses
A person's typical responses are the ways in which they usually respond in a given situation. For example, a person may generally be confident and loud when they are surrounded by their friends, but often become shy and nervous when faced with a challenging or competitive situation, such as a sprint hurdles final race.

Internal / **Constant**

Psychological core
The psychological core is sometimes referred to as the 'real you'. The components of an individual's psychological core are relatively stable and do not often change. They consist of a person's attitude, values, interests, and beliefs. For example, if a person has a particular belief, such as the importance of fair play in sport, they will not alter this in order to fit in with the belief of others.

An individual's personality traits make them react in a certain way in any given situation, so factors such as the environment will not affect a person's reaction. For example, if a person is naturally aggressive they will behave aggressively no matter what the circumstances.

Psychologists have developed ways of categorizing people into different personality types to support the trait approach to personality.

Hans Eysenck suggested that people are either introverted or extroverted:

- **Introverts** are shy people who are happy in their own company.
- **Extroverts** are confident and outgoing. They enjoy socializing and are very comfortable in other people's company.

Type A	Type B
Impatient	Patient
Time-conscious	Relaxed
Competitive	Lazy
Outgoing	Tolerant
Aggressive	Easy-going
Driven	Calm
Forceful	Passive
Focused	Stress-free
Rushed	Laid-back

Matt Jarvis believes that people can be categorized into two types of personality, 'Type A' or 'Type B'. If a person doesn't fit into either Type A or Type B then they are classed as Type AB.

The situational approach to personality

The situational approach to personality is based on the work of Albert Bandura. It is very different from the trait approach because it states that people's personalities cannot be categorized; rather they are influenced by the situations that people find themselves in. This means that how we behave is dependent on our surroundings. For example, a person may be quiet and calm when they are with their family, but they may become aggressive when playing in a competitive situation.

Bandura focused particularly on the concepts of modelling and feedback:

- **Modelling:** This means that people base their actions on the actions of others by observing and copying them. For example, someone who admires David Beckham might watch him play and then try to copy his techniques on the field.
- **Feedback:** When we are given praise or congratulated on our behaviour or performance, we will endeavour to emulate this so that we can receive further positive feedback. Similarly, if we behave badly or our performance is not so good, we will receive negative feedback and will then try to improve so as not to receive such feedback in the future.

The interactional approach to personality

The interactional approach to personality combines the trait approach and the situational approach to personality. It suggests that a combination of an individual's personality traits and the situation that they find themselves in will determine how they react. It also states that on some occasions, the situational factors may supersede the personality traits. For example, a dancer who is typically shy and reserved may uncharacteristically leap and cheer in excitement when given top marks for a performance.

The effects of personality on sports performance

The type of personality that you have may affect the sports that you take part in. For example, an extrovert may enjoy taking part in team activities, such as netball or hockey, whereas an introvert might prefer individual sports where they can work alone, such as cycling or swimming.

There is no evidence to suggest that success in any sporting activity is dependent on the type of personality that you have, however there are significant differences in the way that Type A and Type B personalities conduct themselves in a competitive situation. For example, Type A personalities will strive for the perfect performance and will always aim to win the game.

In contrast, Type B performers are more laid-back and they take part in sport for enjoyment and entertainment rather than to win. Nevertheless, despite a relaxed approach to winning, there have been many successful Type B sports performers, including Roger Federer. He is considered by many to be the world's greatest tennis player, but he is extremely modest and inconspicuous. Yet, he has very high standards, often seeking perfection in his performances, and being over critical with himself when he does not achieve the desired result.

Are you like Roger Federer? He has a Type B personality but is phenomenally successful in his chosen sport.

Measuring personality

Questionnaires are often used as a way of measuring personality. There are two that are commonly used: Eysenck's Personality Inventory (EPI) and the Profile of Mood States (POMS). Observing someone is another way to measure personality.

The results of personality tests are useful to sports performers. For example, if the results of a personality questionnaire indicate that a performer is an introvert, they may be guided towards sports that are less invasive or competitive and be happier and more successful as a result. Personality tests can also be used to predict whether or not a young athlete has the potential to become a future talent in sport.

EPI (Eysenck's Personality Inventory)

EPI measures a person's temperament; their character and how that character presents itself. Eysenck believed that a person's temperament can be split into three main categories:

- Category A: Extraversion/introversion
- Category B: Emotional stability
- Category C: Psychoticism/socialization

Categories A and B can be presented as a diagram.

Hans Jurgen Eysenck.

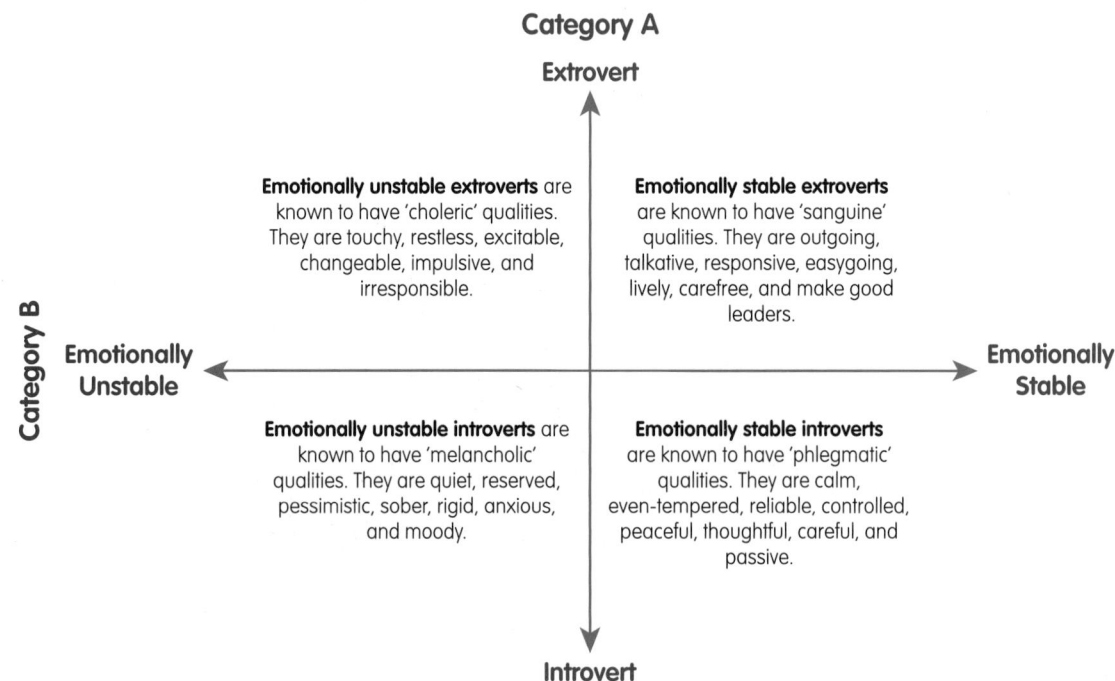

Category A

Extrovert

Emotionally unstable extroverts are known to have 'choleric' qualities. They are touchy, restless, excitable, changeable, impulsive, and irresponsible.

Emotionally stable extroverts are known to have 'sanguine' qualities. They are outgoing, talkative, responsive, easygoing, lively, carefree, and make good leaders.

Category B

Emotionally Unstable ← → **Emotionally Stable**

Emotionally unstable introverts are known to have 'melancholic' qualities. They are quiet, reserved, pessimistic, sober, rigid, anxious, and moody.

Emotionally stable introverts are known to have 'phlegmatic' qualities. They are calm, even-tempered, reliable, controlled, peaceful, thoughtful, careful, and passive.

Introvert

BRONZE

1. Complete the Eysenck personality questionnaire at http://xestia.net/tests/epq.php What sort of personality do you have?

Category C, also known as mastery/sympathy in the online test, is focused on psychoticism and socialization. At the psychoticism end of the scale, a person is liable to experience psychotic episodes, which often involve aggressive behaviour and may include one or more of the following: hallucinations, delusions, and problems communicating with others.

People who behave in a psychotic manner usually display negative personality traits, including inconsiderateness, hostility, recklessness, impulsiveness, and anger. At the socialization end of the scale people display personality traits that suggest they are happy to live their lives in the way that is expected of them by society. They behave according to the values taught to them from a very early age and in line with cultural expectations. Eysenck suggests that the higher the levels of the hormone testosterone, the more likely someone is to display psychotic behaviour.

Profile of Mood States (POMS)

POMS was developed by Douglas M McNair, Maurice Lorr, and Leo F Droppleman in 1971. It is used to assess six dimensions of a person's mood as well as provide an overall rating of psychological distress. The six dimensions are:

- fatigue–inertia
- vigour–activity
- tension–anxiety
- depression–dejection
- anger–hostility
- confusion–bewilderment

Observation

A more simplistic method of assessing personality is by using observational techniques, by observing their traits and behaviours as well as their facial expressions. For example, Joey Barton has been booked and sent off the pitch on numerous occasions for aggressive behaviour during the game. From this an observer might conclude that he is an extrovert and has a Type A personality. However, unless they were able to observe him on and off the pitch, playing football, and at home with his friends and family, they would struggle to decide whether his aggressive behaviour was part of his psychological core, represented his typical response to certain situations, or was a role-related behaviour.

Similarly, if a person constantly looks worried or anxious you can observe that they may suffer from anxiety or depression. However, unless you were able to observe them over a long period of time, watching their 'typical behaviour' in different situations, it would be difficult to say whether they became stressed in certain situations or if they were suffering from a long-term disturbance of their psychological core.

BRONZE

2. Describe the similarities and differences between EPI and the POMS test.

Joey Barton yells at the player from the opposing team in frustration on the pitch. This is the typical unreserved behaviour of an extrovert 'Type A' person.

Unit 3 assignment, part one

Background

You are on work experience with a sports psychologist and have been asked to work with a local coach to analyse the different personality types of each of his players and the effect their personalities have on their performance.

Task

Find out about personality, the different theories of personality, and the effect that personality can have on sports performance, and prepare a presentation for the coach. The presentation should be supported by additional resources, such as a handout of the PowerPoint® presentation, that are suitable for his up-and-coming players to read. You must make sure that you:

Grading criteria to be assessed
1A.1
2A.P1
2A.M1
2A.D1

 **LEVEL 1**

Outline personality and the effect it can have on sports performance. (1A.1)

 **LEVEL 2 PASS**

Using relevant examples, describe personality, including methods of measurement and three different views. (2A.P1).

 **LEVEL 2 MERIT**

Explain three different views of personality, and how personality can affect sports performance. (2A.M1)

 **LEVEL 2 DISTINCTION**

Analyse three different views of personality, and how personality can affect sports performance. (2A.D1)

Tackling the assignment

To achieve a Level 2 Pass, your PowerPoint® presentation and accompanying resources should **describe** personality, the different methods used to measure personality, such as EPI, POMS, and observational techniques, and the three different theories of personality. You also need to describe how personality can affect sports performance.

To meet the Merit criteria you must **explain** the three theories of personality and how personality can affect sports performance. You need to provide lots of detail about each theory and

draw links between the theories and their effects on sports performance. Remember to use lots of sporting examples. To meet the Distinction criteria, you need to go a step further and **analyse** the three different theories of personality and how they affect sports performance. This means you need to provide the positive and the negative effects of personality on sports performance and provide your own opinion about which of the three theories is most appropriate. Again, you should provide lots of examples to back up your arguments.

Meeting the Level 2 Pass criteria

Personality and sports performance

Jodie Evans

Everyone has a different personality. Personality is made up of lots of different characteristics, which make a person individual.

According to some psychologists, there are different types of personality. One of these is a 'Type A' personality. If someone is a Type A, they are always in a hurry. They are also determined to do well, especially if they are involved in sport. The other type of personality is 'Type B'. If a person is Type B they can be quite lazy and relaxed and they are not as determined as a Type A person. I think I am a Type A person.

Albert Bandura was a psychologist who said that the situation a person is in will affect how they behave. He said that we can change depending on who we are with and where we are at the time. He also said that sometimes people will use role models as an example of how they should behave. Someone like Messi, who is a good football player, is a good role model for people who are involved in football and they may want to be as good as him.

Bandura also said that if you are given feedback on how you perform and the feedback is positive, you are likely to perform well the next time so that you can receive the same positive feedback again. It is the same if you perform badly and your coach tells you that you need to improve. You will probably try harder next time.

There are two different ways to measure someone's personality. Both ways involve asking a person questions about their feelings and how they might react in different situations. The first way to measure personality that I have researched is called EPI. This is a huge questionnaire that looks at the different categories of personality. You can find out if you are an extrovert or an introvert by using this questionnaire. An extrovert is someone who is lively and outgoing and has lots of friends, whereas an introvert is the opposite as they like to be alone and are quiet and shy. The questions in the EPI can help people to find out more about themselves.

The second way to measure personality is to use the POMS (Profile of Mood States questionnaire). This was developed by Douglas M McNair, Maurice Lorr, and Leo F Droppleman in 1971.

Jodie has clearly researched personality and has gathered some relevant information on the topic that can be used towards achieving the criteria for this assignment. There are, however, some gaps in Jodie's work which she needs to address before she can be awarded 2A.P1.

Jodie has given a brief description of what she interprets personality to be, but she could have supplied a definition of the term, perhaps the one in the Student Book, by Raymond B Cattel. It would also have been good to see Jodie using Rainer Martens' structure of personality to help with her description of personality.

Jodie mentions Type A and Type B personalities but doesn't link them to the trait theory of personality. I'd like to see Jodie using subheadings to break the text down, so that people reading her work understand how personality types fit into the theories of personality. I would also like to know what other characteristics Type A and Type B personalities have.

I like the way Jodie has categorized herself as a Type A personality, but I would like to see her describe why she thinks she is a Type A personality. I would also like to see examples of sports performers who are Type A and Type B personalities.

Jodie mentions the trait approach and the situational approach to personality but she doesn't mention the interactional approach. This theory should also be described.

When talking about methods used to measure personality, Jodie mentions EPI but she doesn't tell the reader what the initials stand for, who created the questionnaire, and what the different categories are. Similarly, she only briefly describes POMS and hasn't mentioned the third method of measuring personality, observational techniques, at all. Jodie needs to provide much more information if she wants to meet the criteria for 2A.P1.

From a visual point of view, Jodie's handout is a little drab. I would like to see some images or diagrams to support the text. These would make the handout more visually appealing.

Meeting the Level 2 Merit criteria

Unit 3 assignment, part one
Personality and Sports Performance

Samantha Parker

Personality

Personality is a set of traits or characteristics that make all people individual.

Views of personality

There are three views of personality. The first one is the trait view, which was developed by Matt Jarvis. This view says that when we are young we develop traits and these do not change as we get older. The number of traits that we can have might vary, but they could include things like cheerfulness, caring, determination, and aggressiveness. Jarvis said that our traits will make us react in a particular way in certain situations.

There are two main types of personality in the trait view: Type A and Type B. A Type A person may be in a rush, aggressive, and have no patience. This type of person may be suited to sports that require a fast pace, aggression, and determination, such as basketball or rugby. A Type B person can be lazy, calm, and patient. This type of person may be suited to more laid-back sports activities, such as golf or snooker. If a person isn't a Type A or B person, they can be called Type AB as they may have traits from both of the other categories. This type of person may choose any sport as they have a mixture of personality traits.

Another view of personality is the situational view, developed by Albert Bandura. This view is different from the trait view because it says that a person does not fit into a category. Instead, their personality can be affected by the situations they are in. For example, a cricket player might usually be calm and relaxed but if they miss a catch they could become mad with themselves and lose their temper.

The situational view also says that people have role models and copy the behaviour of their role models. For example, a young boy may want to be like David Beckham so he might copy his behaviour. Also, giving feedback to someone can affect their performance in sport. Telling someone they have done well or been successful could make them work to repeat the performance or do better because they enjoy receiving the praise. In the same way, if someone performs poorly and they receive negative feedback (if they miss the ball when batting in rounders for example) they might up their game next time because they don't want to get any more negative comments.

The last view of personality is the interactional view. This view is a mixture of the other two views and says that a person's traits and the situation they are in will make them behave in a certain way. For example, if they are normally shy they might become excited if they do well because the situation makes them happy.

Well done, Samantha. This is a good start to this assignment. I like the way you have illustrated your work with a photograph, which makes it more interesting for the reader. It could be made even more accessible by breaking the information down with more headings though.

Samantha is well on her way to meeting the Merit criteria. She has explained the three views on personality in detail, stating who developed them and including good sporting examples. In order to fully meet the criteria for 2A.M1, Samantha now needs to explain how personality can affect sports performance.

Meeting the Level 2 Distinction criteria

Personality and Sports Performance

Craig Hackett

What is personality?

Everyone has a different personality that is made up of lots of different characteristics or traits. Your personality can have an effect on the type of sport that you decide to get involved in. For example, if you are a shy and quiet person you may choose to go fishing or play golf as those sports mean that you can take your time and be on your own.

Personality has been defined as: 'the visible aspect of one's character as it impresses others: He has a pleasing personality' or 'a person as an embodiment of a collection of qualities: He is a curious personality' (http://dictionary.reference.com/browse/personality).

Views on personality

There are three main theories of personality.

The first theory is called the 'trait view' and was developed by Matt Jarvis. This view states that the way in which a person behaves will depend on the traits or characteristics that they have. These traits are developed at a very young age and stay with the person all of their life. The table below shows the two personality 'types' that Matt Jarvis refers to in his theory. These are called A and B.

Type A	Type B
Forceful	Calm
Aggressive	Patient
Impatient	Laid-back
Determined	Relaxed
Driven	Stress-free

People tend to take part in sports that suit their personality. For example, Wayne Rooney is a typical Type A person as he often displays characteristics such as aggression, impatience, and forcefulness. On occasions, this kind of behaviour can get him into trouble on the pitch, but as these are Wayne's natural characteristics, he will find it difficult to behave any differently. Someone who could be classed as a Type B personality is Roger Federer. He is always calm and composed when playing and when being interviewed post-match. Although he is clearly a determined player who is driven to succeed, his natural personality traits make him a laid-back, relaxed person. This is a completely different personality type to Wayne Rooney and I think the sports that the two men have chosen could be down to their personality traits.

A third strand to this theory is the Type AB personality. This category is for people who do not fit comfortably into either of the other two categories, but instead have several traits from each of them. An example of someone who is a typical AB personality is British heptathlete Jessica Ennis. She has lots of determination, drive, and focus, and this has certainly helped her to become successful in her sport. Despite this, when interviewed about her performances, she is calm, relaxed, laid-back and easy-going, often making a joke about her performance or her training. This shows that Jessica is well suited to athletics because she is able to switch from one side of her personality to the other, and can turn on the drive and ambition when she needs to in order to beat her opponents.

In contrast to the trait theory, the 'situational theory' developed by Albert Bandura states that it is not a person's traits that determine how they will behave, but the situation that they find themselves in. Bandura said that a person's surroundings can have a direct effect on their behaviour. An example of this is football hooliganism. A person who is usually calm and laid-back may lose their temper and become aggressive if they see their friends or family members become involved in an altercation with other football fans. Although they may not have set out to become involved in the trouble, the situation they find themselves in could make this happen.

Bandura also said that two other factors can have an effect on a person's behaviour. These are 'modelling' and 'feedback'. Modelling is when a person will try to imitate someone who they look up to and respect in order to become successful themselves. An example of this is ex-England footballer Jamie Redknapp. His father was involved in football from a young age, played professionally, and is now the manager of Tottenham Hotspur. Jamie has seen his father as a positive role model, which encouraged him to take up the sport and try to be successful. Similarly, Jamie recently encouraged his dad Harry to go for the England football team manager's position. This demonstrates that one person's behaviour can have a direct impact on another's. The same can be said of negative role models. There are often stories in the media of sports stars getting drunk and behaving badly in public. This could have a negative effect on young people who aspire to be like them as they could assume that this behaviour is acceptable or even the norm.

The term 'feedback' refers to the comments given to a performer by their coach, parent or teacher on how they performed. For example, when a trampolinist has completed their routine, they may be given tips on how to improve their performance, such as they need more height or more control when they twist. The type of feedback that an athlete receives can have an effect on future performances. They may feel happy with what has been said if they are given praise and positive comments, which will make them want to repeat their success. Alternatively, if a performer is given negative feedback, they may feel inadequate and be driven not to make the same mistakes again.

The final theory of personality is the 'interactional view'. This view does not conflict with either of the others but incorporates features from them both. The interactional view states that the way in which a person behaves is down to a combination of their individual traits and the situation that they are in. For example, a person who is normally quiet and reserved may become loud and excited in a particularly competitive situation, especially if they are successful. Their natural personality traits may be calm and relaxed but the situation they are in could make them excitable.

Of the three theories of personality, I feel that the interactional approach is the most realistic as it considers both a person's natural make up and the situations they find themselves in. Not all people will change when faced with different situations, but it is possible that a person may be influenced on occasion by other people around them, the atmosphere, and the nature of the situation, how important or competitive it is, for example.

> This is excellent work. Craig has clearly investigated the three theories of personality in great detail and has analysed the components of each, making comparisons and drawing out contrasts between them. I like the way in which he has added his own opinion at the end and has included some solid examples to support his comments. Once he has added details of how personality can affect sports performance, he will have met the criteria for 2A.D1. Well done Craig!

Motivation and its effect on sports performance

Motivation is the need or desire to achieve a goal or certain level of success. A psychology professor called Alan Cox defines motivation as a desire to fulfil a need. Motivation is important to all sports performers because if they lack motivation they will not have the necessary focus and drive to do well.

Influences on motivation

The factors that motivate people to take part in sporting activities generally fall into two categories, intrinsic factors and extrinsic factors:

- **Intrinsic factors** are those that come from within a person. Examples of intrinsic motivation include taking part in a sport because you enjoy being part of a team, because you want to gain experience of competing at a certain level, or because you get a sense of self-worth from your achievements.
- **Extrinsic factors** are external. They can include rewards such as praise, encouragement, trophies, money, or records. They can also include fear of something, such as fear of punishment or loss of status.

Achievement motivation is another way in which sports performers can remain focused and maintain their desire to be successful. By regularly setting themselves realistic and achievable goals, they can remain motivated to do well because they are always striving to achieve something. Achievement motivation is closely linked with intrinsic motivation because it relies on the performer's need to fulfil an internal desire rather than to receive material rewards.

Jessica Ennis was beaten to the title of World Heptathlon Champion by Tatyana Chernova in 2011. This photograph has really spurred Jessica to train harder and focus on the 2012 Olympic title. Jessica said of the photograph, 'That image will stay with me because I don't want to feel like that again. I'm definitely going to get a print of it, but it is already ingrained in my mind. Things like this help you to push yourself that little bit more.'

BRONZE

1. Categorize the following statements as examples of either intrinsic motivation or extrinsic motivation:

   a) 'I love to win competitions. Winning makes me feel so proud of myself.'

   b) 'If I score a goal my mum will give me £10.'

   c) 'I hope I can beat my personal best distance today.'

   d) 'My coach will be really happy if I get through to the final round.'

   e) 'I really want to take home the trophy today.'

   f) 'I want my dad to say "Well done" to me after the game.'

   g) 'I don't want to let my team-mates down.'

SILVER

2. a) Think about a time when you felt really motivated, really 'up for it', and remember what happened.

   b) Now, write a paragraph about the impact of motivation on sports performance, using your own experience as an example.

Three theories of motivation

There are three theories about how motivation can have an impact on performance. These theories are called:

- The trait-centred view of motivation.
- The situation-centred view of motivation.
- The interactional view of motivation.

The trait-centred view of motivation

The trait-centred view of motivation is based on the idea that motivation is a result of what an individual considers to be important and states that the goals we have will determine the way that we behave. It suggests that our internal desires to do well are determined by our general personality traits; by what makes us who we are. According to this theory, the basis for motivation is intrinsic.

The situation-centred view of motivation

The situation-centred view of motivation states that a person's level of motivation is dependent on their surroundings or the environment they are in. This includes any other people present in those surroundings. If a certain environment makes a person feel comfortable, they are more likely to be motivated, whereas if they are in a place where they feel uncomfortable, they may not have the same desire, or motivation, to do well.

One view is that Harry's motivation to study is dependent on his surroundings. He finds it easy to study when he is in the classroom, but much more difficult when he is surrounded by his friends. This is the situation-centred view of motivation.

A contrasting view is that Harry has an intrinsic motivation to study that isn't dependent on his surroundings. This is the trait-centred view of motivation.

The interactional view of motivation

The interactional view of motivation states that a person's level of motivation depends on both their personality and the situation that they find themselves in. This theory also states that communication and interaction with other people can play a part in the level of motivation someone experiences. This is important in sport and exercise as an individual is more likely to be successful if they have the right environment, support from others, and feel happy within themselves. It is also possible that a person might be highly motivated in a particular environment but surrounded by people they do not feel comfortable with. This would require them to be highly motivated from the outset and driven by the goal they want to achieve. For example, if a person wants to achieve a certain goal but finds that they don't like their coach, they could still be motivated to stay with the coach in order to reach their goal, if their desire to succeed is greater than their dislike of their coach.

SILVER

3. Explain the good and bad points of each of the three theories of motivation when considering sports performance.

GOLD

4. Analyse the three theories of motivation, stating which one you think is the most relevant to sports performers and why.

The benefits of good motivation on sports performance

Choosing the right activity

If a performer is motivated to follow in the footsteps of a role model or family member, or motivated by the challenge involved in a particular sport or activity, then they are more likely to succeed. Good motivation therefore plays a crucial role in a performer's choice of activity and if a performer has chosen a sport themselves they will go on to be more motivated to do as well as they possibly can.

Persistence in adversity

Often sports performers encounter difficulties during training or competition, such as illness or injury. The level of motivation a performer possesses has an impact on the likelihood of them succeeding despite these issues.

The benefits of good motivation on sports performance

Pursuing goals

Sports performers are often 'goal orientated'. This means that they focus their effort on achieving set goals in their chosen sport. For example, a track and field athlete may wish to achieve a personal best in the 400 metres in a particular championship event. This may be because they want to improve on their fastest time or because they need to achieve a certain time to be selected for a district, county, or national competition. However, although athletes will always set targets for themselves, their motivation to succeed will have a huge impact on whether or not they are able to achieve their goals.

Intensity of effort

An athlete who possesses high levels of intrinsic or extrinsic motivation will channel all their effort into ensuring that they perform to the best of their ability in order to achieve their goals. As the performer's desire to succeed becomes more intense, so too will the level of effort they put into their training and performance during a match or competition.

Alex Zanardi is an example of a sports performer persevering. Alex is an Italian racing driver and paracyclist. He was in a crash in 2001 and both his legs were amputated, yet he returned to racing less than two years after the accident and, after switching sports to handbiking, won a gold medal in the men's road time trial H4 at the London 2012 Paralympics, at the age of 45.

Goal setting

Goal setting is extremely important for sports performers. Setting goals gives performers something to work towards and helps them maintain purpose and motivation during training and competition, making them more likely to succeed. Goals can be short term or long term, but they should always be SMARTER.

Specific: Targets should be specific; they should set down precisely what you want to achieve. For example, 'I want to run the 100 metres in under 15 seconds'.

Measurable: Targets should be measurable so that you can work out if you have achieved them. For example, it is better to say that your target is to run the 100 metres in under 15 seconds than it is to say that you want to run the 100 metres faster.

Achievable: Goals should be appropriate to the fitness and skill levels of the performer. They should be close enough for us to see, but not so far away that we can't touch them.

Realistic: It is important that we set goals we have the capacity to achieve. All targets need to be challenging so that you have to work hard to achieve them, but they must also be realistic in order for them to serve their purpose and motivate you.

Time-related: Targets should have a time limit on them. For example, 'I want to run the 100 metres in under 15 seconds by the end of August'. If your long-term goals rely on you achieving your short-term goals, then you need to set time limits on your short-term goals in order to reach your long-term goals.

Exciting: Targets should have something exciting about them or relate directly to a reward. For example, your long-term target might be, 'I want to be chosen to represent the county in the English Schools Athletics Championships in June'.

Recorded: All targets should be recorded so that you and your coach can refer to them at any given time. A training diary is the ideal place to record your targets.

BRONZE SILVER

1. Imagine that you are the coach of a local sports team. Your team is lacking in motivation and you have noticed that they haven't tried any new tactics in their game play during the current season.

a) Suggest one short-term and one long-term goal for the team to motivate them to succeed and describe how these goals will motivate the players to do well.

b) Explain how the goals you have chosen can influence motivation and sports performance.

GOLD

2. Analyse the goals you have devised for Activity 1 and how effective they will be for increasing and maintaining the motivation of the team.

The influence of goal setting on performance

By setting themselves goals, sports performers give their training and performance programme structure and direction. They can use their goals to identify areas for development and can focus on these in order to perfect their overall performance. This is referred to as 'mobilizing effort'.

Goal setting encourages performers to persist with their training programme, to keep up the level of effort, because they have a goal to aim for. It also encourages athletes to develop new strategies. If an aspect of an athlete's performance is not working, if they are not meeting their goals, they may decide, in consultation with their coach, to implement a new strategy. For example, a cross-country runner who decides that sitting behind the leading pack for the majority of the race is not putting them in the best position to win might set themselves the goal of changing tactics and attempting to lead the race, extending the gap between themselves and the pack, and winning or beating a rival competitor.

The influence of goal setting on motivation

The desire to become successful in any given sport can be greatly increased if a system of goal setting is implemented. Goals provide direction for behaviour, making an athlete more focused on the tasks they need to complete in order to reach their goals and succeed. Both short-term and long-term goals can increase levels of motivation. Short-term goals provide stepped chunks of progress for the athlete to focus on, whereas long-term goals provide a pathway to ultimate achievement and will keep the performer on track and hungry for success.

Self-confidence

To perform well in sports, you need to think positively, believe in yourself, and believe that you can do what you want to do. In other words, you need to have lots of self-confidence. If you do not have faith in your own abilities you won't have the confidence to take risks, to try a new training technique, or switch coaches if you feel that you are not getting anywhere. Someone who has self-confidence will also admit their mistakes and try to resolve them.

The benefits of self-confidence on sports performance

An example of a sports performer developing a positive game plan is Evander Holyfield. Despite losing his heavyweight world boxing title in November 1992 at the age of 30, he believes that he is able to regain his title despite the fact that he has fought and lost on several occasions. He was quoted in 2010 as saying, 'My goal is to be the undisputed world champion one more time before I let it go. Once I do that, I sit down. And until I do that, I continue to fight.'

Producing positive emotions
Being confident in your own abilities can generate other positive emotions, including pride in your performance and achievements, motivation to become even more successful, hope that you can achieve your goals, and elation when you meet or exceed your targets.

Improving performance
Self-confidence is one attribute that contributes to improving performance. If an athlete does not believe that they can be successful, if one of their peers or their coach tells them that they are weak, and if, for example, they take the criticism to heart, they may not perform well as a result.

The benefits of self-confidence on sports performance

Improving concentration and effort
An athlete is more likely to remain focused on the task at hand and try hard if they believe that they have the ability to succeed. A performer with low self-confidence may lose concentration and become distracted by people around them, by other competitors, the crowd, or their coach. If an athlete has low self-confidence, they are more likely to crumble under pressure and give up at the first hurdle.

Developing positive game plans
Tactics and strategies are important in sport, particularly in invasion games such as rugby. Having self-confidence enables sports performers to have the courage to create or contribute to the creation of a game plan in their sport. For example, a hockey player needs self-confidence to suggest an attacking strategy for use in a particular match and courage to execute the strategy during the game.

BRONZE

1. Imagine that you are preparing for an important competition. With a partner, decide which one of you will practise self-talk and which one will practise imagery. Spend a few minutes alone and practise the technique you have chosen. Then meet up with your partner and discuss your thoughts and feelings.

2. Write a paragraph comparing self-talk and imagery, highlighting the similarities and differences between the two methods for increasing self-confidence.

SILVER

3. a) Think of a situation when you didn't feel confident about your sporting performance and remember what happened.

b) Now, write a paragraph about the impact on sports performance, using your own experience as an example.

GOLD

4. 'Self-confidence is vital for success as a sports performer'. Discuss this statement with a partner and jot down what you consider to be the advantages of having self-confidence if you take part in sport.

Methods for increasing self-confidence

Although some people naturally have an abundance of self-confidence, other people need to work at maintaining and even improving their self-confidence. Some techniques that may be used to increase self-confidence are:

- **Self-talk:** A performer can increase their motivation and improve their self-confidence by using positive 'self-talk'; an internal running commentary of positive reinforcement. For example, a high jumper may talk themselves through the perfect bar clearance while waiting for their turn in a competition.
- **Imagery:** This technique involves sports performers picturing themselves in a particular situation, perhaps executing the perfect performance. They can try to implant this image into their subconscious and then recall it when performing.

Self-efficacy

In order to perform to their full potential and to achieve the outcome they have visualized using imagery techniques, athletes must have confidence in their own ability. Psychologist Albert Bandura refers to this situation-specific self-confidence as 'self-efficacy'. Someone with self-efficacy has a strong belief that they can be successful in a given activity. For example, a student may be a good all rounder at sports, but excel at table tennis. He therefore has self-efficacy when he plays table tennis with his classmates during PE lessons.

Factors affecting self-efficacy

Performance accomplishments
Sports performers can gain confidence in their abilities by focusing on previous positive experiences. For example, if a goal shooter has scored a perfect goal in a previous netball match, this will help them to believe that they can achieve the same success again.

Vicarious experiences
By observing other people's successful performances athletes can become more confident in their own ability. Watching videos of role models perfectly executing a specific skill or watching live demonstrations from coaches and teachers can have a significant influence on a sports performer's self-efficacy, because they can model their performance on their hero's performance and visualize themselves performing the skill to the same standard.

Factors affecting self-efficacy

Verbal persuasion
People who are close to a performer can convince them of their ability. Teachers, coaches, peers, and family members can help performers to believe in themselves by persuading them that they can achieve their goals. This can be of real benefit if the performer is having doubts about themselves or about their performance.

Imaginal experiences
If sports performers imagine what success looks like they can bring it closer to reality. This is similar to the technique of imagery, which is used to increase self-confidence, but whereas performers visualize themselves executing the perfect performance using imagery, here they imagine the feelings and rewards of success.

Coaches and teachers can convince athletes that they can perform well. Andy Murray takes advice from his coach, Ivan Lendl.

BRONZE

1. In order to monitor your self-efficacy you can use a scale like this one:

0	10	20	30	40	50	60	70	80	90	100
Cannot do at all					Moderately certain can do					Highly certain can do

Copy the scale and circle or highlight the number that currently applies to your level of self-efficacy. Over a one-week period, practise the methods that boost self-efficacy and record any changes that occur by regularly monitoring how you feel using the scale. Keep a diary of the experience.

Unit 3 assignment, part two

Background

You have sustained an injury and cannot play sport for several weeks. In order to remain involved with sport while you are in recovery, your coach has suggested that you assist her with a project that she is undertaking. She has asked you to research and report back to her on the influence of motivation, self-confidence, and self-efficacy on sports performance with suggestions as to how to develop these psychological aspects.

Grading criteria to be assessed
1B.2, 1B.3, 1B.4, 1B.5
2B.P2, 2B.P3, 2B.P4, 2B.P5
2B.M2, 2B.M3
2B.D2

Task

Create a handbook or leaflet describing motivation, self-confidence, and self-efficacy, describing ways to develop these psychological aspects and discussing their influence on sports performance. Your handbook or leaflet should:

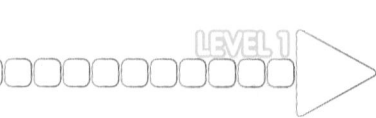 **LEVEL 1**

- Describe types of motivation and the benefits motivation and self-confidence have on sports performance. (1B.2)
- Outline appropriate methods to increase self-confidence in sport. (1B.3)
- Outline factors that influence self-efficacy in sport. (1B.4)
- Outline goal setting, different types of goals that can be set and how these can influence sports performance. (1B.5)

 **LEVEL 2 PASS**

- Describe types and views of motivation and the benefits motivation and self-confidence have on sports performance. (2B.P2)
- Summarise, with relevant examples, methods to increase self-confidence in sport. (2B.P3)
- Describe, using relevant examples, factors that influence self-efficacy in sport. (2B.P4)
- Describe goal setting, different types of goals that can be set, and how these can influence sports performance and motivation. (2B.P5)

 **LEVEL 2 MERIT**

- Discuss the benefits motivation and self-confidence have on sports performance. (2B.M2)
- Discuss how goal setting can influence motivation and the roles of the different types of goals that can be set. (2B.M3)

LEVEL 2 DISTINCTION

- Analyse the benefits motivation and self-confidence have on sports performance. (2B.D2)

Tackling the assignment

To achieve the Pass criteria you need to provide the reader with descriptions. Read the criteria carefully, to make sure you are describing exactly what you are being asked to **describe**, and don't forget to provide examples where you are asked to.

To achieve the Merit criteria, you need to go a step further, not just describing motivation, self-confidence, and goal-setting but discussing them in detail. When you **discuss** something, you examine it, giving arguments for and against.

If you want to achieve a Distinction for this assignment, you should **analyse** the information you are presenting, not only discussing the benefits of motivation and self-confidence but also explaining how they have an impact on sports and what those impacts are. You should justify what you are saying, offer your opinion, and provide examples from sporting situations to back up your analysis.

Meeting the Level 2 Pass criteria

Motivation

Laurel Grantham

Motivation is a feeling that you really want to achieve something. You can be really good at sports but if you don't have any motivation to win, then you will not be successful.

There are two types of motivation, one is internal and the other is external. Intrinsic motivation (internal) is a feeling or desire and can be something like a person wanting to feel good about performing or wanting to enjoy themselves. Extrinsic motivation (external) is where a person is driven to do well because they want to win a prize, like a trophy or some money.

There are three different views of motivation. These are the trait-centred view, the situation-centred view, and the interactional view.

Trait view: This view is based on intrinsic motivation and says that a person has inner 'traits' that make them want to do well in sport. The amount of motivation they have is based on their goals and what they think is important.

Situation view: This view says that how motivated you are depends on the situation you are in at the time. An example is if a person needs to take a penalty shot in football, the pressure of needing to score for their team might make them motivated to do it.

Interactional view: This view says that how motivated you are depends on both your traits and the situation you are in. A person could be really motivated in themselves but they might need a situation, such as a competition, to make them perform really well.

> Laurel has made a good start to this assignment. She has described motivation and self-confidence and has given an accurate summary of the three views of motivation.

Self-confidence

This is different to motivation as you need to have confidence in yourself to perform to the best of your ability. If you are really motivated in training but then lack self-confidence when you perform, you will not be successful. People can be naturally self-confident or they can develop this by improving their concentration and effort and by having good strategies and tactics that they can use in a game.

> Laurel does have more detail to add in order to meet all the criteria for a Pass. She needs to describe the effects that both motivation and self-confidence can have on sports performance. Then she needs to summarize, using relevant examples, the methods that can be used to increase self-confidence in sport. Finally, she needs to describe, again with examples, factors that influence self-efficacy in sport.

Meeting the Level 2 Merit and Distinction criteria

Motivation

Daisy Butler

This is an excellent start to the assignment. I am impressed with the way in which Daisy has structured her analysis of motivation. She has described motivation well, including well-sourced and referenced quotes and examples where necessary. She has begun to add in her own views on motivation and she should continue to do this throughout, alerting the reader of her opinion about each subject covered. She now needs to do the same for self-confidence.

Motivation can be described as: 'something which incites activity'. (http://thesaurus.com/browse/motivation?s=t)

Motivation is a huge factor in whether or not a sports performer is effective. It is not only down to the performer to be motivated, but it is also the responsibility of their coach to help motivate them.

'The ability to motivate and inspire is part of the formula for success. Getting athletes to believe in themselves and achieve comes far easier to some coaches than others. The coach who can motivate is able to generate the desire to excel in their athletes.' (http://sportsmedicine.about.com/od/tipsandtricks/a/qualitycoach.htm)

I agree with this statement because athletes spend a lot of time with their coaches and it is really important that the coach has a positive impact on their athlete, keeping them focused and on track.

There are two main types of motivation. These are:

- Intrinsic motivation
- Extrinsic motivation

Intrinsic motivation is something that comes from inside us. It is an internal desire to be successful for reasons that are built-in, natural, or inherent. A person who is intrinsically motivated wants to take part in sport for pleasure or self-satisfaction, rather than to win a prize or receive praise from others. This does not mean that a person does not like to receive rewards or praise; it's just that the external rewards are not the only things that keep them interested in doing well in their chosen sport. For example, an intrinsically motivated athlete may perform really well in a competition and win a trophy, however they feel more rewarded having completed the event to the best of their ability than for actually receiving a prize for their efforts.

In contrast to this, extrinsic motivation is something that is externally driven. Athletes who are extrinsically motivated are more interested in what they can physically 'get' than how they might feel about their performance.

'Extrinsic motivation refers to motivation that comes from outside an individual. The motivating factors are external, or outside, rewards, such as money or grades. These rewards provide satisfaction and pleasure that the task itself may not provide.' (http://giftedkids.about.com/od/glossary/g/extrinsic.htm)

If an athlete is extrinsically motivated, they are likely to be driven to succeed by the thought that they might win something. An example of this is the Australian cricket team who lost the Ashes for the first time in 24 years on their home turf. They are motivated to win back their title and the cup. England captain Andrew Strauss said: 'We expect them to be very strong, very determined and clearly massively motivated to win back the Ashes and we are going to have to be good enough to overcome it.' (http://www.thenational.ae/sport/cricket/australia-will-be-massively-motivated-says-strauss)

There are many benefits of being motivated to the sports performer. Many coaches and team managers use motivation techniques with their athletes. Motivation can help maintain and improve focus and assist with the development of new strategies. 'Evidence suggests that enhanced motivation promotes learning, performance, enjoyment, and persistence in sport, among other benefits' (McCullagh, 2005).

I agree with the above statement because in order for someone to learn about their sport (be it rules, regulations, tactics, or skills), they need to be interested in the first instance and be motivated to find out more about it. This means that the choice of activity is an important factor in promoting motivation.

For 2B.M2, Daisy has begun to look at the benefits of motivation but she needs to expand on this, discussing the motivational factors that can benefit a sports performer. For example, she could discuss the way in which establishing goals can be motivational and that an increase in the intensity of effort put into training and performance as a result of working towards these goals is a benefit that being motivated can have on sports performance. She then needs to do the same for self-confidence.

To meet the criteria for 2B.D2, Daisy needs to look at motivation and self-confidence in even more detail. She needs to expand on the discussion she wrote to meet the Merit criteria by justifying what she has written with real-life sporting examples. Daisy has begun to offer her own opinion but she needs to do this more frequently, using examples from her own experience to support her opinions.

Arousal and anxiety and their effects on sports performance

There has been a lot of research into the relationship between arousal, anxiety, and performance. Taking part in competitive sports makes many people feel anxious. It can also hype people up. Excessive anxiety and arousal can cause athletes to make mistakes, particularly when they are under pressure. Sports performers therefore need to learn to regulate their levels of arousal and anxiety in order to succeed.

Anxiety

Anxiety is a negative emotional state that determines the level of worry or nervousness an individual experiences.

There are two types of anxiety: trait anxiety and state anxiety.

Trait anxiety
'Trait' is another word for a personality characteristic. Trait anxiety is a fixed or relatively permanent form of anxiety, which people suffer from because their nervous system is constantly active. A person with trait anxiety is generally considered to have an anxiety disorder and will display signs of anxiousness regularly in different, often non-threatening, situations. Trait anxiety is part of an individual's natural make up. It is innate, which means you are born with it.

State anxiety
State anxiety is temporary. It is brought on by specific situations, which make a person feel anxious and activate the nervous system. For example, a competitive swimmer may have high levels of state anxiety before they are called to their starting position, though it usually settles as they begin their race.

There are two types of state anxiety: somatic anxiety and cognitive anxiety.

Somatic anxiety
Somatic anxiety has a physical effect on the body and can make the sports performer feel ill. Symptoms of somatic anxiety can include a dry mouth, a faster heart rate, a stomach upset, a tight chest, and shaking.

Cognitive anxiety
Cognitive anxiety affects the mind and thought processes. It can result in worries and negative thoughts or expectations, such as, 'I might not finish the race' or 'We're going to lose this match'. Cognitive anxiety can make someone quick-tempered or unable to concentrate.

An example of someone who suffers from anxiety is snooker player 'Rocky' Ronnie O'Sullivan. His anxiety has been such an issue that he has withdrawn from important competitions and has even considered retiring from the sport altogether. Despite being involved in competitive snooker for 20 years, Ronnie has never managed to be free of his anxious feelings.

Arousal

This is a physiological and psychological state that a performer should reach before training or competition. It is a state in which the athlete feels alert, awake, and ready for action.

Theories analysing the relationship between anxiety, arousal, and sports performance

There are four theories that analyse the relationship between arousal, anxiety, and performance in sport. These are:

- Drive theory
- The inverted U hypothesis
- Catastrophe theory
- Reversal theory

Drive theory

Drive theory, developed by Clark Leonard Hull, suggests that there is a linear relationship between arousal and performance. As a performer becomes more aroused, their performance level increases.

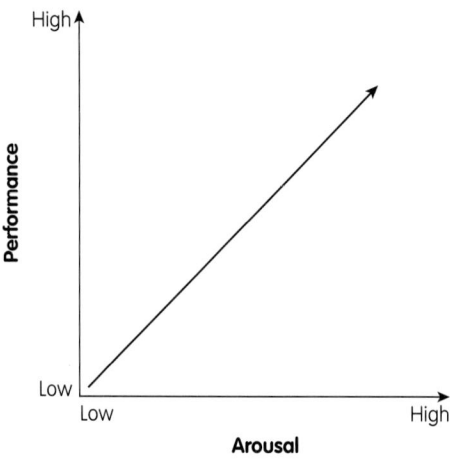

A graph showing the drive theory.

The inverted U hypothesis

The inverted U hypothesis, developed by Robert M Yerkes and John D Dodson, suggests that as levels of arousal increase, performance will improve but only to an optimal point. Following this point, or 'peak', any further increase in the level of arousal will result in the performance steadily declining.

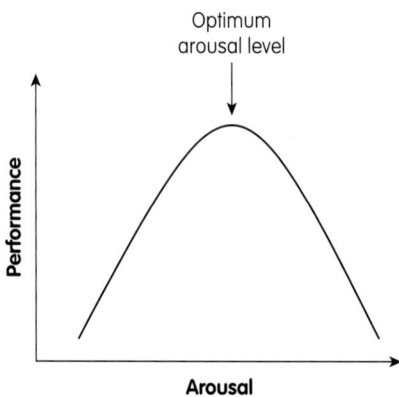

A graph showing the inverted U hypothesis.

Catastrophe theory

The catastrophe theory, developed by Lew Hardy and JA Fazey, works in a similar way to the inverted U hypothesis but it goes further and examines the interactive effects of arousal, cognitive anxiety, and performance. The catastrophe model states that once the optimum level of performance has been reached by the athlete, any further increase in the levels of arousal combined with an increase in cognitive anxiety will cause performance to decline dramatically.

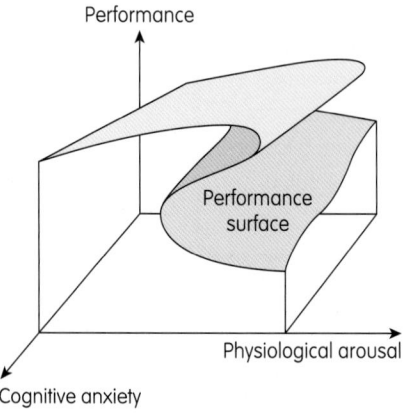

A graph showing the catastrophe theory.

Reversal theory

The reversal theory, developed by Michael J Apter and Kenneth Smith, suggests that the effect that levels of arousal will have on performance depends on the way in which the athlete interprets the arousal. For example, if the arousal is interpreted as pleasant and exciting it will not have a negative effect on the performance, but if it is interpreted as unpleasant and scary then it will have a negative effect on performance.

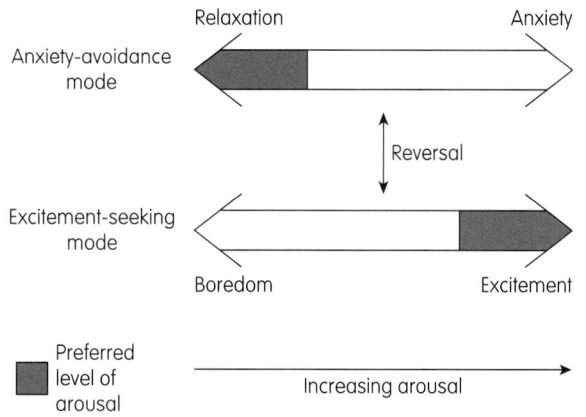

A graph showing the reversal theory.

Controlling anxiety and arousal

Engaging in techniques to control anxiety and arousal will help a performer ensure that their levels of anxiety and arousal do not affect their performance in a negative way.

The imagery technique is useful in controlling anxiety and arousal levels. It involves the performer imagining a relaxing experience, such as sitting on a beach with the waves lapping at their feet, or imagining the perfect performance. Practising the technique implants the image into the performer's subconscious and they should be able to recall it when they become anxious.

Relaxation techniques also help to control anxiety and arousal levels. There are lots of different relaxation techniques, including:

- **Progressive muscular relaxation:** The muscles are contracted for approximately four to six seconds and then relaxed. This method is usually carried out from top to toe (starting with the eyes and moving down the body) or from toe to top (starting with the toes and moving up the body) and can help the performer feel heavy and warm as their limbs relax.
- **Mind-to-muscle techniques, such as meditation:** The performer sits still and quietens their mind by concentrating on their breath. As the mind quietens, the body relaxes.
- **Breathing techniques:** When people are anxious or upset their breathing can become rapid and sometimes erratic. Breathing techniques help to calm breathing and return it to its regular rhythm. One breathing technique is as follows:
  - ❏ Breathe in through the nose and out through the mouth.
  - ❏ Inhale slowly and deeply for a count of four.
  - ❏ Hold your breath for seven seconds.
  - ❏ Slowly exhale through the mouth for a count of eight. And, as you breathe out, try to relax and release all tension from your body. You can also say a positive word, such as 'win' or 'goal', as you breathe out.
  - ❏ Repeat this at least ten times.

BRONZE

1. Describe your levels of anxiety and arousal during training and competition. Are your levels of anxiety and arousal different in training to what they are in competition? Are your levels of anxiety and arousal different at different points during a training session and during competition?

2. Practise each of the techniques for controlling levels of anxiety and arousal.

SILVER

3. Look at the description you created for Activity 1 and assess how valid each of the four theories that analyse the relationship between arousal, anxiety, and performance in sport are by referring to your own experiences.

GOLD

4. Take part in training or competition after you have completed Activity 2. Have the techniques you practised had any impact on your levels of anxiety and arousal and on your performance? Evaluate how valid each of the techniques is using your own experiences as a basis for your arguments for and against.

Unit 3 assignment, part three

Background

As a sportsperson you are continually looking at ways in which you can improve your overall performance. Your coach has decided that, as you are studying the mind and the sports performer, it would be useful for you to research arousal and anxiety and their effect on sports performance. Your coach would like for you to feed back the information that you find.

Task

Grading criteria to be assessed
1C.6, 1C.7
2C.P6, 2C.P7
2C.M4
2C.D3

Prepare a PowerPoint® presentation accompanied by detailed supporting notes highlighting the findings of your research into arousal and anxiety and their effect on sports performance. You must:

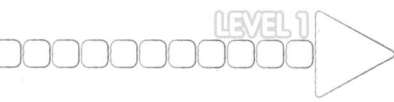 **LEVEL 1**

- Outline different types of anxiety. (1C.6)
- Describe, using two theories, the effect arousal and anxiety have on sports performance and their control. (1C.7)

 **LEVEL 2 PASS**

- Describe, using relevant examples, different types of anxiety. (2C.P6)
- Describe, using four theories, the effect arousal and anxiety have on sports performance and their control. (2C.P7)

 **LEVEL 2 MERIT**

- Assess, using four theories, the effect arousal and anxiety have on sports performance and their control. (2C.M4)

 **LEVEL 2 DISTINCTION**

- Evaluate imagery and relaxation techniques as methods of controlling arousal and anxiety, and in improving sports performance. (2C.D3)

Tackling the assignment

Read the Level 1 and Level 2 Pass criteria carefully to make sure you are describing exactly what you are being asked to **describe**, and don't forget to provide examples where you are asked to.

To achieve the Merit criteria, you need to go a step further, not just describing anxiety and arousal but assessing the effects that they have on the sports performer. When you **assess** something you check out all of the facts and interpret them, giving details of your findings.

If you want to achieve a Distinction for this assignment, you should evaluate imagery and relaxation techniques and the positive effects that they may have on helping to control anxiety and arousal. When you **evaluate** something, you survey all of the facts that you are presented with and use them to classify and calculate the impact they have on the sports performer. As always you should justify what you are saying, offering your opinion and providing examples from sporting situations to back up your evaluation.

Meeting the Level 2 Pass criteria

Kimberley Wolfinden

Four theories of arousal and anxiety

There are four main theories that describe how arousal and anxiety can affect sports performers. These theories are:

Kimberley has made a reasonable start to the assignment. She has covered much of the content required for 2C.P6 and 2C.P7, but there are one or two amendments that she should make in order to fully meet the criteria for a Pass.

Kimberley should begin her assignment with a general introduction, including a description of what anxiety and arousal are. She should also mention who developed each of the theories she describes.

Drive theory:

This theory says that the more excited or aroused a person becomes, the better their performance will be. An example of this is when a netball player begins their warm-up with their team-mates. They may be a little bit excited about the game that they are going to be playing and will feel a small amount of arousal. As the game begins and they get into position, they will feel more aroused and will start to respond to the other players and their opponents. Towards the end of the first quarter, the player could intercept a ball from their opponent and then have a chance at scoring a goal, which could happen as a result of them being very aroused by the situation.

I like the example that Kimberley has used to explain drive theory. She now needs to provide a similar example, ideally each from a different sport, for the other three theories.

Inverted U hypothesis:

This theory says that a person will start to get aroused as they begin their performance and they will eventually reach a high point where they will be at their optimal arousal point. When they are at their optimal arousal level, they will perform really well. After they have reached this point, their performance will get worse as their arousal drops and both will keep dropping until the end of their performance.

Reversal theory:

This theory was developed by Apter and Smith and they say that when a person becomes aroused during sport, they will either feel negative or positive about it, depending on what their personality is like. If they feel that their arousal is negative, this can make them perform badly, but if they think that the arousal feels positive, they will perform well.

Controlling arousal and anxiety

It is important that someone who takes part in sport can control their arousal and anxiety levels so that they do not always have a negative effect on them. One way that an athlete can try to control negative arousal or anxiety is by using imagery. This is where a person imagines that they are in a comfortable, relaxing situation, such as on holiday or in the countryside. This can help to relax them and make them get rid of the feelings of pressure from performing.

As this is a PowerPoint® presentation, Kimberley should consider adding diagrams or pictures to make it more visually appealing to the audience. She could also reduce the amount of text on each slide and place some of it on a page of supporting notes. PowerPoint® slides should contain the essential information; the detail should be provided during the speech that accompanies the PowerPoint® presentation, and recorded on a 'script' for the person giving the speech to use.

Catastrophe theory:

This theory says that as you reach your optimal level of arousal, you will also reach a high level of cognitive anxiety and this will cause your performance to peak and then drop dramatically. When this happens, a 'catastrophe' could occur, such as missing a penalty or losing possession of the ball.

Kimberley has mentioned one of the methods that may be used to control arousal and anxiety. She now needs to describe the other methods that could be implemented.

Meeting the Level 2 Merit criteria

Anxiety and arousal

Rosie Schofield

For this part of the assignment I will be assessing the effects of arousal and anxiety on the sports performer. Arousal and anxiety are both psychological factors that sports performers may encounter when they train or compete. They can sometimes have a positive effect on performance but, if not controlled, they can also be detrimental to performance.

When I was researching this topic, I found that there were four theories of anxiety and arousal. The first theory is known as the 'drive theory' and was developed by Clark Leonard Hull. Hull said that as a person becomes more aroused, their performance improves. This theory is illustrated by the following diagram:

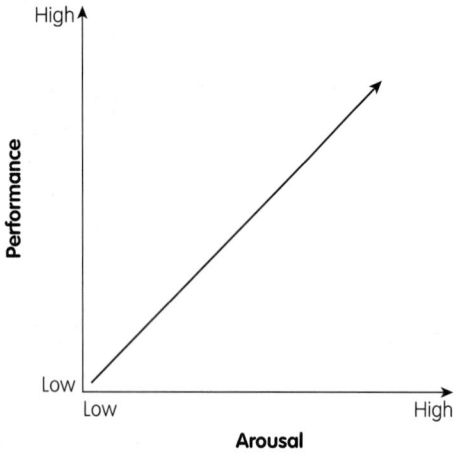

An example of someone who experiences the effects of drive theory is a high jumper. They might enter the competition at a low height and find this easy but as they continue to raise the bar they become more aroused and excited at the possibility of achieving a personal best performance.

As their arousal increases, their performance improves, resulting in a personal best height being achieved.

I believe this theory to a certain extent. However, how can the performance just keep getting better and when does it stop improving?

The next theory that I researched is called the 'inverted U hypothesis'. This was developed by Robert M Yerkes and John D Dodson and is similar to the drive theory, although it states that once an optimum level of arousal has been reached, the performance will drop off. This is represented by the following diagram:

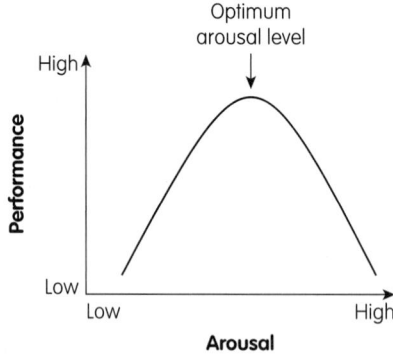

I believe this theory is quite accurate because when I have watched others taking part in a competition I have noticed that they do reach a peak and it is then difficult for them to maintain this level of performance because the moment has gone and they carry on performing at a mediocre level for the rest of the game. I think this is because they have achieved what they wanted to achieve, such as scoring a goal or swimming a fast time, and the rest of the game or competition becomes a bit boring for them.

Rosie has made a great start. She has clearly researched the theories well and has assessed their relevance with regard to the impact arousal and anxiety can have on sports performance. She has also provided great examples from sporting situations to back up what she is saying. If Rosie continues in this way with her coverage of the remaining two theories of anxiety and arousal and goes on to assess the impacts of methods that can be used to control anxiety and arousal, she will meet the criteria for a Merit.

The material we can see here is clearly Rosie's accompanying notes, as the text reads as a speech. To fulfil the task completely, she will need to create PowerPoint® slides to accompany these notes.

Methods used to control arousal and anxiety

Cain South

People who take part in sport can sometimes be affected by negative psychological issues. This can make them underperform and can affect their career in sport. There are many methods that can be used to help to control anxiety and arousal. The ones that I will be evaluating are 'imagery' and 'relaxation techniques'.

'Imagery' means to imagine something that isn't there. When sports performers need to relax and 'zone out' prior to a performance, they can use mental imagery to help them. A situation that they may find relaxing could be sitting on the beach with the waves lapping at their feet. Even though they are not actually there in person, making themselves imagine that they are, can be soothing and relaxing.

In order to use imagery to relax, an athlete would need to find a quiet, comfortable place where they can lie down. They can spend as much time as they like, but about 10–15 minutes is usually effective. They should lie with their eyes closed, picturing a scene where they feel relaxed. They can also think about the sounds that they would hear and the feelings they would feel in this situation.

I think that this technique is effective in helping sports performers to relax as they are able to completely get away from the stress and pressure of the competitive situation that they may be about to face.

'Imagery is a potent method of stress reduction, especially when combined with physical relaxation methods such as deep breathing.' (www.mindtools.com/stress/RelaxationTechniques/Imagery.htm)

A potential negative effect of using imagery to relax when preparing for a competition is that an athlete could become too relaxed and possibly sleepy. They need to have certain levels of arousal so that they can get into the optimum 'zone' (this is referred to in the 'inverted U hypothesis'). If a performer is tired or sleepy following an imagery session, they may not be able to rouse themselves sufficiently to perform to their best ability in a race or competition.

Cain has made a great start to this part of the assignment. He has really grasped the way in which imagery can help sports performers control anxiety and arousal. He has provided good examples and given his opinion on their effectiveness.

In order to further develop his evaluation and to fully meet the criteria for 2C.D3, Cain should find some evidence to support what he is saying about the negative effects of imagery. Is there a sports personality who has used this technique? What is their opinion of it? If Cain does this, and provides the same level of detail for the different relaxation techniques sports performers can use, he will certainly meet the criteria for a Distinction.

Like Rosie, Cain still needs to provide the PowerPoint® slides to accompany these notes.

Unit 4: The Sports Performer in Action

The short-term effects of exercise

Whenever we take part in any form of physical activity, be it walking the dog or running the London Marathon, our body systems undergo a series of changes. These are necessary for our bodies to work effectively and they happen automatically. The changes that happen each and every time we exercise are known as 'short-term responses'; this is because they are reversed once we stop exercising. Many of these short-term changes are really obvious – you can tell if someone has been running because they will be breathing more quickly than normal – but some are more subtle, such as the redirection of blood flow around the body.

The short-term effects of exercise on the musculoskeletal system

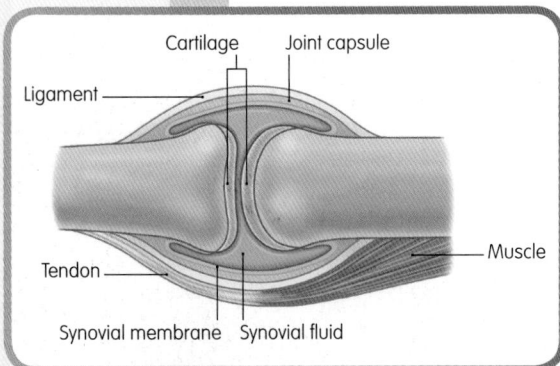

Training can lead to an increase in the amount of synovial fluid in a joint, which reduces the risk of certain injuries.

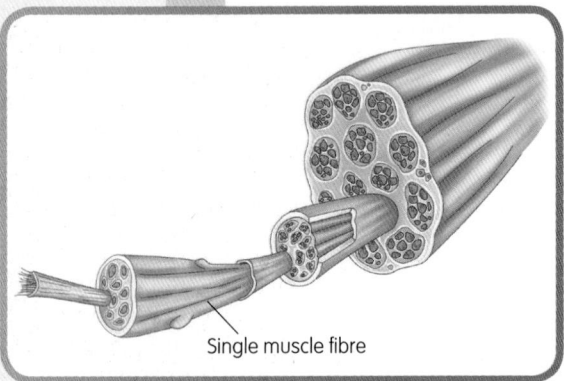

Muscle tears during exercise are common. This is not a bad thing as the small tears repair easily and make the muscle stronger in the long run.

In the short term, exercise has the following effects on the musculoskeletal system:

Increases production of synovial fluid
All the freely movable joints in the body are lubricated by an oily liquid called synovial fluid. This acts like the oil in a car engine in that it prevents wear and tear on the moving parts – in this case, the bones, cartilage, and ligaments. The body adapts to training by increasing the amount of synovial fluid that is present in each joint, nourishing the cartilage by cleansing it and keeping it slippery, reducing the risk of damage to the cartilage, bones, and ligaments.

Increases range of joint mobility
As the body temperature increases, the muscles and connective tissues (the ligaments and tendons) get warmer, and this makes them more elastic, like a rubber band. The warmer they become, the further they are able to stretch without tearing and this allows the joint to move more freely.

There is also an increase in blood flow when we exercise as the heart supplies the working muscles with more oxygenated blood. Movement at the joints becomes easier as a result.

Micro tears in muscle fibres
Each muscle is made up of thousands of individual fibres and, as the muscle works, some of the fibres tear. As the small tears repair, the muscle grows back thicker and stronger.

Encourages formation of new bone
High impact activities, such as running and gymnastics, can encourage new bone formation. Just as muscle tears during exercise, bones are damaged during high impact activities. When this happens, small cells called osteoblasts travel from the bone marrow to the surface of the bone to create a lining. Over time, they convert into osteocytes, which become embedded in the bone and calcify, making the bone thicker and stronger.

Increases metabolic activity
During moderate to intense exercise, the body requires more fuel to supply the working muscles, so the metabolic rate – the rate at which the body burns calories – increases. After reasonably intense exercise (exercising at over 70% of your VO_2 maximum for over 90 minutes) the number of calories your body burns, increases. This effect is most obvious in the first 12 hours following exercise but can be seen up to 24 hours post-exercise.

The short-term effects of exercise on the cardiorespiratory system

As the body undergoes physical activity, the amount of oxygen needed by the working muscles increases. To supply the necessary oxygen, more blood is required and this causes:

Increased heart rate, increased blood flow, and increased cardiac output

The heart rate is the number of times the heart contracts (or beats) per minute. The more quickly the heart contracts, the more blood is circulated around the body and to the working muscles. The increase in heart rate and the increase in blood flow lead, in turn, to an increase in cardio output.

Increased blood pressure

The amount of blood ejected with each contraction of the heart, which is called the stroke volume, increases. When the stroke volume increases, increasing the amount of blood that passes through a blood vessel, extra pressure is put on the walls of the blood vessels, which can be measured as an increase in blood pressure. Increased blood pressure results in a larger delivery of oxygen and glucose to the working muscles, which enables them to work harder for longer periods of time. This is particularly useful when exercising as the performer can train or compete harder for longer durations without becoming tired.

Re-distribution of blood flow

The path blood takes around the body alters when we exercise to make sure that the relevant body parts are receiving the correct amount of blood and nutrients. The arterioles that supply the non-active parts of the body narrow or 'constrict' (a process called vasoconstriction) to lower the amount of blood passing through them. At the same time, the arterioles that supply the skeletal muscles open up (a process called vasodilation) to increase the amount of blood passing through them.

Increased lactic acid

Lactic acid is a chemical compound that builds up in the body during short bursts of high intensity exercise. It is generated when there aren't enough oxygen molecules to completely break down the glucose in the body. It is a waste product, which can cause a burning sensation in the muscles.

Increased breathing rate and increased tidal volume

In order to supply the extra oxygen needed by the blood to fuel the working muscles, the respiratory system has to work harder. One way to increase the amount of oxygen taken in is to breathe more quickly. This is known as an increased breathing rate. Breathing more quickly when we exercise is usually coupled with an increase in the amount of air inhaled and exhaled with each breath, known as the tidal volume or TV.

Sweat production and skin reddening

When we exercise the body gets warmer and the skin heats up. In order to cool down and remove the heat, the body produces sweat, a salty liquid that is excreted from the body.

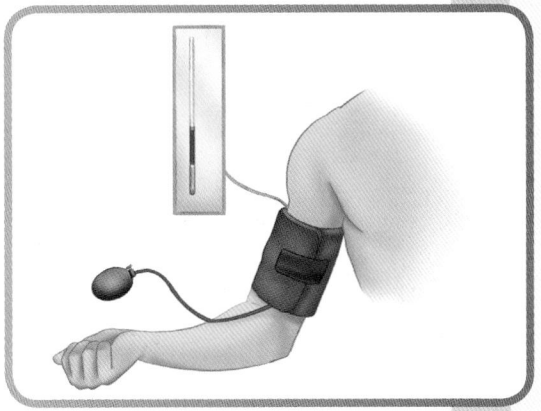

When our blood pressure rises during exercise, it is actually the 'systolic pressure' (which is measured when the heart beats) that increases. This is because the ventricles in the heart contract and the blood on the left side is forced into the aorta and sent around the body to supply the working muscles with freshly oxygenated blood. The 'diastolic pressure' (which is measured when the heart is relaxed, in between heart beats) remains the same following exercise.

BRONZE

1. a) Complete ten star jumps while your partner watches. When you have finished, write down how you felt and what your partner saw happening. Then, change roles and carry out the exercise again. With your partner, compile a list of the changes you think happened inside your body during the exercise.

b) Repeat Activity 1a, replacing the ten star jumps with a ten-minute run.

c) Compare your findings with the findings of other pairs in your group.

2. a) Measure your pulse rate, preferably using a heart-rate monitor, your breathing rate, and your blood pressure while you are sitting in your chair. Then measure your flexibility using the sit and reach test. Record all your results. (Hint: To measure your breathing rate, observe your partner's stomach or chest and count the number of times it rises in 15 seconds. Multiply the number by four to tell you your partner's breathing rate per minute.)

b) Take part in a warm-up, followed by a period of intense activity, such as a 400-metre sprint. At the end of the activity, immediately repeat the four tests and record your results. (Hint: You can actually measure the heart rate and blood pressure at the same time.)

c) Compare your results from before and after the exercise.

3. Obtain the results from Activity 2 for five of your peers. Using the six sets of data now at your disposal (your own and five others), create a graph, table, or chart that allows you to compare the results easily. Which changes happened to all six people (and are therefore true short-term responses) and which changes appear to be unusual (because they only happen to one or two people)?

SILVER

4. Take a look through the short-term responses to exercise you discovered by completing Activities 1 and 2. Create a flow chart showing which physiological responses to exercise happen first and which are secondary responses.

The long-term effects of exercise

If the body is subjected to physical activity on a regular basis, it **adapts** over time. The musculoskeletal, cardiovascular, and respiratory systems undergo a series of changes which help them to cope with the short-term effects of exercise on the body. These changes are called **adaptations** and they are semi-permanent, which means that they are permanent as long as training continues, but that they will be reversed if training stops for any length of time.

The long-term adaptations of each body system relate directly to the short-term responses of that system. This means that, over time, the short-term responses become less evident because the body has adapted to cope with them.

The long-term adaptations of the musculoskeletal system due to exercise

Hypertrophy
Muscles adapt to training by increasing in size. This is called hypertrophy and it occurs because the muscle fibres grow back thicker when the small tears, which happen as a short-term response to exercise, repair.

While you may well be out of breath after swimming six lengths of the swimming pool, the same level of exercise would have much less of an effect on 800-metre swimmer, Rebecca Adlington!

Increased bone density
The bones of the body are put under stress during activity, and so they adapt by becoming thicker and heavier (more dense), which helps to prevent fractures occurring. Osteoblasts travel from the bone marrow to the surface of the bone to create a lining. Over time, they convert into osteocytes, which become embedded in the bone and create a layer of calcium which hardens and replenishes the bone. There is therefore an increase in calcium production following long periods of exercise.

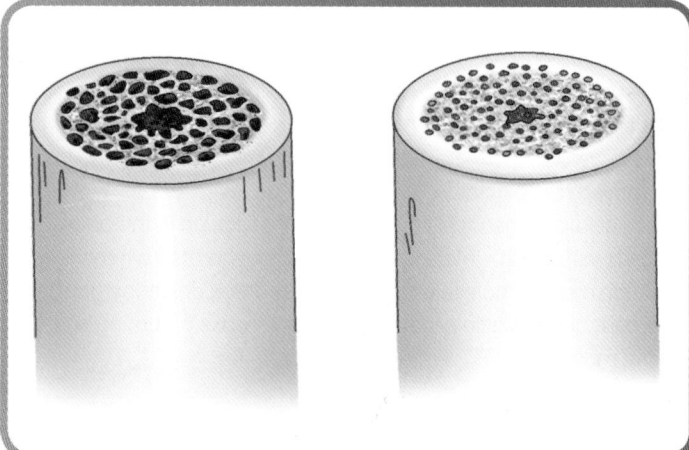

The increased density of the bone on the right, compared with that of the normal bone on the left, helps to prevent fractures occurring.

Increased strength of connective tissue
The tendons (the fibres that attach muscles to bones) and the ligaments (the fibres that connect bone to bone) become stretched as a short-term response to exercise. They adapt by growing thicker and stronger, which helps to prevent them from tearing during activity and reduces the risk of injury.

Increased stability of joints
There are several ways in which our joints can be made more stable through exercise:

- If the muscle mass surrounding a joint increases then the joint is supported more and becomes more mobile. For example, weight-bearing exercises, such as half squats, will help the muscles support the knee joint, which will make it more mobile and stable.

- Losing weight through exercise can also help with joint care because it reduces the pressure placed on the joints.
- Regular flexibility sessions can also help joints move more freely as the connective tissues – the tendons and ligaments – are tensed and then released.

Increased thickness of hyaline cartilage

The ends of long bones are covered in a layer of hyaline cartilage. This acts as a shock absorber, helping to prevent the bones being damaged during physical activity, and the ends of the bones wearing away. Over time, the body adapts by increasing the thickness of the hyaline cartilage to increase the protection to the bones.

Skeletal muscles adapt

After sustained periods of exercise, the muscles in our body adapt to the use of oxygen and become more efficient, for example, at replenishing the working muscles with freshly oxygenated blood and removing carbon dioxide. The capillaries also become more efficient and can therefore work for a longer period of time.

Increased number of mitochondria

Most cells in the body contain mitochondria. These are small cells that burn food to produce energy. Exercise can increase the number and size of mitochondria, making the body more able to burn calories more efficiently.

Decreased risk of osteoporosis

Osteoporosis is a disease characterized by loss of calcium and bone tissue from bones, making them brittle and more likely to break. When we exercise the risk of losing calcium and other tissues from our bones is reduced, making us less likely to develop osteoporosis. Exercise can also build strength and improve balance, making athletes less likely to fall and fracture their bones.

Improved posture

Core muscles within the body, such as the abdominals and the muscles around the lower back area, help to stabilize the back and keep the torso upright. Working these core muscles over a period of time when we exercise can help to improve posture by making the body look taller and leaner. Having good posture can also reduce the risk of developing sciatica, which can cause pain in the back, hip, and thigh regions.

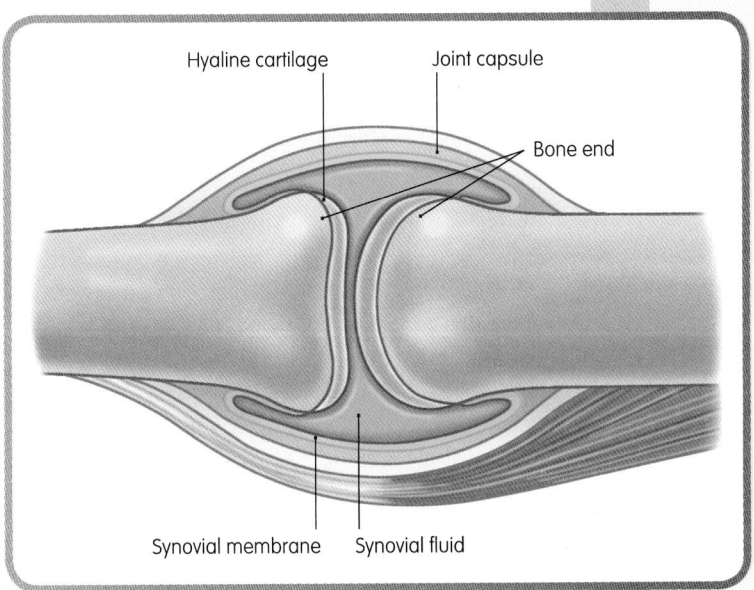

The increase in the thickness of the hyaline cartilage on the surface of joints is an important benefit of exercise.

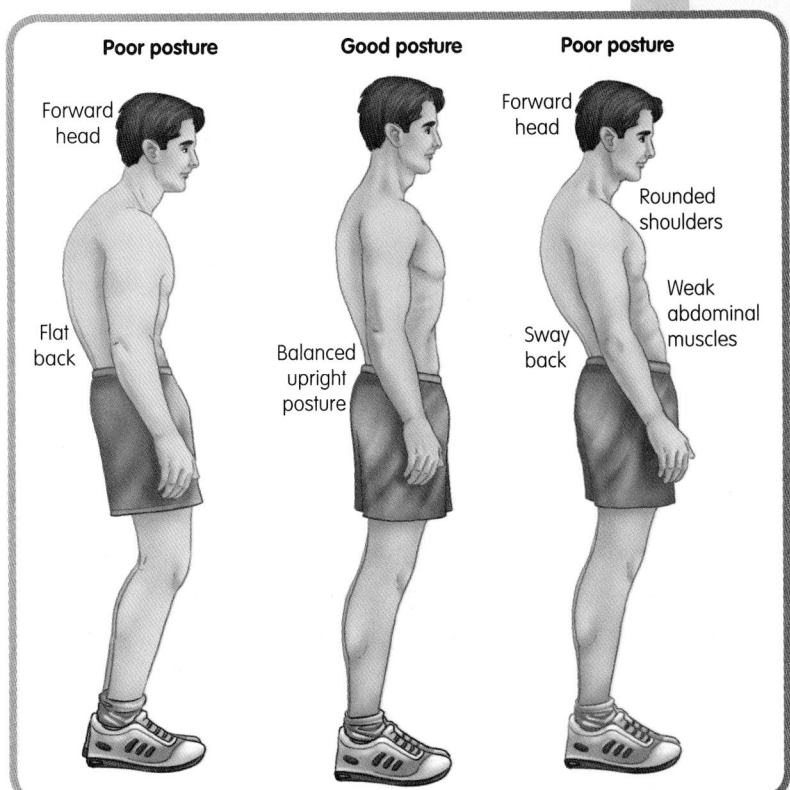

Having good posture means your body is properly aligned. Whatever position our body is in, gravity exerts a force on the joints, ligaments, and muscles. Athletes with good posture have an even distribution of the force of gravity through their body, ensuring that no body part is overstressed.

BRONZE   SILVER

1. Design a poster warning people of the negative effects that not exercising can have on their musculoskeletal system over the long term.

Long-term adaptations of the cardiorespiratory system due to exercise

Increased heart size

The heart has to adapt to cope with the extra demands that are placed on it by regular exercise. The most common adaptation is cardiac hypertrophy, an increase in the size and strength of the heart. In endurance athletes this is typified by an increase in the volume of the left ventricle, the chamber that pumps oxygenated blood to the muscles; whereas power athletes tend to exhibit an increased thickness in the muscular wall of the left ventricle.

Increased stroke volume

Cardiac hypertrophy enables the heart to eject more blood with each contraction, which is known as an increase in stroke volume. In endurance athletes this is because the left ventricle can hold, and therefore eject, a greater amount of blood. In power athletes the increased stroke volume occurs because the thicker muscular wall of the left ventricle enables every last drop of blood to be forced out of the heart and into the aorta.

Decreased Resting Heart Rate (RHR)

When stroke volume increases, the RHR decreases. This is because the body requires a set amount of blood when resting, typically around five litres per minute. When more blood is being ejected from the heart with each contraction (because of an increase in stroke volume), the heart has to contract less often to pump the required amount of blood around the body, hence, the RHR slows. This is shown by the equation:

$$\text{Cardiac output} = \text{heart rate} \times \text{stroke volume}$$

The heart can pump more blood per beat

The heart functions more efficiently and therefore does not need to beat as quickly in order to supply the body with freshly oxygenated blood. This means that the RHR, which is normally around 72 beats per minute (bpm), decreases to anything as low as 40bpm for an elite athlete. Former rower, Sir Steven Redgrave CBE, who won gold medals at five consecutive Olympic Games, was reported to have had a RHR of 40–45bpm at his peak. A reduction in bpm is known as bradycardia.

Decreased risk of hypertension

Hypertension is the name given to high blood pressure. Increased pressure in the arteries can lead to blockages, strokes, and eventually heart failure. Exercising can help to control blood pressure as the acceleration of the blood flowing through the arteries keeps them open and flexible.

Increased vital capacity

Vital capacity, or VC, is the amount of air that can be forcibly exhaled after breathing in as deeply as possible. This can increase following prolonged periods of exercise because the lungs are able to manage greater amounts of oxygen, and gaseous exchange is more efficient.

Increased lung efficiency and gaseous exchange

The lungs become more efficient after prolonged periods of exercise for a number of reasons. The diaphragm and the intercostal muscles become stronger, making inhaling and exhaling easier. There is an increase in the number of alveoli, the small air sacs in the lungs. There is also an increase in VC, which means that more air can be expelled after inhaling, which helps the body get rid of carbon dioxide. As the lungs become more efficient, so does gaseous exchange, which takes place in the lungs. Gaseous exchange ensures that we get the oxygen, which feeds our working muscles and organs, into our blood. At the same time, it removes the carbon dioxide and other waste products that the blood has carried from the working muscles and organs, from our bodies.

Increased maximum oxygen uptake

Maximum oxygen uptake, or VO_2 max, is the maximum amount of oxygen that you can use during exercise when working at your maximum capacity. This is measured in millilitres. Exercising in the aerobic training zone, with a heart rate of between 60 per cent and 85 per cent of its maximum, three to five times a week, can improve your VO_2.

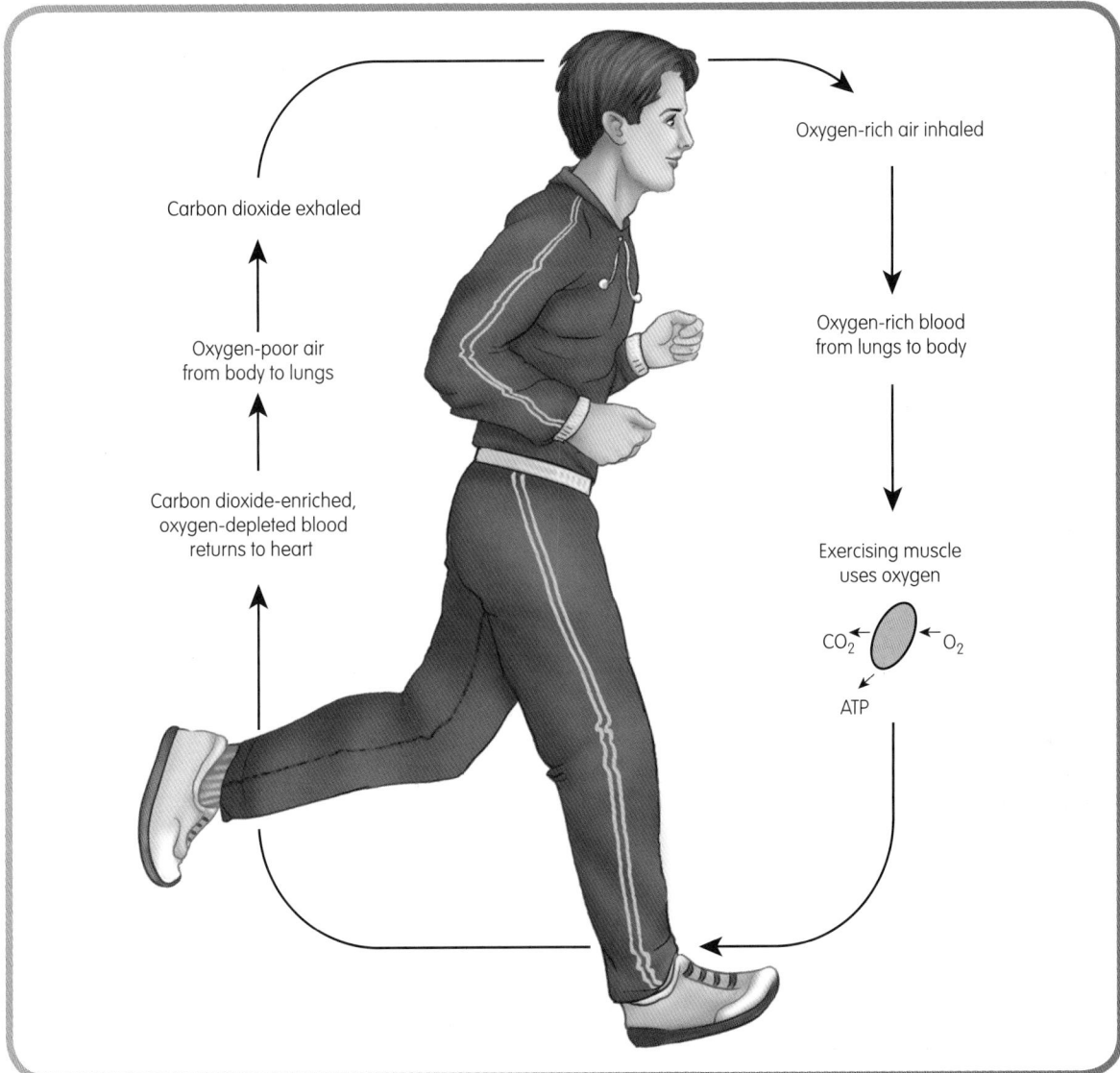

Increasing your VO_2 max means that your body will have a greater capacity for endurance.

BRONZE · SILVER

2. Choose two long-term adaptations of the cardiorespiratory system caused by exercise.

a) Summarize what these adaptations are.

b) Explain how exercise causes them to occur.

3. Create a table, flow chart, or diagram showing how the body's short-term responses to exercise, which you identified in Activity 4 on page 69, lead to adaptations in the long term.

GOLD

4. a) Select one sport from each of the categories below.

Category 1	Category 2
Netball	Table tennis
Basketball	Badminton
Hockey	Trampolining
Football	Dance

b) Analyse the short- and long-term effects of taking part in each of the two sports.

c) Comment on the similarities and differences between the effects of exercise for each sport.

Unit 4 assignment, part one

Background

A fitness consultant you know has been asked by the local hospital to produce a series of leaflets that can be given away in the outpatient department, showing the benefits of regular exercise on the musculoskeletal and the cardiorespiratory systems. They have been asked to consider all participants, regardless of the sports they take part in. You have been asked to create the leaflets on behalf of the fitness consultant.

Grading criteria
to be assessed

1A.1, 1A.2, 1A.3, 1A.4
2A.P1, 2A.P2, 2A.P3,
2A.P4
2A.M1, 2A.M2,
2A.M3, 2A.M4
2A.D1

Task

Design one or more leaflets that contain information about what happens to the body during exercise and the benefits of taking part in sport or exercise on a regular basis. You should include both the short- and long-term effects of exercise on the musculoskeletal and the cardiorespiratory systems. Your leaflet should include pictures, diagrams, and/or photographs to support your work. It should:

 **LEVEL 1**

- Outline two ways in which the musculoskeletal system responds to short-term exercise. (1A.1)
- Outline ways in which the cardiorespiratory system responds to short-term exercise. (1A.2)
- Summarise two long-term adaptations of the musculoskeletal system resulting from exercise. (1A.3)
- Summarise two long-term adaptations of the cardiorespiratory system resulting from exercise. (1A.4)

 **LEVEL 2 PASS**

- Describe ways in which the musculoskeletal system responds to short-term exercise. (2A.P1)
- Describe ways in which the cardiorespiratory system responds to short-term exercise. (2A.P2)
- Summarise, using relevant examples, long-term adaptations of the musculoskeletal system to exercise. (2A.P3)
- Summarise, using relevant examples, long-term adaptations of the cardiorespiratory system to exercise. (2A.P4)

 **LEVEL 2 MERIT**

- Explain responses of the musculoskeletal system to short-term exercise. (2A.M1)
- Explain responses of the cardiorespiratory system to short-term exercise. (2A.M2)
- Explain long-term adaptations of the musculoskeletal system to exercise. (2A.M3)
- Explain long-term adaptations of the cardiorespiratory system to exercise. (2A.M4)

 **LEVEL 2 DISTINCTION**

- Using three different sports activities, compare and contrast how the musculoskeletal and cardiorespiratory systems respond and adapt to exercise. (2A.D1)

Tackling the assignment

Leaflets always look more professional if they have been produced using a computer rather than being handwritten. The leaflet needs to be eye-catching as well as informative, so try and use a mixture of text, tables, graphs, drawings, and photographs. It may be necessary to create a small booklet or a series of leaflets, rather than a single-page leaflet, if you are aiming for a Merit or a Distinction, otherwise you risk not including enough information to show that you are able to compare and contrast the effects of exercise.

To **summarize** something, you need to point out the main facts without going into too much detail. You provide the detail when you **describe** something, when you should paint a picture of what you are discussing for your reader. When you **explain** something, you describe it and then you provide the reasons why it is like it is. When you **compare** two things, you provide the similarities between them, and when you **contrast** two things, you provide the differences or inconsistencies between them.

Meeting the Level 2 Pass, Merit, and Distinction criteria

Responding and adapting to exercise by George Lawrence

The effects of exercise can be separated into short-term changes (which happen each and every training session) and long-term changes (which happen over a period of weeks or months).

Short-term effects on the body

Physical exercise (or training) causes the body to change the way in which it works. The various body systems all respond to exercise to make sure that the body can cope with the demands being placed upon it.

The musculoskeletal system responds to short-term exercise in the following ways:

- **Increase in synovial fluid:** There is an oily substance that lubricates the joints. This is called synovial fluid. When we exercise, the amount of synovial fluid increases making the joint more slippery so that it becomes easier to move around. An example of this from sport is dribbling a ball in basketball. The elbow joint will produce more synovial fluid as the arm pumps up and down to control the ball around the court.
- **Increase in the range of movement at the joint:** There are lots of movements that are possible at the various joints and the range of movement can increase when we exercise. This is because the body gets warmer and the muscles, ligaments, and tendons become more elastic and more stretchy so they can move further.

When we exercise the muscles get warmer and begin to produce more carbon dioxide, increasing the acidity of the blood. If this continues for too long, the body stops working efficiently and the performer has to slow down or stop. To enable the performer to continue working, the cardiorespiratory system responds by increasing the cardiac output (heart rate × stroke volume). This pushes more blood around the body, which delivers more oxygen to the muscles and, crucially, removes more of the acidic carbon dioxide.

At the same time as this is happening, the body temperature begins to increase (because the chemical reactions that produce energy also produce heat). Again, if left unchecked, this heat increase can cause the performer to slow down or stop. To combat this, blood is redirected so that it travels nearer to the skin, where heat can be lost through conduction. The redirection of blood occurs because the brain sends a message to the arteries to get wider where more blood is needed and narrower where less blood is needed. This is called 'vascular shunting' and involves vasoconstriction (narrowing) and vasodilation (widening) of blood vessels.

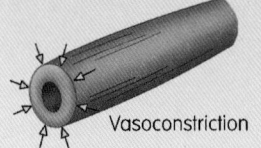 Vasoconstriction

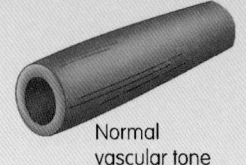 Normal vascular tone

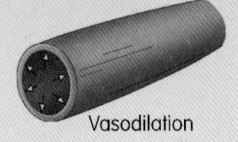 Vasodilation

George has described two ways in which the musculoskeletal and cardiorespiratory systems respond to short-term exercise so has achieved the criteria for 1A.1 and 1A.2 and has begun to meet the criteria for 2A.P1 and 2A.P2. If he continues in this way, describing more short-term responses to exercise and describing the long-term adaptations of the musculoskeletal and cardiorespiratory systems to exercise, he will meet the remaining Level 1 and Level 2 Pass criteria.

George has explained the effects of exercise, by providing examples and using the word 'because', to take his description to the next level. If he continues in this way, he will meet the Merit criteria.

At the moment, George is not meeting the criteria for 2A.D1. If he wants to achieve a Distinction, he will need to choose three different sporting activities and compare the ways in which the body responds to these three sports, and contrast the ways in which the body responds to these three sports. For example, the responses and adaptations that occur within the musculoskeletal system of a footballer will differ from the responses and adaptations that occur within the musculoskeletal system of a golf player. Once warmed up and on the pitch, a footballer will experience an initial increase in blood flow. This occurs as they begin to move around and cover various distances on the pitch. A golf player on the other hand will not have an initial surge of blood flow as the game is evenly paced and no sudden or impulsive movements are made.

George has made a really good start to this assignment but there is still a lot of work to do. The leaflet contains lots of relevant information but I'm not sure about the way it is presented. I think there is too much writing to make a real visual impact. How many people would pick it up and read it if it was on display?

Energy systems

Humans take part in countless different physical activities, ranging from the 100-metre sprint to the Tour de France, and from archery to gymnastics. All activities have one thing in common: they require energy! The human body creates energy in two main ways, either aerobically (with oxygen) or anaerobically (without oxygen), and the energy system used depends on the demands of the physical activity.

The anaerobic energy system

Although the term 'anaerobic' means 'without oxygen', it does not mean that you should hold your breath while taking part in an activity. It simply means that at the point in time when the energy you are using is created there is not enough oxygen present, and this is usually because the short duration of the activity does not allow the body to create enough oxygen. Anaerobic energy production is used during events that last less than 90 seconds and that require power, such as sprinting events, weightlifting, and shot-put.

There are two parts to the anaerobic energy system: the ATP-CP/alactic acid energy system and the glycolysis/lactic acid energy system.

The ATP-CP/alactic acid energy system
The ATP-CP/alactic acid energy system is referred to as the stored or start-up energy system. It provides the majority of the energy athletes use when they perform bursts of high-speed or high-resistance movements lasting up to 20 seconds.

This system relies on stored adenosine triphosphate (ATP, the molecule that produces the energy in all living things) in the muscles that is used up during an intense burst of activity lasting no more than four seconds. ATP returns to normal levels after two to three minutes of rest. Another stored molecule, known as creatine phosphate (CP), helps to replenish the stores of ATP. CP also provides a short burst of energy to enable muscle fibres to contract after ATP has been used up for another 16 seconds. CP is restored through aerobic respiration.

The glycolysis/lactic acid energy system
When the ATP-CP/alactic acid energy system runs out of stored ATP-CP, glycolysis takes place. During glycolysis, glucose stored in the liver and in the muscle cells is converted into pyruvate and the energy released while this happens forms ATP. The ATP then provides energy for the body.

The ATP-CP/alactic acid energy system and the glycolysis/lactic acid energy system work alongside each other during activities lasting 20 to 45 seconds, such as the 400-metre sprint. After 45 seconds, the body relies only on the glycolysis/lactic acid energy system, which is capable of high levels of intensity for up to four minutes.

Unfortunately, the glycolysis/lactic acid energy system prevents waste products from being removed from the body. The lactic acid energy system operates without oxygen, so there is not enough oxygen available to facilitate the removal of waste products from the body. As a result, lactic acid accumulates in muscle cells and blood cells. This is a major cause of fatigue, which eventually slows the athlete down. The more intense the exercise, the faster the rate at which lactic acid builds up to a level that causes high fatigue.

Getting rid of lactic acid after physical activity is a much slower process than replacing the energy stores in the ATP-CP/alactic acid energy system. It may take more than one hour for lactic acid levels to return to their pre-exercise level. Light activity, such as walking or jogging following intense efforts, speeds up the removal of lactic acid. The first ten minutes of active recovery produces the greatest reduction in lactic acid levels.

When the glycolysis/lactic acid energy system is unable to maintain energy requirements, the aerobic system begins to produce energy.

The aerobic energy system

The aerobic energy system requires oxygen, which re-synthesizes ATP to create the energy required. It is used in lower-intensity exercise and provides the energy for most human activity during our lives. It is also important in the recovery from exercise of all intensities.

The aerobic energy system is very efficient and resists fatigue because there is enough oxygen to allow the waste products to be removed from the body. This means that the heart and the lungs, which help to move oxygen around the body, are very important in aerobic activity. It takes longer to overload the aerobic energy system than it does to overload both the anaerobic energy systems, so an aerobic training session must last a minimum of 20 minutes. During more lengthy, low to moderate intensity periods of activity, such as long-distance running, the energy supplied comes from this system.

The glycolysis/lactic acid energy system and the aerobic energy system work alongside each other for activities lasting between four and ten minutes. After ten minutes, the body relies only on the aerobic energy system.

Time scale: 0 s, 5 s, 10 s, 15 s, 20 s, 25 s, 30 s, 35 s, 40 s, 45 s, 50 s, 55 s, 60 s, 90 s, 2 mins, 3 mins, 4 mins, 5 mins, 6 mins, 7 mins, 8 mins, 9 mins, 10 mins, 11 mins, 12 mins, 13 mins, 14 mins, 15 mins

ATP-CP/alactic acid energy system

Glycolysis/lactic acid energy system

Aerobic energy system

- 100m sprint
- weightlifting
- gymnastics (vault)

Competitors in the long jump use the ATP-CP/alactic acid energy system.

- 200m sprint
- 400m/800m
- basketball: fast break followed by a fast recovery

In rugby, players in a rolling maul set up from a lineout use the glycolysis/lactic acid energy system.

- marathon
- steeplechase
- orienteering

Participants in a triathlon use the aerobic energy system.

BRONZE

1. a) Working in a group of four, take it in turns to sprint and time each other. When it is your turn to sprint, explode as quickly as you can from the starting blocks and, at the point when you begin to slow down (even just a fraction), raise your arm in the air. Your partner should stop the stopwatch at this point.

b) Repeat the test but, for the second attempt, try to run at about 80 per cent of your maximum speed for as long as you can. Again, raise your hand when you begin to slow down so that your partner can stop the stopwatch.

c) Look at the data you have collected. What was happening each time you began to slow down?

2. Look carefully at the section on the sporting application of the energy systems and try to come up with a further six activities for each energy system.

SILVER

3. a) Create a bar chart showing the results collected by your group during Activity 1 and then compare these with those of the rest of your class.

b) Who has the most efficient anaerobic energy system? Why?

4. Explain how the anaerobic energy system and the aerobic energy system are used to supply energy to the sports performer for two sports of your choice.

GOLD

5. Looking at your response to Activity 4, explain:

a) The similarities between the way in which the two sports you chose use the anaerobic energy system and the aerobic energy system.

b) The differences between the ways in which the two sports you chose use the anaerobic energy system and the aerobic energy system.

Unit 4 assignment, part two

Background

While on work experience at the local gym, you have been approached by the lead fitness instructor to research the different systems used to supply the body with energy for different sport and exercise activities. Your employer has suggested that you create a poster or a website for clients attending the gym, highlighting the ATP-CP/alactic, glycolysis/lactic, and aerobic energy systems, and their uses in different activities.

Grading criteria to be assessed
1B.5
2B.P5
2B.M5
2B.D2

Task

Design a poster or website that informs the reader of the differences between aerobic and anaerobic activities, and the relative energy requirements of different sports. You should include pictures, diagrams, and/or photographs to show clients how they can investigate the differences for themselves. Your poster or website should:

 **LEVEL 1**

Describe the two main energy systems, including examples of sports that use each system. (1B.5)

 **LEVEL 2 PASS**

Describe the function of the three energy systems in the production and release of energy for sports performance. (2B.P5)

 **LEVEL 2 MERIT**

Using two selected sports, explain how the body uses both the anaerobic and the aerobic energy systems. (2B.M5)

 **LEVEL 2 DISTINCTION**

Compare and contrast how the energy systems are used in sports with different demands. (2B.D2)

Tackling the assignment

The obvious way to tackle this assignment is to produce a poster that can be used as part of a wall display. However, many people prefer to surf the internet in their own time, so you may decide to produce a website instead. Whichever option you choose, it is important to ensure that the information you include is accurate and presented in an eye-catching way. If your poster/website is dull and boring, clients won't look at it in the first place!

And remember, when you **describe** something you need to draw a picture in words for your reader, when you **explain** something you need to provide examples and tell the reader why it is like it is, and when you **compare and contrast** two or more things you need to discuss the similarities and differences between them.

Meeting the Level 2 Pass and Merit criteria

The three energy systems

Marcus Wendle

There are three energy systems. One of these is called the aerobic energy system and it gives us long-term energy. Marathon runners are aerobic athletes because they use oxygen throughout the race, but they are only working at 80 per cent because above this level their body cannot burn oxygen quickly enough to produce energy.

The other two energy systems are anaerobic. They are called the alactic and the lactic systems. These systems are both used when you work without oxygen for a short period of time.

The alactic system is used for short-term activities that are explosive, such as the 100-metre sprint. When sprinters set off from their starting blocks, stored adenosine triphosphate (ATP) in the muscles is used to power them. These athletes are working 'anaerobically' (without oxygen) because they are working at 100 per cent effort but only for a short period of time. Therefore, they can complete their event without burning oxygen to produce energy.

The lactic acid system comes into play when the ATP runs out and is replaced by glycolysis. Glycolysis makes ATP using stores of glycogen in the liver and muscle cells. This much energy is used by sports performers who take part in activities lasting up to four minutes, such as the 800-metre.

> This poster is eye-catching and the use of images will attract clients to read it. It contains a description of the three energy systems in the production and release of energy for sports performance and has therefore met the criteria for 1B.5 and 2B.P5.

> The poster refers to the role of the three energy systems in different sporting activities, so it does go some way to meeting the criteria for 2B.M5 but Marcus needs to go further if he wants to achieve a Merit. He needs to explain how the three energy systems work together within the body during exercises; how one energy system takes over from another because of the demands the athlete is placing on their body. He needs to do this for two sports.

Meeting the Level 2 Distinction criteria

The energy systems used during sports performance

Lacey Trickett

All sports have different demands in terms of the energy they require. For example, a person playing first base in rounders will require a different amount of energy from a basketball player. In this assignment I will be looking at the different energy requirements of sports participants and how they compare and contrast to one another.

To take the two sports participants identified in my introduction, it is necessary to look at the actual amount of energy they use in their respective sports. A first base player in rounders will mainly be stationary during the game as they wait for the batter to miss the ball and the back stop to throw it to them so they can get the batter out on first base. Although they are mainly stationary, they may be required to react quickly to situations within the game. For example, if they are also manning second base they may need to run to this post to receive a catch from a fielder. In order for a first base player to perform these short but rapid movements, they must utilize the ATP-CP/alactic acid anaerobic energy system. This system uses stored ATP to produce short bursts of energy that can last up to 20 seconds. The system does not require oxygen and will enable the first base player to react quickly and powerfully to the situation that they find themselves in.

In comparison, a basketball player may be faced with a similar situation when in what is known as a 'triple threat' scenario. This means that they are in possession of the ball and have a choice whether they pass, shoot, or dribble. In order to execute any one of the three moves, they must also enlist the support of the ATP-CP/alactic acid anaerobic system to generate the short burst of energy required.

> Excellent work! Lacey has really begun to grasp the concept of comparing and contrasting the roles of the different energy systems within different sporting activities. I like the way she has selected two entirely different activities on which to base her analysis. If she can continue to identify further similarities and differences between the two activities and their energy consumptions, and incorporate some examples relating to the use of the glycolysis/lactic acid anaerobic energy system and the aerobic energy system, I feel confident that she will secure a Distinction.

Unit 5: Training for Personal Fitness

Setting goals for a personal fitness training programme

One of the most important aspects of planning a personal fitness training programme is setting goals. These goals provide the overall aim of the fitness programme and therefore become the foundations of any activity that we take part in.

The importance of goal setting

If they are not being met, goals highlight the need for changes to be made to training programmes.

Goals provide a focus for training programmes, helping to motivate and encourage individuals. They help to keep the performer working hard, giving them a better chance of improving their fitness levels or their individual skills.

The positive effects of goal setting on the performer

Achieving goals demonstrates to the performer that their fitness or skill levels have improved. This motivates the performer to set new goals and continue training.

Goals mentally prepare performers for training or competition.

Long-term goals

Setting your long-term goals is the first step in goal setting. For experienced performers, long-term goals are often based around seasons or competitions. The long-term goals for less-experienced performers may simply be to lose weight or to improve their fitness levels.

Long-term goals can be:

- **Outcome goals:** These are based on performance in competition. For example, a netball team might set themselves the long-term goal of reaching the knock-out stages of a competition.
- **Performance goals:** These are based on previous performances. For example, an 800-metre runner might set themselves the long-term goal of matching or beating their personal best in an upcoming competition.

Team players and coaches need to work together to achieve outcome goals.

Medium-term goals

Long-term goals are broken down into medium-term goals. These normally focus on a period of weeks or months, and concentrate on training. For example, a professional football team might set themselves the medium-term goal of improving their aerobic fitness during the pre-season period, between July and August, in order to be ready for the new season.

Pre-season training often involves a lot of hard work.

Short-term goals

Medium-term goals are broken down into short-term goals, which add detail to training programmes. They are often used as incentives to train hard because they are much shorter in duration. For example, a gymnast may set themselves the short-term goal of completing a floor routine during a training session.

Setting SMARTER targets

Effective target setting must follow the SMARTER principle. SMARTER targets are:

Elite gymnasts need to show dedication and commitment to their sport in order to reach the world stage. Setting themselves short-term goals gives them the direction they need for each training session.

Specific
Targets should be specific. You might aim to get fitter but this isn't a specific objective. Instead you need to break your broad aim down into specific objectives, or targets, which are related to the aspect of fitness that you want to improve. For example, if you previously achieved Level 6.3 on the multistage fitness test, your specific target might be to achieve Level 7. It is a good idea to conduct fitness tests before setting specific targets.

Measurable
Targets need to be measurable so that you know if you have achieved them or not. You can also use measurable targets to help you analyse your performance against recognized norms. If your goals are measurable then they automatically become specific.

Achievable
Targets should be appropriate to the fitness and skill levels of the performer. They should be close enough for us to see but not so far away that we can't touch them.

Realistic
It is important that we set targets that we have the capacity to achieve. All targets need to be challenging so that you have to work hard to achieve them, but they must also be realistic in order for them to serve their purpose and motivate you.

Time-related
Targets need to be linked to a point in time by when they should be achieved or it becomes too easy to put them off. By setting a date for re-testing there is a clear end to the phase of training and this can act as a motivation to stay focused. Elite athletes often have a big event as their focus.

Exciting
Targets need to be exciting if the performer is going to spend many hours working towards them.

Recorded
It is important to record targets in order to identify whether or not progress is being made. A performer who records their targets and their progress in a training diary has a constant reminder of what they are aiming for, which can be a very important source of motivation.

BRONZE

1. Write down a long-term goal for your favourite sporting activity.

2. Break your long-term goal down into medium-term goals.

3. Take your first medium-term goal and break it down into short-term goals.

4. Set your own SMARTER targets to help you achieve the short-term goals you set out for Activity 3.

SILVER

5. Assess why each SMARTER target you set for Activity 4 will help you to meet your long-term goals.

GOLD

6. Justify why each SMARTER target you set for Activity 4 will help you meet your long-term goals.

Gathering information to inform your personal fitness training programme

When you are planning a training programme, it is essential to gather information about the performer in order to make the training programme relevant to that performer. This is because each performer has different goals, fitness levels, and a different training history.

Lifestyle: This includes information about how active the performer is in their everyday life and how much time they have to dedicate to a training programme.

Long-term goals

Medical history: It is important to find out if the performer has any medical issues that need to be considered, so performers should always complete a Physical Activity Readiness Questionnaire (PAR-Q) before embarking on an exercise programme.

Physical activity history: It is helpful to know about a performer's previous activity levels so that the personal exercise programme can be planned to suit the performer's individual needs.

Information about the performer

Dietary history and dietary preferences: Diet forms an important part of a fitness training programme. It is therefore important to know about any special dietary requirements a performer might have. For example, are they a vegetarian, a diabetic, or allergic to dairy products? It is also important to find out about a performer's dietary preferences, if there are certain foods they don't like and whether or not their diet is generally poor.

Attitudes and motivation: How the performer feels about undertaking an exercise programme will play a large part in how they approach it. Therefore, it is important to understand their levels of commitment and motivation in order to create an appropriate exercise programme.

Supplement use: Sports supplements are substances taken by people involved in physical activity, particularly bodybuilding, to aid the development of muscle mass or to cause fat loss. Sports supplements can also be used to improve sports performance and recovery from events or training. Any supplements used by a performer should be considered when planning an exercise programme and then monitored throughout, because they might affect the desired outcome. Many available supplements are illegal in professional sports.

Nutritional knowledge: The performer's knowledge and understanding of nutrition and its effects on the body should be considered because it is very important that anyone undertaking an exercise programme is aware of how important diet is in fuelling the body effectively.

BRONZE

1. Use the information on this page to help you design your own PAR-Q.

2. Conduct a fitness interview with the person sitting next to you, using the PAR-Q you created for Activity 1.

Principles of training

The principles of fitness training are rules or guidelines that should be followed by anyone taking part in a training programme. The rules are there to make sure that training is effective and worthwhile, and failure to follow these guidelines could result in a lot of wasted effort and little or no gain in physical fitness.

FITT for SPORT followed by some R&R

As you know from Unit 1, 'FITT for SPORT followed by some R&R' is a way of remembering the principles of training. It stands for:

F	–	Frequency	for	S –	Specificity, and individual differences and needs
I	–	Intensity		P –	Progressive overload
T	–	Time		O –	adaptatiOn
T	–	Type		R –	Reversibility
				T –	variaTion
	followed by some R&R			–	Rest and Recovery

BRONZE

1. Choose three principles of training and describe how you would apply them to a fitness training programme for a sportsperson of your choice.

2. Design a poster that could be displayed in your school or college fitness suite, which describes the principles of training.

3. Describe how the principle of overload would be manipulated to suit both a marathon runner and a 200-metre sprinter.

Frequency
This is the number of training sessions completed per week. You can overload by training more often but be careful not to overtrain.

Intensity
This is how hard the training is. You can overload by training harder each session, by working at a higher heart rate, or by increasing the level of resistance. Information on how to determine exercise intensity is provided on pages 8 and 9.

Time
This is how long each training session is. You can overload by training for longer during each session or, for example, by spending longer on a muscle group.

Type
This is the type of training. You can overload by changing the type of training, for example, by running up hills rather than on a running track.

Specificity, and individual needs and differences
Training should be specific to the activity or sport you are taking part in, the type of fitness required for that sport (aerobic or anaerobic), and to the particular muscle groups the sport uses most.

Progressive overload
Training should get harder as the weeks go by and as the body adapts. If an athlete sticks to the same training plan for a long period of time their level of fitness will plateau and no further improvements will occur. The body needs to be exposed to progressively more challenge in order for it to adapt.

adaptiOn
The body and the working muscles have to be exposed to a level of work that is more difficult than they are used to. By overloading the muscles, they learn to adapt by growing stronger, so that they can cope with increased demands in the future.

Reversibility
'Use it or lose it' is the key phrase here. If a player stops training, either through injury or boredom, fitness levels will begin to decrease. Fitness declines almost three times as quickly as it improves!

variaTion
It is important to vary the training methods used, to maintain motivation and ensure the participant continues to enjoy the training programme.

Rest and Recovery
Each training session should be followed by a period of 24 hours' rest for the muscle groups involved, otherwise muscle fibres can become damaged and injuries can occur.

Designing a fitness training programme

The most important thing to do when designing a fitness training programme is to work with the client. It is no use setting up a programme if it does not suit the needs of the client on a practical day-to-day level. Working with a client is a five-step process.

Step 1: Establish the client's goals

Every fitness programme needs to start with a long-term goal. The two most common goals are to increase muscle strength or size and to reduce body fat percentage (to lose weight). Other goals might be to increase speed or reduce the time taken to cover a set distance, such as a half-marathon. Whatever the long-term goal, it needs to be SMARTER.

Once the long-term goal has been established, the next step is to decide how it will be achieved and to put some medium-term goals in place. For example:

Long-term goal (six months)	Medium-term goal (three months)
To complete a 10-kilometre road race and to complete the event in under 75 minutes, without stopping or walking.	• Increase cardiovascular endurance. • Increase muscular endurance. • Increase speed.

Close attention should be paid to the principles of training (FITT for SPORT followed by some R&R) throughout this process.

Step 2: Assess the client's current level of activity and consider their lifestyle

The most common and effective way of assessing the client's current level of activity and considering their lifestyle is to use a standard screening questionnaire, sometimes called a Physical Activity Readiness Questionnaire or PAR-Q. Collecting this information enables the trainer to tailor the programme to the needs of the individual, in a safe and effective manner. Just because someone looks fit and healthy does not mean that they are ready to take part in an intensive exercise programme.

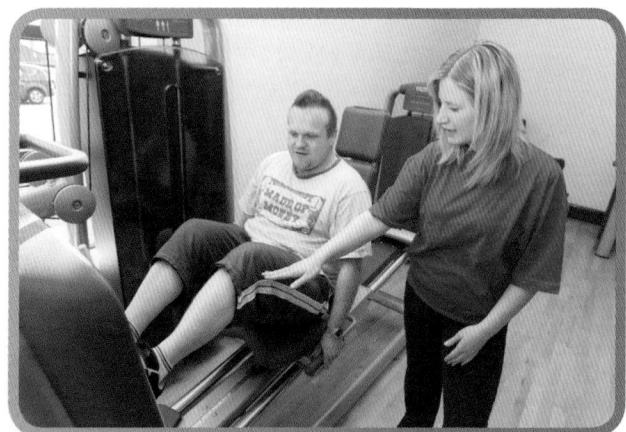

It is important to set goals in order to motivate ourselves and provide focus to our training sessions.

Step 3: Decide which areas of fitness need to be developed

Next, determine which components of fitness (see Unit 1: Fitness for Sport and Exercise, pages 4 to 7) need to be developed to ensure that the client becomes, or remains, fit and healthy. This is likely to include a reduction in the client's body fat content, because this is the most common reason for someone to join a gym. However, for an elite-level athlete it may be much more specific, such as building strength in the abdominal muscles for an international rower, or increasing muscular endurance for a professional cyclist. The key is to ensure that any decisions made at this stage are taken in full consultation with the client.

Step 4: Set the short-term targets that will need to be met in order for the client to meet their long-term goals

The short-term targets will be determined by considering the results of the screening questionnaire, any fitness-test results, and, crucially, the long-term goals of the client. For example, if the client's long-term goal is to run a 10-kilometre race, then the short-term targets should include something like increasing the duration of the training sessions and decreasing the time taken to run a kilometre.

Step 5: Select appropriate activities for the warm-up, main section of the session, and cool-down

A warm-up, in the form of light, continuous physical activity, prepares the body for exercise. An effective warm-up consists of three parts: pulse raising, stretching, and joint mobilization.

The activities in the main section of an exercise session need to suit the requirements of the individual. Using the FITT for SPORT followed by some R&R model will help, because it should ensure that the trainer adheres to the needs of the individual.

Each exercise session should end with a cool-down, in the form of light, continuous physical activity, to reduce the heart rate, remove lactic acid, and prevent blood pooling. An effective cool-down consists of three parts: pulse lowering, static stretching, and developmental stretching.

Creative design

It is important that the training programme is designed in such a way that it avoids barriers to training occurring. In order to ensure the client maintains enthusiasm and motivation, the programme needs to be enjoyable and include interesting activities that encourage commitment and prevent boredom.

To do this, factors such as the client's lifestyle, daily routine, likes and dislikes, the availability of equipment, and the money they have available to spend on training, need to be taken into account. Some activities, such as walking to work, could fit easily into a client's routine. Other activities, such as hill cycling for an elite cyclist, may be more difficult to include because of the potential cost and time involved in travelling to a suitable place to train. There may also be opportunities to include more exciting activities, such as training on a beach to improve strength or running with a weighted backpack.

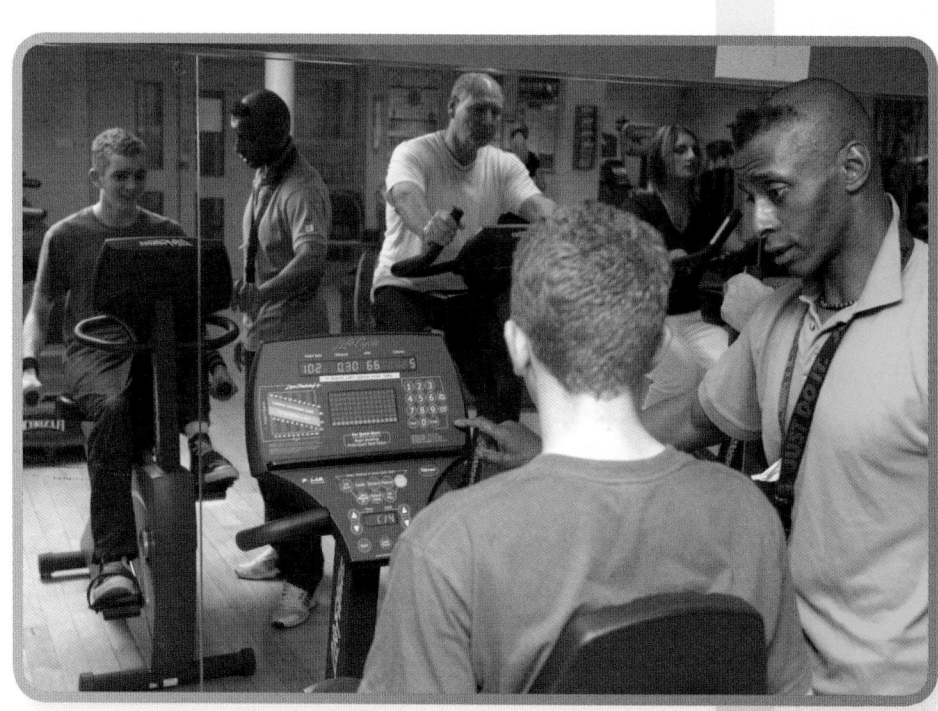

The activities selected to form part of a training session need to be appropriate to the person doing the training to help them achieve their goals.

BRONZE

1. Design a set of SMARTER targets for yourself. They should focus on the first steps you would need to take to achieve excellence in your chosen sport.

2. Design a set of targets for a member of your group. This is even more effective if you choose a partner who you rarely work with. Remember to use a PAR-Q.

SILVER

3. Using a combination of SMARTER targets and your knowledge of the principles of training, design a training programme for your tutor or teacher that demonstrates creative design.

GOLD

4. Suggest ways in which the training programme you designed for Activity 3 could be adapted to suit a professional athlete in the same sport. Justify your decisions.

Unit 5 assignment, part one

Background

As part of the interview process for the job of personal trainer at your local fitness centre, you have been asked to demonstrate your knowledge of the principles of training and your ability to design a fitness training programme.

Task

Design a ten-minute presentation or short speech that can be delivered to a panel of three people at the first stage of your interview. Use yourself as the performer for whom the fitness training programme is being designed. You should provide handouts where appropriate and make sure you:

Grading criteria to be assessed
1A.1, 1A.2, 1A.3
2A.P1, 2A.P2, 2A.P3
2A.M1, 2A.M2
2A.D1

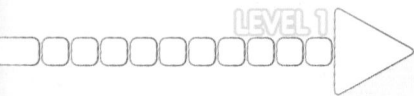 **LEVEL 1**

- Outline personal information for designing a fitness training programme. (1A.1)
- Design a safe four-week personal fitness training programme, with guidance. (1A.2)
- Outline the importance of warm-up, cool down and FITT. (1A.3)

 **LEVEL 2 PASS**

- Summarise personal information for designing a fitness training programme. (2A.P1)
- Independently design a safe six-week personal fitness training programme. (2A.P2)
- Describe the principles of training and their application to the personal fitness training programme design. (2A.P3)

 **LEVEL 2 MERIT**

- Assess personal information for fitness training programme design. (2A.M1)
- Design a safe six-week personal fitness training programme, showing creativity in the design. (2A.M2)

 **LEVEL 2 DISTINCTION**

- Justify the training programme design, explaining links to personal information. (2A.D1)

Tackling the assignment

The most professional way to deliver a presentation in an interview is to produce a PowerPoint® presentation. However, you will need to stand out from the rest of the applicants, so include diagrams, photos, and video footage in your presentation, and make sure that you include everything you have been asked to include.

In order to achieve a Merit, your personal training fitness programme needs to be creative. This means that it needs

to be varied, to include different methods of training, and be interesting for the performer. For example, each week could contain different activities and the location of the training could vary from week to week too.

In order to achieve a Distinction, you must justify why you have designed the training programme in the way that you have by linking each aspect of the training programme to the personal information you have about the performer.

Physical Activity Readiness Questionnaire

Please take a few minutes to answer the following questions.

Name: Kenny King   **DOB:** 27 / 8 / 1996   **Age:** 16   **Sex:** (M)/ F

Occupation: Student   **Have you used a gym before?** (Y)/ N

Emergency contact: Donald King

Relationship: Father   **Telephone number:** 07856 694720

Part A: Medical considerations

It is our professional duty to ask all participants, no matter what age, to complete the following questions. Please tick all those that apply.

☐ Has a family member, under 60, suffered from heart disease, a stroke, raised cholesterol, or sudden death?
☐ Are you a male over 35 or female over 45 and NOT used to regular, vigorous exercise?
☐ Are you on any prescribed medication?
☐ Have you been hospitalized recently?
☐ Have you given birth in the last six weeks?
☐ Do you have any infections or infectious diseases?

Do you have or have you ever had:

☐ Gout ☐ Glandular fever ☐ Heart condition ☐ Stroke
☐ Rheumatic fever ☐ Heart murmur ☐ Diabetes
☐ Dizziness or fainting ☐ High blood pressure (over 140/90)
☐ Epilepsy ☐ Stomach/duodenal ulcer
☐ Palpitations or pains in the chest ☐ Hernia
☐ Liver or kidney condition ☐ Raised cholesterol/triglycerides
☐ Asthma ☐ Arthritis ☐ Muscular pain ☐ Cramps

Do you have any pain or major injuries in the following areas:
☐ Neck ☐ Knees ☐ Back ☐ Ankles

Please give details of any conditions:
_____
_____
_____

If you have ticked any of the above, you need a signed medical clearance from your doctor before starting exercise.

Doctor's signature: _____   **Date:** ___/___/___

I warrant that I am physically and mentally well enough to proceed with usage of the facility.

Client's signature: *Kenny King*   **Date:** 23/9/2012

Part B: Lifestyle and current exercise habits

Are you currently exercising regularly? Yes ☑ No ☐

If yes, please give details below:
* Type of exercise: ____Football____
* Frequency of exercise (times per week): 1 ☐ 2–3 ☑ 3–4 ☐ 5+ ☐

Do you currently drink more than the average amount of alcohol per week (21 units for men and 14 units for women (1 unit = pint of beer/cider/lager or 1 small glass of wine)) Yes ☐ No ☑

Do you currently smoke? Yes ☐ No ☑

Are you, or is there any possibility that you might be, pregnant?
Yes ☐ No ☐

Do you know of any other reason why you should not participate in a programme of physical activity? Yes ☐ No ☑

Summary of personal information

It would appear from the PAR-Q that I am in a perfectly fit and healthy condition, and as a result I see no reason why I should not be allowed to begin a personal training programme. I would recommend that I increase my training from two to three times per week to four to five times per week in order to achieve my fitness goals.

Kenny has listed the personal information he needs to use to design a personal training programme. He has accurately used a PAR-Q in order to ascertain whether or not he is able to begin a personal fitness training programme and has correctly recommended that he is able to start on his training programme. Kenny has therefore met the criteria for 2A.P1. In order for Kenny to meet the criteria for 2M.A1 he needs to assess the personal information provided. To do this he should write more about why he is considered healthy enough to start a fitness training programme and what led him to this conclusion.

Kenny has begun to assess his PAR-Q and has mentioned that he should increase his training to four to five times a week to achieve his goals. Unfortunately, he hasn't mentioned these goals anywhere and I would like to see the SMARTER goal-setting technique used to describe his long-term goals at the bottom of his PAR-Q. I would then like to see an analysis that breaks his long-term goals down into medium-term goals and finally into the short-term goals on which he will base his fitness training programme. He should also describe the activities that should be included in his training programme in order to develop the components of fitness he needs to succeed at football. If he does this, he will meet the criteria for a Merit.

Kenny has shown that he understands the need for a warm-up and cool-down and also understands the principles of training. He has therefore met the criteria for 1A.2 and 1A.3.

The importance of a warm-up and a cool-down

A warm-up is important because it prepares the body for exercise and activity. It should consist of three stages. These are: pulse raising, stretching, and joint mobilization.

A cool-down helps to remove waste products from the body and should contain: pulse lowering, static stretches, and developmental stretches.

When designing a training programme it is important to consider the principles of training.

Principle of training	Meaning	Demonstrated in fitness training programme
Frequency	This is how often somebody trains.	The number of sessions completed each week.
Intensity	This is how hard someone works at their training.	The RPE recorded in the training diary each session.
Time	This is how long you train for.	By how long the session lasts, shown in the training diary.
Type	This is what exercise you do.	The exercises and workouts completed.
Specificity	In order to make training relevant, it must be appropriate for the individual who is performing it and the sport they are training for.	By keeping the exercises relevant to the aims of the training programme.
Progressive overload	It is important to make training sessions harder over time so that the body continues to adapt and benefits from training.	In order to see progression I have increased the weights, reps, speeds, inclines, and distances to develop fitness levels.
Adaptation	This is the body changing as a result of training.	This happens as a result of progressive overload.
Reversibility	If you stop training you lose any gains that you have made.	Hopefully I will not get injured and, therefore, I should not experience reversibility.
Variation	Training methods must be varied to avoid boredom and demotivation.	By changing the exercises and using equipment and the outdoors creatively, I should maintain enthusiasm in the training programme.
Rest and Recovery	If we do not rest, then our body will never fully recover and we could burn out.	Rest days will stop me from burning out and keep me on track to achieve my targets.

Six-week training programme

Week 3 of 6

Monday	Tuesday	Wednesday	Thursday	Friday	Saturday	Sunday
Rest day	10-minute bike ride on level 5 to warm up. Rotations per minute (RPM) = 85 Stretches on the mat, from head down. 20-minute hill-based treadmill session. Level 10 on hill programme 6. Abs session, 3 × 10 of the following: • Leg raises • V-sits • Crunches • Twisting crunches Cool-down	10-minute bike ride on level 5 to warm up. RPM = 85 Stretches on the mat, from head down. Weights session, 3 × 10 of the following: • Chest press 30kg • Lat pull down 30kg • Shoulder press 20kg • Leg press 45kg • Leg extension 25kg • Leg curl 25kg Cool-down	Rest day	10-minute jog on level 7 to warm up. Stretches on the mat, from head down. 20-minute cross-training session with machine set to level 10 on sprint interval programme 5. Abs session, 3 × 10 of the following: • Leg raises • V-sits • Crunches • Twisting crunches Cool-down	10-minute bike ride on level 5 to warm up. RPM = 85 Stretches on the mat, from head down. Weights session, 3 × 10 of the following: • Press-ups • Sit-ups • Swiss ball squats • Swiss ball jack knife • Dumb-bell curls 7kg • Tricep kick backs 7kg • Cuban raises 7kg Cool-down	Game day

Kenny has included the pulse raising and stretching part of a warm-up and he has included a cool-down, but not in enough detail. To ensure his fitness training programme is fully safe, he needs to include all three phases of a warm-up and all three phases of a cool-down.

We can only see one week of Kenny's fitness training programme but it does begin to show creativity. He has included inventive exercises and mixed things up, which will help him avoid getting bored. To fully achieve the criteria for a Merit, the other weeks would need to continue in this way, and I would like to see Kenny go even further and include different methods of training designed to train the components of fitness he needs to succeed at football.

As I have already mentioned, Kenny needs to include the warm-up and cool-down exercises in his plan. He also needs to provide more detail for each exercise. For example, how long should he be spending on the treadmill? How quickly should he be running? Will he set an incline? If Kenny is able to add this detail independently, he will be able to meet the criteria for a Level 2 Merit.

Meeting the Level 2 Distinction criteria

I have selected the activities for the personal training programme because I am fit and healthy and I'm already involved in sport at least two to three times per week. As I have no previous health issues I am confident that I will be able to fulfil the training programme without any problems.

I wish to develop my cardiovascular fitness to achieve a higher level of skill and performance in my chosen sport of football. The training programme aims to help develop both cardiovascular fitness, muscular endurance, and to generally help me to tone up. I have therefore ensured that the programme is specific to my aims and goals.

Over the six weeks, the principle of variation has been applied to help me develop my fitness and avoid becoming bored because I am repeating the same activities over and over again. I have ensured that I have a varied and creative programme that makes the most of all of the equipment that is available in the local gym, as well as including outdoor running and swimming.

In order to ensure that my fitness levels improve I have applied the principle of progressive overload. This means that I have ensured that I am working within a worthwhile range and at a worthwhile intensity to ensure that the training programme has the desired effect. I have increased time, distances, weights, repetitions, and number of sets to ensure that the desired goals are reached.

Rest days have been built into the training programme in order to ensure that I do not burn out and am able to maintain a high level of energy throughout the six weeks.

If Kenny goes on to add a section on his goals and how his programme will help him to achieve them, as well as ensure he fully meets the Pass and Merit criteria, he will achieve a Distinction for this part of the assignment.

Kenny has clearly thought about how he has planned his training programme. There are strong links between the programme and the personal information. He justifies his creativity and shows a strong knowledge of the principles of training.

Exercise-adherence factors

Adherence factors are the things that keep people committed to a course of action; in this case, exercise. The most important adherence factor is overcoming all the barriers that stop people taking part in sport and exercise. When people have managed to do this and find an activity they enjoy taking part in, they are more likely to stick with it. There are then a number of strategies that can be used to strengthen a person's adherence to exercise once they have overcome the initial barriers to participation.

Barriers to adherence

What do you like doing?

Access to facilities plays a large role in our ability to participate. If you live in a town or city that has gyms, swimming pools, and leisure centres within easy reach, then it is fairly easy for you to join up and take part. However, if you live in an area where these facilities aren't readily available then it becomes much more difficult for you to participate. People who live in rural areas often face a 60-minute drive to get to the local swimming pool, for example.

Motivation and commitment: Our level of personal motivation and commitment will have the biggest influence on our ability to remain dedicated to our fitness training. To some people, fitness is a part of their life and they are highly motivated to participate; they find the money, make the time, and make sure they get access to appropriate facilities. Other people find it hard to motivate themselves to exercise and make excuses not to train.

Cost: The cost of joining a health club, gym, or sports team can be expensive. Gym memberships cost an average of £35 a month, with some health clubs charging a lot more to use their facilities. Sports teams often charge more than £200 for a year's subscription. This can lead to people not being able to participate due to the large financial commitment of joining such clubs. Because the cost can be high, many people cannot afford to get fit or think it is an unnecessary expense.

Barriers to adherence

Time: It is difficult to find time in increasingly busy lives to spend a few hours a week working on fitness, because people often put their fitness as a lower priority, behind school, college, work, and family responsibilities.

Emotional barriers: Some people have hang-ups that stop them exercising or mean they really hate certain types of exercise. For example, an overweight person might avoid exercise because they feel silly exercising in front of lots of people who seem much fitter and thinner than they are. In the same way, it is difficult to motivate yourself to take part in activities that you aren't interested in.

Personal injury: Being injured can make it hard or even impossible to train for a certain length of time. When injured, it is important not to participate in sport until fully recovered and then return to training gradually, starting with light training and building back up to full fitness.

Strategies for ensuring adherence to exercise

Setting SMARTER targets is the most effective way for a performer to stay motivated. SMARTER targets help them improve their performance or fitness enough to meet their short-, medium-, and long-term goals. Receiving support from people around them and rewards for meeting targets also helps people to stay focused, maintaining their enthusiasm for the duration of their exercise programme.

Knowing about the benefits of a personal fitness training programme helps adherence. Benefits:
- Provide a focus for training, encouraging motivation.
- Set out what to do in each training session, making it harder to find excuses not to do what should be done.
- Set out a clear pathway for achieving personal training goals.

Strategies for ensuring adherence to exercise

Taking part in enjoyable activities: If you participate in activities that you enjoy, then you will be more likely to continue with your training. When you are working out in the gym, there are going to be activities that you don't enjoy so much. However, thoughtful planning can allow you to hide the least pleasurable activities among the ones you do like, to help you stay committed to your fitness programme.

Rewards for achieving goals: It is important to reward yourself when you achieve the goals that you have set yourself. When elite athletes meet their goals, they are often selected to represent their country or rewarded with medals, cups, trophies, and even cash prizes. People can also reward themselves for doing well, sticking to a training programme, and achieving weight loss or strength goals.

Support and reinforcement can motivate people to achieve their goals. Often people will receive support from friends and family when attempting to achieve their lifelong goals, such as running the London Marathon. People can also receive support from the personal trainer at their local gym, or the coach/manager at their local club. Such people can provide valuable and knowledgeable support for performers, helping them to change their training to achieve a different result or explaining how to perform new exercises that challenge the performer.

 # Remember:

Staying fit does not have to cost the earth. Careful planning, shopping around, and making use of the great outdoors can often save far more than a few pennies.

BRONZE

1. List all the barriers to taking part in a personal fitness training programme that you face.

2. Choose two of the barriers to adherence that you listed for Activity 1 and explain in detail how you could overcome these problems.

Safely implementing a personal fitness training programme

A personal fitness training programme is a training plan designed to improve a person's health, fitness, and performance. It should be designed around a performer's goals, to suit their individual needs. A personal fitness training programme should be completed over a period of six weeks, with a series of fitness tests carried out at the beginning and end of the programme. Thorough planning and careful discussion between a performer and their coach will lead to its effective implementation. There are also a number of other factors to consider when implementing a personal training programme.

Factors to consider when implementing a personal training programme

Importance of commitment: Commitment is considered to be one of the main qualities needed for success in most sports, and this desire to succeed has to come from within the performer. It is important that the performer commits to the training programme in order to achieve their goals.

Factors to consider when implementing a personal training programme

Take part in planned sessions: Taking part in a training session that has been planned is more useful for a performer than taking part in one that hasn't. When entering a gym it is important for the performer to know what they are going to do, when they are going to do it, and how long they are going to do it for. Without direction, training sessions can become meaningless. Circuit training and fitness classes, where qualified instructors provide an intensive session, are run by local leisure centres. These classes are often well attended because people enjoy having someone there to manage their training and provide feedback on their performance.

Gain agreement for any missed sessions: If it is necessary to miss a training session then it is important to get permission from the manager or coach. Remember, if the performer is cancelling a session with a personal trainer it is important to give plenty of notice so that the performer can rebook their training session close to their original appointment and the trainer can fill the performer's slot with another booking.

Record details: The performer should assume full responsibility for recording details of each training session. This will help with motivation for future training sessions.

Follow health and safety guidelines: The performer should always follow health and safety guidelines so that they avoid injury. This includes:
- Wearing the correct training gear.
- Using equipment safely and correctly, for the purpose it was designed for.
- Implementing the correct techniques.
- Following instructions provided by the trainer or leader about personal safety in the training location, be it indoors or outdoors.

Perform to the best of your ability: To get the most out of a training session and to feel a sense of satisfaction when it is finished, the performer must work to the best of their ability throughout.

Hull City FC show their commitment to improving their performance by staying on the pitch at half-time to think about how to improve in the second half.

Training diary

A training diary can record an enormous amount of information about a training programme, including:

- The date, timings, and location of each session.
- Any equipment needed.
- The aims and objectives of each session.
- The type of training completed and FITT details, such as how far or quickly you ran, or how much weight you lifted.
- The percentage of Maximum Heart Rate (MHR) you reached during training or the training threshold you worked in.
- Modifications made to the programme in order for you to meet your targets or to maintain your motivation for training.

Keeping a record of how you felt before, during, and after each training session, how motivated you were, and how well you think it went, will help you to understand how your attitude towards training affects how you train. It is also a good idea to use the Borg Rating of Perceived Exertion Scale (RPE) (see page 9) to measure how hard you have worked in your training session, and to record any barriers to training that you experienced. All this information will help you to see any positive or negative trends that influence your training, which can help inform future planning.

Keeping a record of each training session means that you can track your progress, helping you to determine when you have achieved milestones in your training, and keep you motivated. It is a particularly useful tool in helping you determine if and how the principle of progressive overload has been achieved over the course of a training programme. This information can be used to inform future planning and provide the basis for future training programmes.

BRONZE

1. Find planned training sessions that you could take part in and that could form part of a personal fitness training programme that would help you to meet your targets.

2. a) Thinking about the type of personal fitness training programme that you will complete, write a training diary entry for one session. Remember to include all the information that a training diary should record.

b) After each entry in your training diary, explain why you have included the information that you have. It may be beneficial to use a different coloured pen.

Unit 5 assignment, part two

Background

In order to improve your performance in your favourite sport, you are to participate in a six-week personal fitness training programme.

Task

Implement a six-week personal fitness training programme. Maintain a training diary throughout the programme. Remember to consider your personal exercise adherence factors and your strategies for success before you begin and once you have started the programme. You need to:

Grading criteria to be assessed
1B.4, 1C.5
2B.P4, 2C.P5
2C.M3
2C.D2

 **LEVEL 1**

- Describe two personal exercise adherence factors and two strategies for training success. (1B.4)
- Safely implement, with guidance, a four-week personal fitness training programme, maintaining a training diary. (1C.5)

 **LEVEL 2 PASS**

- Describe four personal exercise adherence factors and four strategies for training success. (2B.P4)
- Safely implement a six-week personal fitness training programme, maintaining a training diary. (2C.P5)

 **LEVEL 2 MERIT**

- Safely implement a successful six-week personal fitness training programme, maintaining a training diary summarising outcomes for each session. (2C.M3)

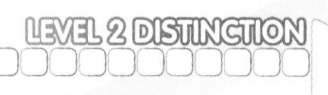 **LEVEL 2 DISTINCTION**

- Safely implement a successful six-week personal fitness training programme, maintaining a training diary to evaluate performance and progress. (2C.D2)

Tackling the assignment

Think about this assignment in two phases: thinking about your personal exercise adherence factors and your strategies for training success and implementing your personal fitness training programme.

It is important to keep a training diary throughout the six-week programme to achieve a Pass. If you want to achieve a

Merit you need to **summarize** the outcomes for each session. This means that you have to write about what you aim to achieve in each training session and about how you plan to achieve it. To achieve a Distinction you need to **evaluate** your performance and progress. This means you have to write about how each training session went, your RPE, and whether or not you achieved your aims.

Meeting the Level 2 Pass criteria

BTEC Level 2 Firsts in Sport

Unit 5 assignment, part two   By Rashid Khan

The barriers to adherence that I have are:

Time
I play football a lot and have school work and chores to do at home, so I don't have lots of free time. I will have to get up early and use my lunch breaks to fit in my fitness sessions.

Cost
I do not have a lot of money so I can't afford to join a gym, so I will need to train outside of a gym.

Access to facilities
There aren't many sports venues near me that I can use so I will have to take advantage of the great outdoors.

Implementing enjoyable activities
I like sport so it will be easy for me to complete my training programme if I keep my training programme varied and activity-based.

Rashid has set his workout well and has begun to describe how each exercise adherence factor affects his ability to commit to an exercise programme. However, Rashid's work is a little vague and very brief. He needs to include a lot more detail about the barriers that affect his participation in exercise. He also needs to explain four strategies that he is planning to use to overcome these barriers and achieve success. If he does this, he will achieve 2B.P4.

Meeting the Level 2 Merit and Distinction criteria

In his diary, Oscar has shown that each week is planned and thought out in advance. His diary also shows a summary of the intended outcomes for each session. If Oscar continues in this way for every training session he completes, he will meet the criteria for 2C.M3.

Training Diary for Oscar Grenieson

Training week 4

Aims for the week: This week I am aiming to increase the time that I run on the treadmill. My main goal is to complete 20 minutes at 10km/h without any rest periods. My weight session will focus on legs – completing the same leg exercises and weights as last week, as these increased from week 2.

Monday 9 September
Session outcomes:
- 10 minutes' cycling at level 4, 60–80RPM. ✓
- Stretching on mat, to include all body parts. ✓
- 20 minutes on the treadmill at minimum 10km/h. Last week I almost managed this but had to drop the speed down in the middle to recover. ✓
- Squats: 40kg, 60kg, 70kg, 80kg, 80kg x 10. ✓
- Leg press: 70kg x 10 x 3. ✓
- Leg extension: 42.5kg x 10 x 3. ✓
- Leg curl: 42.5kg x 10 x 3. ✓

Oscar has clearly appraised his session and shows that he is aware of both his performance and his progress. Oscar also makes reference to his RPE and shows an understanding of this concept. In order to achieve 2C.D2, Oscar needs to make sure that every diary entry is to this standard and that he constantly monitors his progress.

How my session went and notes for next time:
The cardio at the start of the session went really well and I managed to complete 20 minutes without dropping below 10km/h, which is something I did not manage last week. I don't think I left enough time between my run and the start of my weight session as my legs felt tired at the start from all the running. I had a longer rest after my first set of squats and felt OK to continue afterwards.

This weight session went well and I completed all the exercises that I aimed to complete, even though I increased the weight of my squats, leg curls, and leg extensions. Next time I will try to increase the maximum weight that I squat by 5–10kg.

My RPE was high, about 13–14, as I worked really hard to ensure that I completed my 20-minute target on the treadmill, and managed (just) to complete my leg workout.

Reviewing a personal fitness training programme

A fitness training programme should be reviewed both before and after each training session in order to help the performer remain motivated and to find out how well it is going, so that any issues can be resolved quickly. The most important review comes at the end, however, when the six-week programme has been completed. This final review should consider what the client has done and how they feel about their performance, as well as evaluating the progress made, and the effectiveness of the programme. All this information is important for preparing future fitness training programmes.

Modifying a personal fitness training programme to achieve planned targets

It may be necessary to modify a training programme part-way through. For example, if you get injured or miss a couple of training sessions because of other commitments, then it may be necessary to alter the training plan so that you can still reach the targets you have set for yourself by the end of the programme. Changes to facilities or equipment available may also require modifications to be made to your training programme.

An end-of-programme evaluation should include:
- An overall assessment of the programme: How did it go?
- Fitness testing, to establish the performer's fitness levels after the programme (for comparison with their fitness levels before the programme).
- Evaluation: Were the intended targets achieved? Why? Why not?
- Recommendations for future training: What will the next training programme be like? Have the goals changed? Will it include different methods of training? Will it include psychological training techniques?

Focus on strengths

It is important for the personal trainer or fitness coach responsible for working with a performer to pay specific attention to the targets they have successfully achieved. These successes are the reason the performer has been taking part in the training programme and can therefore be used to motivate the performer to continue with their fitness training.

Focus on areas for improvement

Areas in which the performer has not achieved their planned targets need to be given some careful thought. It is important that the reasons for any lack of success are addressed and that these targets are turned into new challenges for future fitness training programmes.

Unit 5 assignment, part three

Background

As a personal trainer, another important part of your job is to review clients' personal fitness training programmes to see how they went. These reviews should focus on the targets set down at the beginning of the training programme, highlighting targets that have been met, and identifying areas for improvement in the future.

Grading criteria to be assessed
1D.6
2D.P6
2D.M4
2D.D3

Task

Complete a review of the personal fitness training programme you have undertaken, using this and your training diary to:

Review the four-week personal fitness training programme, identifying strengths and areas for improvement. (1D.6)

Review the six-week personal fitness training programme, describing strengths and areas for improvement. (2D.P6)

Explain strengths of the training programme and areas for improvement, providing recommendations for future training and performance. (2D.M4)

Justify recommendations for future training and performance. (2D.D3)

Tackling the assignment

Break this part of the assignment down into two phases. First, carry out an end-of-programme review of your personal fitness training programme. Then, stand back and consider the strengths and weaknesses of the original programme. If you were completing the programme again, what would you do again in exactly the same way and what would you attempt to improve?

To achieve a Merit, you need to **explain** the strengths, weaknesses, and areas where your fitness training programme could be improved. This means you need to provide lots of examples from your training diary to support your statements. You then need to provide recommendations for future fitness training programmes and performance.

If you are aiming for a Distinction, you need to **justify** your recommendations. This means you need to offer your opinion on why your recommendations are appropriate and provide reasons or examples to back up your opinions.

Meeting the Level 2 Pass criteria

BTEC Level 2 Firsts in Sport

Unit 5 assignment, part 3   **By Samuel Yates**

After completing my six-week personal fitness training programme I feel that it went quite well.

<u>The strengths of my personal fitness training programme</u>

- The use of activities that are relevant to my sport: I included activities that are specific to my needs as a hockey player, so that the training programme would help me develop my ability to perform.
- Variety of activities: I used a variety of activities, including running, swimming, cross-training, and circuit training, to ensure that I remained interested in my training programme.

<u>The areas of my personal fitness training programme that could be improved</u>

- The intensity at which I performed some of the cardiovascular exercises.
- How often I trained.
- The inclusion of more work targeting sport-specific skills.

Samuel has taken a logical approach to the task and has met the criteria for 2D.P6 because he has described the strengths of his programme and has identified some areas for improvement.

Meeting the Level 2 Merit criteria

The strengths of my training programme

Patrice Traore

Specificity: My training programme was specific to my individual needs, which helped me to improve in my sport.

Progressive overload: At the start of the training programme I found it difficult to run continuously for more than 15 minutes. However, by the end of the six weeks, I was able to run for 25 minutes without stopping or slowing to a walk.

By using a heart-rate monitor I was able to ensure that I was working in the target zone for the duration of my sessions.

Patrice has used the principles of training to explain the strengths of his training programme and how it could be improved. This is a very good idea as it makes his work very clear. If he continues in this way, referring to the remaining principles of fitness and providing recommendations for future training and performance, he will meet the criteria for 2D.M4.

Meeting the Level 2 Distinction criteria

Suggestions to improve my training programme

Patrice Traore

Variation: I did a lot of running outdoors in my training programme and by the end of the six weeks I really did not feel like running any more, even though I did continue. Next time I will try to use a variety of different cardiovascular fitness machines in order to change the type of training I do, because this will help me to maintain enthusiasm for my training, and therefore delay the onset of boredom.

Intensity: Again, I performed a lot of continuous running and although I found it hard, I feel I would have benefited from working at a higher intensity for shorter periods of time. For example, in the future I think interval training would be a more appropriate way for me to meet my targets and increase my fitness to a higher level.

Patrice has shown that he has thought about how his training programme went and the things that made it more challenging to complete. His recommendations of variation and interval training are good, however, his justifications are short on detail. In order to achieve a Distinction (2D.D3), Patrice must go into more detail for both of his recommendations. He needs to include the reasons behind his suggestions, as well as provide more information about how he would overcome these issues in a future training programme.

Unit 6: Leading Sports Activities

Skills and successful sports leadership

Sports leaders can be seen at work in a wide range of different settings and organizations across the world. Sports coaches, fitness instructors, school and college coaches, national club coaches, and amateur coaches are all sports leaders. Essentially, anybody who is responsible for leading a sporting activity can be classed as a sports leader and they will have similar generic skills that enable them to organize and implement training sessions and sporting events successfully. Leaders of more specialized activities will have also undertaken more specialist training in order to be successful in their chosen field.

Core skills

The core skills sports leaders need in order to successfully plan and deliver sporting activities include good communication skills, the ability to organize equipment effectively, and an in-depth knowledge of their activity.

Communication

Communication is one of the most important skills required for planning and leading sports activities and events. There are two main ways in which a sports leader communicates:

1. **Verbal communication:** This is achieved by speaking to people. A leader should be clear and precise in what they are saying. They should keep the information simple and not use too many words, so there is no confusion and the group remains focused throughout.
2. **Non-verbal communication:** This is achieved using lots of different methods, including hand gestures, body language, tone of voice, and facial expressions – anything other than what you actually say to people. Non-verbal communication can be very effective when leading a group, particularly if the environment they are working in is noisy. Some learners also respond better to non-verbal communication (for example, a skill being demonstrated) than they do to verbal communication.

A successful leader also has the ability to listen to their group and deal with any issues or concerns they have about the event or session that is taking place. It is important that the leader is understanding and that members of the group feel that their leader is approachable.

Communication is especially important when coaching young children.

Organization of equipment

Organization is another key skill when planning a sports session or event. Leaders should be aware of both the facilities and the equipment available, and ensure that they have everything in place prior to the session. They should consider the following:

Leaders need to make sure the necessary equipment is available before a session begins.

- **Size of the group:** How many are attending the session? Is more space or equipment needed because the group is large?
- **Condition of the equipment:** Is the equipment safe to use? Has it been maintained to a good standard?
- **Variety of equipment:** Is there something for people of all abilities? Different equipment may be required for people who are disabled or have special educational needs.
- **Return of equipment:** It is important that borrowed equipment is returned in the same condition that it was in when it was taken. This will ensure a positive relationship between the lender and the borrower is maintained and that future hire of equipment is possible.

Knowledge

Perhaps most importantly, sports leaders should have an in-depth knowledge of the skills, techniques, rules, and regulations of the sport or activity they are leading to ensure that they give out accurate information.

Advanced skills

In addition to the core skills that effective sports leaders have, there are also advanced skills that enable a sports leader to provide a high-quality session for participants. These skills include:

Structuring activities

Before any session or event can take place, a detailed and accurate plan should be drawn up. The plan should include the following information:

- **Your goal:** You should have a clear idea of what you want to achieve and what you want the group to achieve by the end of the session. For example, one of your aims might be to get more than ten participants to attend your session; another might be to ensure that everyone who attends makes some progress by the end of the session. You might set yourself an objective, such as, all group members will be able to dribble a basketball using only their right hand by the end of the session, and decide that an expected outcome will be that some members of the group will be able to do this and others will be able to perform a modified version.
- **Content:** Details of what is going to happen during the session will remind you what needs to be covered and ensure that nothing is missed out. For example, a warm-up, followed by passing and shooting skills, followed by a competition, followed by a cool-down.
- **Timings:** It is vital that timings are linked to the content so that everything can be covered in the session, unnecessary delays are avoided, and everyone involved knows what should be happening at all times.
- **Equipment:** A list of the equipment to be used is a useful reminder of what you will need to prepare for the activity. You may also wish to consider any special requirements of people in the group at this point, as different equipment may be required to provide tasks that cater for all abilities.

Topic of lesson: Football – Passing skills		Duration of lesson: 30 mins		Group: Year 7 boys
Lesson objectives: By the end of this lesson students will: • Know how to conduct a pass to someone's feet. • Understand what parts of the foot are used in conducting a pass and how to stand. • Be able to pass and move in a game situation.		**Learning outcomes:** • All must perform a pass to someone else's feet. • Most will be able to move into a space to receive a pass. • Some will be able to do long passes.		**Special educational needs provision:**
Resources required: • 30–40 cones • 3 footballs		**Opportunities for assessment:** • Leader observation • Question and answer		**Gifted and Talented provision:** See differentiation column below.

Time	Activity	Organization (How are the students working? For example, in pairs?)	Teaching points (What exactly are students doing?)	Differentiation
2 mins	Introduction	Students are to sit down in a corner or around me, listening to me explain the lesson and what will be happening.	• Sitting quietly and listening to me.	None.
5 mins	Warm-up	Students should jog around the sports hall three times sticking to the outsides of the cones. When completed, they should all come into a circle, spread out, and perform the flexibility and mobility stretches that I will be doing for them to copy.	• Jogging, not running. • Watching me and copying the stretches. • Keeping quiet.	Students to jog at a speed suitable for their ability and perform only those stretches that they can do comfortably.
13 mins	Skill	Students are to be lined up behind each other in two or more rows, with the students at the front of each row facing each other. The first student passes to the student in the opposite line and then runs to the back of their own line. The receiver then passes the ball to the new person facing them and also runs to the back of their line. This should continue for five minutes. Students should then form a circle and complete two-touch passes, calling the name of the person they are passing to.	• In two or four lines, passing the ball to each other. • Standing in a circle completing two-touch passes.	Divide the class into groups on ability so the quality of the passes is about the same.
2 mins	Plenary	Jog around the hall and stretch off the legs as a cool-down. Then, talk about what the students have learnt during the session.	• Jogging sensibly around the hall. • Watching me and copying the stretches. • Sitting quietly and listening to me. • Answering questions.	Consciously ask them to answer the questions and give hints if they are not answering or answering incorrectly.

An example of a plan for a session.

Target setting

Targets should be set for participants, particularly if the activity is part of a series of sessions aimed at improving skills or techniques in a given sport. For example, if a coach is leading an individual through a series of training sessions, they may wish to set their athlete the target of recording a personal best performance by the end of the season, or of gaining selection for a particular event or squad. Coaches and leaders can also set themselves targets. For example,

6. Write down three SMARTER targets that you want to achieve in your role as a sports leader. For example, you may want to feel more confident when talking to a group by the end of the term.

7. Find an example of a real-life sports leader for each of the skills associated with sports leadership.

8. Choose two sports leaders and list all the skills associated with sports leadership that each of them has. Then, compare the two lists, explaining the differences and similarities.

9. Look at your answer to Activity 8. Based on their skills, which, in your opinion, is the best sports leader and why?

they may want to improve their leadership skills, try different teaching styles or work on using different communication skills. Targets should be SMARTER:

SPECIFIC: Targets should be specific; they should set down precisely what you want to achieve. For example, 'I want to run the 100 metres in under 15 seconds.'

MEASUREABLE: Targets should be measurable, so that you can work out if you have achieved them. It is also better to make these measures specific, wherever possible. For example, it is better to say that your target is to run the 100 metres in under 15 seconds than it is to say that you want to run the 100 metres more quickly.

ACHIEVABLE: Targets should be appropriate to the fitness and skill levels of the performer. They should be close enough for us to see but not so far away that we can't touch them.

REALISTIC: It is important that we set targets that we have the capacity to achieve. All targets need to be challenging so that you have to work hard to achieve them, but they must also be realistic in order for them to serve their purpose and motivate you.

TIME-RELATED: Targets should have a time limit on them. For example, 'I want to run the 100 metres in under 15 seconds by the end of the summer'. If your long-term goals rely on you achieving your short-term goals, then you need to set time limits on your short-term goals to ensure you reach your long-term goals.

EXCITING: Targets should have something exciting about them or relate directly to a reward. For example, your long-term target might be, 'I want to be chosen to represent the county in the English Schools Athletics Championships in June'.

RECORDED: All targets should be recorded so that you and your coach can refer to them at any given time. A training diary is the ideal place to record your targets.

Use of language

The way in which a leader speaks to their group can have an effect on the group's behaviour and their performance. For example, when leading young children, basic, exaggerated instructions with lots of demonstrations will help to make you more easily understood. However, where teenagers and adults are concerned, the information can be more detailed and the terminology more specific.

Evaluation

It is important for a sports leader to evaluate sessions that they run to provide them with feedback on their performance. If a session is unsuccessful, for whatever reason, the leader can work on improving things for the next time that they lead an activity. Equally, if something worked really well, they may want to use this method in the future.

When evaluating a session or event it is important to gather information from everyone involved, including the participants, the spectators, and the helpers, to build an accurate picture of how it went. You might want to ask people about the following:

- **Planning:** How well was the session/event planned?
- **Content:** How suitable was the content of the session/event for the participants? Was there enough/too much going on?
- **Organization:** How organized was the leader before the event and on the day? Did they remain calm?
- **Health and safety:** Were the participants safe? Were there any incidents? If anyone was injured or ill, were they treated efficiently?
- **Personal qualities of the leader:** How appropriate was the leadership style employed? How confident/enthusiastic/motivational/friendly was the leader? How good was the leader at communicating?
- **Achievements:** Did the leader achieve the objectives set out for the session/event?
- **Areas for development:** What could have been done better? What should the leader do next time to make the session/event run more smoothly?

Qualities and successful sports leadership

In addition to all the necessary skills, a sports leader should also possess a range of qualities that make them well suited to working with others in a leadership capacity.

Key qualities

The key qualities needed by an effective sports leader include a smart appearance, enthusiasm, and confidence.

Appearance
A sports leader should always take pride in their appearance and look smart, because they are setting an example to the people in their group. They may also be viewed as a role model by some members of their group.

Enthusiasm
When leading a group or individual, it is vital that the coach or leader is enthusiastic about what they are teaching. In order to motivate the participants and keep them interested, the leader must believe in what they are saying and should try to convey this enthusiasm to their group.

Confidence
A leader should be confident in their ability. This confidence will be passed on to the participants so that they believe their leader knows what he or she is talking about and, therefore, have faith in what they are being taught. A leader may also be required to speak to large numbers of people at any one time and this takes courage and confidence.

Additional qualities

In addition to the key qualities that effective sports leaders have, there are also additional qualities that distinguish successful and effective sports leaders. These include:

Personality
Leaders all have their own individual personalities. However, they must possess certain qualities in order to communicate well with the members of their group.

A leader needs to be confident if they are to hold the group's attention and lead an effective session.

Understanding
There may be occasions when an individual has a delicate issue, which is affecting their performance, that they wish to discuss.

Outgoing and sociable
This is important if they are to get along well with members of the public and communicate with a range of different people.

Approachable
This is important if they want their group to have confidence in them and feel able to talk to them about any concerns.

Leaders should be …

Confident with their authority
Leaders must be able to discipline their group if necessary. This is particularly important when considering health and safety issues.

BRONZE

1. Which of the following statements show an autocratic leadership style, which show a democratic leadership style, and which show a laissez-faire leadership style?

a) Are you warmed up enough now? Would you like to end the warm-up there?

b) Pass the ball and move into a space.

c) Would you like to take a rest now?

d) OK, what would you like to do today then? How about a few stretches to start off with?

e) You must use the correct technique every time if you wish to improve.

2. For each style of leadership, identify a famous sports leader who mainly employs this style.

3. Why is it important for a sports leader to be enthusiastic? Describe the effect that an enthusiastic sports leader could have on a participant. When might participants need an enthusiastic sports leader most?

4. For each of the qualities associated with good sports leadership, find an example of a real-life sports leader who possesses it.

SILVER

5. Choose two sports leaders and list all the qualities associated with sports leadership that each of them has. Then, compare the two lists, explaining the differences and similarities.

GOLD

6. Look at your answer to Activity 5. Based on their qualities, which, in your opinion, is the best sports leader and why?

Motivation

It is important for leaders to motivate the members of their group, because a motivated group is usually more interested and keen to succeed. Motivational techniques that coaches and leaders can use include encouragement, praising the positives, and setting targets for improvement. Leaders should try to be motivational all the time because what they say and do can have a direct effect on the performance of the sportsperson or team.

Humour

Coaches and leaders should enjoy delivering activities and events, and it is really beneficial to have a good sense of humour. A leader who can joke, be light-hearted, and have fun with the group could make their sessions more interesting and stimulating than a leader who is serious all the time.

Leadership style

There are many different leadership styles that sports leaders can use with their groups but the three main ones are:

- **Autocratic (command):** This is a straightforward leadership style where the leader gives out instructions that the group follows. It can be effective when dealing with large numbers of people because there is less chance of the instructions being misinterpreted.
- **Democratic:** This leadership style is more laid-back and, unlike the autocratic approach, the leader involves the group in the decision-making. This approach is effective with smaller groups and, as the group members are asked for their opinion, it gives them a sense of responsibility for the session or event.
- **Laissez-faire:** This is a very relaxed leadership style in which the responsibility for decision-making is largely given to the group. This method can only really be effective if the group members are responsible and experienced, because incorrect decisions could cause problems.

Autocratic (command).

Democratic.

Laissez-faire.

Responsibilities and successful sports leadership

When running a session or event, sports leaders are responsible for all the people involved, the venue, and the equipment being used.

Key responsibilities

The key responsibilities of a good sports leader include conducting themselves professionally, ensuring the health and safety of participants, and making sure everyone is treated equally.

Professional conduct: Leaders must behave professionally and responsibly at all times. Young children often look up to their leader and view them as a role model. Therefore, their actions and behaviour must be impeccable in order to have a positive impact on the members of their group.

Health and safety: A leader must make sure that their group is safe and well while participating in physical activity. This involves duties such as checking that there is a current risk assessment in place and checking that the equipment is in full working order.

Equality: Sports leaders should be aware of equal opportunities and try to ensure that all participants are treated with respect regardless of their age, gender, disability, race, nationality, ethnicity, or national origin. They should encourage members of their group to be polite and respectful to create a good atmosphere.

Wider responsibilities

In addition to their key responsibilities, sports leaders have wider responsibilities which, together, safeguard participants and ensure that sports leaders don't put themselves at risk.

Insurance: It is a requirement that sports leaders have insurance to cover them for any activity that they are leading. This provides reassurance to the participants and their families in case of any accident, and protects the leader should anything go wrong.

Child protection: Sports leaders must make sure that children in their care are safe and not at risk from anyone. It is vital that leaders identify children with problems or those who may be suffering abuse. Children often confide in people that they look up to, and if a child is suffering at home, they may share their burden with their sports coach or leader.

Legal obligations: If you are leading a group of children under 16 years of age, you are legally obliged to seek the permission of a parent or guardian before allowing anyone to take part. Also, if your activity is considered a contact sport, such as football or rugby, participants must not take part in mixed-gender activities and separate-sex practices should be set up.

Ethics and values: Good sportsmanship is about being fair and honest. Sports leaders should encourage the members of their group to respect each other and their opponents, and to abide by the rules and etiquette expected in their sport or physical activity.

Rules and regulations: Leaders should be familiar with the rules and regulations of the sport or activity that they are delivering. They should also ensure that their group members, especially if they are young children, adhere to the rules because this may help to prevent injuries.

BRONZE

1. Taking your own experience and qualifications as a starting point, find out about the next leadership qualification that you could take for a sport of your choice.

SILVER

2. Explain the following responsibilities of being a sports leader, giving examples to support your answer.

- A sports leader should ensure that their athlete(s) abides by the rules and regulations of the relevant sport.
- It is the responsibility of the sports leader to ensure that everyone in their group has an equal opportunity to participate.

Unit 6 assignment, part one

Background

Imagine you are the manager of the local rugby club. You are always looking to recruit new members. At the moment, you are also looking for a suitably qualified coach to lead the under-13 squad. You need someone who can work with children, and who has the right skills and qualities to lead a young side.

Task

Write an article for the sports section of your local newspaper that is designed to encourage applicants for a job like the one outlined in the scenario above. The article should be based around an analysis of the skills, qualities, and responsibilities of sports leaders. Your article should contain:

Grading criteria to be assessed
1A.1, 1A.2
2A.P1, 2A.P2
2A.M1, 2A.M2
2A.D1

 **LEVEL 1**

- Outline the attributes required for, and responsibilities of, sports leadership. (1A.1)
- Describe the attributes of a selected successful sports leader. (1A.2)

 **LEVEL 2 PASS**

- Describe, using relevant examples, the attributes required for, and responsibilities of, sports leadership. (2A.P1)
- Describe the attributes of two selected successful sports leaders. (2A.P2)

 **LEVEL 2 MERIT**

- Explain the attributes required for, and responsibilities of, sports leadership. (2A.M1)
- Evaluate the attributes of two successful sports leaders. (2A.M2)

 **LEVEL 2 DISTINCTION**

- Compare and contrast the attributes of two successful sports leaders. (2A.D1)

Tackling the assignment

In order to meet the criteria for this assignment you need to ensure that you include information about the skills and qualities a sports leader needs to have, as well as information about their responsibilities. For a Pass and a Merit, you need to discuss the skills, qualities and responsibilities of sports leaders in general and then focus in on two examples of people who successfully demonstrate these attributes. If you are not confident about commenting on two famous or well-known sports leaders, you may wish to use

examples of sports leaders that you are more familiar with, such as your PE teachers or college lecturers.

And remember, when you **describe** something you need to draw a picture in words for your reader, when you **explain** something you need to provide examples and tell the reader why it is like it is, when you **evaluate** something you explain it and then give your opinion about it, and when you **compare and contrast** two or more things you need to discuss the similarities and differences between them.

The skills, qualities, and responsibilities of a good sports leader

Jamie Browne

SKILLS	QUALITIES	RESPONSIBILITIES
Good communicator: This is needed because a sports leader needs to tell others what to do. They need to be able to give clear coaching points when showing others how to perform a tennis serve, for example.	Confidence: Sports leaders need to be confident when taking sessions. This is important so that the group feels that the leader knows what they are talking about and means that the group is more likely to show the leader respect.	Health and safety: This is a very important responsibility. Sports leaders need to ensure that all participants are safe and protected from hazards and dangers.

This piece of work is starting to meet the Pass criteria because it includes descriptions of one skill, one quality, and one responsibility of a sports leader. To fully meet the Pass criteria, Jamie needs to extend his table and add more skills, qualities, and responsibilities.

Jamie must make sure that he includes an example for everything he describes. For example, I'd like to see him provide a brief description of a hazard that a sports leader could keep people safe from if she/he follows health and safety guidelines.

The two sports leaders that I am going to describe are my PE teachers. Both teachers are successful in what they do but they are very different. One of them has a very laid-back approach which the group really likes. It allows us to explore things a little more and gives us the confidence to try new things out and not worry if we get them wrong the first time. The other PE teacher has a more organized and direct approach, which also works well. This teacher gives very clear guidance and talks us through the things we need to do to improve the work we are doing, step by step.

Jamie has begun to describe the attributes of two successful sports leaders, but he needs to go into a lot more detail. He needs to describe their specific skills and qualities and how they approach their responsibilities as a sports leader.

Planning and leading sports activities

There are many different sports activities, including individual sports, team sports, and fitness activities. Regardless of the sport, however, all sports activity sessions follow the same basic structure, require the leader to plan carefully before the session, and employ all their leadership skills and qualities to carry out their responsibilities effectively.

The components of a sports activity session

Whatever the sport, all sports activity sessions follow the same basic structure.

Warm-up
Begin with a warm-up activity to set the pace for the rest of the session and help minimize the risk of injury. The warm-up should consist of three phases: the pulse-raising phase, the stretching phase, and the joint-mobilization phase.

Main part
- Introduce the main part of the session by telling the group the aims, objectives, and expected outcomes so participants know what to expect.
- Demonstrate a particular skill or technique and provide participants with an opportunity to practise it. Whatever the skill you are teaching, break it down into bite-sized segments and focus on one segment at a time. For example, if you want to teach the long jump, break it down into the run-up, the take-off, the flight, and the landing. Remember, it may take several sessions to teach all of the segments.
- Allow the group to play a modified game or competition. This is important, particularly for young children, who quickly get bored if they just practise a skill and cannot imagine doing it in a 'game situation'.

Cool-down
It is hugely beneficial for a session to end with a cool-down activity. It may be just a gentle jog and a few stretches, perhaps while seated, but this gives the group a chance to recover from the session and helps to bring both their mind and body back to a resting state.

Planning a sports activity session

When planning a session or event, the following aspects must be taken into consideration. And, remember, even if you have led a similar session in the past you must review each aspect afresh for each new session you lead because some things may have changed.

Resources
- What equipment will you need? Can you access all the equipment you need when you need it? Is it safe to use?
- How long is your session? Have you allocated times to the different parts of your session? Can the planned activities be completed within the time allowed for the session?
- Do you have an appropriate venue for the session? Will the venue be accessible to you before and after the session so that you can set up and pack away the equipment?

Equipment needs to be set up before the session begins.

Participants

- How many people are attending the session? How will you split the group up?
- How old are the people attending the session?
- Are the people attending the session male or female, or will there be a mix of participants? Does your activity require children to work in single-sex groups?
- What ability are the people attending the session? Are they all beginners, or will you have a mixture of experienced and inexperienced participants?
- Do any of the participants have medical or other specific needs? How will you ensure that these are met? Will you need to differentiate the activities?

Demonstrating your skills and qualities and fulfilling your responsibilities as a sports leader

It is important that you demonstrate the skills and qualities of a successful sports leader (see pages 100–104) and fulfil the responsibilities of a good sports leader (see page 105). Sometimes, this involves identifying where you need help. For example, your session might involve a detailed demonstration of a skill you don't perform very well and you might need to find someone reliable to demonstrate it on your behalf.

Will you need help demonstrating skills and techniques during your session?

Measuring successes

Make sure you set targets for yourself so that, when the session is over, you have something to measure your success against. For example, you may set yourself the target of fulfilling the aims and objectives of the session, and meeting the expected outcomes. Or you may set yourself the target of conducting the session safely and in an organized manner.

Health and safety

A leader must make sure that their group is safe and well while participating in physical activity. This involves duties such as:

- Checking that there is a current risk assessment in place, which covers the activity you are doing, in the place you are doing it, with similar participants. If appropriate, you should modify your plan for the session to ensure that the solutions for minimizing risk identified in the risk assessment are in place. If there isn't a risk assessment in place, it is the leader's responsibility to carry one out.
- Checking that the equipment is in full working order and is set up correctly.
- Checking the venue/site to be used for any hazards that may need attention or that participants may need to be made aware of.
- As a leader it is your responsibility to ensure that your sessions are delivered in the safest possible way and that young people in your care are not put at risk. However, there are some activities, such as rock climbing, which are inherently dangerous and participants – or their parents, if they are children – need to give their consent before taking part.

Aims, objectives, and expected outcomes

Every session should have clear aims and objectives that are both measurable and achievable. An aim is something general that you are working to achieve by the end of the session or series of sessions, for example, to improve the over-arm bowling technique of participants. An objective is something specific that you are aiming to achieve, for example, 'By the end of this session, participants will be able to bowl a ball to a batsman using an over-arm technique'.

Each session should have one or more expected outcomes. These are the things that you expect participants to have achieved by taking part in the session. An expected outcome may vary depending on the experience and/or ability of the participants. For example, the expected outcome for one student may be to dribble a basketball in a straight line and the expected outcome for another may be to dribble a basketball around an obstacle.

Leading a sports activity session

Don't forget to keep a record of the session. You could keep a diary or a logbook, record witness testimonies or keep feedback sheets, or use audio or video equipment.

BRONZE

1. Plan a 30-minute rounders session for a mixed-ability, mixed-gender group of Year 11 students.

2. Lead the session you planned for Activity 1.

SILVER

3. Justify why you have included the activities you have in the plan you created for Activity 1.

Reviewing sports activities

Having planned and led a sports activity session, it is important to celebrate your strengths and identify areas for improvement by reviewing your performance. You should then establish a development plan to ensure you improve and become a better leader in the future.

Gathering feedback

In order to accurately review your strengths and areas for improvement, you need to gather feedback on your planning and delivery. This feedback can come from many sources, including:

- **Participants**: People taking part in the session you led can give you vital information that will help you develop as a leader. Were you aware, for example, that you spoke very quietly and some people struggled to hear you? Did you know that you demonstrated each skill too quickly for the participants to fully understand what you were doing? And it's nice to know that the participants welcomed your cheerfulness; you'll work hard to make sure you're smiling during the next session you lead, even if you're having a bad day!

- **Supervisors**: The people who are responsible for overseeing your session will have watched it carefully and should be able to provide you with feedback on how well the session matched the plan you wrote, how you responded to unforeseen circumstances, and how well you demonstrated the skills and qualities of a successful leader.

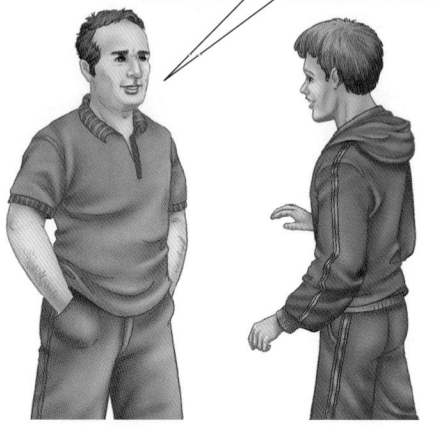

- **Observers**: Although they are not an obvious group to think about, people watching your session – parents or friends, for example – could have experience of planning and leading sports activities and may well have some useful pointers for you that will help you evaluate your own performance.

- **Self-analysis**: Analysing your own performance is crucial for all leaders, from beginners to the most experienced, if you are to make sure that the sessions you deliver are of a consistently high standard. Look at every aspect of the session and be truthful with yourself about how you feel things went. This is not the time to say everything was great and that you achieved or exceeded all your targets. To benefit from self-analysis you need to be critical; you need to be honest about your strengths and the areas of your performance that could be improved.

Questionnaires

Questionnaires or evaluation sheets are often used at the end of a session or workshop when the leader needs the participants to tell them how it went. Questionnaires can contain:

- Closed questions: These are questions that have a yes/no answer or where the participant has to choose their answer from one of the options provided. For example: Do you think that the session was the right length?

  It was much too long   It was a bit too long   Yes, it was just right   It was a bit too short   It was much too short

- Open questions: These are questions that encourage the participant to leave a more lengthy comment about their experience. For example: What did you think about the length of the session?

There are a number of different ways to gather feedback.

Comment cards

Comment cards are similar to questionnaires but not as lengthy and can be more appealing to participants because they are less time-consuming to fill in. A comment card usually contains one or two open questions, with space for participants to write their feedback.

Observation checklist

All sports leaders should be regularly observed by someone with more experience than them, who will record their findings using an observation checklist. The resulting feedback on their strengths and areas for improvement is used to create a plan for their personal development.

Direct verbal feedback

Direct verbal feedback often accompanies written feedback. It is important that it is constructive and positive and, above all, motivates the person receiving it. One successful model for constructive feedback works like this:

- Ask the leader how they feel it went.
- Tell the leader how you think it went.

- Ask the leader what they think they did well.
- Tell the leader what you think they did well, using specific examples.

- Ask the leader what they think they could do differently or better.
- Tell the leader what you think they could do differently or better, using specific examples.

- Agree the next steps together. These could be short-, medium-, or long-term goals.

Analysing your performance

You can use the feedback you gather from different sources to analyse your performance. Consider your leadership skills, your leadership qualities, your responsibilities as a leader, and how well you executed each aspect of your plan, and then identify your strengths and areas for improvement.

Setting targets for development

Once you have established your areas for development it is important to map out a development plan. This is a document that sets down what you will do in a specific time frame in order to improve. Typically, a development plan includes the following information:

- **Aims and objectives:** Clearly stating what you are working to achieve and what steps you are going to take to achieve it. For example, 'I aim to become a PE teacher when I leave university. While at university, I will take every opportunity to develop my experience of sports leadership in preparation.'
- **Goals:** These can be short-, medium-, or long-term goals. They should always be described using the SMARTER goal-setting technique. For example, 'I will achieve coaching awards for six different sports before I leave university, two per year.'
- **Opportunities for training or further development:** Are there training courses or qualifications that will help you achieve your goals? For example, you may have already completed a Level 1 Sports Leaders course but now need to move on to the Community Sports Leaders Award at Level 2. This will enable you to work with groups on your own but under supervision.
- **Possible barriers:** These are the things that will stop you achieving your goals and it is important that you identify them so that you can think of ways to minimize them. For example, you might not have enough money to go on the training courses you would like to attend, so you could consider looking for sponsorship from a local sports club.

BRONZE

1. Thinking about a sports activity session that you have delivered, how could you have gathered feedback about your performance as a leader?

2. Again, thinking about a sports activity session that you delivered, review your performance.

SILVER

3. Create a personal development plan outlining how you plan to improve as a sports leader.

GOLD

4. Justify the personal development plan you created for Activity 3 by explaining why you have made the decisions you have made and explaining the benefits you will reap if you follow the plan.

Unit 6 assignment, part two

Background

You are keen to become a sports leader and, as a favour to you, a local sports coach has given you the opportunity to plan and lead an activity for a group of ten-year-old children. Although the sports coach will be in the vicinity when you are leading your activity, you should create a plan for, prepare, and deliver the activity independently.

Task

Plan two activity sessions for a mixed-ability group of boys and girls aged ten. Your sessions should last approximately 30 minutes and should include a warm-up, skills section, and possibly a modified game. Lead one of the sessions and, afterwards, review your performance, commenting on your strengths, areas for development, and targets for future development. You should:

Grading criteria to be assessed
1B.3, 1B.4, 1C.5
2B.P3, 2B.P4, 2C.P5
2B.M3, 2B.M4, 2C.M5
2C.D2

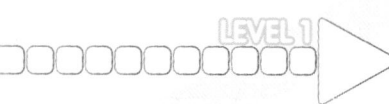 **LEVEL 1**

- Plan a given sports activity. (1B.3)
- Lead a component of a sports activity session, with guidance and/or support. (1B.4)
- Review the planning and leading of the warm-up, main component or cool down, describing strengths and areas for improvement. (1C.5)

 **LEVEL 2 PASS**

- Plan two selected sports activities. (2B.P3)
- Independently lead a sports activity session. (2B.P4)
- Review the planning and leading of the sports activity session, describing the strengths and areas for improvement, and targets for future development as a sports leader. (2C.P5)

 **LEVEL 2 MERIT**

- Justify the choice of activities within the sports activity plan. (2B.M3)
- Lead a successful sports activity session. (2B.M4)
- Explain targets for future development as a sports leader, including a personal development plan. (2C.M5)

 **LEVEL 2 DISTINCTION**

- Justify targets for future development as a sports leader and activities within the personal development plan. (2C.D2)

Tackling the assignment

In order to meet the Pass criteria for this assignment, you should create two session plans containing details of your intended activities, with time allocations. You will need to lead at least one of these activities without help from your teacher or lecturer so you will need to make sure you are confident that you can deliver the plan. You should then review your performance. This can easily be done using a basic form; summarizing what went well, what could have been done better, and describing your targets for future development.

If you're aiming for a Merit you will need to write a commentary to accompany your plan, justifying why you included each

activity. When you justify something, you need to explain why you have done what you have done, with reference to the benefits it will bring. Then you will need to go on to prepare a development plan containing your targets for developing as a sports leader. You should explain each target, telling the reader why you have included it.

If you're aiming for a Distinction, you will need to write a commentary to accompany your development plan, justifying why you have included each target and activity in the plan and detailing the advantages you will gain from them.

Meeting the Level 2 Pass criteria

BTEC PE: Isabella Strong

Lesson topic: Football – Passing

Module: Sports leadership

Lesson duration: 30 mins

Year group: 7

Lesson number: 1

Lesson objectives	Learning outcomes	Special educational needs provision
Know: How to pass a ball **Understand:** How to dribble around cones **Able to do:** Pass and dribble	**All:** Dribble **Most:** Pass **Some:** Pass after dribble	
Resources required	**Opportunities for assessment** Teacher observation Peer observation Question and answer	**Gifted and talented (G&T) provision** See differentiation column

Time	Activity	Organization (How are the pupils working e.g. in pairs?)	Teaching points (What exactly are they doing?)	Differentiation (Other tasks for the more or less able e.g. G&T)
5 mins	**Warm-up** Walk, jog, sprint Stretches for muscle flexibility Joint mobility Starting top to bottom when doing stretches	One big circle All stood around me	To get people stretched well so they don't injure themselves.	
5 mins	**Skill** Dribble in and out of cones	Two groups of three and one group of four	You can use the inside of the foot and the outside of the foot and then you will be able to dribble a lot better and know for the future.	Smaller space between cones for the more advanced, as it is harder to do.
5 mins	**Skill** Passing a ball	Five groups of two	Pass the ball in a pair to each other first with the inside and then the outside of the foot.	More advanced to stand further away from each other.
10 mins	**Warm down and Q&A**	One big group	Ask questions on what we have done in the lesson to make sure they have been listening to me.	Ask harder questions of the people who I believe know more.

Isabella's plan for her football uses a clear format with which to present the lesson content and does just meet the criteria for 2B.P3. However, there are improvements she should make:

- The objectives set are relevant but the outcomes do not accurately reflect the content of the lesson. Isabella needs to think more clearly about which skills are more likely to be achieved by all students, and which students will be able to demonstrate the more difficult skills.
- More detailed outcomes would also be valuable. For example, 'All students will be able to pass the ball accurately using the inside

of the foot along the ground.' This more explicitly explains what is required of participants.
- It would be good to see the 'Resources required' box completed, as thinking through what she will need to lead the session successfully will help Isabella set up efficiently.
- I would like to have seen the participants experience a conditioned game towards the end of the session.

Lesson plan	The plan that I put together was in my view well thought out and linked the different components together. I was able to put clear objectives in the plan, which helped the participants focus on what I wanted them to achieve.
Things that went well	The best part of my session was when I got the participants working in pairs, practising the inside-of-foot pass. I knew this was working well as all participants were very quickly able to demonstrate to me that they could use the correct technique with some degree of speed.
Things that need to be worked on	The areas that I think I need to work on include using participants who are performing skills well to demonstrate to the rest of the group. I was a little shy at times doing this so would sometimes miss it out. Another area that I need to work on is speaking more clearly to the group and waiting for all of them to be quiet instead of talking over them.
Methods used to gain feedback	My tutor observed my session and sat down with me afterwards to go through it all. He told me that I needed to speak a little louder as it was windy, but also slower as I was rushing through the instructions section. I asked five participants what they thought of the session and they all liked it. Their comments included: 'The session was really good because Miss gave simple instructions and I was able to do the tasks.' 'I like football and Miss made it enjoyable. I like practising skills in small groups.' 'The dribbling practice I think was good and I was asked by Miss to demonstrate it to others.'

Isabella's review of her football session is beginning to take shape. She is reflecting on how she felt about the session and taking on board feedback from her supervisor and participants. Isabella now needs to think more about her strengths and weaknesses and comment on these. What went well and why? What didn't go so well and why?

In order to fully meet the criteria for 2C.P5, Isabella also needs to provide targets for her future development as a sports leader. Without these she has only achieved 1C.5.

Meeting the Level 2 Merit and Distinction criteria

It is good to see that Isabella's development plan has a clear goal. By setting her plan out as a table and writing down the impact of each key action she is also explaining each item in her plan. If she continues in this way she should meet the criteria for 2C.M5.

Objective: To become a Level 2 sports leader in football		
Success criteria		
• Successful completion of a Level 2 FA Coaching Award		
Key action (what will I do)	**Impact (why will I do it)**	**Actual outcome (dated) with evidence**
Research into Level 2 coaching awards in football in my area	To see what opportunities are available for me to achieve a Level 2 qualification.	
Seek funding opportunities	To be able to fund the training if it is expensive.	
Carry out some work experience at a local primary school	To gain more experience while waiting to get on a course and also to build my subject knowledge and confidence.	
Check to see if it is possible to work within the PE department at my school	To be able to experience working with different age groups to ensure I keep my options open.	

In my action plan I have decided to include some actions that will get me to explore opportunities to move towards my goal of completing a Level 2 FA Coaching Award in football. The reason why I have included the action point where I will seek work experience opportunities in both primary and secondary schools is because I want to keep my options open as I don't know if I prefer working with younger or older footballers. I think doing both will help build up my confidence in working with all age groups and different ability levels.

Isabella has yet to meet the criteria for 2C.D2 because it is not clear that she understands the reasons why she has decided on each key action. It would be better if she linked each key action to her future careers aspirations more closely. For example, 'The reason why I am exploring work experience in different places with different age groups is because my research into the line of work I would like to go into, as a sports development officer, requires applicants to have had experience of working with different age groups and abilities. Through doing this work experience I think I will give myself a better chance of getting an interview so that I can demonstrate my skills practically.'

Unit 7: Anatomy and Physiology for Sports Performance

Types of muscle

Muscles come in a range of different shapes and sizes. The muscular system refers to all the muscles in the body, from the large muscles of the legs to the small muscles of the hands, and even the tongue (the only muscle in the body that is only attached at one end).

Muscle tissue is made up of individual fibres and the characteristics of these fibres determine the type of muscle. There are three different types within the human body – voluntary muscle, involuntary muscle, and heart muscle – and each type has a specific role in keeping the human body alive, working, and moving.

BRONZE

1. As an aspiring fitness trainer, you need to know about the different types of muscle so that you can design effective fitness training programmes for your clients. You have a basic knowledge of the names and locations of some of the muscles within the body, but you have decided that you need to develop your knowledge of the different types of muscle. Design a poster, which you can show to your clients, that:

- Describes the three types of muscle.
- Gives an example of each type of muscle.
- Explains how each type of muscle is controlled.

2. Create a list of ten jobs that require knowledge of the three types of muscles, for example, a cardiologist.

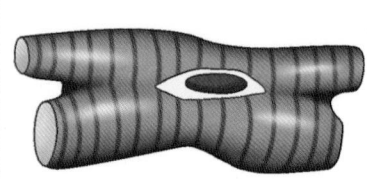

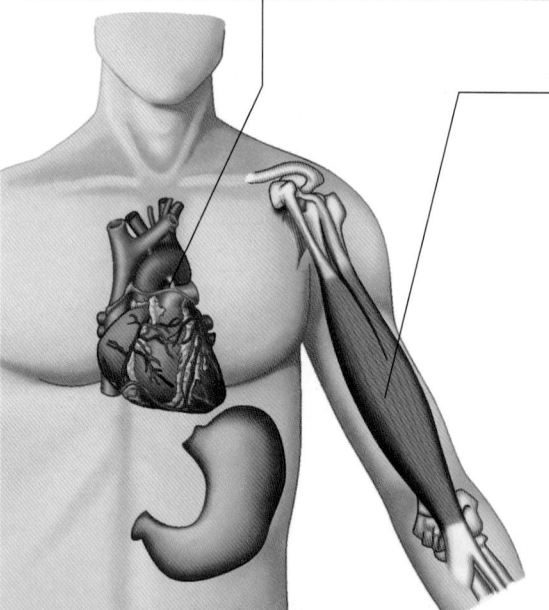

Heart muscle: This is only found in the heart and is not under conscious control. It is also known as *cardiac muscle*. It contracts and relaxes at a fairly rapid rate, which is sustained throughout a person's lifetime, and each contraction forces blood out of the heart and around the body. The rate at which cardiac muscle contracts (the heart rate) is determined by a complex series of chemical reactions, which are controlled by the nervous system.

Voluntary muscle: This type is known as voluntary muscle because you can make it contract or relax, and because you can decide how fast or how powerfully it contracts. It is also known as *skeletal muscle* because it is always connected to the bones of the skeleton. Examples of skeletal muscles include the biceps, triceps, and pectorals. Skeletal muscle is the most important type of muscle for a sportsperson because it is the type of muscle that produces movement, allowing us to run, jump, and throw. When seen through a microscope, the muscle fibres appear as striped lines, which gives rise to yet another alternative name for this type of muscle, *striated muscle*.

Involuntary muscle: This is found within the walls of hollow internal structures, such as blood vessels, and throughout the intestines of the digestive system. It is classified as involuntary muscle because, like cardiac muscle, we have no conscious control over it. Because of its appearance, it is also known as *visceral muscle* or *smooth muscle* and it produces slow, rhythmic contractions that act like a wave pushing substances along, such as food through the intestines or blood through the blood vessels.

The voluntary muscles of the human body

We can consciously control voluntary muscles, also known as skeletal muscles, to produce movement. This enables us to carry out everyday tasks such as walking to school or work and carrying shopping bags. Being able to consciously control our body movements also enables us to take part in a wide range of different sports.

The major muscles of the body

The major muscles of the body are used to produce the movements needed in sport, such as kicking a ball, running, and throwing a javelin. All sportsmen and women should have a knowledge of the most important muscles in the body, and these are shown in the diagram below.

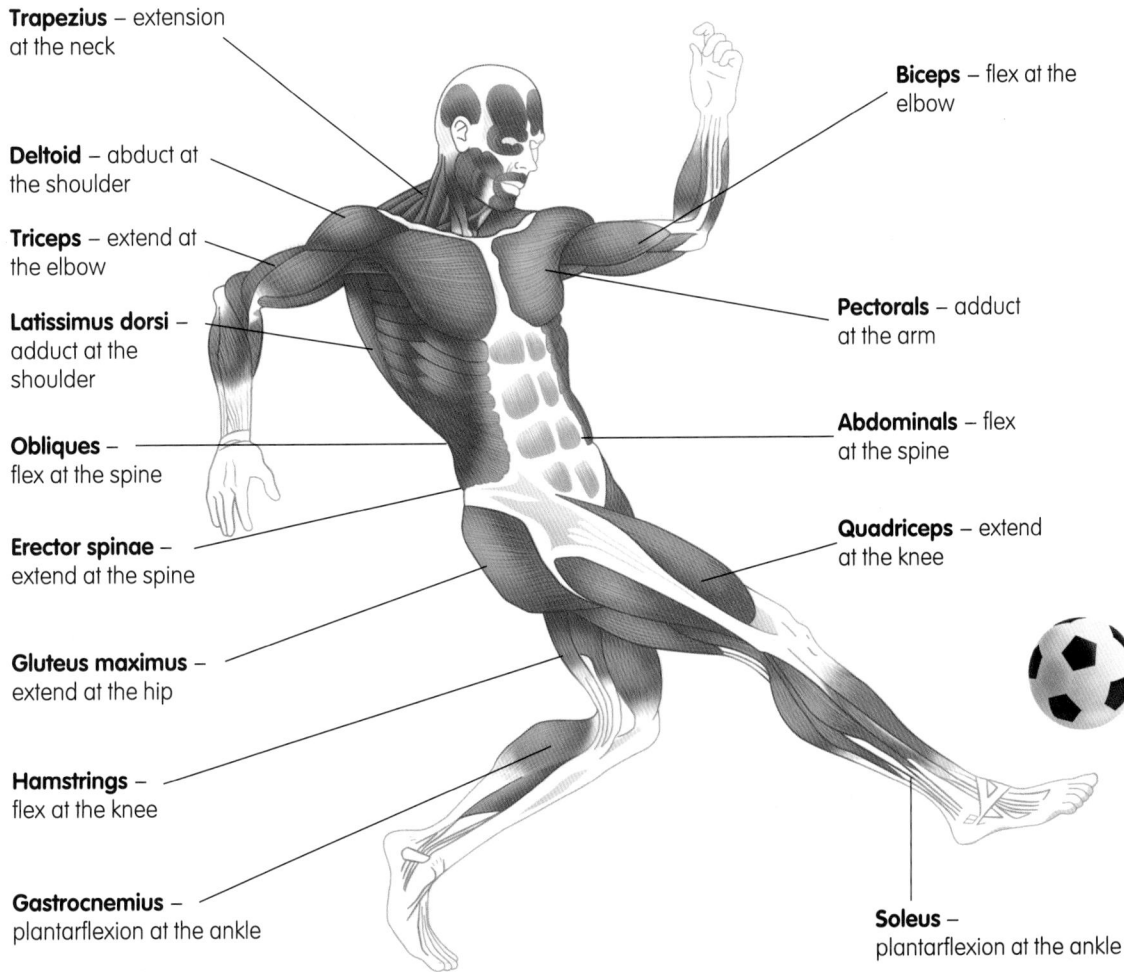

Trapezius – extension at the neck

Deltoid – abduct at the shoulder

Triceps – extend at the elbow

Latissimus dorsi – adduct at the shoulder

Obliques – flex at the spine

Erector spinae – extend at the spine

Gluteus maximus – extend at the hip

Hamstrings – flex at the knee

Gastrocnemius – plantarflexion at the ankle

Biceps – flex at the elbow

Pectorals – adduct at the arm

Abdominals – flex at the spine

Quadriceps – extend at the knee

Soleus – plantarflexion at the ankle

BRONZE

1. Copy the names of the major muscles onto pieces of scrap paper. Then close this book and, in pairs or small groups, stick the labels in the appropriate places on a volunteer. When you have finished, check to see how many you have right.

2. Design a circuit training session incorporating 12 stations, one for each of the major muscles in the human body. For example, you could use a triceps dip station to develop the triceps muscles.

3. Create a poster of a sportsperson in action, such as a gymnast performing a handstand, and label all the muscles that are working.

Voluntary muscle movements

Our skeletal muscles contract to create movement but this movement is created by groups of muscles, not individual muscles, because muscles can only pull, not push. When several muscle groups contract in a coordinated pattern, the result is movement such as the running, jumping, and throwing that we see in sport.

Antagonistic muscle pairs

When a muscle contracts it shortens in length and when it relaxes it gets longer. As a muscle shortens it pulls against the bone it is attached to, causing that bone to move. For example, as the biceps muscle shortens it pulls against the bones in the lower arm, creating movement at the elbow joint. This movement is known as a biceps curl. Then, because the biceps muscle is unable to straighten the elbow, the straightening movement is created by the triceps muscle, which contracts, shortens, and pulls against the bones in the lower arm to straighten the arm again.

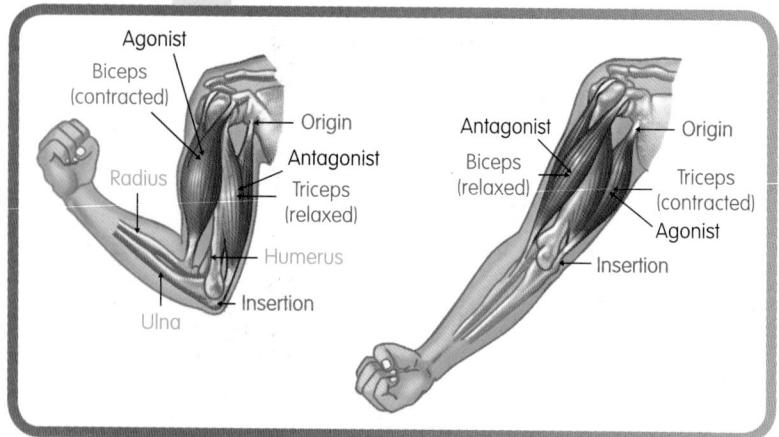

Agonist and antagonist muscles.

When a muscle pulls to create movement, it is called the **agonist** muscle or the **prime mover**. The partner muscle is called the **antagonist** muscle. In the example on the left, the biceps is the agonist when the elbow is bending and the triceps is the antagonist. When the elbow is straightening, the triceps becomes the agonist and the biceps the antagonist.

While all voluntary muscles (except the tongue) work in pairs, some are more obvious than others, particularly during sporting movements. Along with the biceps and triceps pair described above, the most common pairs are:

Rectus abdominus and erector spinae

When running in a hurdles race, the rectus abdominis is the *agonist*, contracting to pull the upper body into a bent position at the waist when jumping over the hurdle, and the erector spinae is the *antagonist*.

Quadriceps and hamstrings

When bending the leg in preparation for kicking a football, the *agonist* are the hamstrings, which shorten in order to bend the leg at the knee joint, making the quadriceps the *antagonist*.

Pectoralis major and trapezius

When playing a forehand drive in tennis, the pectoralis major contracts to produce the movement and is therefore the *agonist*, and the trapezius is the *antagonist*.

BRONZE

1. List three further sporting movements for each of the four antagonistic muscle pairs shown on the page.

SILVER

2. Explain how a muscle can change from being the agonist to being the antagonist during completion of a named sporting movement.

Types of muscle contraction

There are two different ways in which a muscle can work: **isometrically** and **isotonically**, and all movements in sport require a combination of both types of contraction.

Isometric contractions

Isometric contractions occur when a muscle that is working stays the same length. No movement occurs but the contraction helps to stabilize the body. A good example of this takes place during a tug of war (assuming that the teams are evenly matched). The muscles of the arms, legs, back, and shoulders are all working to pull the centre of the rope, and the opposing team, past the winning line; but because the other team is trying to do the same, the muscles in the body are working really hard without producing any movement. Try pushing against a wall and see how the muscles in your upper arms contract.

Isotonic contractions

Isotonic contractions occur when a muscle changes length as it works. When a muscle shortens this is called a **concentric contraction** and when the muscle lengthens it is called an **eccentric contraction**. For example, when performing a press-up, the triceps muscle shortens as you push up from the floor – a concentric contraction takes place – causing the elbow to extend. As you lower yourself to the floor, with gravity pulling you down, the triceps muscle lengthens under tension and an eccentric contraction takes place. If the triceps muscle didn't contract in this way you would hit the floor face first! An eccentric contraction only occurs when the movement is being caused by an outside force, such as gravity or another person.

An example of isometric contractions.

An eccentric contraction takes place in the triceps.

A concentric contraction takes place in the triceps.

BRONZE

1. Describe how the muscles move during a biceps curl. You may want to perform a biceps curl with your bag in your hand to help you feel the contractions. Remember to use the following words in your description:

- contracts
- relaxes
- shortens
- lengthens
- biceps
- triceps
- agonist
- antagonist
- isotonic concentric contraction
- isotonic eccentric contraction
- isometric contraction.

SILVER

2. Copy and complete the table below, listing three physical activities for each type of muscle contraction and the muscles involved:

Muscle contraction	Physical activity	Muscles contracting
Isometric		
Isotonic concentric		
Isotonic eccentric		

 **Remember:**

When a muscle shortens it is called a **concentric contraction**.

When a muscle lengthens it is called an **eccentric contraction**.

Skeletal muscle fibres

Muscles contract at different speeds depending on the movement required. For example, the quadriceps will contract quickly when a person is sprinting and slowly when they are jogging. This change in the speed of the contraction is possible because each muscle is made up of hundreds (and sometimes thousands) of different fibres that can be divided into two categories: fast-twitch muscle fibres and slow-twitch muscle fibres. Sports coaches and other professionals in sport need to understand the difference between the two types of muscle fibre so that they can help sportspeople to train correctly, and avoid fatigue and injury.

Slow-twitch muscle fibres

Slow-twitch muscle fibres are used in low-intensity activities and endurance events, such as the marathon. They work aerobically, which means they need oxygen to produce energy. The oxygen is used in the mitochondria of the muscle cell (the engine room) to produce the energy required to make the muscle work. Slow-twitch fibres (also known as type I fibres) contract at a slow rate and produce a relatively low amount of force. This means that the fibres can work continuously for long periods of time without becoming fatigued. Type I fibres are also used during the recovery periods of intense activity, such as when jogging around the pitch in rugby, rather than when sprinting or making the tackle.

Slow-twitch muscle fibres:

- work aerobically and use oxygen to produce energy
- work at a constant pace for a long period of time
- become fatigued less quickly than fast-twitch muscle fibres
- contract at a slow speed
- produce low force
- are red in colour.

Fast-twitch muscle fibres

In broad terms, fast-twitch fibres are suited to fast, explosive activities that last for less than two minutes and which require a maximum power output for a short period of time. Fast-twitch muscle fibres can be subdivided into two further types: type IIa and type IIb. Both are white in colour.

Type IIa muscle fibres

Type IIa muscles fibres are suited to activities that require fast, repetitive contractions for between 30 and 120 seconds. A good example of a sporting activity that employs type IIa muscle fibres is the 800-metre race, which lasts around one and a half minutes for elite athletes. The muscle fibres need to contract quickly, but need to be able to sustain a high contraction speed throughout the race. Characteristics of fast-twitch type IIa fibres include:

- The ability to contract at a high speed (though not as fast as type IIb muscle fibres).
- The ability to generate a medium to high force.
- The ability to work aerobically for short periods of time.
- The ability to resist fatigue for up to two minutes.

Type IIb muscle fibres

Type IIb muscles fibres are pure fast-twitch fibres, which are used when maximum power output and speed are required, during a 100-metre race or when competing in a powerlifting event for example. While type IIb muscle fibres are able to produce an explosive amount of force, they do become fatigued very quickly due to the build-up of lactic acid. Characteristics of type IIb fast-twitch muscle fibres include:

- They are only able to work anaerobically (without oxygen).
- The ability to contract at a very high speed (considerably faster than type IIa fibres).
- The ability to produce explosive power.
- The ability to generate an extremely high force.
- The inability to resist fatigue due to the build-up of lactic acid.

Each person has a mixture of both fast- and slow-twitch muscle fibres. However, some people have more of one kind of muscle fibre than the other, making them more suited to certain kinds of physical activity than others. Type IIa fibres are relatively uncommon in humans so most people have a combination of type I and type IIb fibres.

BRONZE

1. Compile a list of ten famous sportsmen and sportswomen. Rank them, placing the person you think will have the highest percentage of fast-twitch muscle fibre at the top and the person you think will have the highest percentage of slow-twitch muscle fibre at the bottom.

SILVER

2. As a fitness coach you need to be able to identify the predominant twitch muscle fibres used in different physical activities so that you can direct people to the activities that are most suited to their physiology. List five activities based on the predominant twitch fibre used for that activity for each of:
- Fast-twitch type IIa
- Fast-twitch type IIb
- Slow-twitch
- A mixture of fast- and slow-twitch.

3. The government has expressed concern that not enough people are taking part in physical activities to maintain and/or improve their health. Design a circuit-training session that can be used to develop all three of the twitch fibre types.

Recruiting different skeletal muscle fibre types

Muscles contract at different speeds and with different force depending on the movement required. For example, the quadriceps will contract quickly when a person is sprinting and slowly when jogging, while the bicep will generate a low force when lifting a light object, such as a cricket ball, and a high force when lifting a heavy object, such as a heavy dumb-bell. This change in the speed and strength of the contraction is possible because the different twitch muscle fibre types are recruited and put to work when needed.

Slow-twitch muscle fibres produce a relatively low force and are therefore used when a low power output is needed; when either a low speed of contraction or a low strength of contraction is required, when running a marathon or when jogging during a football match for example. Slow-twitch muscle fibres are the only type of muscle fibre that can work in isolation. This means that it is possible to have slow-twitch muscle fibres working while fast-twitch muscle fibres of both types are not working.

Fast-twitch muscle fibres cannot work in isolation. Once the intensity of an activity increases beyond the point at which slow-twitch muscle fibres can work alone, the fast-twitch type IIa muscle fibres are recruited into action. This means that during activities such as an 800-metre race or a medium-paced run back into position during a hockey match, the muscle output is produced by a combination of slow-twitch muscle fibres and fast-twitch type IIa muscle fibres.

In order to produce all-out maximum power or explosive force, it is necessary to also recruit the fast-twitch type IIb muscle fibres. Therefore, in events such as shot-put or long jump, the power output from the muscles is generated by recruiting all three muscle fibre types, starting with the slow-twitch muscle fibres, moving on to the fast-twitch type IIa muscle fibres, and finally the fast-twitch type IIb muscle fibres. It is only during a maximum power output situation that all of the muscle fibres within a muscle will be recruited and put to work.

Very few sporting activities rely heavily on one particular twitch fibre type, so it is necessary to be able to determine which muscle fibre types are being used at any one time. Look at the graph. It shows the relative usage of the different muscle fibre types for a wing attack during a netball game.

It is clear from the graph that the slow twitch fibres are always working, since they are always recruited first. However, at various points, additional twitch fibres are recruited to cope with the demands of the game:

At point 1: The wing attack is jumping to compete for a high ball. This burst of power requires the use of all the muscle fibre types.

At point 2: The wing attack is marking her opponent and is running back to defend, but not running at full speed. Therefore the type IIb fast-twitch muscle fibres are not being used.

At point 3: The wing attack is walking around in the centre area while the ball is in her team's defending third. Since she is not allowed in that area she is not directly involved in the game and therefore does not need to move at a fast pace. Moving around slowly requires only the use of slow twitch fibres.

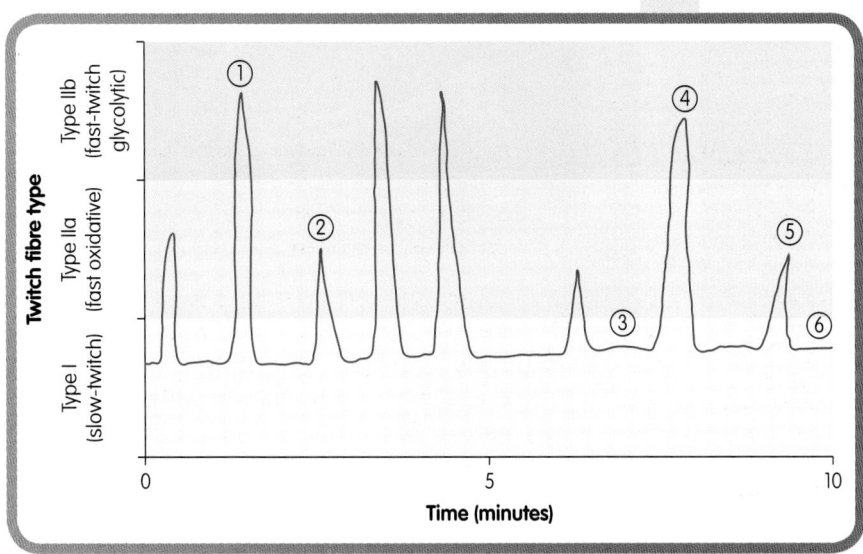

A graph showing relative usage of the different muscle fibre types for a wing attack during a netball game.

The skeletal system

The skeleton is the framework of the body and gives a person their shape. It consists of 206 bones, which are held together by ligaments at the joints. The bones are divided into five main types and each has a special function.

The major bones of the body

In order to understand the skeletal system, it is important to remember the names of all the major bones of the body.

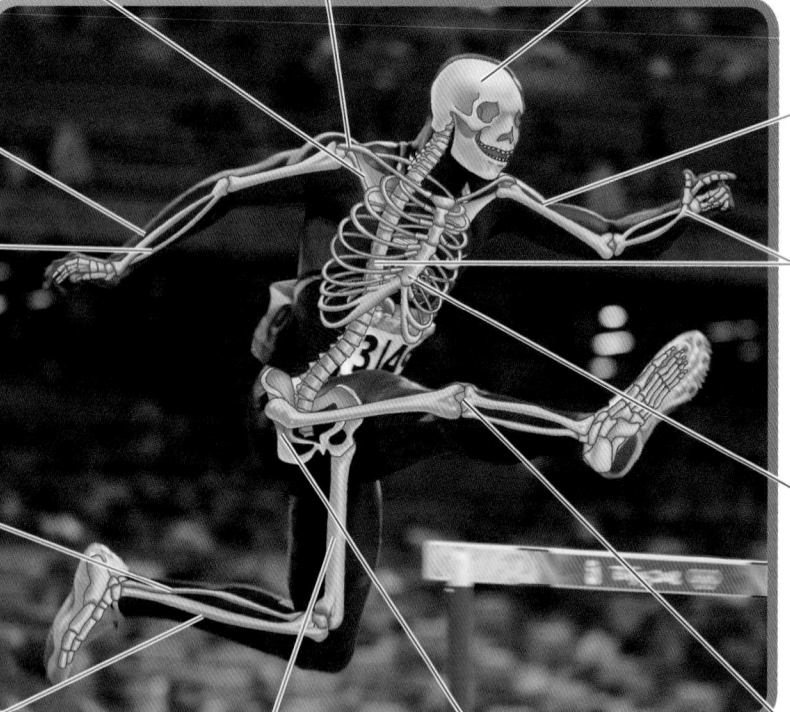

Scapula: situated at the back of the body, connecting the arm to the central skeleton. The scapula is a **flat** bone.

Clavicle: also known as the collar bone, the clavicle supports the shoulder and connects the upper arm to the main part of the body. The clavicle is a **flat** bone.

Skull: made up of 28 bones, eight of which form the cranium, which protects the brain. These are **flat** bones.

Radius: one of the bones in the lower arm. It rotates around the ulna to allow movement. The radius is a **long** bone.

Humerus: also known as the 'funny bone', the humerus is situated in the upper arm. It is a **long** bone.

Ulna: situated in the lower arm. It rotates around the radius to allow movement. The ulna is a **long** bone.

Carpals: found in the wrist, carpals glide across one another to enable the wrist to move in multiple directions. They are **short** bones.

Fibula: the smaller of the two lower leg bones. The fibula is a **long** bone.

Sternum: a **flat** bone that lies in the centre of the chest and has ten pairs of ribs attached to it.

Tibia: also known as the shin bone, this is one of the two bones situated in the lower leg and is the larger of the two. The tibia is a **long** bone.

Femur: the longest bone in the body, the femur is situated in the upper part of the leg and is a very strong bone. It is a **long** bone.

Pelvis: also known as the hip, the pelvis connects the legs to the body and provides protection for the lower internal organs. It is a **flat** bone.

Patella: also known as the knee cap, this is a small bone situated between the upper and lower leg. The patella is not connected to any other bones. It is a **sesamoid** bone.

Different types of bone

Bones are divided into five types: long, short, flat, irregular, and sesamoid.

- **Long bones:** These are found in the arms and legs; the femur and humerus are two examples. They are greater in length than they are in width. The ends of long bones are covered in a layer of articular cartilage, a tough outer layer that both protects the bone from wearing away and at the same time reduces friction in the joint. Long bones are used as levers to create large movements such as running and swimming.
- **Short bones:** These are found in the ankles, feet, wrists, and fingers. The carpals and tarsals are two examples. They are cube shaped and are light but strong. They are associated with small, precise movements but are also required for movements needing strength, such as a handstand.
- **Flat bones:** These are strong, flat plates that provide protection for major organs such as the brain, heart, and lungs. They also provide attachment for muscles. The scapula and the skull are flat bones.
- **Irregular bones:** These bones are very unusual in shape. Examples include the bones of the vertebral column and some of the facial bones.
- **Sesamoid bones:** These bones are usually oval in shape. They are found where a tendon passes over a joint and are imbedded in the tendons. Their role is to protect the tendon from damage during movement or impact. Examples include the patella (kneecap) and some of the bones in the feet and hands.

BRONZE

1. Copy the names of the major bones onto pieces of scrap paper. Then close this book and, in pairs or small groups, stick the labels in the appropriate places on a volunteer. When you have finished, check to see how many you got right.

2. Copy and complete the table below, identifying what type of bone each one is. Is it long, short, flat, irregular, or sesamoid?

Bone	Type
Clavicle	Flat
Ulna	
Femur	
Patella	
Cranium	
Tibia	

The vertebral column

The vertebral column, also known as the spine, consists of 33 vertebrae. The vertebrae form a hollow column, called the vertebral column, which contains and protects the spinal cord. It is also flexible to allow the body to bend and twist. Each vertebra has a hole in the centre which allows the spinal cord to pass through it. The vertebrae are irregular bones and are separated by discs of cartilage, which act as shock absorbers. The vertebral column is made up of five sections.

Cervical (7 vertebrae)

Thoracic (12 vertebrae)

Lumbar (5 vertebrae)

Sacral (5 fused vertebrae)

Coccyx (4 fused vertebrae)

The rib cage

The ribs are flat bones. They form a cage, which surrounds the heart and lungs to provide protection. The rib cage consists of 12 pairs of ribs, separated into groups:

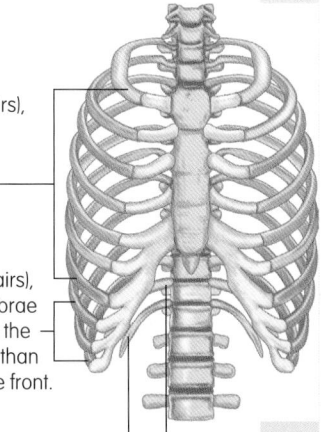

The true ribs (7 pairs), attach at both the front and back to the sternum and the vertebrae respectively.

The false ribs (3 pairs), attach to the vertebrae at the back and to the ribs above, rather than the sternum, at the front.

The floating ribs (2 pairs), attach only at the back and appear to 'float' at the front.

The axial and appendicular skeleton

The human skeleton can be divided into two parts: the axial skeleton and the appendicular skeleton.

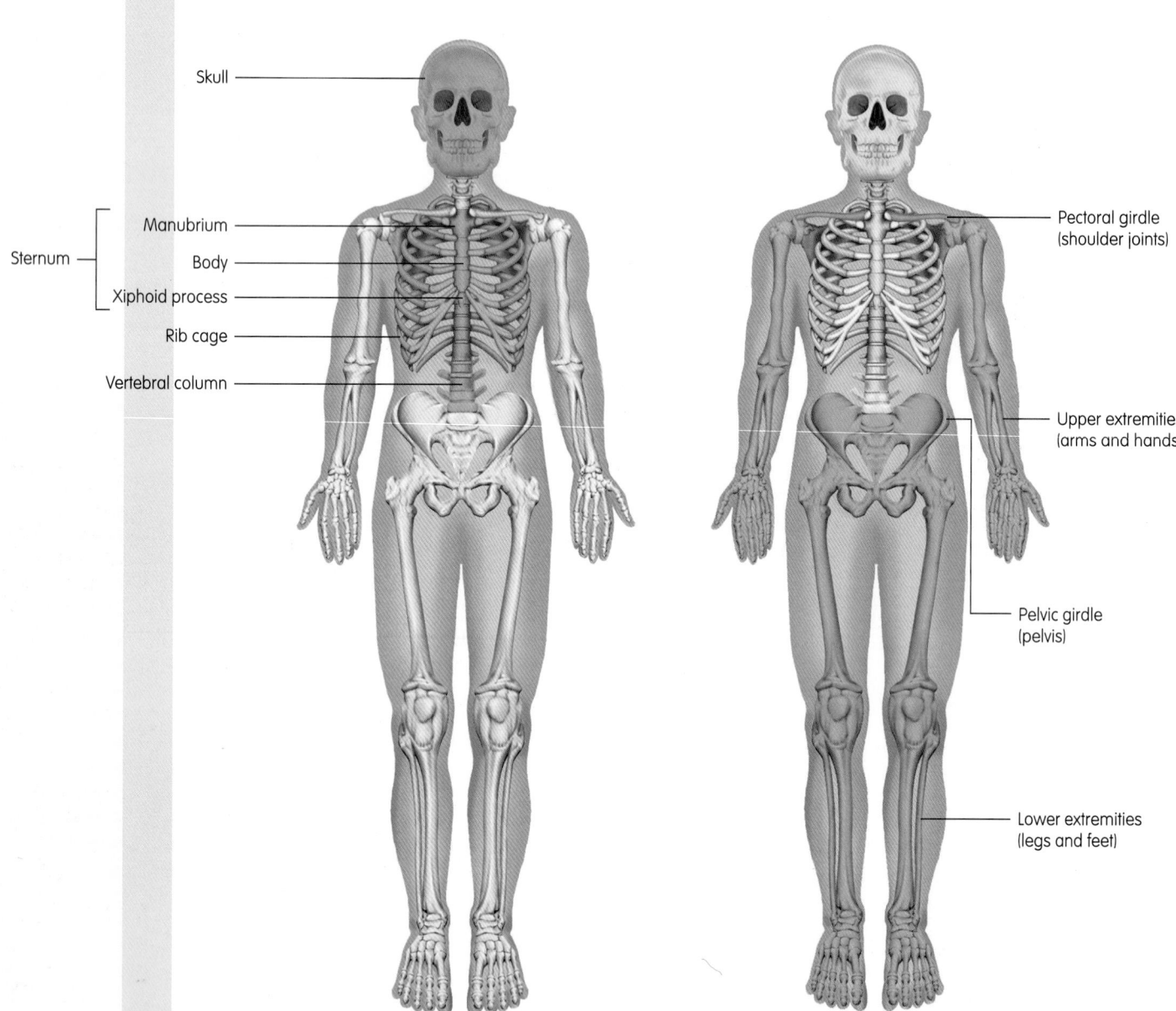

The axial skeleton

- Skull
- Sternum
  - Manubrium
  - Body
  - Xiphoid process
- Rib cage
- Vertebral column

The appendicular skeleton

- Pectoral girdle (shoulder joints)
- Upper extremities (arms and hands)
- Pelvic girdle (pelvis)
- Lower extremities (legs and feet)

BRONZE

3. Which sport-related occupations do you think require knowledge of the skeleton and bones? Try to come up with as many ideas as you can.

The functions of the skeletal system

The skeleton not only gives the body its shape, it also performs six very important functions. These are: protection, muscle attachment and movement, shape, support, blood production, and the storage of minerals.

Protection

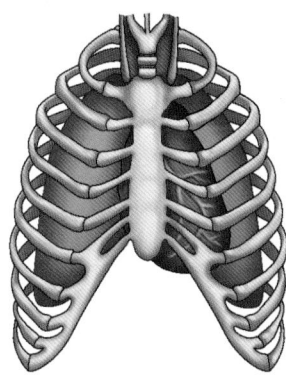

Some parts of the body are delicate and can be damaged easily. The skeleton helps to protect them by providing a shield around them. Examples of this are the rib cage and sternum, which protect the heart and lungs. They ensure that the vital organs do not get damaged during a rugby tackle or when taking a hit in boxing.

Muscle attachment and movement

The bones of the skeleton give the muscles something to attach to. Muscles work by contracting, and as they get shorter, they pull on the bones. This action allows the body to move in a range of directions, particularly if the joint that attaches the bones is freely movable. In sport, this function is vital. Generally people who have longer bones in the legs are likely to have a longer stride pattern, which can be particularly useful when running long distances.

Shape and support

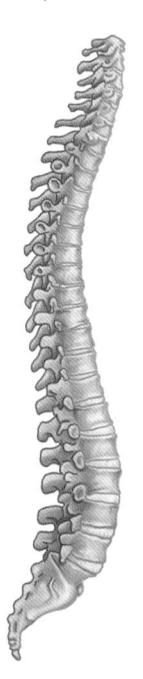

Without the rigid framework that the skeleton provides, the body would be a mass of soft tissue. It gives the body its shape and also provides support, holding vital organs in place. For example, the shape of the vertebral column gives the body height and the rib cage supports the lungs. The shape of the skeleton can often dictate a person's success or failure in sport. For example, people who are tall and thin are likely to be better at the high jump than those who are short, while those who are short and wide are likely to make a better prop in rugby than someone who is tall and thin.

Blood production and mineral storage

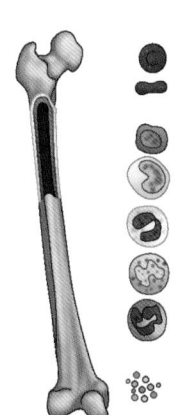

Some of the larger bones contain bone marrow. Red and white blood cells and platelets are formed in the marrow cavities. Some of the bones where this process takes place include the humerus, ribs, and femur. Bones also provide storage sites for minerals such as calcium, phosphorous, sodium, and potassium, which can then be used in multiple chemical reactions when needed. An athlete with a high red blood cell count can work aerobically for longer, because it is red blood cells that transport oxygen around the body. This is particularly useful for endurance athletes.

BRONZE

1. Design a poster illustrating the functions of the skeleton in relation to a sporting situation. It could show, for example, how the skull protects the brain during a rugby tackle.

SILVER/ GOLD

2. Put together a reasoned argument as to whether or not the following statement is true:

'No matter how much a person eats, exercises, or diets, there is a limit to how much they can change their body shape.'

Types of joint

A joint is a point where two or more bones meet. There are over 100 joints in the human body and they are classified by the amount of movement they allow. The three types of joint are: fixed, slightly movable, and freely movable.

Where two or more bones meet, there is a layer of smooth cartilage that prevents them from rubbing against one another. Tough, fibrous straps, called ligaments, hold the bones at a joint in place. Ligaments are elastic to allow movement at the joints.

Fixed joints

Fixed (fibrous) joints, also known as immovable joints, are located in areas of the body where movement is not beneficial. For example, the bones in the skull have fixed joints. The bones in fixed joints usually link together or overlap and are held together by tough connective tissue. Other examples of fixed joints are the pelvis and the fused joints in the sacrum.

Slightly movable joints

Slightly movable (cartilaginous) joints allow a small amount of movement. They are held together by tough ligaments and are connected by cartilage. The pads of cartilage between the vertebrae make the joints slightly movable as they prevent the bones from jolting when a person runs or jumps. The joints between the ribs and sternum are other examples of slightly movable joints.

Freely movable, or synovial, joints

Freely movable (synovial) joints are the most common type of joint found in the human body. They allow the bones at the joint to move freely. A freely movable or synovial joint, such as the knee joint, has the following main components:

BRONZE

1. a) How do synovial joints differ from other joints?

b) Identify the six most commonly used synovial joints in the body and name a sporting action that involves the use of each of them.

c) Choose one of your sporting actions and explain how the joint moves during the three phases of the action, during preparation, execution, and follow-through. For example: When preparing to perform a chest pass in netball, the elbow joint is 'flexed'. The humerus is close to the radius and ulna in preparation for passing the ball horizontally. When executing the chest pass and releasing the ball the elbow 'extends' and the radius and ulna move away from the humerus. During the follow-through phase the elbow extends further as the ball is pushed away from the body and towards its intended target.

Bone ends: A layer of smoother, slippery hyaline (also known as 'articular') cartilage covers the ends of bones to form a cushion, which prevents the bones from rubbing.

Joint capsule: This is made up of the synovial membrane and fibrous tissue and encases the joint, preventing the synovial fluid from leaking out. It also protects the joint by holding the bones together.

Ligaments: These are strong yet elastic fibres that stretch across the joint and hold the bones in place, by attaching one bone to another. Their strength enables them to withstand sudden stresses, protecting the joint from dislocation during impact.

Bursa: this is a fluid-filled sac which floats around inside the joint, reducing friction between the tendon and the bone.

Muscle

Tendons: These white fibrous cords of connective tissue attach muscles to bones and are found towards the end of the muscle tissue. They are made from collagen and so are tough and strong.

Synovial fluid: This is a clear, slippery substance that oozes from the synovial membrane and nourishes and oils the joint, preventing friction.

Synovial membrane: This is the lining inside the joint capsule. It secretes a runny liquid called synovial fluid, which nourishes and lubricates the joint.

Synovial joints

The majority of joints in the body are freely movable or synovial. There are several types of synovial joints in the body, allowing a range of movement possibilities. For example, the shoulder joint can move in more directions than the knee joint, yet they are both synovial joints. The range of movement depends on the shape and size of the bones at the joint and the ligaments that keep them in place.

Gliding joint: This type of joint allows a small amount of movement in all directions because the ends of the bones are flat and move in a gliding motion over each other. This type of joint is found in the small bones of the hands and feet, where the bones glide over each other at the intercarpal and intertarsal joints, when you cross your fingers and toes for example.

Ball and socket joint: This is the most movable joint in the body. The wide range of movement is made possible by a round-headed bone, which fits into a socket. Examples of this type of joint are the hip and the shoulder.

Condyloid joint: This joint has one bone that has a rounded bump on the end, which fits into a hollow cavity on the other. Movement at this type of joint is similar to the movement that takes place at saddle joints. Examples of condyloid joints are those in the wrist and at the base of the skull.

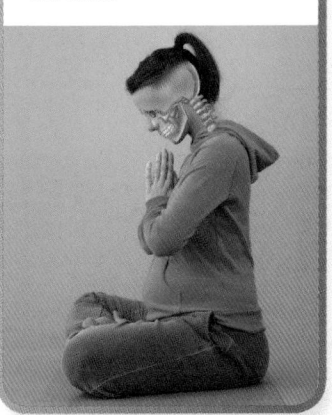

Saddle joint: As the name of this joint suggests, the ends of the bones are shaped like saddles and they fit closely together. The movement range at this type of joint is forward and backward, and side to side. An example of this type of joint is the carpo-metacarpal joint of the thumb.

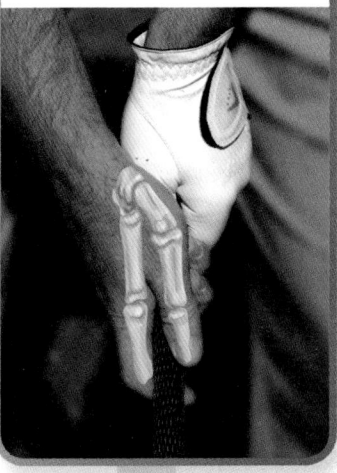

Hinge joint: This type of joint can only move in one direction and works in a similar way to a hinge on a door. The bones can move towards and away from each other as one bone has a pulley-shaped end that fits into a hollow in the other bone. Examples of this type of joint are the elbow and the knee.

Pivot joint: This joint only allows rotation. It consists of a cylindrical surface at one end, which rotates within a ring-like structure made of bone and ligament. This is similar to a wheel rotating around its axis. Examples of pivot joints in the body are the atlas and axis vertebrae (the cervical vertebrae) in the neck, and the joint that attaches the radius to the ulna in the lower arm.

BRONZE

1. Research the six main types of synovial joint and provide an illustrated description of each one.

SILVER

2. Choose two synovial joints. For each, draw or download images of four physical activities that require movement at that joint and then explain what is happening. Remember to:
- Name the articulating bones.
- Describe the movement that is taking place.
- Name the type of synovial joint.
- Explain the ways in which the joint allows the movement to take place.

Movement at the joints

There are ten major types of movement possible at joints.

Flexion: This is when a joint is bent and the two bones either side come towards each other.

Extension: The joint is fully stretched out or straightened.

Abduction: This is a sideways movement where a body part is taken away from the centre line of the body.

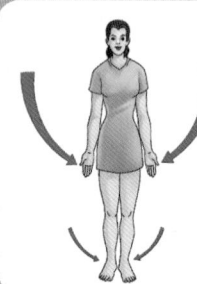

Adduction: This is the opposite of abduction, when a body part is moved towards the centre line of the body.

Rotation: This is a spinning or turning movement, where part of the body rotates around an imaginary axis. The rotation can be inwards or outwards.

Circumduction: This is when a bone or bones rotate fully around an axis to complete a full circle of movement. For example, in order to complete a circumduction at the shoulder joint to bowl a cricket ball, the arm has to go through a full combination of movements; it has to flex, extend, abduct, and adduct.

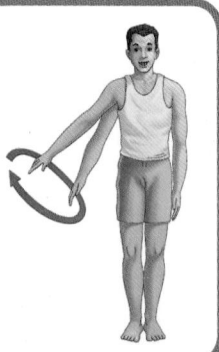

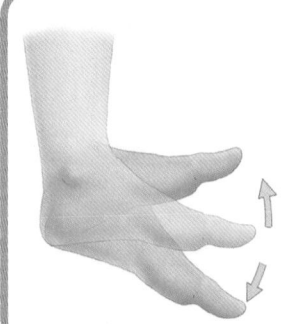

Plantarflexion: This is when the ankle joint moves, increasing the angle between the top of the foot and the tibia, when pointing your toes.

Dorsiflexion: This is when the ankle joint moves, decreasing the angle between the top of the foot and the tibia, when lifting your toes.

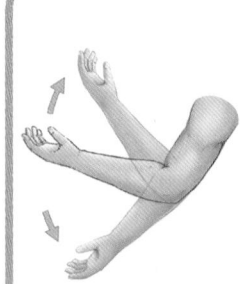

Elevation: This is when part of the body moves upwards, such as when lifting an arm.

Depression: This is when part of the body moves downwards, such as when lowering an arm.

BRONZE

1. Copy and complete the table below, which shows the types of synovial joints in the left-hand column and the six different ways that joints can move across the top. Tick the appropriate boxes to show which movements occur at which joints.

	Flexion/ extension	Abduction/ adduction	Rotation	Circumduction	Elevation/ depression	Plantarflexion/ dorsiflexion
Ball and socket						
Hinge						
Pivot						
Saddle						
Condyloid						
Gliding						

Remember:

Abduct means to take away from the centre line of the body.

Adduct means to bring towards the centre line of the body.

SILVER

2. Add a sporting example to each box in the table above where you have a tick. For example, the front crawl arm action requires flexion (and extension) of the hinge joint at the elbow.

Types of cartilage

There are three different types of cartilage found in the human body, and each type has a specific purpose that can be related to movement and sporting activity.

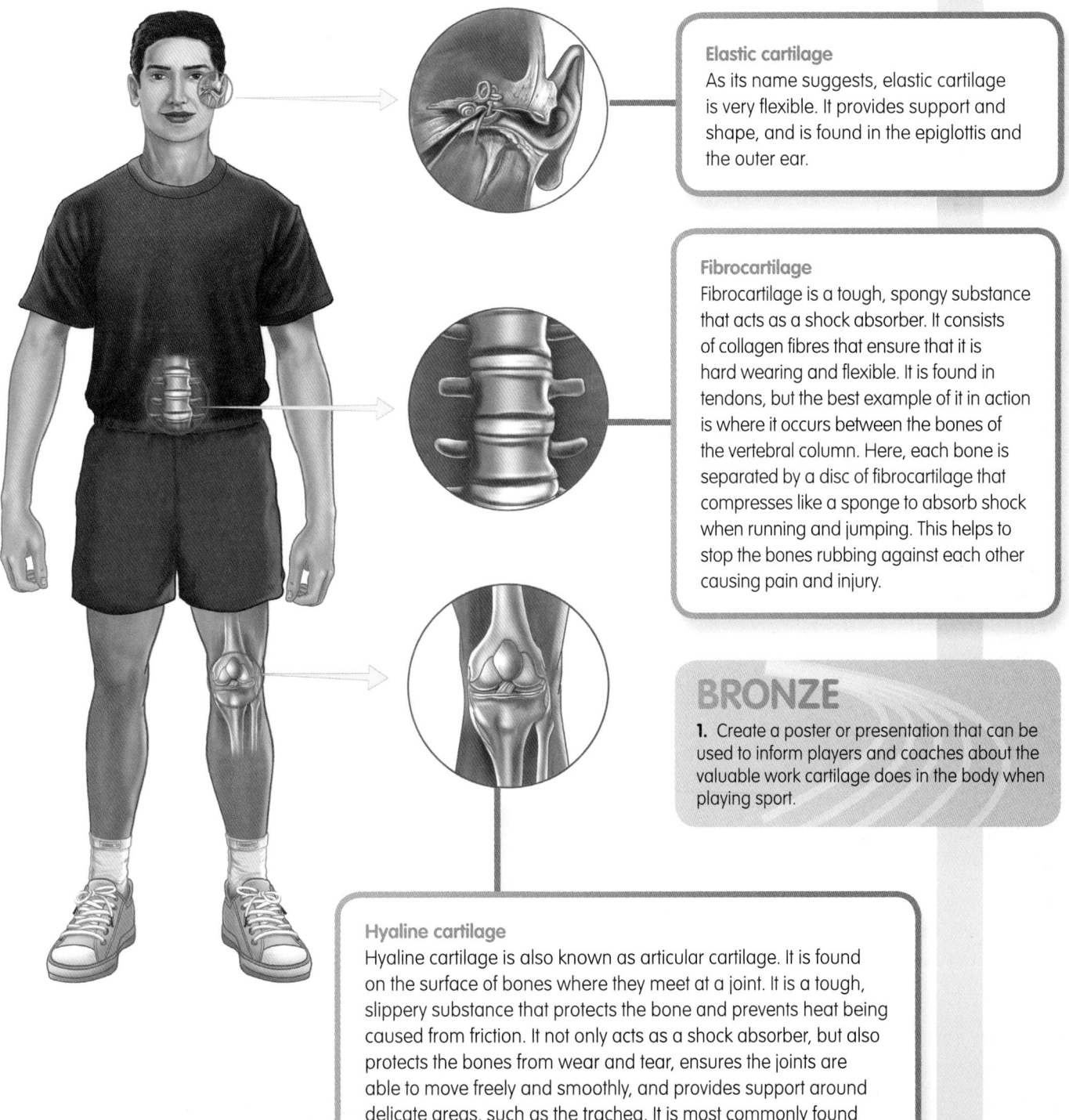

Elastic cartilage

As its name suggests, elastic cartilage is very flexible. It provides support and shape, and is found in the epiglottis and the outer ear.

Fibrocartilage

Fibrocartilage is a tough, spongy substance that acts as a shock absorber. It consists of collagen fibres that ensure that it is hard wearing and flexible. It is found in tendons, but the best example of it in action is where it occurs between the bones of the vertebral column. Here, each bone is separated by a disc of fibrocartilage that compresses like a sponge to absorb shock when running and jumping. This helps to stop the bones rubbing against each other causing pain and injury.

BRONZE

1. Create a poster or presentation that can be used to inform players and coaches about the valuable work cartilage does in the body when playing sport.

Hyaline cartilage

Hyaline cartilage is also known as articular cartilage. It is found on the surface of bones where they meet at a joint. It is a tough, slippery substance that protects the bone and prevents heat being caused from friction. It not only acts as a shock absorber, but also protects the bones from wear and tear, ensures the joints are able to move freely and smoothly, and provides support around delicate areas, such as the trachea. It is most commonly found covering the ends of long bones, but it also exists in the trachea (windpipe) and bronchi (where the trachea joins the lungs).

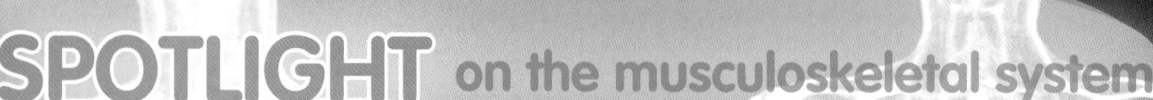

SPOTLIGHT on the musculoskeletal system

BRONZE

1. Design a poster illustrating the different types of bones and their functions within the body.

2. Create a PowerPoint® presentation about the three main types of joint. Highlight the differences in the structure, location, and movement possibilities of each type.

3. Create a booklet that can be handed out at a sports awards evening or another similar event. It needs to highlight all of the major muscles in the body. Remember to show views from both the front and back of the body.

SILVER

4. Create a booklet about four different types of physical activity and the movement that takes place at two synovial joints during each.

5. Design a webpage containing information on the muscular system. You should include a section about the three different types of muscular contraction and give an example of each type of contraction taking place in a sporting movement. Use pictures and diagrams to make your webpage visually stimulating.

GOLD

6. Choose four different physical activities, such as a team sport, a racket sport, an athletics event, and a gymnastics event. Then, for each activity, analyse the movements occurring at four different synovial joints, such as the shoulder, hip, elbow, and knee joints. Try to make comparisons and explain the differences between the four activities. For example, you might say that the flexion occurring at the elbow when throwing a javelin is similar to, but less pronounced than, the flexion at the elbow that takes place during a short throw-in during a football match. This is because the javelin throw requires more power.

The cardiovascular system

There are three main components of the cardiovascular system:

- The heart: the pump that forces blood to flow through the blood vessels.
- The blood vessels: the pipes through which the blood flows.
- The blood: the medium for moving oxygen, nutrients, and waste products around the body.

The heart

The heart is about the size of a closed fist and lies within the chest cavity just left of centre. The left-hand side of the heart is bigger than the right-hand side. The left-hand side needs to pump blood all the way around the body, whereas the right-hand side only pumps blood to the lungs, which are relatively nearby.

The heart is made up of four chambers. The top two chambers are called the **atria** and the bottom two are called the **ventricles**. The two sides of the heart are separated by the **septum**.

The heart contains valves that play an important role in preventing blood flowing backwards. On the right-hand side of the heart, situated between the right atrium and the right ventricle, is the **tricuspid valve**. On the left-hand side of the heart, the **bicuspid valve** is situated between the left atrium and the left ventricle. When the heart contracts and blood is ejected from the ventricles, it also passes through the semilunar valves. The **semilunar valves** are situated at the openings of the pulmonary artery and the aorta, which deliver blood to the lungs and the rest of the body, respectively.

Essentially, the heart has four main blood vessels that link it to the lungs and the rest of the body. These four blood vessels allow the heart to operate as a dual-action pump that keeps a constant supply of oxygen entering the body and provides a way of expelling carbon dioxide. The four main blood vessels are:

- The **pulmonary veins** deliver oxygenated (oxygen rich) blood from the lungs to the left atrium of the heart. They are the only veins in the body that carry oxygenated blood; all the other veins carry deoxygenated blood.
- The **aorta** is the largest artery in the body and delivers oxygenated blood from the heart to the rest of the body.
- The **venae cavae** (superior and inferior) are the largest veins in the body and carry deoxygenated blood from all over the body to the right atrium of the heart.
- The **pulmonary artery** carries deoxygenated blood from the heart to the lungs. It is the only artery in the body that carries deoxygenated blood; all the other arteries carry oxygenated blood.

Because the heart is a muscle it also requires its own blood supply in order to function. So, while the pulmonary vein and the venae cavae flow into the chambers of the heart, other blood vessels – called **coronary arteries** – flow to the heart to provide it with the oxygenated blood it requires to contract and pump the blood flowing through it.

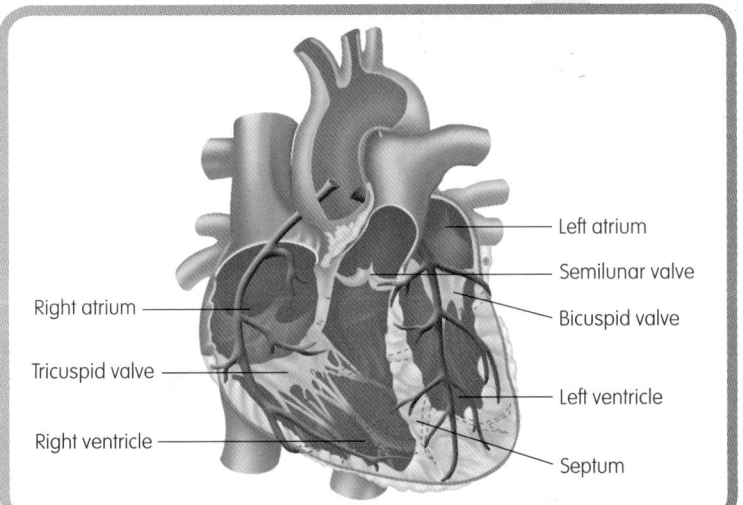

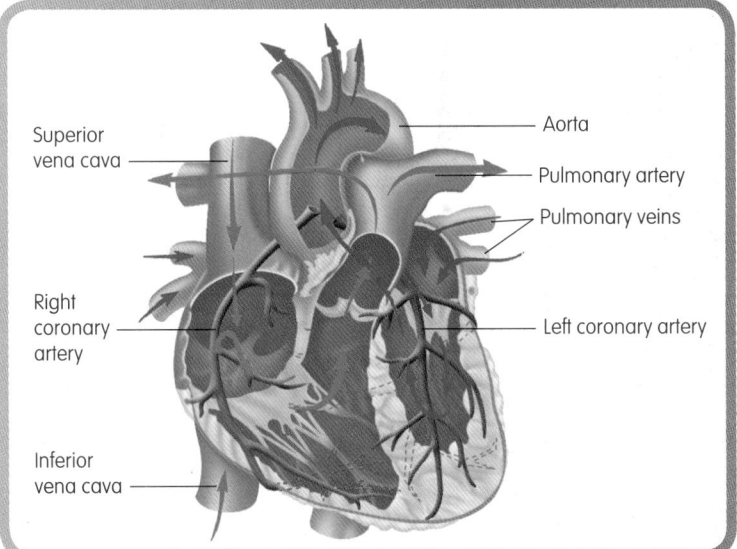

BRONZE

1. Present the information about the heart on this page in a more visual and interesting format. You could create diagrams, rhymes, or even a rap. But, whatever you decide on, make sure you include the following:

- The anatomical make-up of the heart, the chambers.
- The valves contained within the heart.
- The major blood vessels leading to and from the heart.

Blood vessels

The structures of the three main blood vessels found in the body are different because they each carry blood under different conditions. There are actually five types of blood vessel, but arterioles are simply small arteries; and venules are simply small veins.

Arteries and arterioles

An artery has three layers: an outer layer of tissue, a muscular middle layer, and an inner layer of epithelial cells. Arteries are tough on the outside and smooth on the inside. They carry oxygen-rich blood away from the heart to all parts of the body, under high pressure and at high speed, so they have thick walls, which can cope with this pressure. Arteries have a pulse, which allows us to monitor our heart rate. Arterioles are smaller versions of arteries that branch off to form a link between arteries and capillaries.

The only exception is the pulmonary artery, which is the only artery that carries deoxygenated blood, from the heart to the lungs.

Veins and venules

Veins are similar to arteries but, because they transport blood at a lower pressure and at a slower pace, they are not as strong. Like arteries, veins have three layers: an outer layer of tissue, a middle layer of muscle, and a smooth inner layer of epithelial cells. However, each of these layers is thinner than those found in arteries. Veins transport deoxygenated blood back to the heart via a process called venous return, with the exception of the pulmonary vein, which transports oxygenated blood from the lungs to the heart. Veins have valves to prevent blood flowing backwards, unlike arteries, which do not have any valves. Venules are smaller than veins and provide a link between the capillaries and the veins.

Capillaries

Unlike the arteries and veins, capillaries are very thin and fragile. Their walls are only one cell thick and blood cells can only pass through them in single file. The exchange of oxygen and carbon dioxide takes place through the thin capillary wall. The red blood cells inside the capillary release their oxygen, which passes through the wall and into the surrounding tissue. Meanwhile, the tissue releases its waste products, such as carbon dioxide, which pass through the capillary wall and into the red blood cells. This means that capillaries deal with both oxygenated and deoxygenated blood. Capillaries are the link between arterioles and venules.

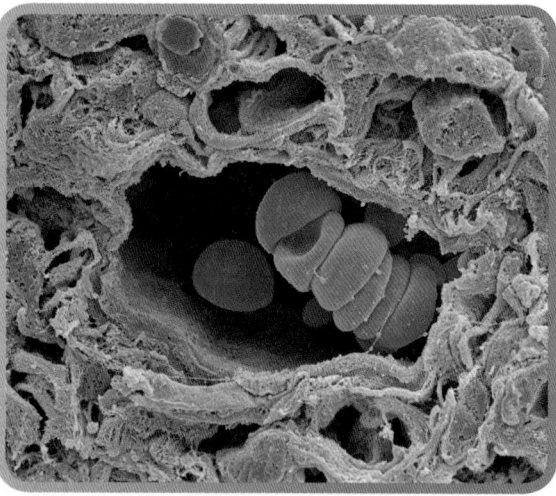

Red blood cells in an arteriole.

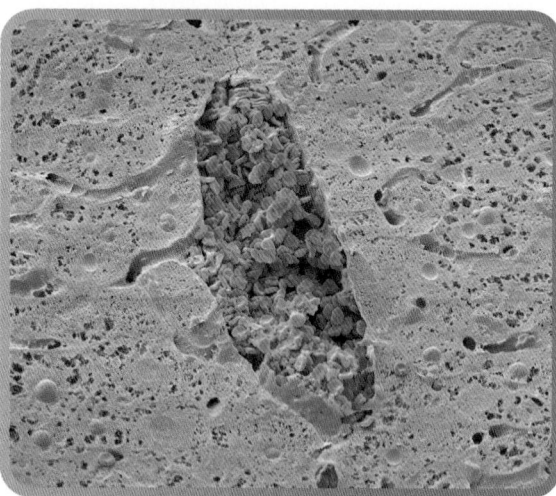

A vein in the liver, filled with red blood cells.

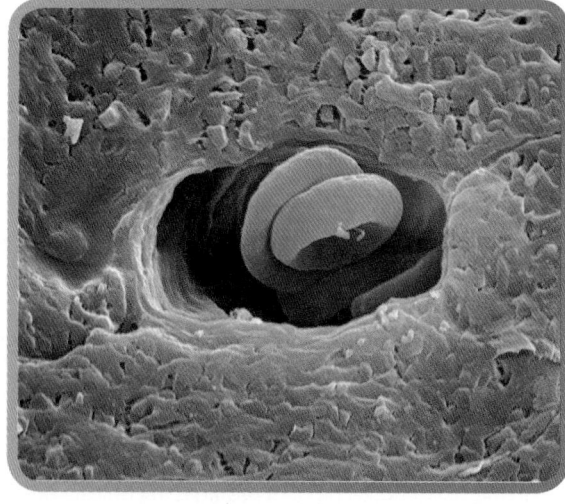

A capillary near the heart containing red blood cells.

BRONZE

2. Using the information on this page, draw a diagram showing the structure and function of the three main blood vessels. Your diagram should show the differences in the thickness of vessel walls, internal diameter, blood pressure and direction of blood flow between the vessels, as well as information about the specific job they each do.

The functions of the cardiovascular system

The main role of the cardiovascular system is to transport oxygen and nutrients to all the tissues in the body, and to remove waste products, such as carbon dioxide, from them. However, the cardiovascular system also helps to regulate body temperature and plays an important role in fighting disease and infection.

Circulation of oxygen
The cardiovascular system transports oxygen around the body to the working muscles and the vital organs. The oxygen attaches to haemoglobin (the red blood cells), which carries it through the bloodstream. The oxygen is then deposited at the muscles and vital organs, where it is used to create energy.

Circulation of carbon dioxide
Once the oxygen has been delivered to the muscles and vital organs, the haemoglobin then attracts carbon dioxide and transports it back to the lungs to be breathed out. Carbon dioxide is a waste product, which is produced when oxygen is used to create energy.

Blood clotting
When the blood vessels become damaged they leak blood. If this blood leak is not stopped, the body will eventually become short of the blood needed to transport oxygen to the vital organs. To stop the leakage, plasma in the bloodstream is delivered to the site of the wound, where it thickens like glue and plugs the hole. This process is described as blood clotting.

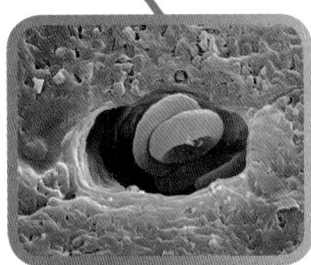
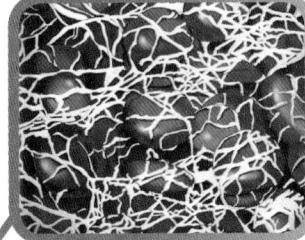
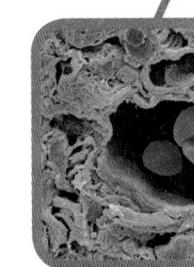
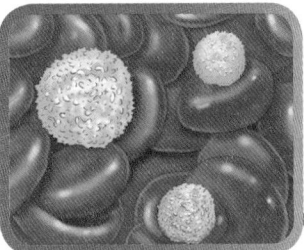

Protection against infection
The bloodstream contains both red blood cells and white blood cells. White blood cells fight infection. When the body detects disease or an infection, the cardiovascular system delivers a plentiful supply of white blood cells to the affected area and the white blood cells fight the disease or infection.

Provision of nutrients and hormones
All cells within the body require a steady supply of nutrients and hormones for them to work properly. These nutrients and hormones help the cells to grow and function and are delivered to the cells by the cardiovascular system.

BRONZE

1. Imagine you are a red blood cell, a white blood cell, or a plasma cell and write about the different things that could happen to you in a day or create your 'day in the life of…' as a cartoon. Whichever you choose, make sure it is clear what the specific role of the cell you have chosen is.

Regulation of body temperature

Body temperature can be subdivided into internal temperature and external temperature. The most important of these is internal body temperature, because it controls the efficiency of the internal organs. If internal temperature rises or falls rapidly, there can be serious consequences such as hypothermia or heat exhaustion.

The cardiovascular system is responsible for helping to maintain the body's internal temperature at a constant 37°C. It does this by regulating the flow of blood to certain blood vessels. This process is known as thermoregulation and it is controlled by the brain.

If your external body temperature rises because it is a hot day or your internal body temperature rises because a lot of energy is being produced by your muscles or you are ill, your body needs to act to stop your internal temperature rising too high. It does this through a process called **vasodilation**. The smooth muscles surrounding the blood vessels leading to the skin's surface relax. The arterioles dilate (increase in diameter), allowing more blood to reach the capillaries, so that heat in the blood can escape through the skin via radiation. In addition, the sweat glands in the skin secrete sweat, which cools the body as it evaporates from the skin.

If your external body temperature decreases because it is cold outside, it slowly causes your internal temperature to decrease. If this is not controlled then hypothermia sets in, which can cause the body's vital organs to stop functioning. To combat this the blood vessels **vasoconstrict**. The arterioles contract (decrease in diameter), decreasing the flow of warm blood to the capillaries, and reducing the amount of heat that can escape through the skin via radiation. The warm blood that is diverted away from the capillaries stays in the body's core and helps to maintain a healthy internal temperature for as long as possible.

If your internal body temperature drops too low, heat can be generated through shivering. This, often involuntary, action is the body's way of protecting itself. In order to shiver, muscles must contract and relax rapidly and, in doing so, the engine room of the cell that produces the energy needed to fuel the movement also produces heat, which can raise the internal body temperature.

Thermoregulation is helped by the layer of subcutaneous fat that lies beneath the surface of the skin. This acts as an insulator, helping to keep body heat in when it's needed.

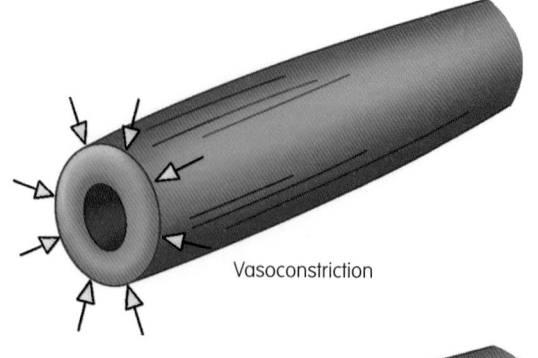

Vasoconstriction

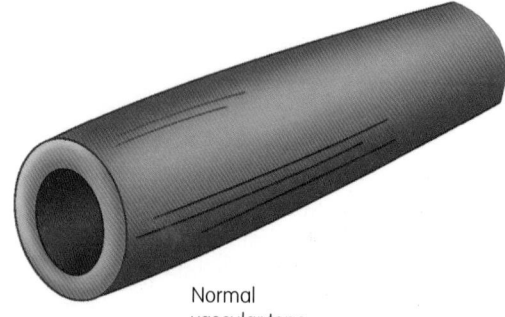

Normal vascular tone

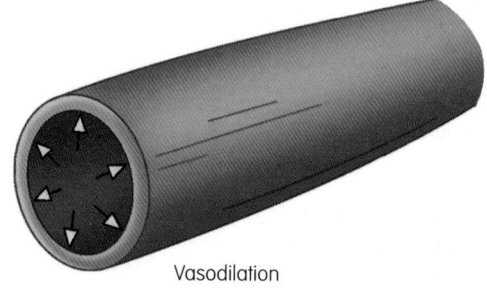

Vasodilation

BRONZE

2. Plan a five-minute presentation to describe the process of thermoregulation. Remember to mention:

- vasoconstriction
- vasodilation
- smooth muscles
- blood vessels
- the skin's surface.

The respiratory system

The respiratory system works to bring about the actions in the body that we call 'breathing'. Breathing is the means by which oxygen from the air is brought into the body.

The structure of the respiratory system

Air passes into the body through the **nasal cavity**. The air is warmed by the many blood vessels in the nasal cavity. Impurities such as dust are removed as the air passes through the nasal hairs, which are called cilia, and the mucus in the naval cavity. The mucus also moistens the air.

The **trachea**, which is also known as the windpipe, carries the air we breathe towards the next part of the respiratory system, the bronchi. It is strengthened by rings of hyaline cartilage, which protect it during impact and stop it from collapsing.

The **pleural membranes** line the lungs and the thoracic (chest) cavity. They are covered in a layer of pleural fluid, an oily substance that reduces friction between the lungs and the surrounding tissues.

The **bronchi** are smaller tubes that branch off the trachea and carry the air towards the bronchioles.

The **alveoli** are tiny air sacs that have a very important role to play in making sure the oxygen from the air we breathe in gets into the bloodstream.

The **bronchioles** are tiny tubes that are spread across the entire surface of the lungs. They carry the air towards the alveoli.

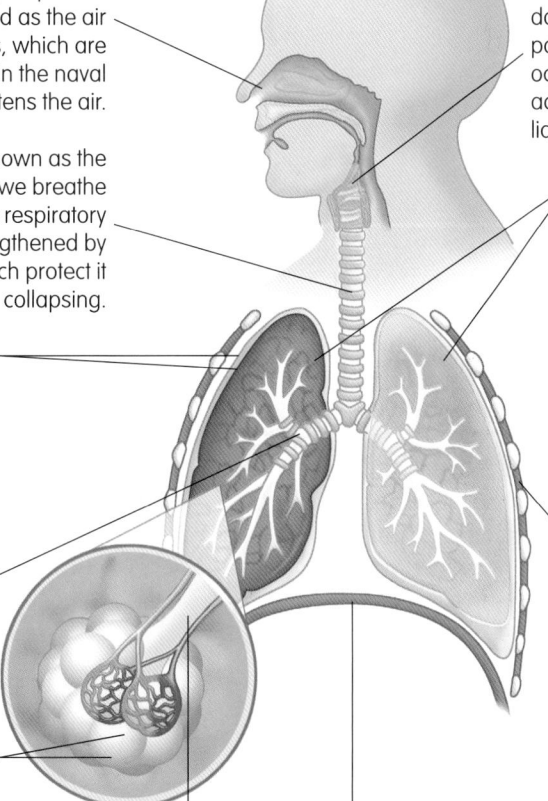

The **epiglottis**, a small flap of elastic cartilage at the top of the trachea, acts as a gateway, ensuring that air passes down to the lungs, and food and drink pass into the digestive system. Choking occurs most often when the epiglottis acts incorrectly, and passes food or liquid into the trachea.

The **lungs** are the key to the respiratory system. They inflate and deflate – just as a balloon does when you blow it up and let the air out – raising and lowering the air pressure in the body and allowing air to pass into and out of the lungs. Once inside the body, the oxygen in the air is passed into the bloodstream and the carbon dioxide in the body is passed out through a process called gaseous exchange.

The **intercostal muscles**, found between the ribs, contract and relax during the breathing process. In doing so, they raise and lower the rib cage, which increases and decreases the volume of the chest cavity. This changes the air pressure in the lungs, allowing air to pass in and out of the body.

The **diaphragm** is a sheet of muscle dividing the chest cavity and the abdominal cavity. It is pulled downwards to stretch the lungs, thereby decreasing the pressure in them and allowing them to fill with air. When the diaphragm relaxes, it returns to its original bell-like shape, which decreases the volume of the lungs and forces air out of the body.

BRONZE

1. a) Explore your respiratory system by identifying the parts of your anatomy that allow you to breathe. Breathe in and out slowly, and write down what you can feel.

b) Compare your findings with a partner's. What similarities and differences have you noticed?

2. The respiratory system is often compared to an upside down tree. Draw a diagram to illustrate this comparison. Think about the different thicknesses of branches on a tree and what you find at the end of branches.

3. Read about the mechanics of breathing and gaseous exchange on page 138 and then answer the following questions.

a) Imagine you are an oxygen molecule. Using all your knowledge and understanding about the structure and function of the respiratory system, describe your journey from the air to the blood of a human.

b) Now imagine you are a carbon dioxide molecule and describe your journey from the blood of a human to the air.

The mechanics of breathing

When we breathe in, our rib cage rises. This is because the external intercostal muscles contract and lift the ribs upwards and outwards. At the same time as this is happening, the diaphragm – a large sheet of muscle separating the abdomen and chest area – contracts and flattens out. These two actions make the volume of the chest cavity bigger, reducing the amount of pressure in the lungs. The pressure in the air around us is now greater than the pressure in the lungs and air rushes into the lungs to equalize the pressure. We call this **inspiration**.

When the air pressure in the lungs is the same as the air pressure in the air around us, the external intercostal muscles and the diaphragm relax and the internal intercostal muscles contract. The diaphragm becomes dome shaped. This reduces the volume of the chest cavity and increases the pressure in the lungs. The pressure in the lungs is now higher than the pressure in the air around us and, therefore, air pushes out of the lungs to equalize the pressure. In other words, we breathe out. We call this **expiration**.

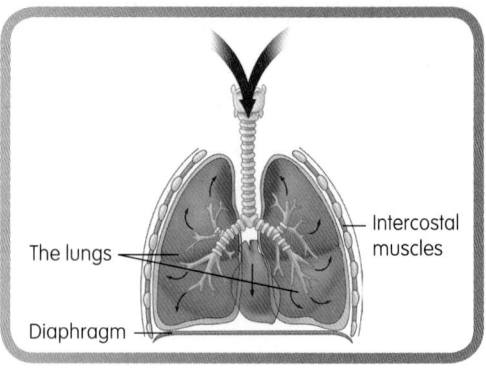

Inspiration.

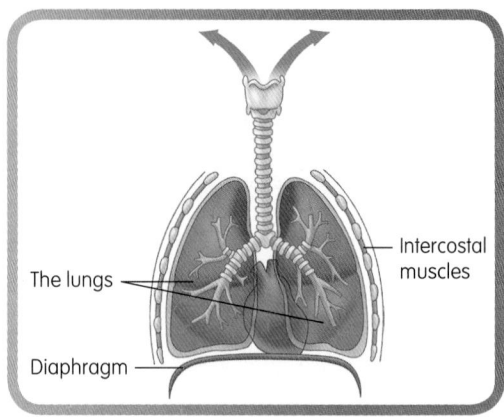

Expiration.

Gaseous exchange

We breathe so that gaseous exchange can take place. Gaseous exchange ensures that we get the oxygen that feeds our working muscles and organs into our blood. At the same time, it removes the carbon dioxide, which the blood has carried from the working muscles and organs, from our bodies. Gaseous exchange takes place at the alveoli in the lungs. There are millions of alveoli in the lungs; so many, in fact, that if you flattened them all out you would cover the area of half a tennis court!

The alveoli have capillaries running across them. These are the part of the cardiovascular system where the exchange of oxygen and carbon dioxide takes place. Because the walls of the alveoli are so thin, oxygen and carbon dioxide can move between the alveoli and the capillaries; that is, between the respiratory system and the cardiovascular system.

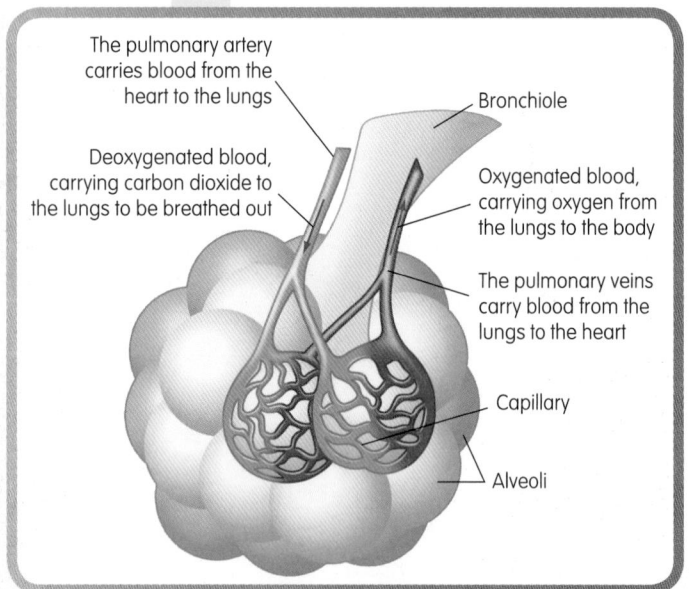

The pulmonary artery carries blood from the heart to the lungs

Deoxygenated blood, carrying carbon dioxide to the lungs to be breathed out

Bronchiole

Oxygenated blood, carrying oxygen from the lungs to the body

The pulmonary veins carry blood from the lungs to the heart

Capillary

Alveoli

A bronchiole and alveoli.

Diffusion is the term used to describe how molecules move from an area of higher concentration to an area of lower concentration. Oxygen and carbon dioxide can move between the alveoli and the capillaries because of diffusion.

- The concentration of the oxygen in the alveoli that has just been breathed in, is higher than the concentration of the oxygen (in the blood) in the capillaries that has been circulated around the body. Therefore, the oxygen molecules move from the alveoli to the capillaries; from the area of higher concentration to the area of lower concentration.

- The carbon dioxide moves in the opposite direction. The concentration of the carbon dioxide in the capillaries is higher than the concentration of the carbon dioxide in the alveoli, and so the carbon dioxide molecules move from the capillaries to the alveoli; from the area of higher concentration to the area of lower concentration.

SPOTLIGHT on the cardiorespiratory system

BRONZE

1. Build a model of the respiratory system. It should show:

- The structure of the respiratory system.
- How we breathe.
- How gaseous exchange takes place.

2. Research and then create a visually stimulating diagram that depicts the functions of the cardiorespiratory system, and gives a short description of each. Remember to include the key functions that link the cardiovascular and respiratory systems.

SILVER

3. In pairs, decide which of you is going to take on the role of the cardiovascular system and which of you is going to take on the role of the respiratory system. Then, using your hands and any other objects that you think might help you, show how the two systems work together to supply the body with oxygen.

GOLD

4. The local rugby club has signed up for a six-week training programme at your local fitness centre and the head coach has asked that all players are provided with information on how the body's systems work. You have been asked to assist the fitness instructor by focusing on the cardiovascular and respiratory systems. The coach is very keen that the players understand how these systems operate, how they work together, and how they have equally important roles in making them better, more efficient players. To ensure that this happens, you need to include clear, accurate examples in your presentation and run through various exercises that will develop the players' efficiency further. You will need to mention the supply of oxygen and the removal of carbon dioxide.

External exam practice

Tackling the exam

You can decide to take the exam when you are ready. It will be completed on a computer and will last one hour. There are a total of 50 marks available and the number of marks for each question is shown in brackets. Depending on the number of marks you get, you will receive one of the following grades for the unit:

- Distinction at Level 2   • Merit at Level 2   • Pass at Level 2   • Level 1   • Unclassified.

The exam contains different types of question and some sample questions for you to practise are provided below.

1. Which of the following is NOT a function of the skeleton? (1)

   a. Support ◯

   b. Blood production ◯

   c. Blood clotting ◯

   d. Movement ◯

   e. Shape ◯

   f. Mineral storage ◯

2. Where in the body would you find articular cartilage? (Tick all that apply) (1)

   a. In the outer ear ◯

   b. Between the bones of the vertebrae ◯

   c. At the ends of long bones ◯

   d. Around the trachea ◯

3. Link the type of muscle to its alternative name. (3)

Heart muscle	Skeletal muscle
Voluntary muscle	Cardiac muscle
Involuntary muscle	Smooth muscle

4. Give an example of a sporting activity in which flexion and extension are continually repeated. (1)

5. State the functions of the cardiorespiratory system. (4)

6. One of the functions of the cardiovascular system is 'blood clotting'. Explain this process. (2)

7. Below are incomplete descriptions of some of the structures of the respiratory system. Complete the descriptions by inserting the name of the structure being described. (6)

   a. Air passes into the body through the _____. The air is warmed by the many blood vessels in the nasal cavity. Impurities, such as dust, are removed as the air passes through the nasal hairs, which are called cilia, and the mucus in the naval cavity. The mucus also moistens the air.

   b. The _____, a small flap of elastic cartilage at the top of the trachea, acts as a gateway, ensuring that air passes down to the lungs and food and drink pass into the digestive system. Choking occurs most often when the epiglottis acts incorrectly and food or liquid passes into the trachea.

   c. The _____, which is also known as the windpipe, carries the air we breathe towards the next part of the respiratory system, the bronchi. It is strengthened by rings of hyaline cartilage, which protect it during impact and stop it from collapsing.

   d. The _____ are smaller tubes that branch off the trachea and carry the air towards the bronchioles.

   e. The _____ are tiny tubes that are spread across the entire surface of the lungs. They carry the air towards the alveoli.

   f. The _____ line the lungs and the thoracic (chest) cavity. They are covered in a layer of pleural fluid, an oily substance that reduces friction between the lungs and the surrounding tissues.

8. The statements below relate to points on the graph. Match the statements to the correct points on the graph. (3)

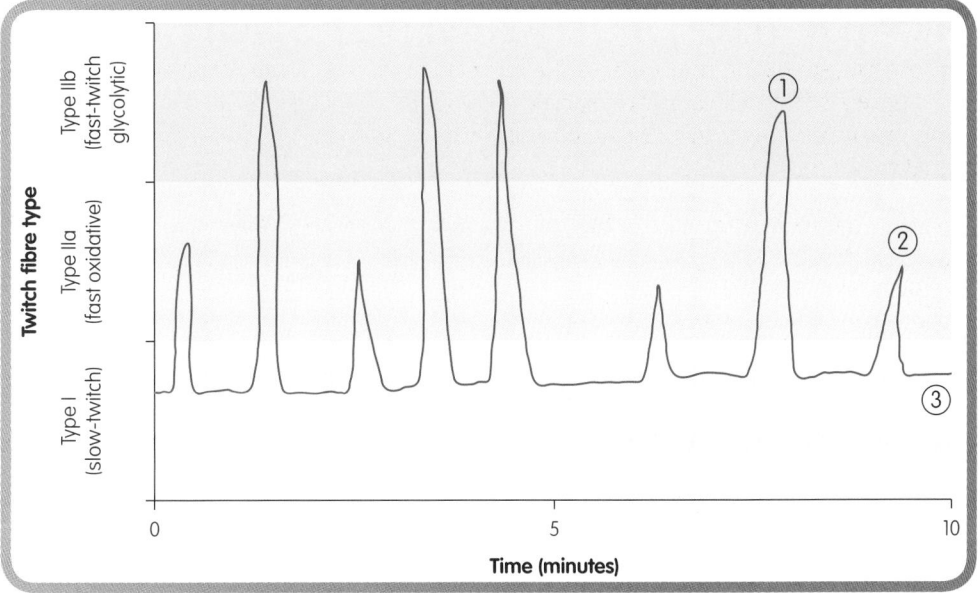

A graph showing relative usage of the different muscle fibre types for a player during a football game.

The footballer is moving at a medium to fast pace along the wing to provide an outlet for a pass.

The footballer is jumping to head the ball.

The footballer is jogging back into position after a goal has been scored.

9. Label the components of the diagram below. (6)

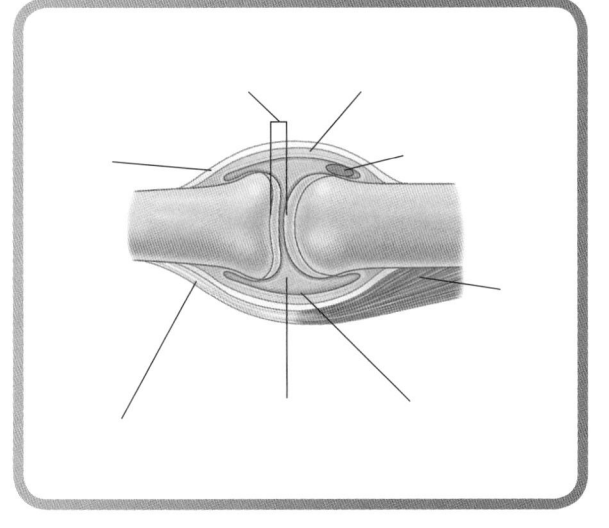

10. Which is the predominant muscle fibre type being used in the activity shown in the photograph? (1)

Unit 8: Promotion and Sponsorship in Sport

Reasons for the promotion of sport

We've all seen how many people get very excited about major sports events such as the FIFA World Cup or the Olympic Games. But what causes this excitement and loyalty? Promotion – the publicizing and selling of a match or event – is one of the key reasons why people become enthusiastic about sporting events, whether it's a small community sports initiative or the RBS 6 Nations Rugby tournament. Ensuring an event captures the public's imagination is, in itself, enough to justify promoting sporting events but there are also other reasons why sport is promoted.

The annual RBS 6 Nations Rugby tournament is always well promoted.

Economics

High-profile sports events have the potential to generate substantial sums of money, for the promoters, the participants (if they are professional and are paid to compete), and also the government in the form of taxes. Top performers, such as Usain Bolt, can earn up to £7 million a year from race fees and product endorsements!

Events also bring economic benefits for local businesses in the area where they are staged. The FINA World Swimming Championships, held in Manchester in 2008, is estimated to have generated £7 million for the city and when the UEFA Cup was held in the city in the same year, it is believed to have generated £11 million.

Community sport often brings people together and helps develop a feel-good factor in a community.

Community sport

Promotion is used by many organizations, such as sport development units, to engage local communities in healthy activities and to make sure the benefits of sports are well known and understood.

Getting local communities involved in sport and physical activity has many benefits, not only those associated with health. If people are active and engaged in community projects – such as playing for, or volunteering at, local clubs – they are often more motivated and generally more content. A positive community, where people from different generations and different backgrounds spend time together, is a far nicer place to live, with lower crime rates and fewer incidents of anti-social behaviour.

Why promote sport?

Healthy living

Many national organizations, such as government departments and the National Health Service (NHS), run promotional campaigns to make the nation more aware of the benefits of following a healthy lifestyle, eating more healthy foods, and exercising regularly.

A healthy nation benefits everyone. Taking part in sport and other forms of physical activity helps keep people generally fitter. Fitter people are often happier and healthier, which reduces the pressure on NHS services and saves the country money. A healthy nation is also more productive at work, as people work more efficiently when they are functioning at their peak and have fewer days off work due to sickness.

A healthier nation cuts down the demands placed on the NHS and reduces costs.

Social inclusion

Many social inclusion or anti-crime initiatives are centred on sport. Sport distracts people from other things, so it is often used to engage members of society who are on the verge of offending or have already committed minor offences and who are heading for a life of crime. Training and taking part in sport gives people a focus for their energy, fills up their spare time, and helps instil a sense of discipline and a sense of belonging. Sport is also an excellent tool for promoting active citizenship and developing personal responsibility. Many young people who have managed to turn their lives around have acknowledged the influence sport has had on them; that it has helped keep them on the straight and narrow.

Boxing is just one sport that gives young people the opportunity to channel their energies into a worthwhile activity. Here, James DeGale, Kevin Mitchell, and JJ Bird pose with local youngsters at the Times Amateur Boxing Club in London.

Creating local and national identify

When an individual or a team does well, promotion of the success can generate pride in a community or in the country as a whole, generating a feel-good factor that often spreads beyond those people who are actively interested in sport.

The 2012 Olympic torch relay was a great example of this. Many worthy members of the community were selected to run with the torch and large numbers of spectators turned out to cheer the runners on their journey. Not only did the relay bring people together, but it also benefited many businesses, which saw an increase in takings when the torch passed through their communities.

Natasha Sinha carries the Olympic Torch in Greenwich as part of the London 2012 Olympic torch relay.

BRONZE

1. Identify one example of a sports promotion for each reason discussed above, and describe what form the promotion took and what its purpose was.

The role of the media in promoting sport

One of the most effective ways of promoting sport is via the media, which includes television, radio, adverts, leaflets and posters, local and national newspapers, magazines, websites, and social media tools, such as Twitter and Facebook.

The relationship between the media and sport is complex. Promoters and the media have a very profitable relationship, with promoters paying media outlets to advertise their events and the media paying promoters of large events for the privilege of screening live footage. Yet promoters also rely on the media to promote their events and communicate the results of matches and tournaments for free because the media has airtime or column inches to fill. The danger is that the media will turn on a participant, a team, or a tournament because it makes a good story.

Advertising using the media

Promoters will carefully choose the type of media they want to use to promote their event and the image of the event they want to project. They start by considering who their target audience is and how they can best reach them. Large-scale events, such as the London Marathon, are promoted nationally through a variety of media, whereas smaller events with smaller budgets that are of interest to a local community, may only be promoted in the local press.

A central part of any promotional campaign is establishing an image for a sport or a particular event. Logos and slogans, which are designed to reinforce key messages, are particularly powerful tools and promoters of top sporting events spend many hours and a great deal of money making sure they get the branding right.

Getting it right?

The BBC promotes the annual Sports Personality of the Year (SPOTY) award extremely well each year. It promotes the evening via the internet, on its own BBC sports programmes, and has regular updates on BBC Radio 5 Live. In this way, the promotion reaches the target audience – members of the public with a wide-ranging interest in sport – through a variety of different media to maximize the message, but it manages to do so without paying for advertising outside of the BBC, keeping the cost of promotion down. The image it uses stays pretty much the same from year to year, although the personalities up for the top award do change. This ensures continuity from year to year and strengthens the brand.

Boxers Amir Khan and Junior Witter show off their title belts as part of the BBC Sports Personality of the Year in 2006 and 2007.

Will it work?

The logo for the 2014 Commonwealth Games, to be held in Glasgow, will become far more prominent as the games approaches, as will many other aspects of the promotional campaign. However, the Commonwealth Games already has its own website with a mission statement about how the games will be organized and delivered, and people are being encouraged to follow the build up via Twitter. Why not keep a close eye on developments and see if the Glasgow 2014 Commonwealth Games achieves its aims?

Mission statement and vision

Our mission

Our mission is to organise and deliver the Glasgow 2014 Commonwealth Games in a way that fully realises the aspirations of the Glasgow Bid and the contractual obligations of the Host City Contract – on time and on budget.

Our vision

Our vision is to stage an outstanding, athlete-centred and sport-focused Games of world-class competition, that will be celebrated across the Commonwealth, generate enormous pride in Glasgow and Scotland, and leave a lasting legacy.

The media as commentator

Many sports events or initiatives make the most of any opportunity to get free promotion. This includes the coverage they get from media sources such as:

- BBC Radio 5 Live.
- Talk Sport.
- Coverage in mainstream news.

An excellent example of the power of the media was the rise, fall, and rise again of David Beckham some years ago.

Beckham was built up to an almost god-like status during the run up to the World Cup in 1998, but his dismissal from the pitch during the match against Argentina during the tournament was the start of a media campaign that attacked him. Nearly all the blame for England's exit from the tournament was laid at his feet and he was regularly abused in the media.

Slowly though, Beckham's reputation was restored, mainly as a result of his performances on the pitch, and the media was almost totally behind the decision to make him England captain in 2000. His rehabilitation was complete after his famous last-minute free kick against Greece in 2001, securing England's qualification for the 2002 World Cup. This time the media coverage he received was extremely positive.

David Beckham continues to attract considerable publicity, most recently as an Olympic Ambassador for the 2012 Olympic Games. This is a far cry from the backlash he received at the hands of the media in 1998.

BRONZE

1. Select a sports event or initiative of your choice and research how the media promoted and reported on it.

The effects of promoting sport

Promotion can have many positive impacts on spectators and participants. It raises awareness of events and ensures bigger and better spectacles and opportunities to compete. For example, locating an event close to a fan base is important. When local Nottingham boy Carl Froch won the IBF super-middleweight world title at the Capital FM Arena in Nottingham in May 2012 he was roared on by thousands of fans from his home town, making the fight not only thrilling for spectators, but amazing for the participant and commercially successful for the promoter. While these are extremely important benefits, it is important to remember that promotion also brings downsides, such as excessive entry prices for spectators and an increase in the pressure on performers to succeed.

The effects of promoting sport on spectators

The downside of promotion

If a sporting event is going to be popular and can expect wide press coverage and a lot of spectators then it will probably attract a sizeable promotional budget and will, consequently, be widely promoted. If a sporting event is well-promoted and well-organized, most spectators will be happy. But large events that have been heavily promoted do have downsides for spectators:

- **Cost:** Entry fees, travel costs and the cost of merchandise, food, and drink are generally higher for bigger events. Promoters need to cover the cost of paying performers' fees, venue hire, advertising, and possibly the cost of policing the event, but they also need to make a profit. Both costs and the expected profit are higher for bigger events.

- **Availability:** It is often possible to watch large events on the television or listen to coverage on the radio, but for die-hard fans there is nothing like attending a live sporting event. Often, the bigger an event, the harder it is to get tickets. The massive interest in tickets for the London 2012 Olympic Games meant huge numbers of people were unable to get tickets and were extremely disappointed. Spectators can also suffer if the timing of the event is scheduled to benefit the television audience rather than those who have bought tickets to see the match live, as thousands of Liverpool football fans found out to their cost when faced with travel chaos after the FA Cup Final at Wembley in May 2012. Train cancellations and engineering work resulted in many fans having to make alternative travel arrangements, incurring additional costs and inconvenience.

- **Accessibility:** The location of major events can be a problem, especially if spectators have to travel long distances to attend them. For example, supporters, particularly those from the north of England, find it difficult to travel to Wembley Stadium in north-west London and often face traffic problems and parking issues. The size of stadia also limits the number of people who can watch an event, as there are often more people wanting tickets than there are tickets available.

- **Under-represented groups:** Promoters target advertising at the groups of people they think are most likely to attend their event. As a result, potential spectators from under-represented groups – including families, people with disabilities, and ethnic minorities – are often ignored by advertising campaigns, don't attend, and continue to be under-represented as a result.

The psychological effects of promotion

Promotional campaigns aim to maximize awareness and engage individuals as well as communities, therefore, they target their advertising campaigns at particular target markets to try and get their messages across as effectively as possible. To help them do this, they often recruit sports stars to help publicize events. Examples such as Shane Warne promoting the Cricket Ashes Series and Nick Faldo promoting the Ryder Cup spring immediately to mind.

Promoters always try to use stars who are seen as positive role models. Using sports stars, like Dame Kelly Holmes and Sir Chris Hoy, who have a clean-cut image that focuses on their hard work and dedication to their sport gives further credibility to the event or sport being promoted.

Sports stars are also used to promote products. Linking the image of a famous, high-achieving sports star with a brand encourages people who want to be like that sports star to buy the products they are promoting. This benefits both the athlete and the brand. The products athletes promote range from merchandise connected with their sport, such as replica kits or pens, pencils, and key rings, to everyday brands, such as cereals, razors, and sandwiches, as well as sports-related clothing.

David Beckham at the launch party to promote Adidas Originals clothing by James Bond.

Elizabeth Simmonds, James Goddard, Rebecca Adlington, Liam Tancock, and Gemma Spofforth promote Speedo swimwear.

Spectators can benefit from the psychological effects of promotion. They often feel part of something special, especially if the promotion includes someone they admire and identify with; someone they feel they have a personal connection with. Going to the same event, wearing the same clothes, and eating the same food as someone they admire can boost a person's sense of belonging, their self-esteem, and their sense of well-being. For example, Amir Khan grew up in Bolton and he has a large following among similar inner-city communities, who like to see their own opportunities reflected back at them in this boy-made-good.

Yet promotion has a darker side. Ultimately, promoters want to make money and they use role models and brand sponsorship to manipulate people into attending the event they are organizing or buying the product they are selling. The fan is an endless source of cash. Just think about how regularly football clubs change the design of their shirt. It isn't because the old design is looking tired and old fashioned. It's because they want to push 'real' fans into spending a large sum of money on the new shirt just so they continue to belong to the inner core of supporters. And at approximately £45 per shirt this can be very expensive for a family with football-mad children.

England football players model the new England Umbro Performance Perfected shirt.

BRONZE

1. Identify a high-profile sports event that has taken place recently or is soon to take place and describe how you think the way it has been promoted may have affected spectators. Remember to consider both the positive and negative effects on spectators.

The effects of promoting sport on participants

Promotion doesn't just affect spectators. It also affects participants, and the effects of promotion on sport can be both negative and positive for participants.

If more events are planned and run, there are increased opportunities for people to compete.

The competition on places is likely to be less fierce, which means people of varying abilities will take part and develop experience that may help them develop as athletes.

If the competition for places is less fierce, the overall standard of competitors at many events may decrease, making them less attractive to top athletes and players who can choose to stay away. This may, in turn, reduce the pull of the event for spectators.

Well-promoted events, such as the London Marathon and the Great North Run, are very popular with participants.

Participants work hard to secure an opportunity to compete and the high value put on places gives the participant a real sense of being special and taking part in something unique.

Popular events have to select participants in some way. They may hold a lottery, establish entry standards, or hold a qualifying competition. There will always be some would-be participants who will be disappointed they can't take part.

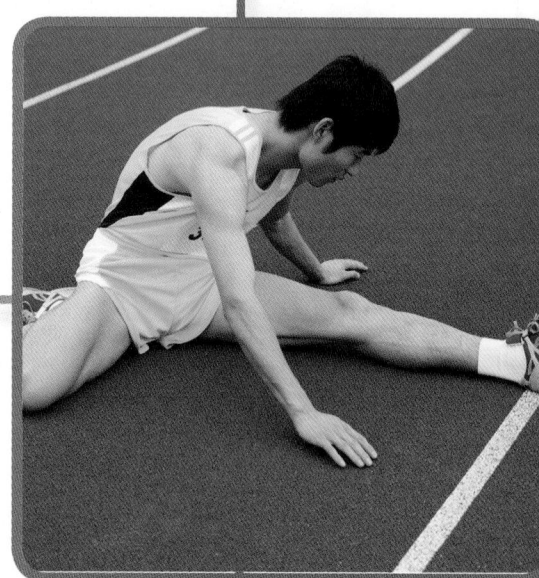

Good promotion can increase the coverage of under-represented sports.

Increased coverage may result in an increased awareness among the general population and the number of opportunities to participate at all levels may increase as a direct result. Televising events, such as the Women's FA Cup Final or the Paralympics, can act as the catalyst to attract girls into football and disabled people into sport.

The promoters behind the increase in coverage may begin to make demands on participants, changing times of competitions to suit the sporting calendar or television schedules. And there are always many more sports that never receive the significant promotion they often deserve. Are you aware that the England Women's Cricket team regularly competes in a women's version of the Ashes, while their rugby-playing compatriots are often successful in the Women's 6 Nations Rugby competition?

Well-promoted events can raise the profile of participants.

Success at a well-promoted event can make an athlete famous. An example of this is the female GB swimming team, and particularly Rebecca Adlington, after their successes at the Beijing Olympics in 2008. A famous athlete can then benefit financially from their sporting success through sponsorship deals.

Fame does have its downsides, and can place an athlete under an uncomfortable level of scrutiny, as Rebecca Adlington discovered after her success in Beijing. The media attention and subsequent intrusion into her personal life disrupted her training and she underperformed for a considerable period after the games.

Events that are well promoted and generate considerable interest often favour the home team or individual and make life very difficult for the away team. Promotion can also turn one team into the favourite and the other into the underdog.

There are numerous examples in the FA Cup each year where lower-league teams triumph over teams from higher leagues.

Being the favourite is not always good for participants. Home advantage didn't do Bayern Munich much good in the 2012 Champions League final. Was the level of expectation just too high for the German players?

As an event becomes more popular there is often a growth in the number of participants.

More opportunities to participate is obviously positive for participants. For example, with the rise in popularity of running, most towns and cities now hold an annual 10-kilometre (or longer) distance race, which means that both serious runners and those who want to take part for fun or to raise money for charity can take part in several races a year.

An increase in the popularity can lead to excessive demand for places at more high-profile events and sometimes a lack of demand for places at smaller, less high-profile events. For example, applications each year for the London Marathon far exceed the places available.

SILVER

3. Identify a sporting event you are familiar with and assess all aspects of the way the media promoted it. Make sure you cover:

- The key message(s) being communicated.
- The different media used and why they were chosen.
- How imagery was used.
- The effects of the promotion on spectators and participants.
- Your opinion on whether the promotion was successful or not.

BRONZE

2. Identify an example of a sports promotion that you think has impacted positively or negatively (or both) on participants. Outline the effects and explain why you think they occurred.

Unit 8 assignment, part one

Background

You are an active volunteer at your local club, which is looking into running a large-scale competition to boost income and raise awareness of the club in the region. A small working party, which you are part of, has been formed to look into the feasibility of putting on the competition. The first task for the working group is to find out about sports promotion.

Grading criteria to be assessed
1A.1, 1A.2, 1A.3 2A.P1, 2A.P2, 2A.P3 2A.M1

Task

Prepare a report on the issues surrounding the promotion of sport. The report should:

- Describe two different reasons for the promotion of sport. (1A.1)
- Describe the role of the media in the promotion of sport. (1A.2)
- Describe the effects the promotion of a selected sporting event has on spectators. (1A.3)

- Describe four different reasons for the promotion of sport. (2A.P1)
- Explain the role of the media in the promotion of sport. (2A.P2)
- Explain the effects the promotion of a selected sporting event has on participants and spectators. (2A.P3)

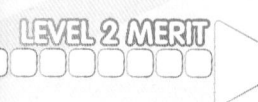

- Assess the role of the media in the promotion of two selected sporting events. (2A.M1)

Tackling the assignment

You have been asked to prepare a report for the committee and an innovative way to tackle this part of the assignment would be take on the role of a reporter and write a newspaper or magazine article or, better yet, prepare a report for radio or television. You could include interviews with participants and spectators to meet the criteria for 2A.P3.

Whichever method you decide to use, you will need to ensure that your **descriptions** paint a sufficiently detailed picture. Your **explanations** should explain why things are as they are, with 'because' appearing prominently in your answers. And, your **assessment** needs to judge the value and impact of the media in the promotion of two sporting events, so you will need to examine both the positives and the negatives and then draw your own conclusion about the media's role. Most importantly, you should use lots of examples throughout.

Promoting Sport

by Linda O'Donnell

The media can be used to promote sport in a variety of ways for a variety of reasons. In this article I am going to explore the ways it can be used to raise awareness of the benefits of sport as part of a healthy lifestyle. An example of this is the 'Change for Life' campaign run by the NHS, which is aimed at families and focuses on the importance of eating well and exercising regularly, so that the chances of getting obesity-related diseases, such as heart disease, some cancers, and type 2 diabetes, are reduced in later life.

Eat well   Move more   Live longer

The campaign has a very distinctive logo (see above) and includes advice specifically aimed at families, with a separate section for adults. It includes information on food intake, fitness activities, and advice on cutting down on alcohol for adults.

The campaign is promoted through a television advertising campaign and an interactive website at www.nhs.uk/Change4Life/Pages/change-for-life.aspx. Many of the adverts were on during prime time television, which meant that they had maximum exposure and reached as many people as possible. It was also supported by a poster campaign in major towns and cities.

The target audience for the campaign was families in general, although the campaign focused mainly on families who were inactive and who weren't eating a healthy diet. It was hoped that the television adverts and poster campaign would be an effective way to target this group, with the website a useful reference tool for families who wanted to find out more.

The local sport development unit (SDU) ran a series of activity days based on the Change for Life campaign, promoting it via their website, monthly newsletter, and a series of adverts on the local radio station. This culminated in a family 'It's a Knockout'-style event in the main city park, which attracted over 40 families and 500 spectators. They used a local swimmer and a local gymnast to help promote the event, both of whom represented Team GB at the London 2012 Olympics. This added to the attractiveness of the event as both of them are excellent role models and very fit!

There was a range of merchandise on sale on the day, such as t-shirts and fridge magnets, and all the participants and spectators were given a series of meal sheets and activity cards to use at home.

The SDU produced a summary of the activity days and the 'It's a Knockout' event, which looked at many aspects of the campaign, including its impact on the participants and spectators of the 'It's a Knockout' event.

Linda has made a great start, presenting the information clearly and concisely, although breaking the content up using sub-headings would make it even easier to read. She has also combined the 2A.P1, 2A.P2, and 2A.P3 criteria effectively. She is well on the way to achieving all three, but she does have more work to do.

Linda has discussed one reason for the promotion of sport, encouraging healthy living. To fully achieve 2A.P1 Linda needs to replicate this level of detail for three other reasons for the promotion of sport, and she needs to give other examples of the role the media plays in promoting sport to meet the criteria for 2A.P2.

To achieve 2A.P3 Linda needs to go into a lot more detail about the effects the promotion had on spectators and participants. She has indicated that the SDU has already done this, so there should be plenty of data for her to work with, or she could interview some of the participants and spectators and use her findings from those interviews in her article.

Bradley Mickleson

SPORT EVENT 1: REGIONAL RUGBY FINAL

Bradley has developed a good framework from which to work, although the ultimate key to his success will be how he presents the information verbally to pull his presentation together.

How the event was promoted:

1. Posters around town and in sports centres.
2. Clip on regional BBC news programme.
3. Article in local press.
4. Radio coverage of the event on the day.
5. Pre-match promotion on Rugby Football Union (RFU) website.

- Set the scene.
- Mention date, venue, teams, scores, etc.
- Show newspaper cuttings and RFU webpage.

Effects of promotion on spectators:

1. The event was a sell-out, with 1700 spectators in attendance. This is a record crowd, over 500 more than any other final in previous years. This meant that there were long queues at the toilets and refreshment stalls.
2. Despite large numbers, spectators reported that access was good, parking fine, and facilities excellent. Parking was free, which offset the price of the admission tickets.
3. Each primary school in the area that was involved in the tag rugby festival, was given free tickets.

4. There was an international player in attendance, which went down well with spectators. Many said it was the highlight of the day and reflected well on the organizing club.
5. Interest from non-traditional rugby fans was high. Many reported they would attend club matches again in the future.

- Focus on the effects of the media promotion used and quote some of the spectators who commented that they saw the event advertised on TV and radio.
- Build on the fact that different media outlets were used: TV, radio, internet, and newspapers.
- Stress the high attendance and sales figures (merchandise and catering).
- Emphasize the impact of the free tickets for schools on the attendance figures and sales figures.

Bradley has covered many of the factors required to meet the criteria for 2A.M1, although he hasn't yet made any references to negative aspects of the promotion. For example, did a sell-out crowd mean that some spectators couldn't get tickets or were most of the tickets given away free to schools? Bradley needs to replicate this level of detail when he discusses the effect of the positives and negatives of the promotion on the players, and provide an assessment of a second sporting event.

Sources of sponsorship

There are very few events nowadays, either locally or nationally, that don't attract some form of sponsorship. It's commonplace for individuals, teams, and events to tap into sponsorship opportunities to help pay for training, equipment, or prize money. In return for financial support, the sponsor's logo is heavily promoted by the person, team, or event being sponsored.

Private-sector sponsorship

Sponsorship can come from a range of sources and focus on varying levels of performance. The most common form of sponsorship is from private companies or individuals, such as a builder's merchant sponsoring a regional cricket team or a bank sponsoring a national league or competition.

Private-sector sponsorship can be local, regional, or national.

Large multinational companies from the private sector, which sell their goods and services across the world, also sponsor international or global events. For example, BMW sponsors many golf tournaments worldwide and BNP Paribas sponsors many tennis tournaments.

BMW promotes the Asian Open, 2008.

BMW promotes the Italian Open, 2012.

Remember:

It is possible to draw a distinction between international events (events that are promoted in more than one country) and global events (events that are promoted around the world).

BRONZE

1. Identify three regional, three national, three international, and three global private-sector sponsors. Do not repeat examples you have already come across in this book.

SILVER

2. Choose one regional, one national, one international, and one global example from the list you created for Activity 1, and describe what the sponsorship deal consists of. Don't forget to consider what the individual, team, or event spends the money that they receive on and what the sponsor gets in return.

Public-sector sponsorship

The public sector can also be a valuable source of sponsorship, often in the form of a grant. A grant is the name given to money that the state gives to people or organizations for a specific purpose. Although much of this funding is aimed at elite performers, many local authorities will support promising athletes in their area to help with training, travel, competition, or coaching costs.

UK Sport

For elite performers, one of the most important funding programmes is administered by UK Sport. This is called the World Class Performance Programme, which receives funding from the National Lottery.

The fund gives financial support to Olympic and Paralympic athletes, helping them with training costs and sport science support for example. This funding is distributed by the receiving athlete's governing body.

In addition, athletes can apply for a personal award, which is paid directly to them. This fund can help towards living costs and other expenditure linked to their training. The level of financial support each athlete receives is mainly determined by the level at which an athlete is capable of performing.

TASS

Another funding initiative, this time aimed at age-group athletes who are not yet performing at senior level, is TASS, the Talented Athlete's Sponsorship Scheme. TASS supports approximately 600 athletes a year with up to £3500 support each.

One, now famous athlete, who benefited from TASS funding is Rebecca Adlington, who has gone on to Olympic and World Championship success!

BRONZE

3. Go to www.uksport.gov.uk/pages/how-the-funding-works and answer the following questions:

a) How are the athletes 'banded' on the scheme?

b) What are the maximum awards for the three different bands?

c) What is the average Athlete Personal Award for a Podium athlete?

d) What is the average Athlete Personal Award for a Development athlete?

4. Find out as much as you can about TASS and prepare a three-minute presentation on the scheme.

SILVER

5. Find out about an individual, team, or event that has secured private-sector sponsorship and summarize:

a) What sponsorship they receive.

b) Who provides it.

c) What it helps them do.

d) What they are required to do in return.

e) What it has helped them achieve.

Securing private-sector sponsorship

Securing a sponsorship deal is not easy. There are a number of hurdles that need to be overcome before, hopefully, a sponsorship deal that the individual, team, or event being sponsored and the sponsor both agree to.

IDENTIFY NEEDS

The individual, team, or event organizer must prepare a proposal for the prospective sponsor. Before writing the proposal, the needs of both sides must be considered:

- What does the athlete or event need? New kit, a training venue, or money to pay for transport to and from matches?
- What does the sponsor want? Positive exposure in the media or a venue for corporate hospitality?

PREPARE A STATEMENT OF BENEFITS FOR THE SPONSOR

The proposal should include an outline of the type of benefits the sponsor will get from the deal. These can include:

- The sponsor's name on kit.
- The sponsor's name on equipment.
- A mention in the media.
- An acknowledgment in interviews.
- Priority tickets for high-profile events.

APPROACH THE SPONSOR

The individual, team, or event organizer needs to approach the prospective sponsor with a proposal. This is often a written proposal initially, which may be followed up by a face-to-face meeting to further discuss the proposal and iron out any issues or concerns.

BRONZE

6. Imagine you are a talented sportsperson, hovering just under national level. You need access to better facilities, better coaches, and help from sports scientists to step up to the next level. You have secured a TASS grant but you still need approximately £3000 to help pay for everything and have decided to apply for private-sector sponsorship from a local business. Prepare your proposal.

Ethical issues arising from sponsorship

Ethics are principles of moral conduct. Sponsorship links sport and business, and can have a powerful impact on those that come into contact with it so it is important that ethics are considered at every stage while a sponsorship deal is negotiated and planned and especially during the roll-out. There are many ethical issues relating to sponsorship to consider.

Sports marketing

Sports marketing is big business – David Beckham is estimated to have earned over £26 million in 2012 from marketing deals alone, including deals with Adidas and Samsung – and companies need to make ethical decisions when they choose athletes to sponsor. They need to balance the needs of the athlete (to be free from too much pressure from the media so they can perform) with the needs of their business (to get their product noticed by as many people as possible in the most effective way).

Overall, most sponsors think very carefully about the image their athletes portray and by and large behave in an ethical and professional manner. However, some organizations that sponsor events are accused of unethical behaviour.

An example of this is the US-based company Proctor and Gamble (P&G), which still tests many of its cosmetics on animals. P&G were one of the main sponsors for the London 2012 Olympics and Paralympics held in the UK, where animal testing on cosmetics was banned in 1998. Using animals to test the safety of cosmetics is seen by many to be in direct opposition to the Olympic principle to 'uphold universal fundamental ethical principles and promote a peaceful society'.

Sponsors may also, perhaps unwittingly, make too many demands on an athlete. For example, in the build up to the London 2012 Olympics, the diver Tom Daley was accused of letting his media commitments get in the way of his training and preparation.

And who can forget the Wayne Rooney saga. Wayne and his wife, Coleen, were said to be experiencing marital problems after it was revealed that Wayne had used the services of prostitutes. Despite outrage from parents' groups, who said he was setting an appalling example to children, his four key sponsors said they would not drop him as it was a 'private matter'. Were Wayne's sponsors behaving ethically or were they happy to receive the extra publicity from the scandal?

Positive and negative influences of individuals

Companies want to sponsor sportspeople because they believe their brands will be made to look bigger, healthier, and more successful if they are linked with people who excel in sport. They use the sportspeople they sponsor in huge advertising campaigns which, in turn, makes the footballer or cyclist being sponsored a household name and a role model. Role models can have both positive and negative influences on those that follow their every move. Sportspeople who have received a lot of money from a company therefore have a responsibility to act ethically as their behaviour is carefully watched by a huge number of people.

The majority of athletes, such as Sir Christopher Hoy and Dame Kelly Holmes, take their responsibilities as role models very seriously. However, there are others who are less conscientious.

Scandal never seems to be far from FIFA president Sepp Blatter. Recent examples of gaffs made by Blatter include his comments about gay football fans in Qatar and his dismissal of racism issues in football despite the evidence. His behaviour and subsequent accusations of corruption within FIFA saw many of FIFA's sponsors voice their concerns. Coca Cola, which has a £304 million deal to 'partner' FIFA, described the corruption allegations as 'distressing and potentially damaging', although their protestations fell short of a withdrawal of support.

Ethics and the individual

Codes of conduct

Ultimately, companies want to sponsor sportspeople who have a clean-cut image and all major sponsorship deals now contain clauses in them to ensure that the athletes or organizations being sponsored are clear about the standard of behaviour expected of them.

Tiger Woods was heavily sponsored prior to the well-publicized problems in his private life, but many companies withdrew their sponsorship deals when Tiger began to attract attention for all the wrong reasons. The energy drink company Gatorade didn't want their product associated with a negative role model, and decided to drop him from their marketing campaigns.

The link between sponsorship and addiction

The alcohol, tobacco, and gambling industries used to be some of the bigger sponsors of sporting events, teams, and athletes. But then governments began to establish strict rules on which products and brands could be used in sponsorship campaigns and, over time, these rules have become stricter and stricter. This is because they felt it was their ethical duty to stop companies suggesting that their unhealthy and addictive products were healthy by promoting them alongside sport.

For example, the names of cigarette brands used to be emblazoned across Formula 1 Grand Prix cars and team garages, but tobacco advertising in the European Union was banned by the 2005 EU Tobacco Advertising Directive. Although tobacco advertising was banned on TV during the 1990s the Directive bans tobacco advertising in the print media, on radio, and over the internet. It also prohibits tobacco sponsorship of cross-border events or activities, although this is only at European level.

The influence of sponsors

Sponsors plough huge sums of money into sport and this gives them a lot of power, not only over the individual athletes they sponsor, but also on the governing bodies of sports, the timing and location of events, and even the rules and regulations of competition.

The days when most football games kicked off at 3pm on a Saturday are a thing of the past. SkySports pumps huge sums of money into the game and, because they wanted maximum exposure for their televised games, persuaded the Premier League to move games to Sundays, Mondays, and, sometimes, to Saturday lunchtimes. Even the Rugby 6 Nations now takes place on some Sundays and a game was even played on a Friday night in 2011, although the experiment was scrapped in 2012! The question is, how far is it ethical for companies to exert this much power over sport?

Ethics and companies

Regulating sponsorship and advertising

Governing bodies are very aware of the ethical grey areas when it comes to sponsorship and sport and they issue codes of practice to their members to ensure that ethical issues are covered in sponsorship deals. For example, the FA provides football clubs with a guide containing regulations about advertising on players' kit.

All advertisements, including those associated with sports goods and products, are governed by the Advertising Standards Authority (ASA). The ASA is a self-regulating organization, which means that it has been set up by the advertising industry to regulate the content of adverts, sales promotions, and direct marketing in the UK. The ASA only regulates the advertisements themselves and not the actual sponsorship deals. The ASA deals with complaints and can apply a range of sanctions on advertisers if needed. These include having future adverts vetted before they are run or removing trading privileges from companies that break its guidelines. In 2011, the ASA changed or banned over 4500 adverts. This included banning an advert for Cheltenham Ladies Day, by the bookmaker Paddy Power, after receiving complaints that the advert was degrading and hateful.

Does sponsorship by unethical companies tarnish the image of major sporting events?

Many multinational corporations make unethical decisions in their desire to make money, so should they be encouraged by promoters to sponsor major sporting events and advertise their brands? For example, Adidas is the only sportswear company that was allowed to produce clothing with the London 2012 logo on it and it will make vast sums of money from this relationship. Yet many of the workers who make the clothes are paid appallingly low wages and are abused and exploited.

The relationships between the sponsors and the organizers of the London 2012 Olympic and Paralympic Games were also perceived as unethical by some. London 2012 attracted high-profile sponsors, including Coca Cola, Visa, Adidas, and British Airways. Although their sponsorship money helped make the games a tremendous success, the number of hospitality tickets allocated to the major sponsors and their partners meant that many members of the public were unable to get tickets to watch their favourite events. The exclusive deals struck by the sponsors were also seen by many as damaging, especially to local communities. For example, while McDonald's was the only branded food provider allowed inside the stadia, local businesses nearby were faced with prosecution if they used the Olympic branding. Café Olympic in East London was even forced to change its name!

ASA ✓

157

The impact of sponsorship

Sponsorship deals have different impacts, sometimes positive and sometimes negative, on:
- The organization providing the sponsorship.
- The individual, team, or event receiving the sponsorship.
- The spectators.

BRONZE

1. The examples of the impacts of sponsorship on sponsors and the individuals, teams, and events sponsored provided are all positive. Can you identify any negative impacts and explain why they may occur?

2. The examples of the impacts of sponsorship on spectators provided are all negative. Can you identify any positive impacts and explain why they may occur?

GOLD

3. a) Choose an example of sponsorship of an individual, team, or event in sport and note down as many impacts, both positive and negative, this sponsorship has.

b) Working with a partner, compare and contrast your examples of the impacts of sponsorship on sport with their examples.

Hint: Remember to focus on the *impacts* the sponsorship has had and not on the sponsorship deal itself, although you may need to summarize the deal to set the scene for your partner.

Impacts on the sponsor

Sponsors may generate greater product recognition, which should lead to higher sales and an increase in profits.

Sponsors may be associated with success, raising their profile, and providing them with an opportunity to tap into the feel-good factor generated by that success.

Sponsors may be seen in a positive light by spectators, enhancing their reputation and increasing their exposure to their target markets.

Sponsors may get access to priority seats or be provided with other hospitality opportunities, which they can use to help them to secure deals with prospective customers or partners.

Impacts on the individual, team, or event being sponsored

An individual may get financial support to help pay training costs, employ sport science support, or fund warm-weather training opportunities, improving their chances of success.

A team may be able to sign a top star, which may increase their chances of success and attract more spectators, which may, in turn, attract bigger and better sponsorship deals.

A team or an event may be able to improve their facilities, making it more enjoyable for spectators to attend and hopefully increasing the crowd.

An event or competition may be able to attract more media coverage, which may lead to wider audiences and, ultimately, may lead to more people getting involved with the sport at grass-roots level. This helps sports survive in an increasingly competitive environment.

An event may be able to attract higher-profile competitors, and thereby attract bigger crowds and make a higher profit.

Impacts on the spectators

Top venues may be chosen to host an event, which may result in high travel and admission costs for spectators.

The timing of events may change to suit the demands of the media or the sponsor, which could inconvenience spectators.

Coverage of events may be limited to those media outlets that have bought the rights to them, limiting access for fans. For example, many boxing matches are now pay-per-view. This may mean that fewer new supporters become involved in a sport as exposure to the population in general is limited.

Unit 8 assignment, part two

Background

You are an active volunteer at your local club, which is looking into running a large-scale competition to boost income and raise awareness of the club in the region. A small working party, which you are part of, has been formed to look into the feasibility of putting on the competition. The next task for the working group is to find out about the role of sponsorship in sports promotion.

Grading criteria to be assessed
1B.4, 1B.5
2B.P4, 2B.P5
2B.M2, 2B.M3
2B.D1

Task

Prepare a presentation exploring the sponsorship in sports promotion, looking at the different sources of sponsorship and the ethical issues relating to sponsorship of sporting events. Your presentation should:

- Outline public, private, regional and national sources of sponsorship. (1B.4)
- Outline three different ethical issues which can arise from sponsorship of a given sports individual, team or event. (1B.5)

- Describe public, private, regional, national, international and global sources of sponsorship available, including procedures involved in securing sponsorship. (2B.P4)
- Describe the range of different ethical issues which can arise from sponsorship of a selected sports individual, team or event. (2B.P5)

- For two selected sports individuals, teams or events, summarise information on their sponsorship. (2B.M2)
- Explain ethical issues which can arise from sponsorship of a selected sports individual, team or event. (2B.M3)

- Compare and contrast the impact of sponsorship on two selected sports individuals, teams or events. (2B.D1)

Tackling the assignment

The list above makes it clear what you need to cover in your presentation but, as you progress onto the Merit and Distinction criteria, make sure you choose examples to explore that you are interested in *and* which provide you with enough information to cover the criteria in sufficient depth.

As with other assignments, you need to make sure that:
- Your **descriptions** are clear, detailed and concise.
- Your **summaries** are brief but include all the important points.

- Your **explanations** include reasons why something is an issue and include the word 'because'.
- Your work **comparing and contrasting** explores similarities and differences.

This is a great opportunity to focus on your favourite players and/or teams, so make the most of it!

Meeting the Level 2 Pass criteria

SPONSORSHIP
by Chun Lin

There are various possible sources of sponsorship:

1. PUBLIC-SECTOR SPONSORSHIP

Public-sector funding mostly comes in the form of financial support, such as Awards for All funding, which offers grant aid of between £300 and £10,000. It is available to voluntary and community groups, as well as others, for projects that are designed to improve communities and the lives of people who live within them. It's a Lottery-funded grant programme.

Players within clubs may also benefit from grant aid provided by the local authority, which allocates funds up to the value of £5000 to support and develop local sportspeople.

For age-group players who are performing at a high standard, there is always TASS (the Talented Athlete's Sponsorship Scheme), which helps fund such aspects as coaching fees, strength and conditioning work, and sport medicine support. This support can be worth up to £3500 a year. Players need to be competing at national or international level and be nominated by their national governing body in order to access this funding.

ETHICAL ISSUES

With any sponsorship deal clubs need to be aware of ethical issues. Some of the main ones are:
- Obtaining sponsorship from organizations that are linked to gambling, tobacco products, and alcohol.
- Making sure advertising standards are adhered to.
- Considering carefully the role of local sports stars to help promotion, especially if they have been involved in any activities that might be seen as negative.
- Making sure that any national governing body codes of practice are adhered to.

> Although this is only a snapshot of Chun's work it is clear that she has started to cover the key elements of public-sector sponsorship. If Chun replicates this standard for private, regional, national, international, and global sources of sponsorship, she will be awarded the 2B.P4 criteria.

> Chun has gone off the boil here. Although the points she raises are valid, she has only identified them and not described them. She needs to go into far more detail if she is going to meet the criteria for 2B.P5. For example, she needs to describe what the advertising standards are and give an example of where a sports star has attracted negative publicity to an organization or event.

Meeting the Level 2 Merit criteria

TIGER WOODS CASE STUDY
Rod Wilson

Tiger Woods is a great example of a sportsman who maximizes sponsorship opportunities, despite his fall from grace in 2009.

In 2009, Tiger was confirmed as the world's first athlete to make a million dollars. Although some of this income came from winning golf tournaments, Tiger has made a fortune from endorsement and sponsorship deals, such as his deal with TAG Heuer (watch makers) in 2005, when the world's first professional gold watch was launched.

In 2006, this was followed by a new six-year contract, which he signed with EA Sports (the company behind his video game series), and which was quickly followed in 2007 by a deal to become an ambassador for the Gillette Champions marketing campaign. The deal is believed to be worth between $10–20 million and also features Thierry Henry and Roger Federer.

In 2009, Tiger was involved in a minor car crash that triggered a series of events that meant he received a lot of bad publicity. As the story unfolded, many of Tiger's sponsors deserted him, including the communications company AT&T and the car maker General Motors, who announced that Tiger's free access to their vehicles was being removed.

The decisions to drop Tiger were made because the bad publicity surrounding him was seen as potentially damaging to the sponsors' reputations, especially as much of the bad press was linked to family disagreements and extra-marital affairs. Sponsors, especially in America, are very conscious of family values, so allegations of this nature were seen to be tarnishing their images if Tiger continued to be associated with their brands. In 2011, Tiger secured his first big sponsorship deal since his downfall, with Rolex, with the company obviously feeling that his reputation was back on track.

> It looks like Rod is a keen golfer, so choosing Tiger as an example is a good choice. He has effectively combined the criteria for 2B.M2 and 2B.M3 as he has started to summarize Tiger's sponsorship deals and has explained an ethical issue that arose as a result of his behaviour. Good stuff Rod!

> To fully achieve the criteria for 2B.M2 Rod now needs to summarize the information on the sponsorship of another individual, event or team. And, to fully meet the criteria for 2B.M3 he needs to explain a range of other ethical issues.

Meeting the Level 2 Distinction criteria

Comparing and contrasting the impact of sponsorship — Felicity McMahan

| SEMI-PROFESSIONAL FOOTBALL CLUB | | PREMIER LEAGUE FOOTBALL CLUB | |
Similarities	Differences	Similarities	Differences
Shirt sponsorship deal	Deal with local law firm worth approximately £120,000 per year	Shirt sponsorship deal	Deal with a global brand worth approximately £400 million over five years
Match-day hospitality package	Cost £50 per person: 200 places available	Match-day hospitality package	Considerably more expensive at approximately £125 per person: 8000 spaces available
	Individual players are sponsored		Individual players are not sponsored
Community project sponsors	No charity support	Community project sponsors	Manchester City Football Club choose charities to support

As the table shows there are many similarities between both clubs, although there are differences as well.

There will also be similarities and differences between the impacts of the sponsorship of the two clubs, with the impacts mainly based on the level of income each club receives. The impact of large and lucrative sponsorship deals for the Premier League club will mean that they will be able to attract top-level players, which should help them win trophies. This will, in turn, help them attract more sponsors and better players.

The semi-professional club, on the other hand, will attract far less sponsorship. As the example shows, this club has a local sponsor and the sums are far less than those received by the Premier League club from sponsorship, although £120,000 a year will help considerably when it comes to paying the players. The players are also sponsored as well, which will bring much needed income into the club and may help the players with travel costs as many of them will be combining playing with other jobs.

Again, both clubs have hospitality facilities but the cost and number of places available varies drastically and the impacts will, again, vary according to the income generated. If the semi-professional club sold all their places they would generate £10,000 per match while the Premier League club would generate £1 million per match!

The differences in income generation will impact on many things, including expectation levels among fans and sponsors. Sponsors paying high amounts will expect the club to be successful and therefore on television regularly, while the semi-professional club will not have this pressure. Also, success will mean the club plays more matches, which will impact on supporters as they will have to pay more to watch their club and will probably have to pay far higher admission prices.

Felicity has made a really good start here, outlining the similarities and differences in a table that she can refer to. She clearly understands the impacts these similarities and differences have, although she still needs to comment further on such things as increased media coverage and match schedule changes in order to meet the criteria for 2B.D1. It is a promising start though.

Planning the promotion of a sports event

Planning a sports event is complex and time consuming, even without considering the way the event is to be promoted. But good event organizers know that you forget promotion at your peril. Without a strong plan for promotion even a well-organized event is likely to fail, because no one will know about it.

There are a number of things that need to be taken into account to ensure a sports event is promoted effectively.

The aims and objectives of the event

Once you have clearly established the aims and objectives of the event you will be able to ask yourself key questions that will ensure the promotion is appropriate and effective, such as:

- Who are the target audience?
- Which types of sponsor may be interested in supporting the event?

Remember:

An aim is something that you intend to achieve by the end of a promotional campaign, such as 'To raise awareness of the new facilities at an existing sports centre'. An objective is a small step that helps you achieve the aim, for example 'To carry out a radio advertising campaign to showcase the new facilities and the opportunities they provide'.

For example, two local fun runs in adjacent towns could have very different aims. The aim of one could be to get families and older adults to increase their activity levels while the aim of the other could be to get young people and local celebrities raising funds for a local charity. And an objective for the fun run that aims to increase activity levels could be to promote the event in local workplaces.

Leaflets

Posters

Adverts on local radio

Adverts in local newspapers

Advert in a school, club, or local authority newsletter

The choice of media

Once you know what you want to promote and who you want to promote it to, it is time to decide how to promote it. You need to consider these questions:

- What forms of media does your target audience access most frequently?
- What skills and experience do you have to draw on and what will you need to pay a professional to do?
- How much money do you have to spend on promotion and what can you buy for that money?
- What can you reasonably achieve in the time available?

Press releases

Using a mailing list to send out emails, text messages, or leaflets

Social media, such as Facebook or Twitter

ADVERT ON A SCHOOL, CLUB, LOCAL AUTHORITY, OR BUSINESS WEBSITE

Promotional film posted on the internet or burned onto DVD

Fact:

A press release is a statement about something that could be viewed as newsworthy. It is written by the people or organizations that wish to promote an event and it is sent to the media in the hope that journalists will write or broadcast a story about the event and draw attention to it. A press release should contain all the facts a journalist might need to prepare a story and provide them with something exciting to encourage them to write a story.

Sponsorship

Securing sponsorship is never easy, but it is well worth the effort.

Firstly, you will need to identify a potential sponsor. Your local chamber of commerce may have a list of businesses willing to sponsor events, you may have connections with a local business, or you may know of a business that would benefit from the advertising sponsoring your event could provide.

Once you have chosen a potential sponsor, you need to:

- Identify the sponsor's needs.
- Prepare a statement of benefits for the sponsor.
- Approach the sponsor.

More information on securing sponsorship can be found on page 155.

 Remember:

The Data Protection Act controls how personal information is used by organizations to ensure that it is kept confidential, safe, and only used for the purpose for which it was intended. For example, if an athletic club collects the names and email addresses of members of the public who attend an open evening they must ensure that the list is kept secure, is only accessible by nominated members of the club, and the information is only used for the purpose for which it was given. The club cannot pass the information on to another club or to a local business for example, as this would be a breach of data protection, which is a serious offence.

Timeline

Producing a timeline of key actions that need to be completed will help keep the campaign on track and ensure that all promotional opportunities are maximized. The promotional campaign should be coordinated by one individual, who will liaise with their team and the team responsible for planning and organizing the whole event.

Evaluation questionnaire

All events should include an element of evaluation – whether this is conducted via interviews, comment cards, surveys, or questionnaires – and there should be the opportunity to gather feedback from participants on the promotion of the event as part of this process.
Questions can focus on how well the event itself was promoted:

1. Where did you hear about the event?
2. How could the event have been promoted more successfully?

Questions can also focus on gathering information that will help you promote a similar, but better, event next time:

3. What local newspapers and websites do you access?

Or you might take the opportunity to ask a question that will help you fulfil your obligations to your sponsor:

4. Would you like to receive promotional literature from our main sponsor?

You should also ask other members of the events team what they thought of the way in which the event was promoted:

5. Do you think the event was promoted effectively? If not, what could be done to make it more effective in the future?

'Reviewing a sports event' on pages 234–236 contains more information on how to gather feedback on a sports event.

BRONZE

1. Write a short press release, of no more than 150 words, for a half-term activity week for children from disadvantaged backgrounds. The scheme is funded by a local charity and sponsored by a baker's shop in the town. It aims to give the children a fun week, introducing them to new sports and developing their understanding of healthy eating. The scheme will take place on your school site and is free. A local market trader is also donating free fruit each day.

SILVER

2. You are still working on the half-term activity week you wrote the press release for in Activity 1, but step backwards a few weeks and imagine you haven't yet persuaded the baker's shop in town to sponsor the event. Write to the owner of the shop explaining what you would like in terms of sponsorship and what you will be able to do in return for their support.

Reviewing a promotional plan

It is always good practice to review all aspects of an event, including the effectiveness of the promotional plan. A review should focus on three areas: strengths, areas for improvement, and recommendations for the future.

What about the promotion went well?

Were the aims and objectives met? Did the promotion come in on budget? How effective was the planning and organization?

Why did these things go well?

What evidence do you have from the feedback provided that these things went well?

What about the event didn't go so well?

Are there examples of the outcomes of the promotion not meeting the planned aims and objectives? Were there problems with the planning that caused issues with the promotion itself?

Why didn't these things go well?

What evidence do you have from the feedback provided that these things didn't go well?

Remember:

Reviewing your event doesn't have to be a negative experience. There is every chance that you will have exceeded expectations.

Recommendations

What recommendations can you make for future promotions?

Building on your successes and analysing your weaknesses, can you suggest alternative ways in which the promotion for the event could have been carried out? What have you learned that will influence the way you promote an event in future?

Can you justify your recommendations?

Can you provide at least one reason why each of your recommendations will improve things?

BRONZE/SILVER/GOLD

1. Three events have taken place and, after each event, an area for improvement was identified.

a) Give one or more recommendations for improvements that could be made next time the event is held.

b) Explain your recommendation(s).

c) Justify your recommendation(s).

Area for improvement	Recommendation(s) for improvement	Explanation	Justification
The event did not attract a sponsor and therefore ran at a loss of £1000.			
The event only attracted 50 participants rather than the 130 you were hoping for.			
You don't have any feedback from participants.			

Unit 8 assignment, part three

Background

You are an active volunteer at your local club, which is looking into running a large-scale competition to boost income and raise awareness of the club in the region. A small working party, which you are part of, has been formed to look into the feasibility of putting on the competition. The work you have done so far has been well received by the club's committee and they have decided to put on the event. You have been asked to plan the promotional campaign.

Task

Write a plan for a promotional campaign for a sports event. You will need to decide on the aims and objectives of the event, choose the media you will use to advertise the event, and consider gaining a sponsor. You should also compile a timeline to help you implement the plans successfully and consider how you will gather feedback on how the promotional campaign went after the event. Finally, you will need to review the promotional campaign.

Grading criteria to be assessed
1C.6
2C.P6
2C.M4
2C.D2

- Create, with guidance, a plan to promote a given sports event or scenario. (1C.6)

- Independently create a plan to promote a selected sports event or scenario, describing strengths and areas for improvement. (2C.P6)

- Explain strengths of the plan and areas for improvement, providing recommendations for future promotion. (2C.M4)

- Justify recommendations for future promotion of a selected sports event or scenario. (2C.D2)

Tackling the assignment

When writing your plan, remember that you need to work independently because if you receive help from your teacher you will only be able to achieve a Level 1.

You should, by now, be very clear what is required when you are asked to 'describe' or 'explain' something, but you may

not have had to 'justify' anything before. When you **justify** something, you need to support your recommendations with well thought through reasons why following them will improve things.

PROMOTION PLAN

Produced by Dorothy Westcott

Our event

A family hockey activity day

Aims of the event

There are various aims of the event. These are:
- To recruit new members for the junior teams.
- To recruit new members for the senior teams.
- To recruit new volunteers to help with coaching and administration duties.
- To provide a fun and safe environment.
- To generate funds for the hockey club, in particular to help fund the under-17 squad tour to Holland.

Media and promotion

The event is going to be advertised via:
- Posters in local sports centres, pubs, shops, and community centres.
- Information is going to be posted on the club's website.

Press release

If we send the local newspaper a press release, they have agreed to write a story about the event one week before. It will be accompanied by a photograph of our junior international (Jodie Jones), who has just been picked to captain the England team in the next international match versus Germany.

The text of the press release is as follows:
Little Frecklington Hockey Club is running a family activity day on Saturday 27th June 2012 at their ground in Station Road. The event is being sponsored by JCM Sportswear and the club has a fantastic range of activities planned for the day.

The day starts at 10am, with a display of hockey skills by the under-17 squad. The display will be led by the new England captain Jodie Jones, who is the first player from Little Frecklington to have this honour.

The club welcomes all ages and abilities and hopes they will not only recruit new members but will also help their fund-raising drive to support the under-17s, forthcoming tour of Holland. The tour will help the team's development and should ensure we produce future regional and national players.

Further details can be obtained by calling the club event coordinator on 07765 674036
or by visiting the club's website: www.LFHockeyClub.co.uk.

The plan Dorothy has prepared so far is detailed, but she has a lot more work to do before she meets the criteria for 2C.P6.

I would like to know more about the sponsorship deal she has secured with JCM Sportswear. What benefits will the sponsor be getting in return for their sponsorship? How much money will the club receive from JCM Sportswear and how are they spending the money? What did Dorothy do to secure the sponsorship? I also want to see her timeline and her plans for gathering feedback on her promotion. Finally, Dorothy has not yet described any strengths or areas for improvement.

Once all this is in place, and if Dorothy's teacher can confirm that she has produced her plan independently, she will meet the criteria for 2C.P6.

Meeting the Level 2 Merit and Distinction criteria

JUNIOR BADMINTON TOURNAMENT STRENGTHS AND AREAS FOR IMPROVEMENT BY GLEN ROE

FEATURE OF PLAN	STRENGTH OR AREA FOR IMPROVEMENT	REASONS WHY	RECOMMENDATION FOR FUTURE PROMOTIONAL CAMPAIGNS	JUSTIFICATION
Two sponsors secured for the event	A definite strength	This is a strength because to secure one sponsor would be good, but to get two is even better. This means that the event will definitely break even because the sponsorship deals will pay for the hire of the sports hall and the purchase of the trophies.	This can't really be improved on, although it will be important to check after the event that the sponsors are happy with what they got in return. Both have their names included in the tournament programme: one sponsor will have its name on the trophies and the other will be presenting the awards. Both will feature in the tournament write up on the club website, so I think they will both be happy.	
The advertising timeline	Area for improvement	This is a real area for improvement because the promotional campaign doesn't really have a timeline. Because the event is an annual one, the club coach is happy to follow the previous year's format, even though this year is very different because we have: • sponsors • media coverage • an advertising plan. With this change in format it's important to have a timeline to follow so that deadlines are met and problems identified with enough notice so they can be addressed.	I recommend we: 1. Spend time at the start of the promotional campaign planning the timeline and checking it out with someone who has a background in promotion. 2. Monitor it every week to make sure everything is on track. 3. Amend the timeline if needed, adapting it to meet any changes in circumstances.	These recommendations are needed because the promotional plan needs more structure. We have already missed the deadline to get a press release published and the press have also indicated that they won't have enough staff to cover the event on the day. This will limit the exposure of the event and may disappoint both sponsors, who think the press will be covering it. It is also important because this is the first promotional plan I have produced and a timeline would give me more focus and direction.

Glen has used a very simple format to present his work and it is very good. Although we can only see a sample of his work it is clear that he understands the level of detail required to meet 2C.M4 and 2C.D2, and it is good to see that he has gone into depth when making recommendations. His justifications also have a clear rationale. If Glen continues in this way, the 2C.M4 and 2C.D2 criteria are well within his capabilities.

Unit 9: Lifestyle and Well-being

Physical activity and well-being

Most people are aware of the need to lead a healthy lifestyle, which includes eating the right foods and taking regular exercise, but it is often difficult to know exactly what a healthy lifestyle looks like in practice. How much exercise do we need to take part in to be healthy? To help people make the right choices, the Department of Health, the government department responsible for England's health and well-being, produces recommended guidelines outlining the amount of physical activity adults and children should take part in for a healthy lifestyle.

The Department of Health's recommended guidelines for physical activity say that:

Adults aged 19–64 should try and be active daily, doing:

- At least two-and-a-half hours of moderate-intensity aerobic activity every week, such as cycling or fast walking OR one hour 15 minutes of vigorous aerobic activity, such as running or a game of tennis every week OR a combination of moderate and vigorous aerobic activity, such as two 30-minute runs plus 30 minutes of fast walking.
- Muscle strengthening activities on two or more days, working all the major muscle groups.

These guidelines are also applicable to older adults, aged 65 or over, who are generally fit and have no health conditions that limit their mobility.

Children and young people aged 5–18 need to do:

- At least one hour of physical activity every day, consisting of a mixture of moderate-intensity aerobic activity, such as fast walking, and vigorous aerobic activity, such as running.
- On three days a week, undertake muscle- and bone-strengthening activities.

Ways to increase physical activity in daily life

There are some very obvious ways in which a person can increase their level of physical activity. They can go for a bike ride, jog around the local park, or go for a swim at the local swimming pool. But are there some less obvious ways?

Perhaps surprisingly, everyday chores, such as vacuuming the house, can be classed as physical activity, especially if they are done a bit more quickly than normal. Other, less conventional, ways to increase physical activity levels include:

Swimming is a great way to contribute to your weekly activity target.

These young people are enjoying a serious workout as part of their one-hour-a-day target.

Digging holes, raking leaves, and cutting the grass are all great ways to increase physical activity levels, especially if traditional sports are not for you.

BRONZE

1. Find out what the recommended physical activity levels are for children under five, including toddlers and babies.

2. Compile a list of activities that are considered to be:

a) Moderately aerobic.

b) Vigorously aerobic.

c) Muscle strengthening.

d) Bone strengthening.

- Spending time in the garden every week, pulling weeds, cutting the grass, sweeping up the leaves, and tidying the flower beds can get the heart pumping faster than normal.
- Walking to the shops and then walking back is far better than using the car or taking the bus. If the shops are too far away to make this feasible, you could take the bus and get off a stop earlier than usual.
- Using the stairs, at the office or in a large department store, rather than a lift or escalator, is a great way to raise your heartbeat and get the blood pumping around your body.

Integrating physical activity into everyday life is often easier said than done, especially in today's world where people are often busy at work or school or helping with family chores. Therefore, everyone needs to give careful thought as to how and when they will exercise.

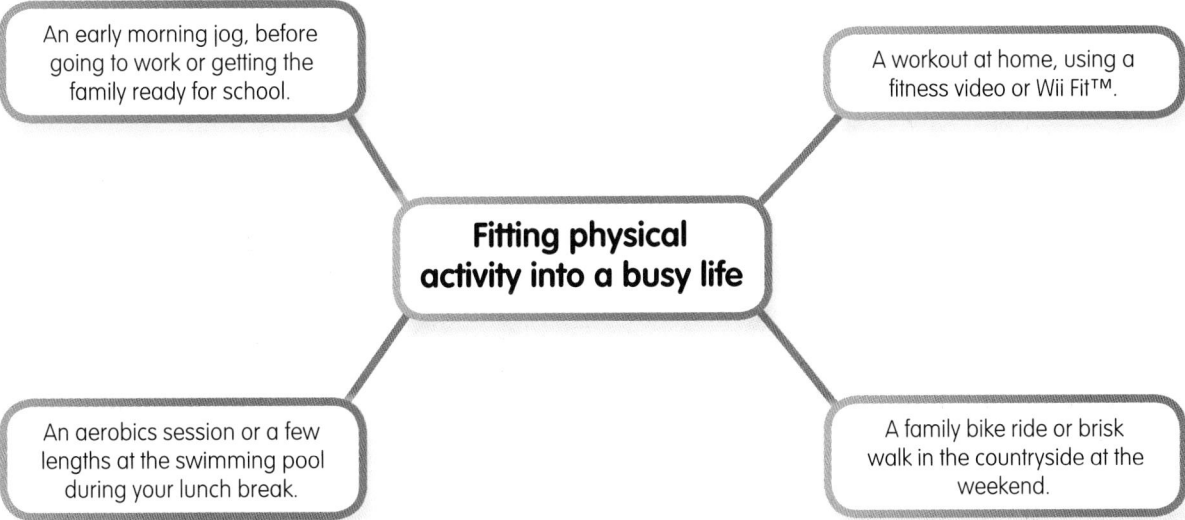

An early morning jog, before going to work or getting the family ready for school.

A workout at home, using a fitness video or Wii Fit™.

Fitting physical activity into a busy life

An aerobics session or a few lengths at the swimming pool during your lunch break.

A family bike ride or brisk walk in the countryside at the weekend.

BRONZE

3. Read Suzie's story. What recommendations can you give to Suzie to help her increase the level of physical activity in her life, bearing in mind the government's physical activity guidelines for an adult?

Suzie is a working mum with two children aged seven and nine, whose husband works away all week. Her daily routine is to get her children ready for school, drive them to school, go to work as an office manager, do the daily shop, pick the children up from school, cook them tea, and then relax in front of the television, as well as help with their homework if necessary.

On Saturdays, Suzie and her husband take the children to a dance class and on Sundays spend the day doing household chores that have been neglected during the week.

Although her days are very hectic Suzie feels as though she is not doing enough exercise, especially as she was a keen swimmer when she was younger. She struggles to do any exercise in the evenings, although her parents have offered to look after the children once a week if that would help.

SILVER

4. Explain each of the recommendations you made to Suzie in Activity 3, stating clearly why your suggestions will help her increase her level of physical activity.

GOLD

5. If Suzie challenged some of your recommendations could you justify them? Note down how you would convince her that your suggestions will increase her physical activity levels and will fit in with her busy life.

Unit 9 assignment, part one

Background

You have recently been appointed as a trainee health promotion officer with a local authority. The health promotion team are busy developing lots of schemes and have decided to produce a new magazine covering a range of lifestyle and well-being issues, which will be available for free at local leisure centres.

<table>
<tr><td colspan="1">Grading criteria
to be assessed</td></tr>
<tr><td>1A.1, 1A.2
2A.P1, 2A.P2
2A.M1
2A.D1</td></tr>
</table>

Task

Write a magazine article for the first edition about recommended levels of physical activity and the ways in which people can increase the amount of physical activity they undertake. Your article should:

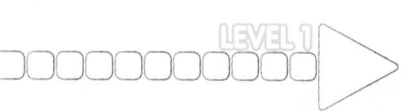 **LEVEL 1**

- Describe how much physical activity adults and children and young people should do to benefit their health. (1A.1)
- Summarise three ways in which a selected individual could increase their level of physical activity. (1A.2)

 **LEVEL 2 PASS**

- Assess whether three selected individuals are undertaking sufficient physical activity to benefit their health. (2A.P1)
- Make recommendations for how three selected individuals could increase their physical activity levels. (2A.P2)

 **LEVEL 2 MERIT**

- Explain recommendations for how three selected individuals could increase their physical activity levels. (2A.M1)

 **LEVEL 2 DISTINCTION**

- Justify recommendations for how three selected individuals could increase their physical activity levels. (2A.D1)

Tackling the assignment

You need to present your article in such a way that it appeals to a wide audience, including young people and adults. Using graphics or presenting the information pictorially may help you to do this.

You could base your assessments and recommendations on real people that you know, including people in your class, friends and family, or you could make up some case studies to get your message across. Remember, if you are going to use real people, check that they are happy to be included in your article first.

Whatever methods you decide to use, ensure that your descriptions are clear and that your assessment includes a full review of each person's current level of activity. Then, when you make your recommendations, include explanations to support the recommendations you are making, and justify them by showing clearly why the changes you are recommending need to be made, referring back to the health benefits wherever possible.

Meeting the Level 2 Pass criteria

Be Healthy
by being active

Matty Shackell

Are you getting enough exercise? Do you actually know what sort of physical activity you should be doing... and for how long?

If the answer is no, read on!

If the answer is yes, still read on – just to check you've got it right!

The government, through the Department of Health, produces guidelines that outline how long different age groups should be exercising for and what type of activities they should do.

If, for example, you are an adult aged between 19 and 64 you should be doing at least two and a half hours of moderate intensity aerobic activity every week and muscle-strengthening activities on two or more days, working on all the major muscle groups, such as the legs, back, chest, etc.

Moderate activity could include activities such as cycling, fast walking, aqua aerobics, and hiking. The sorts of activities you can do to strengthen muscles include lifting weights or heavy gardening tasks, such as digging and shovelling.

You can also

> This is a good start by Matty. As long as he adds to the answer by indicating how much time Wilf needs to exercise for and includes a similar level of detail about the guidelines for young people, he will achieve 2A.P1 and 2A.P2.

To help show how these guidelines can be applied, let's have a look at some of the health promotion team's current activity levels...

Team-mate 1:

Wilf the
van driver

Wilf has been with the team for years. He drives the van, our promotional vehicle that tours the city, and is the office comedian. He is 42 and a big lover of the great outdoors, spending most weekends hiking in the Derbyshire countryside. He reckons he spends at least four hours every Sunday walking up hills and down dales. Apart from that though, Wilf does little else. He used to have an allotment but gave it up some years ago. He lives in a flat in the city so doesn't have a garden and his walk to work only takes three minutes!

Our assessment of Wilf

We are all a bit disappointed with Wilf, as he should be doing far more physical activity. It's good that he hikes most Sundays, especially as he walks for about four hours and this is likely to be at moderate intensity. However, he hasn't done any muscle strengthening work since he gave up his allotment, and this is something that Wilf needs to address.

Wilf could go to the gym during his lunch break or help out some of his mates down at the allotment with the digging at least twice a week. He could also do some push-ups in the office, when nobody is watching!

> This is a great way for Matty to present his work and his assessment of whether Wilf is taking sufficient physical activity is spot on. He has made some sound recommendations as well, so if this level of detail is replicated for two other people he should be awarded the 2A.P1 and 2A.P2 criteria.

Meeting the Level 2 Merit and Distinction criteria

Summary of recommendation for the team's administrator, Mandy (aged 31)

Lucy Spear

- Mandy does little moderate or vigorous activity, so we are recommending that she either does two-and-a-half hours of moderate activity per week, such as aqua aerobics or brisk walking, or one hour 15 minutes of vigorous activity, such as jogging or fast swimming, per week.
- Mandy doesn't do any muscle strengthening activity at the moment, so we are recommending that she joins the other girls in the team in the gym at least twice a week and attends one of the yoga sessions run by our yoga instructor on Wednesday lunchtimes.

> **I have produced a table for Mandy to refer to, just in case she forgets why we are suggesting what we are suggesting!**

RECOMMENDATION	EXPLANATION	JUSTIFICATION
Attend aqua aerobics session every Thursday evening: 7 pm – 8 pm.	This has been recommended because the activity is of moderate intensity and should be sufficient to raise Mandy's heart rate and get her into a bit of a sweat.	I have made this recommendation for three reasons: 1 It counts towards Mandy's two-and-a-half hours of moderate intensity aerobic activity per week. 2 Mandy likes swimming, therefore aqua aerobics seems ideal as it combines the moves of land-based aerobics, which are often easier in the water, with water-specific movements. 3 Mandy lives near the pool, so she can walk there and back, adding more physical activity to her week.
Join our walking group twice a week (Mondays and Fridays) in the local park. Each session lasts approximately 45 minutes.	Again, this activity is of moderate intensity so will have a similar effect to the aqua aerobics. The two sessions per week will give Mandy a total of two and a half hours of moderate intensity aerobic type activity per week. This is the recommended minimum total.	I have also made this recommendation for three reasons: 1 Mandy will need no equipment to take part. 2 Two other members of the team take part, so Mandy will be able to join in with friends. 3 Mandy enjoys walking and used to walk her children to school before she returned to work. As the walks are conducted at a brisk pace they are ideal, moderate intensity exercise and should be free from risk with little chance of her injuring herself.
Join the gym. I have prepared a weight training programme for Mandy that covers her major muscle groups and recommends that she trains at least twice a week.	Mandy does no muscle strengthening activity so this recommendation will address this. She doesn't do any vigorous aerobic activities either, such as a contact sport, so a full muscle group weight training programme is just what Mandy needs.	There are two reasons why I have suggested weight training for Mandy. They are: 1 She does no muscle strengthening work, so a full weights programme is a good way to ensure all her major muscle groups are used. 2 Mandy doesn't like any of the alternatives I suggested and, as her husband is a member of the gym, travelling to and from it will be easy. He can also help supervise Mandy during the early part of her programme and encourage her to attend.

> Lucy has presented her work clearly and concisely. She has also applied the assessment verbs, 'explain' and 'justify', well. If she repeats this level of detail for two other individuals, Lucy will meet the criteria for 2A.M1 and 2A.D1.

Healthy eating

One of the most important aspects of a healthy lifestyle is eating the right sorts of food. And if the right sorts of food are cooked in a healthy way and eaten in the right quantities then your healthy diet can significantly contribute to your health and well-being. But what makes a healthy diet?

Nutrients

The human body needs a wide range of nutrients to perform, live, grow, and thrive, and a healthy diet contains a balance of the following six essential nutrients.

Carbohydrates

There are two main types of carbohydrate: simple carbohydrates and complex carbohydrates.

Simple carbohydrates or simple sugars are found in foodstuffs such as refined sugar, sweets, and biscuits, although they can also be found in more nutritious foods, such as fruit and milk. It is more beneficial to get simple carbohydrates from nutritious sources, because foods like milk and fruit also contain vitamins, minerals, and fibre, which are all vital to a healthy diet.

Simple carbohydrates.

Complex carbohydrates or starches can be found in bread, pasta, and rice and are more beneficial to the body than simple carbohydrates. As with simple sugars, some foods containing complex carbohydrates are healthier than others. Refined grains, such as white flour and white rice, are processed, which removes some of the nutrients and fibre. Fibre aids digestion and also makes you feel full for longer so that you are less likely to want more food.

Both simple and complex carbohydrates should be eaten in moderation as part of a healthy, balanced diet. Carbohydrates provide the body with the energy you require to carry out daily activities and exercise.

Complex carbohydrates.

Fats

There are two main types of fat:

Cakes contain saturated fats.

- **Saturated fats**, which are normally solid at room temperature, should be eaten in moderation as large amounts can increase the level of cholesterol in the blood and increase the risk of heart disease. Saturated fats are found in foodstuffs such as butter, cheese, and fatty meats.
- **Unsaturated fats**, which are normally liquid at room temperature, are found in olive oil and oily fish, such as salmon and sardines. Unsaturated fats are considered much healthier than saturated fats.

Avocados contain unsaturated fats.

Fat performs various important roles in the body, including:
- Protecting internal organs.
- Providing an additional source of energy.
- Helping to transport fat-soluble vitamins, such as vitamins A, D, E, and K, around the body.

Water

Water is a vital part of any diet and performs many roles, such as transporting nutrients around the body, removing waste products, lubricating joints, and regulating body temperature through sweating. In fact, water makes up approximately two-thirds of the human body!

Water is an essential part of a healthy diet.

Protein

Protein is found in foods such as chicken, fish, eggs, and grains. It cannot be stored in the body, so you need to eat protein daily. It plays an important role in helping the body grow and in maintaining and repairing body tissue.

Eggs are a good source of protein.

Spinach is a good source of vitamins and minerals. It contains beta-carotene, folic acid, potassium, iron, vitamin B6, vitamin C, calcium, and magnesium.

Vitamins

Vitamins are an essential part of a balanced diet. They perform many roles, including:

- Helping keep skin, hair, bones, teeth, and blood cells in good condition.
- Helping the body to process carbohydrates and fat into energy.
- Helping tissue and bone form in the body.

Vitamins can be found in a variety of foods. A balanced diet of breads, cereals, fruits, vegetables, red meat, fish, poultry, dairy products, legumes, seeds, and nuts will ensure that you get a satisfactory amount of the vitamins your body needs.

Minerals

Minerals, such as calcium, iron, and sodium provide a range of benefits for the body. For example:

- Calcium helps develop strong bones and teeth. Milk and oily fish are great sources of calcium.
- Iron helps the brain and nervous system function effectively and helps to produce haemoglobin, a blood product that helps fight infection. Iron can be found in red meat, grains, and eggs.
- Sodium helps many cell processes to be performed, but too much sodium can contribute to high blood pressure and heart disease. Sodium can be found in many processed foods and salt.

The nutrients that the body needs are classified as macro nutrients or micro nutrients. Macro nutrients – carbohydrates, fats, proteins, and water – are needed in large quantities. Micro nutrients, such as vitamins and minerals, are needed in smaller quantities.

The following quantities of nutrients are recommended for a healthy diet:

BRONZE

1. Copy and complete the table below, listing as many foods as you can think of for each component of a healthy diet.

Component	Foods
Carbohydrate	
Fat	
Protein	
Water	
Vitamins	
Minerals	

2. Dehydration is a potential risk for athletes, particularly those taking part in aerobic activities in warm weather. Find out how much water an adult should consume in one day and how much water a child should consume in one day.

50–60% carbohydrates

1.5–3 litres of water per day

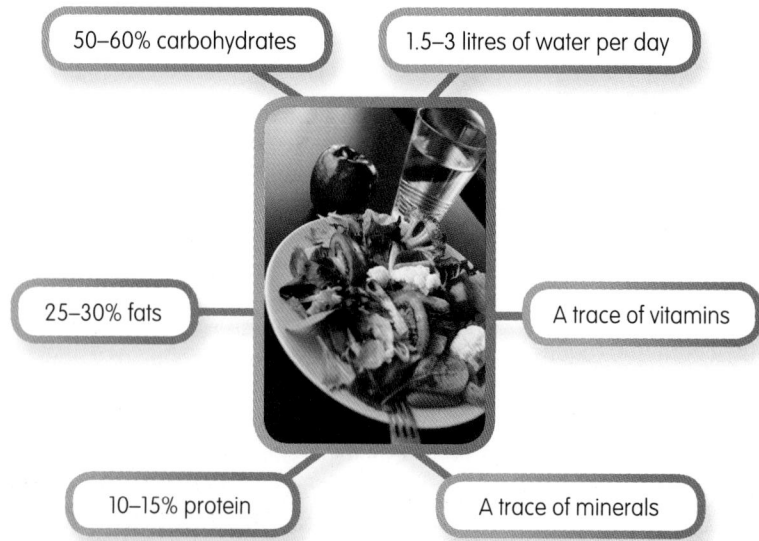

25–30% fats

A trace of vitamins

10–15% protein

A trace of minerals

The eatwell plate

To help people develop healthy eating habits, the government, through the Food Standards Agency, has developed the 'eatwell plate', which informs people about how much of each type of food they should be eating.

The eatwell plate applies to most people, regardless of their weight or ethnic origin, but it does not apply to children under two years of age because they have different nutritional needs. After the age of two, however, children should be encouraged to eat the same type of foods identified in the eatwell plate and in the same proportions.

An excellent source of vitamins, minerals, fibre, and carbohydrates.

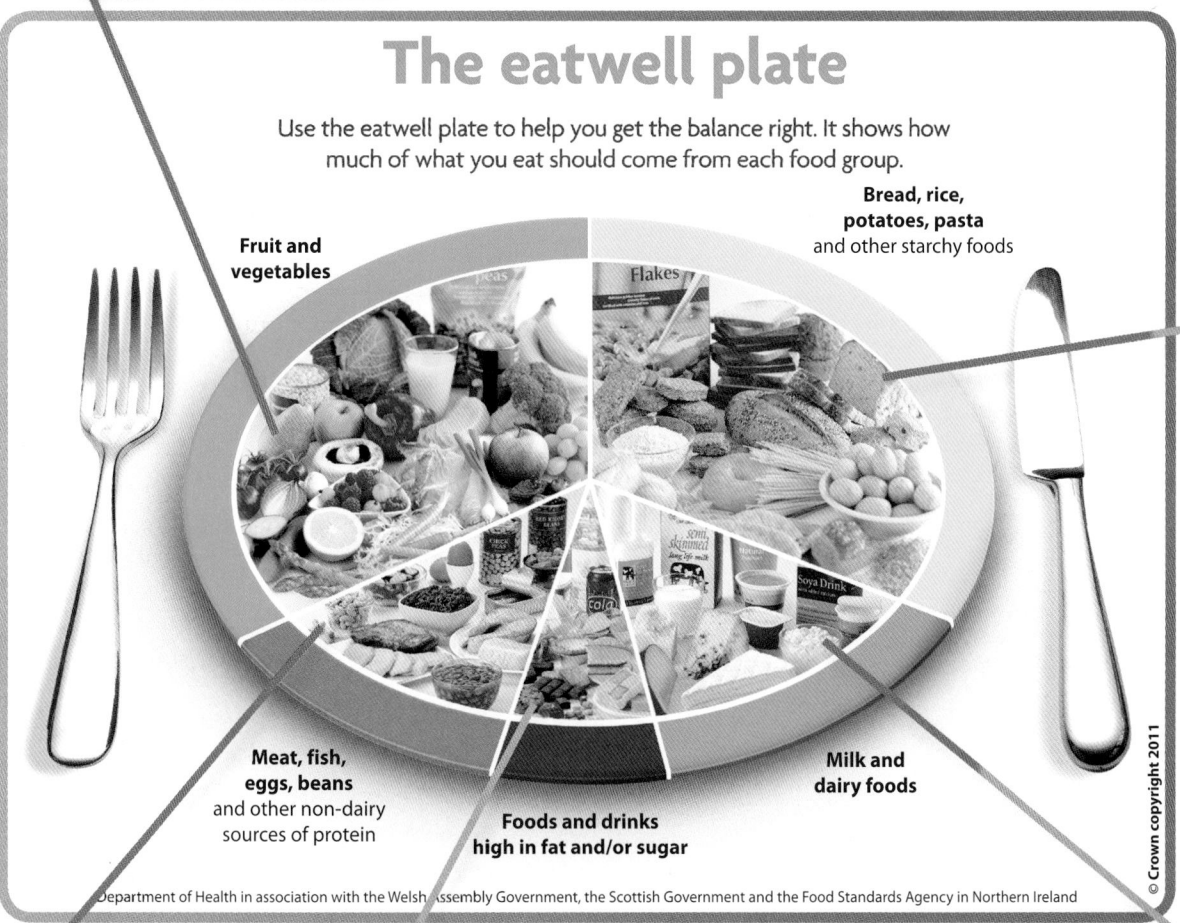

The eatwell plate

Use the eatwell plate to help you get the balance right. It shows how much of what you eat should come from each food group.

Fruit and vegetables

Bread, rice, potatoes, pasta and other starchy foods

All excellent sources of carbohydrates and minerals.

Meat, fish, eggs, beans and other non-dairy sources of protein

Foods and drinks high in fat and/or sugar

Milk and dairy foods

© Crown copyright 2011

Department of Health in association with the Welsh Assembly Government, the Scottish Government and the Food Standards Agency in Northern Ireland

Great sources of protein.

A small amount of food high in fat and sugar provides the fat and sugar the body needs, but it is vital not to each too much.

Provide the body with fat, protein, and vitamins.

BRONZE

3. Five meals are described below. For each meal:

- Draw a plate containing the meal, broken into its consistent food groups.
- Compare the plate you have drawn with the eatwell plate. Is the meal healthy or unhealthy?

a) Pepperoni pizza, chips, and a Fanta Orange drink.

b) Spaghetti bolognaise and a glass of milk.

c) Chicken salad and blackberry tart, with a glass of water.

d) Baked potato with cheese, beans, and salad, with a glass of fruit juice.

e) Baked cod, baked potato, peas, and broccoli, with a glass of water.

SILVER

4. Next to each plate you drew for Activity 3, explain how you would make the meal healthier.

Eating a healthy balanced diet

A healthy, balanced diet is important for everyone. It gives us the nutrients and energy required to complete everyday tasks as well as enjoy an active and varied social life. It helps us fight illness when it occurs and also helps us maintain mobility and independence in later life.

A healthy, balanced diet is especially important for sports performers, ensuring they can train and compete to their maximum and helping them to recover from exertion and rehabilitate after injury, as well as helping to prevent illness from occurring.

A central part of a healthy diet is ensuring that the energy we consume, through the food we eat, matches the energy we use.

Healthy eating habits

There are a number of tips you can use to help you develop healthy eating habits:

1 Eat a variety of foods, ensuring that all the macro and micro nutrients your body needs are included in the right proportions.

2 Avoid foods that are high in fat, particularly saturated fat. Opt for low-fat alternatives wherever possible.

3 Avoid too many processed foods, such as breakfast cereals, packet sauces, and pizza, as they often contain high levels of fat, sugar, and salt.

4 Eat more fruit and vegetables. Five portions of fruit and vegetables a day is ideal.

5 Eat breakfast. It's a great way to kick-start your metabolism, the chemical reactions that take place in the body's cells that convert the fuel in the food we eat into the energy we need to function effectively.

6 Consider healthier ways to cook food, such as grilling and steaming rather than frying.

7 Watch how many calories you eat. Excess calories are stored by the body as fat.

8 Manage your portion sizes. Most things are OK in moderation.

9 Eat regularly. Going short of food for long periods can lead to binge eating and opting for sugary snacks!

10 Eat the right foods and drink the right fluids in their recommended quantities, giving your body the nutrients it needs to function effectively.

Measuring your weight

A person's weight is often used as an indicator of whether or not their diet is healthy and balanced.

Body Mass Index (BMI) is a way of calculating whether or not your body is of an ideal weight. BMI is a test designed for men and women over the age of 18, and although people under the age of 18 can use it, the results should not be taken to have any significant meaning.

According to NHS Direct (UK):

- If your BMI is less than 18.5kg/m² you are underweight for your height.
- If your BMI is 18.5 to 24.9kg/m² you are an ideal weight for your height.
- If your BMI is 25 to 29.9kg/m² you are over the ideal weight for your height.
- If your BMI is 30 to 39.9kg/m² you are obese.
- If your BMI is over 39.9kg/m² you are very obese.

To calculate your BMI:
Measure your weight in kilograms.
Measure your height in metres (so 182cm is actually 1.82m)
Calculate your BMI using the following formula:

$$BMI = \frac{weight\ (kg)}{height\ (m) \times height\ (m)}$$

If more than 25 per cent of a boy's weight or more than 32 per cent of a girl's weight is fat then they are classified as obese. Body fat can be measured using special scales, available in gyms and health clubs, which measure the percentage of fat, water, and muscle tissue in your body.

Maintaining a healthy weight

The food that we eat provides us with energy and the key to maintaining a healthy weight is ensuring that energy in, equals energy out. If your energy intake and energy expenditure is the same, then your weight should be steady. In order to lose weight, the energy intake must be reduced or the energy expenditure increased. To gain weight, energy expenditure should be less than energy intake.

Energy is measured in joules or kilojoules. Food energy can also be measured in terms of the nutritional or 'large' calories it contains. One calorie (Cal) has the same energy value as 4.186 kilojoules (kJ).

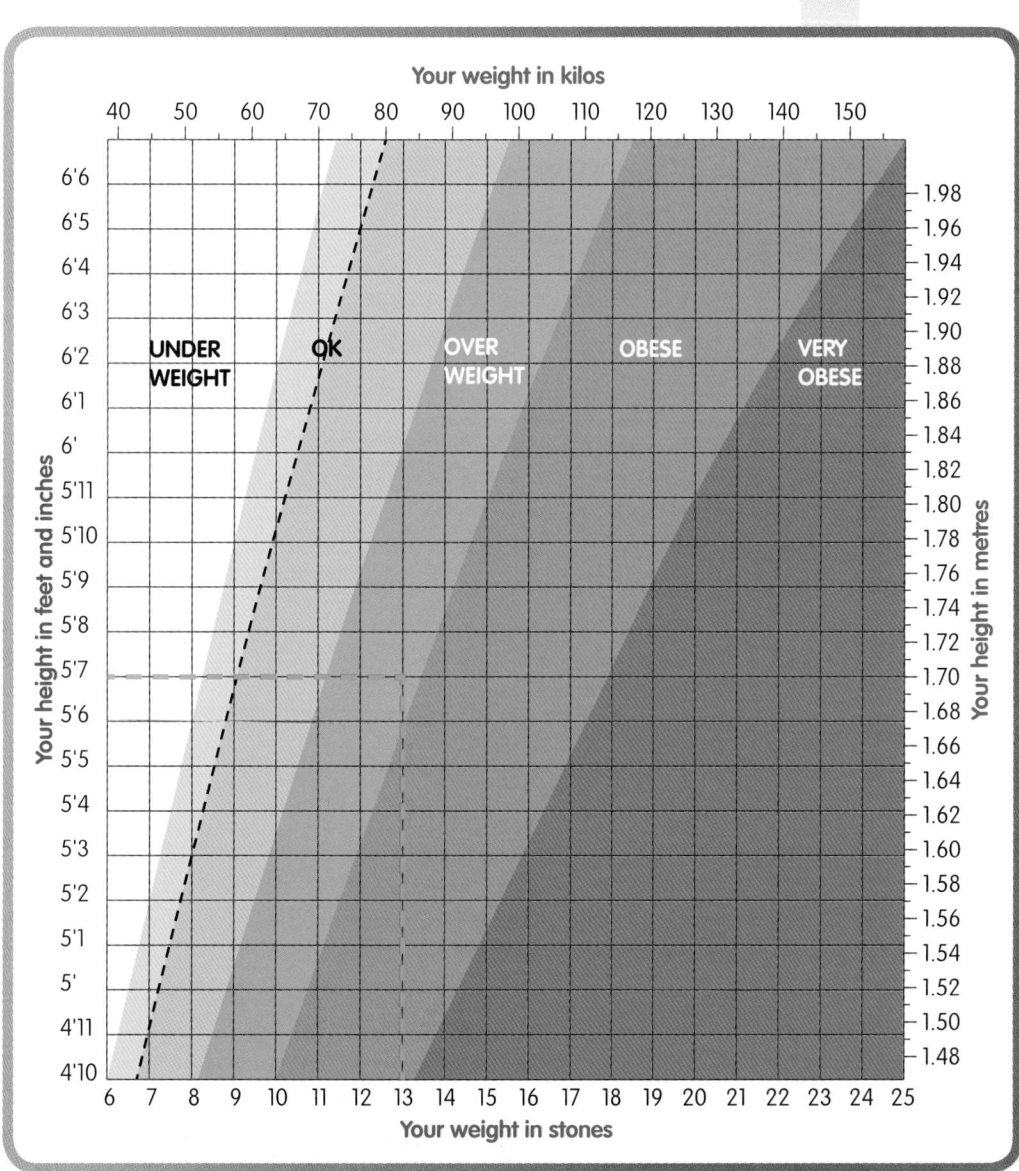

This height–weight chart can be used as a guide to determine whether a healthy adult is overweight.

How much energy food contains depends on its components. Fats and alcohol are the most energy-dense components. This is why they should only be consumed in moderation, particularly if you are overweight or obese. Below is the energy value per gram of some food components:

- Fat: 37kJ (9 Cal)
- Alcohol: 29kJ (7 Cal)
- Carbohydrates: 16kJ (4 Cal)
- Protein: 17kJ (4 Cal)
- Water: 0kJ (0 Cal)

Basal Metabolic Rate (BMR)

A person's Basal Metabolic Rate, or BMR, is the minimum amount of calories they need in order to function when at rest. If someone takes part in sport they will require more calories than someone who spends their time watching television, in order to provide the energy that they need to perform. There are a variety of factors that can have an effect on your BMR. These are:

- Age
- Size
- Gender
- Body composition
- Illness
- Dieting

An easy way to calculate BMR is to multiply your weight (in kilograms) by ten. For example, if your weight is 45kg, then your BMR is 450.

Another way to measure BMR is to use the Harris-Benedict equation. This method uses a formula that involves height, weight, age, and gender. It is more complicated than multiplying your weight by ten but the results are more accurate.

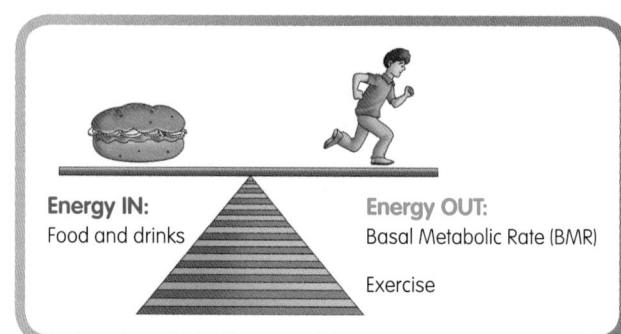

Energy IN:
Food and drinks

Energy OUT:
Basal Metabolic Rate (BMR)

Exercise

W = weight in kilograms H = height in centimetres A = age in years

BMR for males $= 66 + (13.7 \times W) + (5 \times H) - (6.8 \times A)$
BMR for females $= 655 + (9.6 \times W) + (1.8 \times H) - (4.7 \times A)$

Despite a person's BMR having an impact on their individual energy requirements, rough guidelines for the daily energy requirements have been developed:

- 15-year-old boys   11,500kJ (approximately 2700 Cal)
- 15-year-old girls   8800kJ (approximately 2100 Cal)
- Adult men   10,500kJ (approximately 2500 Cal)
- Adult women   8400kJ (approximately 2000 Cal)
- Older men   8800kJ (approximately 2100 Cal)
- Older women   8000kJ (approximately 1900 Cal)

BRONZE

1. Find out your weight and calculate your BMI.

2. Find two food labels, one from something healthy, such as a cereal bar, and one from something unhealthy, such as a packet of crisps. Find out how many calories are in each item and then find out how much exercise is required to burn the calories off.

SILVER

3. Using the same two food labels that you used for Activity 2, compare the nutritional values of each food and explain which is better for you and why.

BRONZE

4. Find out how each of the factors listed above (age, body composition, size, illness, gender, and dieting) affects a person's BMR.

5. a) Calculate your BMR.

b) Calculate your energy intake on an average day.

c) Calculate the amount of energy you expend on an average day.

d) Using your calculations, decide whether you are taking in enough energy to sustain your daily activities, or if you are eating too little or too much.

Eating for sport

Sports performers must not only eat a healthy and well-balanced diet, they must also ensure that their diet is specifically tailored to their sport, training regimes, and competition schedules. For example, the cyclist Bradley Wiggins consumed approximately 8000 calories a day during the 2012 Tour de France, ensuring he had the necessary fuel in his body to complete each stage of the race! Athletes competing in anaerobic sports, such as sprinting, and strength-related sports, such as the shot-put or discus, will eat slightly fewer carbohydrates than athletes competing in endurance sports.

BRONZE

1. Choose one famous sportsperson and find out how their diet supports their training and competition requirements.

SILVER

2. Create a three-day meal plan for an athlete of your choice. The plan should cover the day before, the day of the competition, and the day after. It should include breakfast, lunch, and dinner, as well as all drinks and snacks.

Before training and competition

When preparing for physical activity, athletes must carefully consider what foods they eat. When preparing for aerobic exercise, athletes must load their bodies with energy-providing foods, such as carbohydrates, two to four hours before they begin in order to maximize their stores of glycogen. This process is often referred to as 'carbo-loading'. It is also important to drink plenty of fluids before taking part in sports to avoid becoming dehydrated.

Different diets for different sports

Not all sports performers follow the same diet plans. Some performers, such as weightlifters, may follow a high-protein diet. Foods that contain lots of protein are generally low in fat and carbohydrates, which allows athletes to build and repair muscle tissue as well as lose excess fat. Athletes following a high-protein diet should aim to consume around one gram of protein per one pound of body weight.

In contrast, endurance athletes may follow a high-carbohydrate diet. Approximately two to three days before an important race, long-distance runners will carbo-load to ensure that there is a large amount of glycogen in their muscles in order to sustain them during the lengthy period of performance ahead.

During sport

Sports competitors should ensure that they drink plenty of fluids, in the form of water or a sports drink, so that they remain hydrated. If the activity is lengthy, a snack may also be required. Foods that are easy to digest and that contain carbohydrates for energy, such as low-fat cereal bars or bananas, are best. Foods that contain protein may also be eaten because they will help to repair muscle damage.

After sport

Sports drinks are popular among athletes, particularly after performing, because they help to rehydrate the body and replace the body's store of energy. They are better for athletes than water because they contain carbohydrates and electrolytes, such as sodium and potassium, which have been lost in sweat and therefore need replenishing. Potassium can also help to speed up the recovery process.

Within one to two hours of completing physical activity carbohydrates may also be eaten to replace energy, as well as protein to help repair muscle tissue.

During rest periods

Athletes often schedule a rest period of two to four weeks per year into their training programmes. During this time, they should try to eat a nutritious, well-balanced diet containing plenty of easily digestible, starchy foods. They should also ensure that they begin each day with a good breakfast to kick-start their metabolism and drink plenty of fluids to remain hydrated.

Supplements

Although we can get most of the energy we require from food, some sports performers supplement their diet with vitamins, minerals, energy bars, and protein drinks to enhance their performance or to aid recovery. For example, creatine monohydrate allows an athlete to train harder for longer periods with less recovery time.

Most supplements are legal but some athletes are tempted to take illegal substances, such as anabolic steroids, to improve their performance. If caught using this kind of supplement, sports performers may be banned from taking part in their sport for a period of time and their reputation may never recover from the scandal.

Monitoring and assessing your diet

As we have seen, a healthy, balanced diet is extremely important for a sports performer. It is therefore important for an athlete to assess their diet on an ongoing basis to determine what food and drink they are consuming, when they are consuming it, and how it compares to what they should be eating. A good way for a performer to monitor their energy and nutritional consumption is to keep a food diary.

How many kilojoules or calories are contained in the food and drink consumed.

The type of food and drink consumed.

How many grams of protein, carbohydrates, and fat are consumed.

Any supplements taken.

A food diary is used to keep a record of what we eat and drink each day, and should include details of…

The quantity of food and drink consumed.

A daily energy target in kilojoules or calories.

The times at which food and drink are consumed.

A comparison between the energy target and the energy consumed.

How you are feeling about your diet. This information can help to inform future meal planning. If, for example, a sports performer is feeling full of energy and positive about their weight after eating a particular way for a week, they can look back on this and use the same foods to create a similar effect in the future.

Here is an example of a food diary:

Monday **Target calorie consumption:** 1500 calories **Actual calorie consumption:** 1258 calories	7:30am	1 x grapefruit (1g protein, 0% fat, 0% carbohydrates) 1 x glass of water	100 calories
	10:00am	1 x cereal bar (6g protein, 0% fat, 21g carbohydrates) 1 x diet cola	110 calories
	1:00pm	1 x jacket potato (180g) (4.2g protein, 0.1g fat, 46g carbohydrates) Tinned tuna fish (200g) (54g protein, 1g fat, 0g carbohydrates) 1 x glass of water	198 calories
	4:00pm	1 x banana (1.3g protein, 0.3g fat, 21g carbohydrates)	100 calories
	7:30pm	Spaghetti bolognaise (240g) (17g protein, 5g fat, 43g carbohydrates) 1 x glass of orange juice (1.7g protein, 0.5g fat, 25g carbohydrates)	750 calories
		Feelings: I was hungry in the morning so had my cereal bar. I felt stuffed after my evening meal. I am wondering if I should eat a larger meal at lunchtime so that I can eat less at dinner and don't feel so full when it is time for bed. **Food groups:** My diet contained some fruit but not enough vegetables. There were sufficient bread/cereals/potatoes included but I needed more dairy products. I also ate some meat and fish, which was good. Generally though, I had a reasonable balance of the food groups required.	

Analysing your diet

Once you have collected information about your diet, it is time to examine it closely.

You can compare your diet with what you know about the requirements of a healthy, balanced diet and any special requirements you might have if you are training or competing in sport for example. You can also compare your diet with relevant guidelines, such as the government recommendation that we eat five portions of fruit and vegetables a day, the recommended daily energy intake, and the eatwell plate.

One way to analyse your diet is to complete a paper-based dietary analysis questionnaire but many fitness centres also have dietary analysis software, which can analyse a client's diet and recommend improvements. The instructor or personal trainer will talk to their client and run tests to find out about things such as their eating habits, their blood cholesterol levels, and their BMI. The instructor can then recommend ways in which the client could change their diet, for example, to lower their cholesterol levels.

Acting on recommendations

When you have collected information about your diet and analysed it using either a questionnaire you have created yourself or dietary analysis software, it is time to use the findings to inform your diet and energy intake in the future.

A dietary analysis will identify strengths in your diet and areas for improvement. For example, it might tell you that you are not drinking enough water when you are training, so you can plan to drink more at these times. It might tell you that the amount of saturated fat in your diet is too high, so you can work to prepare your meals in a different way in order to reduce their saturated fat content. It might tell you that you aren't eating enough protein and carbohydrates after you have exercised, so you can adjust when you eat these to ensure your body gets the nutrients it needs when it most needs them. It could also show you that you are eating too many 'ready-meals' or processed foods, and that you should aim to eat more fresh foods, which are rich in vitamins and minerals, instead.

Making improvements can be pretty painless if you address each area for improvement little by little, such as replacing a chocolate bar snack with a fruit alternative, by including at least one vegetable with your evening meal, or by only eating chips once per week.

1 medium apple   2 broccoli florets   2 halves of canned peaches

1 handful of grapes   1 medium banana   3 heaped tablespoons of peas

1 medium glass of orange juice   7 strawberries   3 whole dried apricots

5 A DAY

Just Eat More
(fruit & veg)

www.doh.gov.uk/fiveaday

3 heaped tablespoons of cooked kidney beans   16 okra

NHS

BRONZE

1. a) Design a questionnaire that will ascertain the dietary habits of a classmate, friend, or family member.

b) Ask someone to complete your questionnaire and return it to you for analysis.

2. Using the information provided by the questionnaire, design a healthy meal plan for seven days. Your plan should include breakfasts, lunches, and dinners, as well as fluids and healthy snacks.

SILVER

3. Describe how your meal plan relates to the eatwell plate and other dietary recommendations.

4. Describe the dietary changes you have recommended to your classmate, friend, or family member.

GOLD

5. Justify the dietary changes you have recommended to your classmate, friend, or family member in Activity 4, explaining why their diet has to change in the ways you have suggested. Remember to refer to healthy eating habits, weight, BMR, calories in, and energy expended.

Unit 9 assignment, part two

Background

The new lifestyle and well-being magazine has been well received by the community and the second edition is eagerly anticipated. The health promotion team decide to focus the next edition on healthy eating and dietary planning, and you have been asked to produce a series of articles.

Grading criteria to be assessed
1B.3, 1B.4, 1B.5
2B.P3, 2B.P4, 2B.P5
2B.M2
2B.D2

Task

Write a series of articles that cover a wide range of dietary information and use real-life examples to exemplify healthy meal plans that can be used by members of the community. You must:

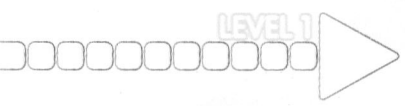

- Describe the functions of the essential nutrients and why a healthy diet is important for a healthy lifestyle. (1B.3)
- Collect dietary information for a selected individual for one day, documenting via a food diary. (1B.4)
- Design, with guidance, a healthy meal plan for a selected individual for one day, specifying the type and amount of food to be consumed. (1B.5)

- Explain the functions of the essential nutrients and why a healthy diet is important for a healthy lifestyle. (2B.P3)
- Collect dietary information for a selected individual for one week, documenting via a food diary. (2B.P4)
- Independently design a healthy meal plan for a selected individual, for one week. (2B.P5)

- Design a healthy meal plan for a selected individual, for one week, making reference to the eatwell plate, and describing suggested recommendations for change. (2B.M2)

- Justify the design of a healthy meal plan for a selected individual, for one week, justifying suggested recommendations for change. (2B.D2)

Tackling the assignment

As with your first article, you need to present the information in a way that appeals to a wide audience. Basing your articles around a case study is a good way to tackle the assignment. You could begin by explaining the functions of essential nutrients and why a healthy diet is important for a healthy lifestyle. You could then move on to look at the food diary to show what a person is currently eating, describe their new meal plan, and then link the recommendations you are making with the information you began with to justify the changes you are suggesting.

And don't forget that you must work independently to meet the criteria for 2B.P5.

Meeting the Level 2 Pass, Merit, and Distinction criteria

DIETARY PLANNING

Laurie Hines

Here at the health promotion team we have been collecting dietary information from other members of the council, using a paper-based food diary, so we can help design healthy meals for them. One member of staff,

Sandra, has kindly agreed to let us use the information we have collected for her as material for our dietary planning case study. Thanks Sandra!

MONDAY	Breakfast	Bacon	128 calories
		Egg	92 calories
		Beans	197 calories
		Orange juice	44 calories
	Lunch	Pepperoni pizza slice	290 calories
		Sausage roll	240 calories
		Chocolate cookie	275 calories
		Can of orangeade	164 calories
	Dinner	Spaghetti bolognaise	600 calories
		Garlic bread	100 calories
		Can of orangeade	164 calories

Laurie has clearly collected lots of information about Sandra's diet and is well on his way to meeting the criteria for 2B.P4, but there are several things he could do to improve the food diary. For example, he doesn't record the amounts of food and drink that Sandra consumes and he doesn't detail absolutely everything she eats. He doesn't mention what she had on her toast for example. Also, he hasn't noted the timings of Sandra's meals, how her food was cooked, or how she felt about the food and drinks she was consuming. Did she eat each meal at the same time each day, for example, and did she have any snacks between meals? All this information needs to be added to the food diary to help Laurie produce a healthy meal plan.

Based on the information I collected for Sandra I have planned a range of meals for her for one week.

DAY ONE

Breakfast:
- Porridge with a handful of fruit, such as blueberries.
- Two scrambled eggs on wholegrain toast, with mushrooms and tomatoes.

Morning snack:
- A handful of dried fruit or fresh fruit.

Lunch:
- Salad with mixed leaves, tomato, red onion, avocado, bean sprouts, carrot, apple, beetroot, cucumber, and feta cheese, with an optional olive oil and balsamic vinegar dressing.
- Chicken breast or turkey with rice.

Afternoon snack:
- Fresh fruit, for example, apple or banana.

Dinner:
- Lean meat, such as a steak, vegetables, and a medium potato.

Evening snack:
- Low-fat yoghurt.

1 glass of water with each meal.

This is an excellent meal plan for Sandra. If Laurie repeats this standard of work in his meal plans for the rest of the week he will easily achieve the criteria for 2B.P5.

As Sandra is a keen distance runner I was slightly surprised by the findings of her food diary, so I suggested plenty of changes to her diet. Her original diet contained far too much fat, too few complex carbohydrates, and a lack of fruit and vegetables. She was also eating approximately 3500 calories a day and, although she was training every other day, this was approximately 500 calories more per day than she needed. This explains why her weight had increased by one-and-a-half kilos over the past two months.

The meal plan I have produced replicates the requirements of the eatwell plate. As Sandra is a runner and trains three times a week I have ensured she has approximately 60 per cent carbohydrates, 25 per cent fat, and 15 per cent protein in her diet, as well as the necessary range of vitamins and minerals. I have also made sure Sandra drinks plenty of water. Her overall calorie intake is approximately 2000 on the days she doesn't train and 3200 on the days she does.

The changes I have suggested will ensure Sandra:

- Has the correct quantity of nutrients in her diet to allow her to train and compete well (the carbohydrates and fats are important here) and sufficient protein to maintain and repair her muscles and other body tissues.
- Keeps her weight constant, by matching her calorie intake to her calorie expenditure. This is especially important as Sandra will need more calories on the days she trains, which will be predominantly in the form of carbohydrates.
- Consumes sufficient fluid to

From what we can see of Laurie's work he clearly demonstrates that he understands the requirements of the 2B.M2 and 2B.D2 criteria. His recommendations lead on well from his initial findings, reflect the requirements of the dietary guidelines, and he has justified his suggestions by linking them into Sandra's training needs and weight management. If Laurie continues to produce work of this quality and depth, the Merit and Distinction criteria are well within his grasp.

The health risks of smoking and drinking excessive alcohol

Following a healthy lifestyle is not only about eating the right foods and taking plenty of exercise. It's also about understanding the health risks and negative effects of harmful lifestyle factors, such as smoking and drinking alcohol, and implementing techniques to reduce or eliminate them. Smoking and drinking alcohol have a significant impact on sports performance, so a thorough understanding of the effects are especially important for athletes.

The health risks associated with smoking

The health risks associated with smoking are well documented. Government websites and anti-smoking campaigns, such as Smokefree, outline the harmful effects smoking can have on the body. Despite this, however, there are still plenty of people who continue to smoke.

It is estimated that approximately 100,000 people in the UK die each year due to smoking, mainly from smoking-related diseases, such as cancer, and other diseases that affect blood circulation, breathing, and the functions of the heart. The life expectancy of a long-term smoker is about ten years less than a non-smoker.

Health issues associated with smoking include:

- Cancers caused by the poisons that are contained in the tar in cigarettes, which is deposited in the lungs. These poisons can cause lung cancer. They can also get into the bloodstream and be transported to other parts of the body where they can also cause cancer.
- Circulation problems caused by the chemicals in cigarettes, which damage the lining of the blood vessels, causing them to harden. This hardening can result in strokes, coronary heart disease, and aneurysms (swollen arteries, which can burst, causing internal bleeding).
- Breathing problems, such as bronchitis (where the respiratory passages are affected) and emphysema (where the alveoli, or air sacs, in the lungs are damaged).
- A dulling of the sense of taste and the sense of smell, which can lead to a reduced enjoyment of food.
- An increased risk of contracting other diseases, including dementia, gum disease, tooth loss, and osteoporosis.

The health risks associated with excessive alcohol consumption

Millions of adults in the UK drink alcohol sensibly, and the government, via the National Health Service (NHS), regularly reinforces key messages regarding safe levels of alcohol consumption to help people ensure they do not drink too much.

The most recent advice is:

- Men should drink no more than 21 units per week, and no more than 4 units per day.
- Women should drink no more than 14 units per week, and no more than 3 units per day.
- If you've had a heavy drinking session, avoid alcohol for 48 hours.

A unit of alcohol is the scale used to measure the volume of pure alcohol in an alcoholic drink. One unit of alcohol is defined as 10 millilitres in the UK.

However, despite the advice, many people consume excessive amounts of alcohol, running the risk of serious health problems, including:

- Alcohol poisoning, which can cause lung damage (if you inhale your own vomit) and even lead to a heart attack.

- Liver disease: It's estimated that alcohol is responsible for approximately 30,000 deaths in the UK per year through liver cirrhosis.
- Cancer: Excessive drinking can cause cancers, because alcohol is converted by the body into a toxic chemical called acetaldehyde that can damage your DNA, hindering the body's ability to repair damaged cells, such as those in the liver and other essential organs.
- Mental health: Alcohol can alter the brain's chemistry and lead to depression, anxiety, and hallucinations.
- Weight gain: The high calorific content of many alcoholic drinks can lead to weight gain and, in turn, the health risks associated with obesity, such as heart disease, problems with joints, and high blood pressure.
- Strokes: The increase in blood pressure that can occur as a result of excessive alcohol consumption can increase the risk of having a stroke.
- Stomach ulcers and gastrointestinal complications: Alcohol, even in moderation, makes the stomach produce more acid than normal, which in turn can inflame the stomach lining. This can result in pain, vomiting, diarrhoea, and, in extreme cases, can cause internal bleeding.

1 unit	1 unit	1 unit	1 unit	1 unit
1/2 pint of ordinary strength beer, lager, or cider	1 small glass of wine	1 single measure of spirits	1 small glass of sherry	1 single measure of an aperitif

Excessive drinking can also lead to many social problems, such as aggression, missing work because of a hangover, and many domestic problems. Alcohol abuse is frequently quoted as a cause when families and relationships break up.

The effect of smoking and alcohol consumption on sports performance

The effects of smoking

Smoking interferes with the body's ability to function in a number of ways. Firstly, tobacco smoke affects the lungs so that they work less efficiently and so the body isn't able to pick up the amount of oxygen it needs when it is working hard. Secondly, tobacco smoke contains a chemical called carbon monoxide, which gets into the bloodstream and inhibits it from picking up oxygen. It also contains other chemicals that affect the circulation of blood. They make the blood vessels smaller so that they are less able to carry oxygen when the body is burning up large amounts of energy.

In short, if you smoke your body has less fuel and the fuel it does have is transported less efficiently to those areas that need it when you are taking part in sport. Because of this, smokers tend to have less energy and also find it harder to maintain high levels of fitness than non-smokers.

The effects of alcohol

Alcohol affects the body's ability to turn food into energy, slows down reaction times, increases body heat loss, and reduces endurance. For example, if you have alcohol 24 hours before exercising you are more likely to develop muscle cramps.

The relaxant properties of alcohol can affect your sporting ability long after you've finished drinking. Alcohol slows down the information processing ability of the brain. This, in turn, affects your reactions, coordination, accuracy, and balance – all the things that are important for staying on top in any sport.

After exercising the body needs to be rehydrated. It's not helpful to drink alcohol straight after a match or event as this will dehydrate the body further.

BRONZE

1. a) Using the information below, and any other reference material you can find, work out how many units of alcohol Jack and Jill drank last week.

Jack	Jill
Monday: two pints of lager	Monday: two glasses of wine
Tuesday: Nothing	Tuesday: one glass of wine
Wednesday: Nothing	Wednesday: two glasses of wine
Thursday: two pints of lager and one measure of whisky	Thursday: two glasses of wine
Friday: six pints of lager	Friday: two small gin and tonics
Saturday: four pints of lager and two measures of whisky	Saturday: two glasses of wine and two vodka and tonics
Sunday: Nothing	Sunday: one glass of wine

b) Describe how Jack and Jill's weekly consumption of alcohol compares to recommended safe limits.

2. Carry out research to find out what effects excessive alcohol consumption had on the lives and football careers of Paul Gascoigne and Tony Adams.

Techniques to stop smoking and cut down on alcohol consumption

Quitting smoking or reducing your alcohol consumption isn't as easy as it may sound. The addictive nature of both cigarettes and alcohol means that a variety of techniques and strategies are often needed, with various organizations and professionals around in the background to offer support, guidance, and motivation.

Quitting smoking

There are many techniques to help people stop smoking. They include:

Your local NHS Stop Smoking Service

This is a free service and research suggests that people are up to four times more likely to quit smoking if they use the service than if they try using willpower alone. The service includes support from a trained advisor, either on a one-to-one basis or in a group, who gives advice on nicotine replacement products and other techniques that may help. The service also includes the use of a carbon monoxide monitor to measure levels of the chemical within the body, which is a great motivational tool to help people see the benefits of giving up smoking.

Patches, gums, and other medicines

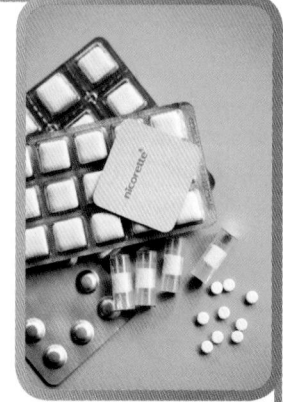

The craving for nicotine is one of the hardest aspects of stopping smoking to cope with. Giving up smoking can cause nicotine withdrawal symptoms, such as headaches and irritability. Gums, patches, and other medicines can be used to help manage these withdrawal symptoms. Some are available from the NHS with a prescription, while others can be bought over the counter at a chemist.

Alternative techniques

Hypnotherapy and acupuncture are also used successfully to help people give up smoking. Hypnotherapy uses the power of suggestion to help focus the unconscious part of the mind to help people quit smoking. Acupuncture, on the other hand, involves inserting thin, solid needles into acupuncture points on the skin, stimulating certain functions in the body, which can change the experience of smoking, making the taste unpleasant or the smell off-putting.

Cutting down on alcohol consumption

Support and advice for cutting down on your drinking can be found from a variety of sources, including your doctor and www.drinkaware.co.uk. Some of the ways in which people can cut down on their alcohol consumption are to:

drinkaware.co.uk
for the facts about alcohol

Use support counselling services or support groups where you can discuss your problems. Sharing your concerns with other people who are trained to help you or who are going through the same thing can help.

Have alcohol-free days. The current advice is to have at least two alcohol-free days per week.

Keep track of the number of units of alcohol you drink and keep within the recommended limits.

Get watered, not slaughtered.

Plan activities that don't involve drinking.

Use smaller glasses and only drink with your evening meal.

Avoid getting into rounds where it is harder to control what you are drinking.

Drink non-alcoholic drinks or low-alcohol alternatives.

Unit 9 assignment, part three

Background

The health promotion team run an annual well-being roadshow, visiting local schools, community centres, and health centres to promote many aspects of their work. The roadshows have a theme each year and this year the focus is on the health risks associated with smoking and excessive alcohol consumption. You have been asked to produce information that can be presented at the roadshow.

Task

Prepare information for the general public about the health risks associated with smoking and excessive drinking and explore ways in which people can stop smoking and reduce their alcohol consumption. The information should:

Grading criteria to be assessed
1C.6, 1C.7, 1C.8 2C.P6, 2C.P7, 2C.P8 2C.M3

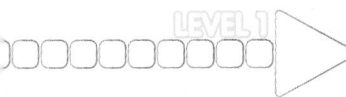

- Describe four health risks associated with smoking. (1C.6)
- Describe four health risks associated with excessive alcohol consumption. (1C.7)
- Describe one technique an individual can use to stop smoking and one technique to cut down on excessive alcohol consumption. (1C.8)

- Describe four health risks associated with smoking and effects of smoking on sports performance. (2C.P6)
- Describe four health risks associated with excessive alcohol consumption and effects of alcohol consumption on sports performance. (2C.P7)
- Explain two techniques an individual can use to stop smoking, and two techniques to cut down on excessive alcohol consumption. (2C.P8)

- Compare and contrast different techniques used to stop smoking and for cutting down on excessive alcohol consumption. (2C.M3)

Tackling the assignment

This assignment gives you the opportunity to be innovative, using a range of methods to present your work. You could prepare a short film, a rolling PowerPoint® presentation, annotated posters, or leaflets. Think about what you do best and choose the most effective method(s) of communication to get your message across.

Whatever method(s) you choose, make sure your descriptions are clear and concise, your explanations give sound reasons why you are stating what you are stating, and that, when you compare and contrast the different techniques used to stop smoking and cut down on excessive alcohol consumption, you look at the similarities and differences between the techniques and explain your reasoning.

Meeting the Level 2 Pass criteria

• Kerri Drayton

The health risks associated with smoking

The health risks associated with smoking are generally well known, but do you <u>really</u> know what damage smoking does to your heath?

Smoking is known to create problems with blood circulation throughout the body, which in turn reduces the amount of oxygen that reaches the major organs of the body.

This is because the chemicals in the smoke damage the lining of the blood vessels, which in turn makes them become harder. Smoking also deposits a substance called plaque in the blood vessels. The two problems combine to narrow the arteries and restrict blood flow. Over time, this can cause problems with the heart and can also result in a stroke.

The health risks associated with excessive alcohol consumption

In addition to the social problems excessive drinking can cause, it can also affect your health. One example is cirrhosis of the liver, where the normal tissue in the liver is replaced by scar tissue. Eventually the liver is unable to function normally and can no longer break alcohol down into water that is then passed out of the body in urine.

Quitting smoking

Many smokers want to give up but struggle to do so because smoking is addictive. One way to quit is to get advice and support from one of the organizations designed to help smokers give up, such as the NHS Stop Smoking Service. Here, trained advisors can offer support and give advice on nicotine replacement products.

> This is a good description by Kerri. To fully achieve 2C.P6 and 2C.P7 Kerri needs to maintain this level of detail for three other health risks associated with excessive alcohol consumption. She then needs to describe the effects smoking and excessive alcohol consumption have on sports performance.

> Kerri has only briefly described one technique to help someone stop smoking, and needs to provide a lot more detail to achieve 2C.P8. The criteria require her to explain the technique, so Kerri needs to explain *why* this technique may work. For example, having a dedicated advisor means the person wanting to quit has one-to-one support and attending support groups can work because it provides an opportunity to benefit from other people's experience and encouragement.

Do you want to cut down on your alcohol consumption but are unsure about the best way to go about it?

Two possible ways...

Have at least two alcohol-free days per week

Drink non-alcoholic or low-alcohol drinks

Francis has made a fair attempt to compare and contrast the two techniques used to cut down on alcohol consumption, but has chosen two techniques that are pretty similar. If he had chosen two more contrasting techniques, perhaps two alcohol-free days and attending counselling, he would have had more material to work with. Francis also needs to compare and contrast two different techniques used to stop smoking to meet the criteria for 2C.M3.

These two methods are pretty similar, although there are some subtle differences.

The similarities are that neither involve cutting out alcohol altogether, which many people find difficult. They both rely on you to be disciplined though, making sure you schedule at least two alcohol-free days into your week and checking that the drinks you are consuming are either free from alcohol or contain low levels of alcohol.

The main differences are that one method (alcohol-free days) means no alcohol at all, while the other means that alcohol can be consumed but only if it is a low-alcohol alternative. The low or non-alcohol alternative may appeal to people who see drinking as an important part of their social life.

A sensible approach would be to combine the two, maybe drinking non-alcoholic drinks for a minimum of two nights and then drinking low-alcohol alternatives on other occasions throughout the week.

Francis Gould

The impact of drugs on health and sports performance

Although the potential health risks are well known and the penalties are harsh, there are still some athletes who are prepared to use performance-enhancing drugs in an attempt to improve their performance. But at what cost?

The impact of performance-enhancing drugs on sports performance

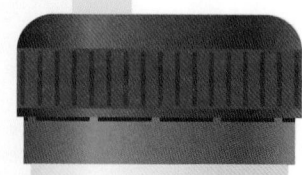

Anabolic steroids

Anabolic steroids are probably one of the most common drugs used in sport. They mimic, or copy, the male hormone testosterone and can improve endurance and stimulate muscle growth.

What are the effects on sports performance?

- They help performers train harder and for longer periods.
- They help performers with their recovery time, helping them train more often.
- They can help build muscle mass, often increasing performance in sports that need strength and short bursts of power.

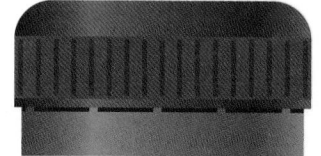

Erythropoietin (EPO)

Erythropoietin (EPO) is a naturally-occurring hormone, which is produced by the kidneys. It stimulates the production of red blood cells, which carry oxygen within the blood. It can be manufactured artificially and injected into the body.

What are the effects on sports performance?

- An increase in oxygen to the muscles, which increases the performer's aerobic capacity.
- Allows the performer to delay the onset of fatigue.

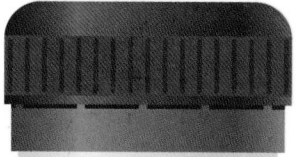

Human growth hormone (HGH)

Human growth hormone (HGH) is an anabolic hormone that occurs naturally in the body. It is produced by the pituitary gland and stimulates the growth of muscle, cartilage, and bone.

What are the effects on sports performance?

- It increases muscle size and can improve performance in sports that need strength and short bursts of power.
- It allows tired muscles to recover more quickly, again allowing a performer to train harder and more often.

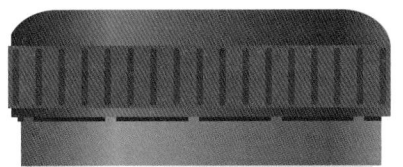

Diuretics

Diuretics help with weight loss and speed up the elimination of drugs from the body by increasing the volume of urine produced by the kidneys.

What are the effects on sports performance?

- Diuretics can help performers, such as boxers or jockeys, lose weight quickly.
- They may also help performers who have taken a banned substance and need to get it out of their system quickly.

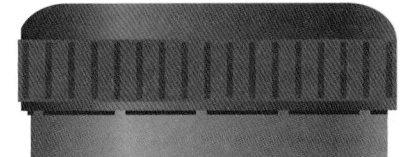

Beta blockers

Beta blockers are a type of medication that block the effects of adrenaline. They help the heart work more efficiently, reduce the heart rate, and limit anxiety.

What are the effects on sports performance?

- They allow performers to stay calm, letting them focus more effectively.
- They help performers to have steadier hands, a real advantage in sports such as snooker, darts, shooting, and archery.

The harmful effects of performance-enhancing drugs

Although taking performance-enhancing drugs may provide benefits, there are plenty of negative or harmful health effects to take into consideration. These include:

Taking anabolic steroids can cause an increase in aggression and lead to kidney failure if they are taken for a prolonged period of time. Side effects for men include developing prominent breasts, baldness, acne, and infertility, while for women they can lead to increased body hair, baldness, or a deeper voice. Anabolic steroids can be addictive and can also cause high blood pressure, heart disease, and cancer.

Other effects of performance-enhancing drugs can include irrational behaviour, mood changes, and other mental health issues.

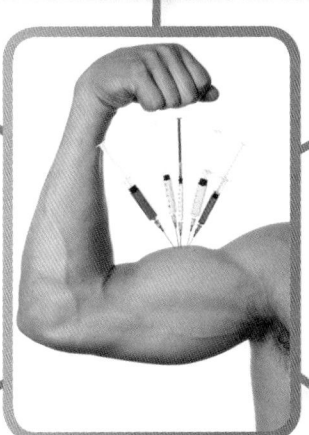

Taking diuretics can cause dehydration and the negative health effects associated with this, such as fatigue, poor concentration, headaches, and dizziness.

Healthy people who take beta blockers are placing themselves at risk of lowering their blood pressure and heart rate to dangerous levels. They also increase the risk of depression and can lead to vivid dreams, sleep disturbance, and breathlessness.

Taking EPO can cause heart problems or increase the chances of a stroke.

Taking HGH can lead to joint pain, muscle weakness, and excessive fluid retention.

BRONZE

1. Unfortunately there are plenty of performers who have been caught using performance-enhancing drugs. See if you can identify a few and describe the benefits you think the performer was hoping to gain from taking the drug.

How performance-enhancing drugs can affect different types of sport

Athletes who compete in endurance events, such as the Tour de France or distance running, may be tempted to take EPO because increasing their red blood cells allows their muscles to function more effectively over a long period of time.

Sports where weight limits are a key consideration, such as boxing or horse racing, may be affected by the abuse of diuretics. Boxers, for example, are known to shed a considerable amount of weight before a weigh-in in order to make the stipulated limit for their weight classification.

Athletes performing in sports that require strength and power, such as the javelin, the shot-put, and the high jump, may be tempted to take anabolic steroids because they would benefit from an increase in muscle size and strength.

Beta blockers have been found to be a problem in sports where concentration and a steady nerve are required. The calming effects they have on the participant, allowing them to keep a steady hand in sports such as shooting or archery, are beneficial.

HGH helps increase muscle size, so competitors in events such as bodybuilding may be tempted to use it, although its use in sport was banned in the late 1980s.

Why do some performers take the risk?

Despite the potential health effects and the possibility of receiving a lengthy ban from competing, some participants aren't deterred from taking performance-enhancing drugs. Why?

The reasons are numerous, and only the individuals concerned can really explain their actions, but some of the reasons given in the past include:

- **Pressure from the coach or coaching team to succeed:** Many athletes have been introduced to drugs by their coach in order to help them improve, which enhances the reputation of the coach as well as the athlete.
- **Desire to win at all costs:** Many performers are driven by the need to succeed, whether this is for the glory or for the financial rewards that many sports afford. Taking performance-enhancing drugs can improve performance levels more quickly than traditional training, so taking them can be seen as a shortcut to success.
- **Being unaware of the health risks:** Some athletes, especially in their early years, are not fully aware of the potential health risks so they are not put off by the down sides of taking performance-enhancing drugs. This is far less of an issue nowadays as most sports have extensive player education programmes that warn of the dangers of drugs.

SILVER

2. Which performance-enhancing drugs will have most impact on the performance of a football or hockey player?

GOLD

3. Watch the following clip of David Millar on YouTube: http://www.youtube.com/watch?v=v SAAUO_tbY, and summarize why David resorted to taking performance-enhancing drugs.

Unit 9 assignment, part four

Background

The health promotion team have been approached by their local county sport partnership (CSP) to help support a drugs awareness programme aimed at gifted and talented athletes in the area. You have been asked to produce information that can be used as part of the drugs awareness programme.

Grading criteria to be assessed
1D.9
2D.P9
2D.M4
2D.D3

Task

Prepare a presentation or information sheets about the impact of performance-enhancing drugs on health and sports performance. The presentation or information sheets should:

 **LEVEL 1**

- Describe two different types of drugs and their impact on sports performance. (1D.9)

 **LEVEL 2 PASS**

- Describe four different types of drugs and their impact on sports performance. (2D.P9)

 **LEVEL 2 MERIT**

- Evaluate the impact of four different performance-enhancing drugs on performance in four different types of sport. (2D.M4)

 **LEVEL 2 DISTINCTION**

- Discuss, using relevant examples, why some individuals may resort to using performance-enhancing drugs in sport. (2D.D3)

Tackling the assignment

Your presentation or information sheets need to **describe** four different performance-enhancing drugs to an appropriate level of detail so that the young athletes clearly understand what the drug is and its impact on sports performance.

When you **evaluate** each performance-enhancing drug, make sure you cover both the potential 'positive' and negative effects of each drug on a particular sport or group of sports, making sure you pair a different sport or group of sports with each drug.

When **discussing** why some individuals resort to using performance-enhancing drugs in sport you need to use relevant examples. Quotes from the athletes themselves, as well as the national governing bodies for their sports, and comments from journalists and other interested parties will really bring your presentation to life.

Meeting the Level 2 Pass and Merit criteria

Drugs: A mug's game!

Danni Butterworth

There are various performance-enhancing drugs you need to be aware of, as you may be tempted to use them as you progress through your sporting life. We all know taking drugs is a mug's game, but being better informed will enable you to understand the dangers and make the right decision.

In this leaflet we will look at four different types of performance-enhancing drugs, starting with:

Anabolic steroids

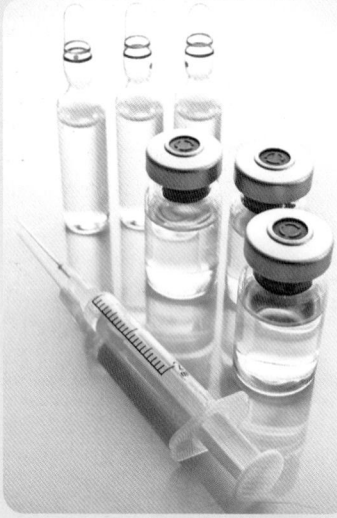

Anabolic steroids are a man-made version of the male hormone testosterone. They are legally available, but only through prescription as they are used medically to treat a variety of conditions that cause a loss or wastage of muscle mass.

The testosterone within steroids helps the body use proteins more effectively, which in turn helps build muscle. Steroids also delay fatigue, which means that performers can train harder and longer as well as recover more quickly, which in turn lets them train more often.

Steroids are taken in either pill form or injections, and doses taken by steroid abusers are often 10 to 100 times higher than those taken legally.

There are many health risks associated with taking and abusing steroids. For men, there is a greater chance of infertility, some have been known to develop breasts, and incidents of severe acne are common. Women who take steroids can develop a deeper voice, also suffer from baldness, and have an increase in body hair.

Many steroid users who try to quit can experience mood swings, depression, and increased aggression.

The impact of taking steroids on a sport such as power lifting are clear. They will help the lifter train longer and harder, putting them at an advantage over other competitors who are 'clean'. They will also help the abuser to train more often because the steroids aid recovery, again giving them an advantage over others who need more time to recover between training sessions.

Danni has described anabolic steroids and their potential effect on power lifting well. She has also looked at the possible positives and negatives of steroids, using a sport to support her views. If Danni continues with this level of detail for another three drugs and evaluates their impact on different sports she should meet the criteria for 2D.P9 and 2D.M4.

Meeting the Level 2 Distinction criteria

Richie Easton

Why do participants take drugs?

1. Due to the pressure placed on them to succeed, which may come from coaches or agents.

2. To improve their performance, making them more successful.

3. For the financial rewards of winning, getting sponsorship deals, etc.

4. Due to a lack of awareness of the negative health effects, because of poor education.

5. Because of their own desire to win at all costs.

I like Richie's approach. He has summarized very briefly why performers may take drugs, but has then researched the topic and found some powerful examples. The video is great discussion material, although the key to Richie meeting the criteria for 2D.D3 is how he presents it and manages the discussion that emerges from his presentation. There will be plenty of opportunity for Richie to consider and comment upon the possible pressure Millar received from the cycling coaches and his team, the financial benefits that followed his success, and the general adulation he received being a key member of a powerful team.

Richie also needs to find similar examples to support the other items on his PowerPoint® slide, although more than one is covered by the David Millar case study.

When I talk about pressure to succeed I will show the video clip of David Millar (www.youtube.com/watch?v=v_SAAUO_tbY, which contains some bad language), who was banned for taking EPO in 2004. It's a powerful video because it explains that he felt as though he was obliged to take drugs.

I will talk about the impact on him: how he lived a lie, the culture of drugs in his team, the effect on his personality, the increase in glory that followed.

I will also issue a newspaper article from the Guardian (www.guardian.co.uk/sport/2004/jul/02/cycling.tourdefrance2004?INTCMP=SRCH), which discusses how his ban has now been overturned and the positive environment he encountered when he became part of Team GB.

Unit 10: Injury and the Sports Performer

Risks and hazards

A hazard is different from a risk. A hazard is anything that could potentially cause harm or injury to a person. A risk is the likelihood of harm or injury actually occurring. When planning a sports session, the teacher, coach, or leader needs to ensure that all hazards are kept to a minimum and, if any minor hazards cannot be eliminated, that they are pointed out to participants. They must also assess the risk of injury or harm coming to the participants and do everything they can to reduce that risk. Teachers, coaches, and leaders should make every effort to keep participants safe from harm and injury.

BRONZE

1. a) Look at the picture above and identify as many hazards as you can. There are ten to find.

b) Categorize each hazard you have identified, as to whether there is a high, medium, or low risk of it causing harm or injury to the players.

2. Identify the hazards and risks associated with a sporting area in your school or college. It could be an indoor basketball court or a synthetic pitch.

People-related risks and hazards

Risks and hazards from people are those created by the participants taking part in a sport or physical activity. They include:

Inappropriate warm-up or cool-down: Failing to warm up or cool down properly increases the risk of a performer sustaining an injury. A warm-up should include three phases: a cardiovascular phase that raises the heart rate and gets the blood flowing quicker; a stretching phase that improves the flexibility of the muscles, and; a joint mobilization phase that loosens and increases the range of movement at the joints. A cool-down should have two phases: a gentle aerobic phase, which gives the heart a chance to gradually slow down before returning to its resting rate and the muscles a chance to relax, and; a stretching phase, which stops the build up of lactic acid in the muscles and helps to prevent immediate cramping or soreness the following day.

Physique: It is important that players have a suitable physique for the sport they are participating in or the position they are playing in, and many sports ensure that participants compete against opponents of a similar physique. Sometimes this is by age category, such as in under-19s football, and sometimes it is by weight category, as in boxing. Having the correct physique for your sport or position reduces the risk of injury during contact with your opponents.

Arsenal's Eduardo suffered a horrific leg break following this tackle from Martin Taylor of Birmingham City in February 2008.

Alcohol: Drinking alcohol or taking recreational drugs before taking part in sporting activities can be very dangerous for the participant and others. It can have many negative effects that include:
- Loss of control, including the ability to concentrate, react quickly, and maintain good balance.
- Increased aggression.
- Increased fatigue, which in turn affects the level of performance.
- Masking pain that may be indicating that injury is taking place.
- Increased heat loss.

Overtraining: When you train, your muscles are worked hard, and in some cases microscopic muscle tears weaken the muscle fibres. This is natural, and the body heals itself and becomes stronger as a result. However, if you overtrain, your muscles do not have time to repair fully, and the microscopic tears become bigger and bigger, weakening the muscle as a whole and leading to long-term injury.

Technique: Participants with poor technique are more likely to suffer from injuries than those with a good technique, because their movements are less efficient and less accurate. Energy is wasted on simple movements, which leads to even poorer technique because of fatigue. This is particularly likely to lead to injury in high-risk sports, such as climbing. In addition, poor technique in sports such as weightlifting can lead to injuries like back pain, sprains, and strains.

Behaviour of other participants: When a sporting activity involves other people, for example, when you are playing a team game, it is important that the other participants do so responsibly and safely. Injuries can be sustained when opponents perform dangerous tackles or behave in other inappropriate ways.

Skill level: Participants with a low skill level often suffer from injuries because they attempt movements that they are not capable of. For example, a large proportion of injuries in skiing occur because participants lose control when skiing on terrain that is above their skill level. Having a low skill level does not in itself lead to injury; it is the low skill level coupled with over confidence that leads to injury.

Jewellery: Participants should not wear jewellery when taking part in sporting activities because it can potentially cause injury to the wearer and others around them. For example, if a basketball player is wearing a bracelet an opposing player could get their finger caught in it while attempting to steal the ball.

BRONZE

3. Carry out research and then write two short paragraphs describing why 'physique' and 'overtraining' present a risk and a hazard to people.

Equipment-related risks and hazards

Risks and hazards from equipment are the risks and hazards related to something we are using or wearing during sporting activity.

- **Inappropriate clothing and footwear:** Wearing the wrong clothing and footwear, or clothing or footwear that doesn't fit properly, can dramatically increase the risk of injury in many sports. For example, in football, wearing the wrong studs on wet surfaces can result in serious – but avoidable – injuries if players slip and fall into one another.
- **Incorrect use of equipment:** Often participants have the correct equipment, but use it incorrectly. For example, wearing shin pads is only useful if they are worn on the front of the leg with the socks pulled up to keep them in place. Unfortunately many players do not do this, which leads to the shin pads being in the wrong position at the critical moment.
- **Lack of protective clothing or equipment:** Failing to wear the correct protective clothing or to use the correct protective equipment can make a participant vulnerable to injury. In football, shin pads protect the tibia, which can be on the receiving end of significant kicks and blows because tackling is one of the main methods of intercepting the ball.
- **Faulty or damaged equipment:** All equipment must be checked before it is used. If it is faulty or damaged it can cause serious injury to the participant using it or any people nearby. For example, playing with a tennis racket that doesn't have a suitable grip can injure a player's hand, as the racket could slip around causing blistering, and it can also injure people nearby if it flies out of the player's hand and hits a spectator.
- **Incorrect use of equipment:** Protective clothing and equipment are only useful if they are worn/handled correctly. For example, wearing a helmet while riding a horse or playing goalkeeper in hockey is essential, but if the helmet straps are not fastened correctly the helmet will fall off during sudden movement, which increases the likelihood of a head injury.

BRONZE

4. Carry out research into the protective clothing and equipment used in a sport of your choice. Then, write no more than 200 words explaining why it minimizes the risks and hazards involved with taking part in that sport.

Environment-related risks and hazards

Risks and hazards from the environment are those risks and hazards that are all around us.

- **Cold weather:** During cold weather it is important that participants try to stay warm and dry because heat loss increases when we are cold and damp. Several layers of thin clothing are better than one thick heavy one and are also easier to add or remove when exercising. The thin layers help trap heat and reduce the amount that escapes. In very cold weather it is also advisable to wear a hat because as much as 50 per cent of total body heat can be lost from the head and neck. If the body's core temperature drops below an acceptable level you will suffer from hypothermia, which, if not treated, can lead to death. In addition, when muscles are cold they do not move or stretch freely. Stretching a cold muscle unexpectedly is likely to lead to a muscle strain injury.
- **Rain:** Excess water can lead to flooding and muddy pitches, which increase the risk of slipping and, therefore, the risk of injury.
- **Hot weather:** Taking part in sporting activities in hot weather can increase the risk of injury to the performer. It is harder for the body to cool itself down in hot weather, which can lead to heat stroke or heat exhaustion and even death. Participants are also at risk of sunburn. Drinking lots of fluids is essential in hot weather to avoid dehydration, and staying out of the midday sun is advisable.
- **Playing surfaces:** Prior to a sporting activity playing surfaces must be checked to make sure that play is safe, the surface hasn't been damaged, there is nothing for participants to trip over or slip on, and that there are no other dangerous objects – such as stones – that could come into contact with the participants and injure them. It is more important to check outdoor playing surfaces carefully but indoor playing surfaces should also be checked every time they are used. Wearing suitable clothing can sometimes reduce the risk of injury on a particular playing surface – for example, wearing tracksuit bottoms on an AstroTurf® pitch can reduce the risk of skin abrasions for a goalkeeper.

There are many different risks associated with climbing in cold weather.

BRONZE

5. This page details some of the risks and hazards associated with the environment but there are others. Research another environmental hazard and give an account of why participants are at risk from this while taking part in sport.

Rules, regulations, and legislation

Whether you are taking part in sport at a competitive level or simply enjoying sport as a pastime with friends, there are rules, regulations, and legislation in place to protect you from injury.

Put simply, rules are statements of what you are and are not allowed to do in a given situation. Rules can be formal or informal. Formal rules, for example rules that are introduced by a governing body of a sport, are often called regulations. Legislation is the name given to rules and regulations that have been made into law by the government of a country.

Regulations

Regulations in sport are important. They:

- **Maintain a safe environment:** By ensuring that equipment, playing surfaces, and players' behaviour are appropriate, regulations minimize the risk of injuries happening.
- **Protect participants and those leading the activity:** By establishing a code of conduct, regulations help to ensure that players do not injure each other, or put referees and other officials in danger.
- **Minimize injury by enforcing rules that specify the safety equipment or protective clothing that must be used:** For example, the rules of football state that all players must wear shin pads in a game, and the rules of ice hockey require all players to wear a helmet.
- **Minimize injury by enforcing rules that specify how a facility or location should be used:** For example, a school might not allow slide tackling on a synthetic pitch, to reduce the risk of grazes and burns, or a ski resort might close a particular slope due to the risk of an avalanche.
- **Require a risk assessment to be carried out:** A risk assessment ensures that risks have been considered and potential hazards identified and controlled where possible. Potential risks to players from each other, from the activity, from equipment, and from the environment are identified, classified as high, medium, or low risk, and then minimized where possible.

Legislation

The Health and Safety at Work Act 1974
All workers have a right to work in places where risks to their health and safety are properly controlled. Your employer is responsible for health and safety, for making sure you aren't hurt while you are doing your job and that you don't get ill because of your job, but it is also your responsibility to look after your own health and safety.

Management of Health and Safety at Work (Amendment) Regulations 1994
These regulations require employers, including self-employed people, to ensure that risk assessments have been carried out so that employees and people associated with a business or a place of work are adequately protected. These regulations cover a wide range of scenarios, including those relating to young people and expectant mothers, and imminent or serious dangers.

Health and S
What y

All workers have a right to work in places
controlled. Health and safety is about sto
Your employer is responsible for health a

What employers must do for you

1 Decide what could harm you in your job and the precautions to stop it. This is part of risk assessment.

2 In a way you can understand, explain how risks will be controlled and tell you who is responsible for this.

3 Consult and work with you and your health and safety representatives in protecting everyone from harm in the workplace.

4 Free of charge, give you the health and safety training you need to do your job.

5 Free of charge, provide you with any equipment and protective clothing you need, and ensure it is properly looked after.

6 Provide toilets, washing f and drinking water.

7 Provide adequate first-aid facilities.

8 Report injuries, diseases a dangerous incidents at wo our Incident Contact Cent
0845 300 992

9 Have insurance that cover in case you get hurt at wo or ill through work. Displ hard copy or electronic co the current insurance certi where you can easily read

10 Work with any other empl or contractors sharing the workplace or providing employees (such as agency workers), so that everyone health and safety is protec

Your health and safety representatives:

Other health and safety contacts:

HSE

Health and Safety (First-Aid) Regulations 1981

These regulations require employers to provide adequate and appropriate equipment, facilities, and personnel to enable first aid to be given to employees if they are injured or become ill at work. These regulations apply to all workplaces, including the self-employed and those with fewer than five employees.

Safety of Sports Grounds Act 1975

Following a number of major accidents at sports grounds it became clear that the structure and management of these venues needed to be controlled. This Act placed the control with local authorities and the Fire Safety and Safety of Places of Sports Act 1987 made it a duty of local authorities to enforce the Act.

The Children Act 2004

This Act supports the government's Every Child Matters programme, which was designed to ensure that all organizations involved in safeguarding children – including district councils, Primary Care Trusts, Youth Offending Teams, and schools – work together to improve the well-being of all young people.

aw

eed to know

to their health and safety are properly tting hurt at work or ill through work. t you must help.

t you t do	If there's a problem
w the training you have ed when using any items your employer iven you.	1 If you are worried about health and safety in your workplace, talk to your employer, supervisor, or health and safety representative.
reasonable care of your and other people's health safety.	2 You can also look at our website for general information about health and safety at work.
pperate with your employer ealth and safety.	3 If, after talking with your employer, you are still worried, phone our Infoline. We can put you in touch with the local enforcing authority for health and safety and the Employment Medical Advisory Service. You don't have to give your name.
someone (your employer, rvisor, or health and safety esentative) if you think the k or inadequate precautions utting anyone's health and ty at serious risk.	

HSE Infoline:
0845 345 0055

HSE website:
www.hse.gov.uk

Fire safety
You can get advice on fire safety from the Fire and Rescue Services or your workplace fire officer.

Employment rights
Find out more about your employment rights at:

www.direct.gov.uk

h and Safety Executive

Following the Hillsborough disaster, various new rules, regulations, and legislation were introduced.

Control of Substances Hazardous to Health (COSHH) 2002

Using chemicals or other hazardous substances at work can put people's health at risk, so this law requires employers to control exposure to hazardous substances and protect both employees and others who may be exposed to them to prevent ill health.

BRONZE

1. Choose a sport or physical activity that you take part in regularly. Then, write down as many rules and regulations as you can think of that have been designed to control the way you behave and protect you from injury.

SILVER

2. The Hillsborough disaster occurred on 15 April 1989, when 96 Liverpool fans were crushed to death on the terraces of Sheffield Wednesday's stadium. Find out as much as you can about the Hillsborough disaster, and the Taylor Report that followed, and explain the health and safety rules, regulations, and legislation that were introduced as a result.

Unit 10 assignment, part one

Background

Your school or college is due to hold a sports day for Year 6 students from the local primary school and you have been asked to assist in the preparations for the event. Planning such events needs to be done very carefully as health and safety is of paramount importance. Everybody involved in the planning and delivery of the sports day needs to be aware of the potential hazards and any preventative strategies that can be used, as well as the rules, regulations, and legislation that apply to the event.

Task

Prepare an informative document to be given to the teachers from the local primary school that clearly identifies the potential hazards and any preventative strategies that can be used at the sports day, as well as the rules, regulations, and legislation that apply to the event. Your document can be presented in any format you wish and should include:

Grading criteria to be assessed
1A.1, 1D.7
2A.P1, 2D.P7
2D.M3
2D.D3

 **LEVEL 1**

- Describe two different risks or hazards that relate to each topic of people, equipment and the environment respectively. (1A.1)
- Outline reasons for having health and safety rules, regulations and legislation in sport. (1D.7)

 **LEVEL 2 PASS**

- Explain three different risks or hazards that relate to each topic of people, equipment and the environment respectively. (2A.P1)
- Discuss reasons for having health and safety rules, regulations and legislation in sport. (2D.P7)

 **LEVEL 2 MERIT**

- Explain how two selected rules, regulations or pieces of legislation help maintain the health and safety of participants in a selected sport. (2D.M3)

 **LEVEL 2 DISTINCTION**

- Analyse the impact of two selected rules, regulations or pieces of legislation on participants in a selected sport. (2D.D3)

Tackling the assignment

One way to approach this assignment is to create a webpage that illustrates the risks and hazards associated with a school sports day. You could include links to video footage of hazardous situations (making sure you include a range of different risks and hazards), with information about how the rules, regulations, and legislation that apply to the event help to ensure the safety of those involved.

To meet the Pass criteria, you must explain different risks and hazards, and **discuss** reasons for health and safety legislation. To do this, you will need to provide a broad overview of the topics, make a suggestion, and then follow it up with further, relevant information.

To move up to a Merit you need to **explain** health and safety legislation as it relates to a specific sport. This requires you to demonstrate a greater understanding of health and safety legislation and, more importantly, to *apply your knowledge* to a specific circumstance, such as how the Fire Safety and Safety of Places of Sports Act 1987 is used to prevent a repeat of the 1985 Bradford Stadium Fire.

If you are aiming for a Distinction, you need to **analyse** legislation. You are expected to research rules, regulations, and legislation in depth and then conclude how effective it really is in maintaining health and safety. For example, has the Fire Safety and Safety of Places of Sports Act 1987 actually been effective in preventing fires at major sports stadiums over the last 25 years?

Meeting the Level 2 Pass criteria

Emily Harris

People factors

Inappropriate warm-up and/or cool-down

If students do not warm up or cool down properly they are at risk of injury and that is a hazard. They could pull a muscle or even break a bone if their body is not coping or is straining because they have not stretched properly. A good warm-up consists of mobility, flexibility, and cardiovascular exercises. A cool-down needs to be very slow and simple, for example, an easy jog and a few stretches.

Physical fitness

Students who are not physically fit or prepared are more likely to get an injury. Students need to be aware that they should only push their bodies as far as their physical fitness will allow. For example, your body will not be able to cope with the intense training required to play a full season of football if you did not train in the break between the end of the last season and the beginning of the new season.

Physique

A student's physique has an impact on how well they perform in different sports. For example, if somebody has quite a big build then they are probably more suited to shot-put or discus, and if they have a much smaller build they may be better at sprinting or long-distance running.

Environment Factors

Weather

The weather can have a major impact on the safety of an activity or an event. This is true of both extremes of heat and extremes of cold. For example, if the London Marathon takes place on a particularly hot day, then the risk of dehydration is increased, which event organizers would need to be prepared for. If the event takes place on a particularly cold day, then participants may well suffer from hypothermia.

This webpage shows a sound understanding of the risks and hazards associated with people, but 2A.P1 does require a total of nine risks or hazards to be explained (three each for people, environment, and equipment hazards), which means that Emily falls short of meeting the Level 2 Pass criteria at the moment.

While Emily's example of dehydration due to hot weather during the London Marathon is an appropriate example of how weather can present a hazard, I am not convinced of her point regarding hypothermia. It is unlikely that even the British weather in April would be cold enough to cause hypothermia, particularly for the runners who will be generating body heat as they move. However, it is a largely irrelevant point, since the task clearly asks students to produce an informative document that can be given to teachers prior to a sports event for Year 6 students. I would have preferred Emily to give examples of potential risks and hazards presented by equipment, people, and the environment at a Year 6 sports event.

Meeting the Level 2 Merit criteria

Year 6 Sports Day

BTEC Level 2 Unit 10 assignment, part one   **Luke Norton**

The 2012 Year 6 Sports Day will feature a number of different events and competitions, including athletics, badminton, and football. Each activity has important safety rules, which must be followed. These are shown below:

Football

Within the football tournament, players will compete in mixed teams of six-a-side, though please note that in future years players will compete in single-sex teams due to FA (Football Association) regulations, which prevent mixed teams after the age of 11 years.

As per FA regulations, all players must wear shin pads, knee-length socks, and football boots. Studs must be of the moulded astro-turf type. This is to ensure that all players are safe and that the risk of injury is reduced. Not wearing shin pads leaves the legs exposed during a tackle, and due to the varying degree of players size and strength at age ten, a smaller player could easily be injured through contact with a larger opponent. The wearing of shin pads greatly reduces the risk of injury during collision, because it spreads the impact over a wider area.

Luke has started this piece of work off very well. Presenting the information in a booklet is a very good decision, because parents and teachers can carry it with them on the day of the event. The booklet is also a useful document to refer to if players arrive not wearing the correct equipment.

Luke has clearly referenced the FA rules regarding safety equipment, and in particular the wearing of shin pads. He has then explained the rationale for wearing such protective items. Luke has also given parents, teachers, and players food for thought in terms of future competition between boys and girls. Luke's explanation of the use of shin pads is more detailed than his point about the gender of players competing against each other, and I would like to have seen him develop this further by explaining why boys and girls do not compete against each other in contact sports after primary school. So, although Luke has discussed two examples of rules and regulations relating to football, he has only explained one of them fully and to meet the criteria for 2D.M3 he will have to add to his explanation about girls and boys competing together.

Meeting the Level 2 Distinction criteria

I particularly like James' approach to this assignment. His booklet clearly sets out the rules and regulations that apply to the Year 6 sports event, but he's taken the opportunity to share his thoughts on his own favourite sport as well, F1 Racing. The great advantage of this is that it has opened up an opportunity for him to really analyse the impact of rules in his sport. To meet the criteria, James has been asked to analyse the impact of *two* selected rules in a sport, but he has gone further and covered *three* rules. Better yet, he's concentrated on the rule changes that relate to improving safety for the drivers involved, rather than some of the more innocuous rule changes. James' ability to see the advantages and disadvantages of each rule, along with his efforts to give his own opinion on the rules' impact on the sport, clearly meet the requirement to analyse the rules and regulations. The best example of this is his point that the third new rule (no short-cuts) was not actually needed, since the stay on the track rule already exists. As such, I am happy that James has met the Distinction criteria for this assignment.

And finally…

BTEC Level 2 Unit 10 assignment, part one

James Carson

The previous pages in this booklet set out the rules and regulations as they relate to the Year 6 Sports Day event, but out of interest I wanted to share my thoughts with you all on my favourite sport: Formula 1 (F1) Racing. Rule changes occur every year in most major sports, but F1 rules seem to change more than most. Here are my thoughts on the rule changes for the 2012 F1 racing season, which begins with the Australian Grand Prix in March.

There have been several rule changes that affect the design and build of the car, ranging from changes to the exhaust set up, to the shape of the car's nose, and even to the type of traction that is allowed. However, I am more concerned with the rule changes that affect the way the car is driven.

Safety cars

Ever since I began watching F1 racing, the safety car has been a prominent feature. Whenever there's a crash or something similar, the safety car is sent out onto the track. The rule has always been that no-one is allowed to overtake the safety car and so many drivers and teams use this rule to 'close the gap' between themselves and the cars in front. The result is that the field becomes more cramped, which can be great at the restart. However, it also means that those drivers who are in front of the safety car (usually the race leaders) end up closing in on the back markers, who then inevitably get in the way at the restart. The new rule states that drivers *can* overtake the safety car (although they still can't overtake the car in front of them). This means that at the restart, all of the 'back markers' will be past the safety car, and so the race leaders will have an open road in front of them. This will hopefully mean that the top drivers tussle a bit more throughout the race. It should also mean that there are fewer accidents after a restart, which creates excitement for spectators, but is very dangerous for the drivers. I'm looking forward to seeing how this one pans out!

The 'one-move' rule

This new rule states that drivers who move to the side to defend their position – by blocking the overtaking route to a car behind – must, if they move back to their original position, leave at least a car's width between themselves and the edge of the track. This will stop drivers swerving around on the track quite so much, and it is hoped this will also reduce the risk of high-speed crashes at the end of the main straight on each track. However, it is also important to note that this has been a 'gentleman's agreement' between drivers for several years, since none of them want to be either the cause or victim of a high-speed crash. The problem, as I see it, is that now it's been made an official law, the race marshals will have to police it. How on earth are they going to spot (on a TV replay or from the control tower) whether a driver has left a full car's width between themselves and the edge of the track or whether they've left an inch or two less than is required. This one, I predict, is going to lead to lots of challenges from team managers in the pit lane. I wouldn't be surprised if it's repealed for the 2013 season.

Banning short cuts

What a complete and utter waste of time this rule is going to be! The idea behind it is to stop drivers taking a short cut at corners on their way to the pit lane, so as to reduce the risk of collisions. Drivers sometimes do this to save themselves some time, and since the difference between first and third place is sometimes less than three seconds, time is of the essence. The best example of this was last season (2011) when Sebastian Vettel cut out a bit of the track on his way back to the pits during a practice session in Korea last year to save himself some time. However, the rule in F1 has always been that 'drivers must stay on the track at all times'. As such, race stewards could simply have imposed a penalty on Vettel for his short cut and other drivers would have been deterred from copying him. Surely it's better to enforce the rules that already exist than bring in new ones?

Causes of injury

All injuries are the result of a physiological cause or a psychological cause. Physiological causes can be either intrinsic or extrinsic. Intrinsic injuries occur when an athlete becomes injured as a direct result of taking part in sport. Extrinsic injuries are caused by external factors, such as the equipment or other participants, and not the sports performer themselves.

Both physiological and psychological causes of injury can be prevented if appropriate precautions are taken.

Inappropriate loading

Ensuring that the intensity of the activity being undertaken is suitable for the athlete is vital in preventing injury. A performer should make sure that the intensity of their training sessions increases slowly, 'loading' the body according to the pressure it can handle. However, injuries can occur if an athlete 'overloads' their body and puts it under intense pressure; for example, a sprinter who normally works at 50 per cent of their maximum speed suddenly increases to 80 per cent of their maximum speed. Performers are likely to overload when they return to sport after a forced break, for example, if they have been ill. They do not realize that their body has taken a step backwards in terms of fitness and train too hard, too soon, on their return.

Gravity

If the force of gravity, the force exerted on the body by the Earth, is greater than the opposing force provided by a performer's muscles, then the performer will collapse to the ground. This is particularly evident when landing after a jump, when taking part in the high jump, or when landing after jumping for the ball in a line-out for example. As gravity pulls the performer back towards the ground, incorrect foot placement on landing can reduce the force that the muscles are able to apply, causing the joints to collapse and possibly resulting in knee and ankle injuries.

Extrinsic factors

These are external factors, such as equipment and other people, that are often beyond an individual's control. For example, being knocked over in an ice hockey match by a poorly skilled opponent is not something the performer can directly control. Similarly, if a pole vaulter's pole breaks while she is in the air, it is highly likely to cause injury but is not something that can be anticipated.

In some cases, external factors relating to equipment can be controlled, because often it is the incorrect use of the equipment that causes injury. For example, not setting the trampoline up correctly could cause serious injury if it collapses during a performer's routine. In this instance any injury could easily have been avoided if the equipment had been properly checked before use.

Overuse

Overuse injuries are directly related to overtraining, when the performer has not allowed a suitable rest period between training sessions or competitive fixtures. The wear and tear placed on muscles, joints, and connective tissues is too great, and the lack of recovery time means that the body is put under stress before it has had time to recover, resulting in injury.

Physiological causes of injury

Levers

In order for a part of the body to move, the relevant muscles and bones need to work together as a series of levers. A lever consists of the following three components:

- The pivot (or fulcrum): The point about which the lever rotates.
- The load: The force applied by the lever.
- The effort: The force applied by the user of the lever system.

If the lever is not balanced, for example if the load is too heavy or the effort is not great enough, an intrinsic injury, such as a sprain, strain, or even a fracture, may occur.

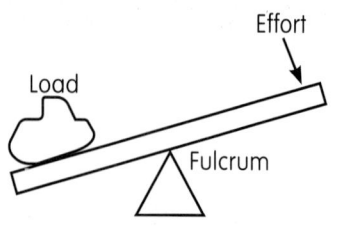

Alignment

It is important for sports performers to have good alignment because poor alignment can put a strain on the body and can lead to intrinsic injuries. If an athlete has poor balance, they may put more weight on one foot than they do on the other, causing discomfort and eventually injury. Therefore, it is important that an athlete maintains good posture when training and performing, making sure that they keep a straight back to avoid injuries and/or strains.

Stress

Being in a stressful situation can lead to injury because of the physiological effects of stress on the body. Stress leads to an increased heart rate, which can cause fatigue to occur earlier than usual. More seriously, stress causes the body to release adrenalin. An appropriate amount of adrenaline can improve performance, but when too much adrenalin is released a performer will find it hard to perform fine movements, which means that twists and sprains are more likely to happen. Stress also reduces concentration levels.

Personality

Each person has their own unique personality and there may be aspects of a person's personality that make them more likely to injure themselves. For example, trait anxiety is a fixed or relatively permanent form of anxiety, which people suffer from because their nervous system is constantly active. It can lead to poor concentration, particularly in stressful situations, which makes accidents and injuries more likely. A rock climber with trait anxiety is likely to panic at some point, reducing their ability to place their hands and feet safely while climbing. In some cases, trait anxiety can cause a person to freeze, which can put people trying to help them in danger too.

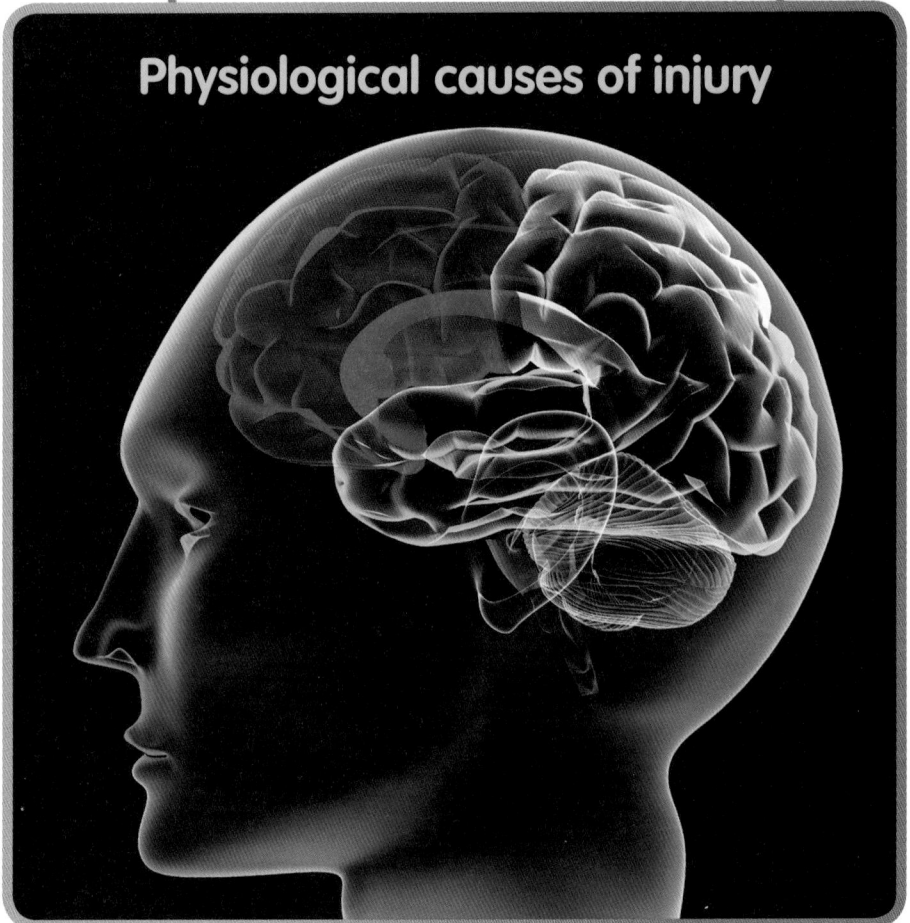

Physiological causes of injury

Reduced concentration

To be able to perform at a high level, a performer's mind and body must be prepared and ready to cope with the physical demands of the situation. A lack of concentration can lead to trips, falls, and other mistakes, which can result in physical injury. The effects of poor concentration are greater the more dangerous the activity.

BRONZE

1. a) Make a list of four different injuries that you or a member of your family has suffered.

b) Categorize each injury as having a physiological or a psychological cause.

SILVER

2. Choose a sport and for three of the most common injuries in the sport, give a detailed account of why they occur.

Types of injury

People who take part in sport and exercise are at risk of developing injuries. Injuries sustained by sports participants can be categorized as basic injuries or complex injuries.

Basic injuries

Basic injuries cause damage to the skin or muscles, and include:

- **Strains** occur when a muscle or tendon is overstretched or torn. A strain can cause pain, swelling, and muscle weakness.
- **Sprains** occur when a ligament is overstretched or torn. Sprains can cause pain, bruising, and swelling.
- **Bruising** occurs when the skin is banged or bumped and tiny blood vessels are broken, causing the area to become red or purple as it fills with blood.
- **Grazes** happen when a slight abrasion, or rubbing, of the skin causes the surface layer of the skin to come off, leaving the area raw and tender.
- **Cuts** are caused by lacerations to the skin and always result in external bleeding. Common causes of cuts include contact with another player's studs in rugby or football or colliding with a sharp object on the pitch.
- **Blisters** are small areas of raised skin with either air or blood trapped underneath. They can be extremely painful, and are usually caused by ill-fitting clothing/footwear, which rubs against the skin's surface.

Complex injuries

Complex injuries can be divided into overuse injuries and acute injuries.

Overuse injuries often occur when a sports performer pushes themselves hard over long periods of time and continuously puts the same muscles, bones, and joints under pressure. Examples of this type of injury are:

- **Tendonitis:** The tendon becomes inflamed because lots of pressure is put on it. The tendon can become painful and movement in that area becomes uncomfortable. Tennis elbow and golfer's elbow are common names given to specific examples of tendonitis.
- **Shin splints:** Tiny fractures in the surface of the tibia cause pain and swelling. Shin splints are common in any sport involving running.
- **Osgood–Schlatter disease:** This is a common injury in young performers aged between 9 and 16 years of age. It is caused by overuse of the joint during a growth spurt as a result of excessive running and jumping, and is characterized by pain just below the patella (kneecap).

Acute injuries are injuries that reach a crisis quickly. Acute injuries that occur as a result of sport and exercise include:

- **Fractures:** This is the word used to refer to broken bones. There are many types of fracture, but they are generally categorized as 'open' or 'closed'. With an open fracture, a fragment or fragments of bone pierce through the skin causing an open wound. A closed fracture happens when the bone is broken but does not penetrate the surface of the skin, so no wound is visible, other than swelling and bruising around the area.
- **Dislocations:** Two bones become separated or misaligned at a joint, causing deformity, intense pain, and swelling.
- **Concussion:** This is a mild brain injury caused by a blow to the skull. Concussion can cause temporary unconsciousness, a headache, and a loss of short-term memory. Vomiting and nausea are also common.
- **Spinal injuries:** The spinal cord is damaged, causing reduced movement and sometimes paralysis. Spinal injuries can occur following a blow to the back. For example, a bad fall in gymnastics could result in a spinal injury.

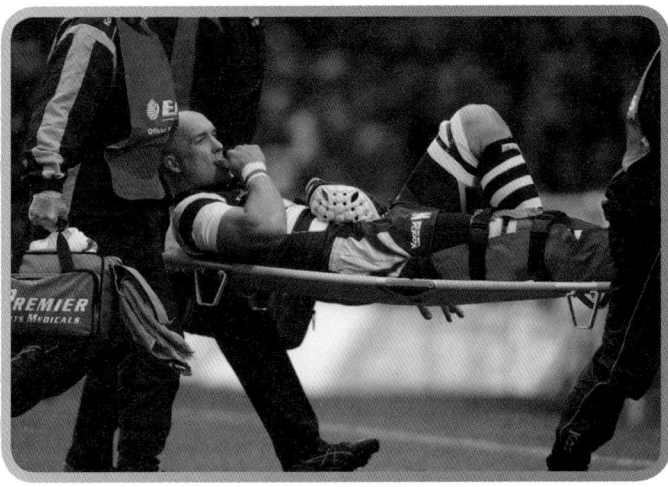

Nathan Budgett of Bristol is stretchered off with a suspected broken leg in a rugby union match.

French rugby player Yannick Jauzion sporting a bruised eye.

American footballer Michael Lewis is helped from the field while suffering from concussion.

Footballer Kevin Davies looks down at his dislocated finger.

Wales' Lee Byrne receives treatment for what could be a sprained ankle.

BRONZE

1. Discuss, with a partner, which sports performers are most likely to suffer from overuse injuries and why.

2. For each activity in the table below, name an injury that participants may suffer and classify the injury as either basic or complex.

Sport	Injury	Basic or complex?
Football		
Rugby		
Tennis		
Netball		
Swimming		

Types of illness

When participating in sport it is important that performers recognize the potential threat posed by illness. Not only are some illnesses associated with sports participation but careful consideration should also be given to what effect illness may have on a performer should they become unwell during training or competition.

The following illnesses are associated with sports participation and should be monitored closely when sport or exercise is undertaken:

- **Asthma** is a respiratory disorder that affects the lungs. When someone suffers an asthma attack the air passages to the lungs become narrow and normal breathing becomes difficult. Symptoms of asthma include shortness of breath, wheezing, coughing, and chest tightness. Asthma attacks can be very mild but they can also be life-threatening.
- **Heart attacks** occur when the blood vessels that supply the heart with blood become blocked. This can be caused by a build up of cholesterol, which makes it difficult for the blood to pass through. Symptoms of a heart attack often include chest pain, sweating, and shortness of breath.
- **Viral infections** such as flu, are caused by the presence of a virus in the body. Any part of the body can be affected by a viral infection and most antibiotics do not help with the symptoms. These symptoms can vary but may include a high temperature, nausea, and tiredness.
- **Hypoglycaemia** occurs when there is a low blood sugar level in the body. People who suffer from diabetes can also suffer with hypoglycaemia. Symptoms include sweating, weakness, and confusion.

 **Fact:**

Although some sports, such as swimming, are said to be beneficial for asthma sufferers, this is not the case with one particular type. Exercise-induced asthma, or EIA, is a condition that can occur after several minutes of vigorous aerobic exercise. People who suffer from EIA should ensure that they warm up before they exercise and gradually increase the intensity of their activity.

BRONZE

1. Discuss the possibilities of the illnesses above occurring as a result of physical activity. Which people are most at risk of suffering from these illnesses during physical activity?

SILVER

2. What does EIA stand for and how can this affect a sports performer? What should people who suffer from EIA do to ensure that it does not affect their performance?

SPOTLIGHT on injury and illness

BRONZE

Completing these activities will help you to achieve a **Level 2 Pass** in your assignment.

1. a) Choose two injuries (one basic and one complex) and one illness associated with sports participation, and find out as much as you can about them. For example, what are the signs or symptoms to look for and what is the correct treatment?

b) Find a partner and act out the injuries and illnesses you have chosen. Your partner has to guess what they are.

SILVER

Completing this activity will help you to achieve a **Level 2 Merit** in your assignment.

2. For the injuries you researched for Activity 1, create a poster describing the injuries and showing how they can be caused in a sporting context. Your poster should make it clear what the difference is between a basic and a complex injury.

GOLD

Completing this activity will help you to achieve a **Level 2 Distinction** in your assignment.

3. Create a short video or storyboard for two complex injuries other than those you have researched in Activities 1 and 2. Your video or storyboard should analyse the relationship between the two injuries. For example, are there any similarities or differences in the way they are caused or the way they are treated?

Responses to injury

The human body responds to injury both physiologically and psychologically. Sometimes the effects of injury are obvious, such as when bleeding occurs, but sometimes they are not immediately apparent, such as in depression or with a loss of self-confidence.

Physiological responses to injury

Physiological responses are generally quite easy to spot, and are usually evident immediately or at least within 24 hours of the injury occurring. They include pain, swelling, redness, an increased temperature, and a loss of movement around the site of the injury.

Pain

Pain is the most obvious physiological response to injury. The cells that have been damaged by the injury release chemicals and these chemicals react with the pain receptors in the muscle or joint, sending a message to the brain that something is not right. Pain is the body's way of telling the performer to stop moving in order to prevent further, more serious injury.

Physiological responses to injury.

Swelling

When a muscle or joint is injured, the body responds by sending fluid to the area to repair the damage. The additional fluid is delivered via the bloodstream, and is responsible for flushing out the chemicals causing the pain. However, a portion of the fluid then remains to allow the white blood cells in the fluid to fight the ensuing infection. The fluid takes up space in the muscle or joint and so the injured part of the body swells to accommodate the fluid.

Reduced range of movement

Over the short to medium term there is often a reduced range of movement around a joint due to the swelling caused by an injury. As the swelling subsides, the range of movement gradually increases, assuming that there has not been a complete fracture of the bones at the joint or a dislocation of the joint.

Redness

The redness around an injury is caused by the increased blood flow to the damaged area. Blood vessels vasodilate, open wider, to allow more blood through, and this pushes them closer to the skin, making the skin look redder. In addition, the injury could have caused internal bleeding (bleeding that takes place beneath the skin), which will also increase the redness of the area.

Heat

The area around the injury will increase in temperature due to the increased blood flow to the damaged area.

Psychological responses to injury

Psychological responses to injury are often more difficult to spot and are usually more long-term than physiological responses. They may well be apparent immediately, such as a performer crying in frustration, but it is more likely that they will be spotted in the days, weeks, and months after an injury has occurred, and can be much more difficult to overcome than a physiological injury.

Immediate psychological responses to injury
The immediate psychological responses to injury can include anger, and in some cases distress, as the performer very quickly becomes aware that they will not be able to take part in physical activity for a while. If you watch athletes on television you will see the angst on their faces in the first couple of minutes after an injury has occurred. These feelings can last anywhere from a few minutes to a few days.

Psychological responses to physiological injuries.

Long-term psychological responses to injury
Long-term psychological responses to injury build up in the days and weeks following a serious injury. They are caused when a performer realizes they will not be able to participate for quite some time, and include:

- **Loss of self-confidence:** Many performers begin to doubt themselves and, because the injury takes time to heal, they begin to wonder if they will be able to perform as well as they did prior to the injury. In many cases, it is this lack of confidence that leads to initial under-performance or over-zealousness when they return to competition.
- **Lowered self-esteem:** Coupled with a loss of self-confidence, lowered self-esteem is characterized by a performer feeling that they are not good enough to be part of their team anymore, and that team-mates are beginning to doubt their ability and performance levels. Similarly, an individual performer may have similar feelings towards their coach, or may begin to feel that opponents are significantly stronger and more skilled than they are.
- **Frustration:** Often the desire to get back to performing as quickly as possible leads to an athlete becoming frustrated with the speed of their recovery. It is common for a player to try to make a comeback too soon, which invariably leads to a repeat of the injury (or at least a different but related injury), which keeps the performer out of action for even longer.
- **Depression:** As the three psychological responses outlined above become stronger, performers often become depressed. This results in a much longer recovery time, as depression causes loss of appetite and energy, which means that training sessions become ineffective. A negative spiral occurs, because as depression leads to an increase in recovery time; an increase in recovery time leads to further or deeper depression. If performers find themselves in this position, they generally need to seek medical advice.

BRONZE

1. Create a poster showing the physiological and/or psychological responses to injury.

SILVER

2. Research two famous sports players who have had to retire after injury. Produce a short report explaining the physiological and psychological effects of the injuries that caused them to retire.

Management of physiological injuries

The treatment and management of an injury will differ depending on its severity. In some cases, little or no treatment is required, while in other cases a long-term rehabilitation plan has to be designed. However, regardless of how serious an injury may be, you should always use the SALTAPS procedure when dealing with an incident.

Remember:

If you are not a qualified first aider, you should always ensure that an injured player or performer seeks appropriate medical advice as soon as possible. This may be from a first aider, a hospital, or a physiotherapist. Sometimes the most serious of injuries can occur from the most minor of incidents.

SALTAPS

SALTAPS describes the stages involved with assessing an injury. With the exception of 'stop play', the stages should only be carried out by an appropriately qualified first aider. You should not move on to the next stage until both you and the injured performer are satisfied that the current stage has been fully completed. For example, you should not touch the area until you have looked at it first and are happy that it looks alright to touch. SALTAPS is not an alternative to seeking medical advice, and if at any point you are unable to move on to the next stage, then you should seek urgent medical attention, either by calling for an ambulance or by taking the injured participant to Accident and Emergency.

Stop play
The first step is to stop play, so that other players are safe and so that attention can be given to the injured player.

Ask
Check how the player feels. It is useful to ask them to rate the level of pain they are experiencing on a scale of one to ten (1 = no pain; 10 = severe pain), to give you an indication of how serious the injury could be. Remember that just because a person can feel no pain, this doesn't mean the injury is not severe. Shock may mean that a person doesn't feel pain until later on.

Look
Check the injured area to see how serious the injury could be. However, don't be fooled. Just because something looks like a minor injury, it doesn't mean that it is.

Touch
Touch the affected area if the player will allow you to. Be very gentle. If a leg or an arm is fractured, it is sometimes possible to feel the fracture. Also, while touching the injury, ask the performer if they can feel that you are touching it. If they can't, it is likely to be a more serious injury.

Active movement
Ask the player to move the affected limb. For example, if it is a leg injury, ask them if they can move their toes and feet first and then ask them if they can move their whole leg.

Passive movement
If the player cannot move the limb on their own, ask them if you can move it for them. Does moving it increase the pain? Is there a sufficient range of movement at the joint?

Stand up
If all other stages are completed to both your satisfaction and the player's, the last stage is to ask the player to stand up. This is particularly the case if it is the leg or foot that is injured. You may need to support the player's bodyweight as they get up. Sometimes this stage will show how serious an injury actually is, because putting bodyweight on an injured area will often cause extreme pain and a player may be in denial about the extent of the injury until they try to put weight on it.

Basic first-aid treatments

Some minor injuries can be treated immediately or over a few days with simple first-aid techniques. However, if after a few days, there has been little or no improvement, the injured person should always seek professional medical help.

PRICE
Sprains and strains, which are both soft tissue injuries, are both treated using the PRICE method:

P = PROTECT: Prevent further injury occurring by protecting the injured area.
R = REST: Rest the injured area.
I = ICE: Apply an ice pack to the affected area.
C = COMPRESSION: Apply gentle but substantial pressure to the injury.
E = ELEVATION: Raise the injured body part above the level of the heart.

Hot and cold therapy
Alternating between an ice pack and a heat pack stimulates the blood flow to the injured area. As the area cools the blood flow decreases, and as it heats up the blood flow increases. Stimulating the blood flow improves the delivery of endorphins (to relieve the pain), white blood cells (to fight any infection), and red blood cells (which carry oxygen and aid the healing process) to the site of the injury. Hot and cold therapy reduces stiffness and soreness, but it also decreases the likelihood of muscle spasms, which cause the muscle to contract and can make an injury worse, because the pain receptors are less likely to be stimulated.

Sports creams
Sports creams contain medication to help the healing process and to stimulate blood flow. Sports creams should never be used on broken skin, because they usually have a burning effect, which causes pain and can delay recovery.

Support strappings
There are all manner of support strappings available for sports injuries, but all have one thing in common: they are used to restrict the amount of movement possible at the affected area. For example, using a tubigrip strapping on an ankle injury prevents the ankle from moving through its full range of movement, reducing the stress on the muscles, ligaments, and tendons. This can help to reduce recovery time. Strappings should not be confused with protective plastic supports, which are there to *prevent* injury, rather than aid recovery.

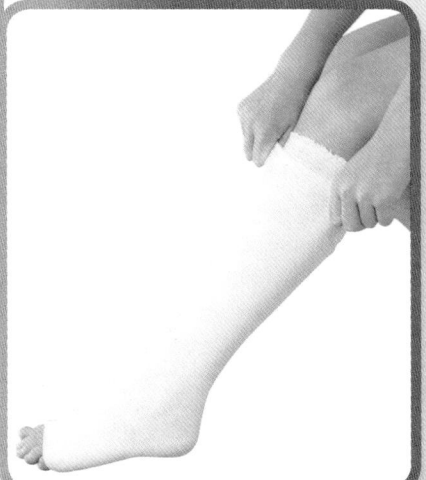

BRONZE
1. Produce a poster that explains the 'PRICE' method of treating a sports injury.

SILVER
2. Write an account of how hot and cold therapy would be used to treat a specific injury received while involved in a sport of your choice.

GOLD
3. Analyse the different treatments available for a specific injury received while involved in a sport of your choice.

Management of psychological injuries

The management and treatment of psychological injuries is much more complex than the management and treatment of physiological injuries and is well beyond the scope of this book and the Level 2 BTEC course. However, what follows below is a suggestion of how to manage the psychological *effects* of a physiological injury.

One of the most common approaches to managing a psychological injury is goal setting. Many performers also find that relaxation techniques help them avoid dwelling on their injury.

Goal setting

The key point in psychological recovery from a physical injury is to see the process of recovery as active, not passive. Athletes who simply sit and wait for an injury to heal invariably find that the recovery takes longer than they expected. In contrast, taking an active role in *promoting* the recovery helps a performer to focus their mind on the positive; on the small steps they are taking, rather than the negative. And, in doing so, the performer can see that they are making progress towards a full recovery. There are three key components to this process:

1. Write down a structured recovery plan, which includes minor targets or goals that can be reached along the way. For example, you could set a date for a plaster cast to be removed or a date for completing a 100-metre walk.
2. Be flexible in your approach and don't throw your recovery plan away because you didn't reach one of your goals on time. Instead, adjust the next two or three stages of your recovery plan and extend the timeline slightly. Allow yourself permission to change your goals if they prove unrealistic.
3. Find support, from a friend or family member who will allow you to discuss your frustrations, or from a coach who will help you to plan your recovery. If possible, seek support from people who have suffered the same injury and take their advice.

Relaxation techniques

Relaxing the mind effectively can aid recovery because it prevents frustration and anger building up, which can stop the downward spiral into depression. There are many relaxation techniques you can try, including hypnotherapy and acupuncture, but there is a very simple technique that you can practise without help from someone else: visualization, which is also known as mental imagery.

Find a quiet place to sit or lie comfortably and imagine yourself performing successfully and without injury. Visualize yourself running hard, jumping high, or scoring a winning goal. Doing this effectively enables your mind to work with your body to promote the healing process, because you will begin to *feel* that you can accomplish your goals.

BRONZE

4. Imagine that you have suffered a long-term physiological injury, such as a fractured tibia, and write a structured recovery plan.

5. Practise the visualization relaxation technique and, afterwards, describe how you think it would help you overcome an injury.

SPOTLIGHT on responses to injury and management of injuries

BRONZE

Completing these activities will help you to achieve a **Level 2 Pass** in your assignment.

1. Work with a partner to role play the scenarios below. Take it in turns to be the casualty.

a) You are playing football in the school playground at lunchtime and your friend sprains his ankle. Demonstrate how SALTAPS helps you to deal with this situation.

b) A team-mate collapses after colliding with an opponent in a game of rugby. His leg hurts very badly and he cannot stand up. Demonstrate how PRICE helps you to deal with this situation until medical help arrives.

SILVER

Completing these activities will help you to achieve a **Level 2 Merit** in your assignment.

2. Working with a partner, imagine that one of you is a sports therapist and the other is an interviewer who is asking questions about how to treat a specific injury. The sports therapist should give a detailed account of how to deal with a psychological injury, while the interviewer should ask probing questions to extract the relevant information. Then swap roles and repeat this for a physiological injury.

GOLD

Completing these activities will help you to achieve a **Level 2 Distinction** in your assignment.

3. You are working for a governing body in your favourite sport. Identify a problem area relating to health and safety within your sport and create a new rule to solve this issue and prevent further injuries from occurring. Justify your new rule to a partner.

4. For an injury of your choice, give a detailed account of how and why the injury is likely to occur, linking the cause of the injury to its severity.

Unit 10 assignment, part two

Background

Your school or college is due to hold a sports day for Year 6 students from the local primary school and you have been asked to assist in the preparations for the event. Planning such an event needs to be done very carefully as health and safety is of paramount importance. Everybody involved in the planning and delivery of the sports day needs to be aware of the potential hazards, common injuries, and any preventative strategies that can be used, as well as the rules, regulations, and legislation that apply to the event.

Grading criteria to be assessed
1B.2, 1B.3, 1B.4, 1C.5, 1C.6
2B.P2, 2B.P3, 2B.P4, 2C.P5, 2C.P6
2B.M1, 2C.M2
2B.D1, 2C.D2

Task

Prepare a short video or PowerPoint® presentation that can be played on a loop throughout the sports day. Your video or PowerPoint® presentation should inform parents about the causes of injury in sport, and about injuries and illnesses and their treatment. It should:

- Outline three different physiological, and three psychological, causes of injury in relation to sport. (1B.2)
- Describe two basic injuries associated with sports participation. (1B.3)
- Describe two types and signs of illness associated with sports participation. (1B.4)
- Describe the physiological and immediate psychological responses to injury in sport. (1C.5)
- Describe how to manage physiological and immediate psychological responses to injury in sport. (1C.6)

- Explain three different physiological, and three different psychological, causes of injury in relation to sport. (2B.P2)
- Describe two types of basic injury and two different types of complex injury associated with sports participation. (2B.P3)
- Explain four types and signs of illness associated with sports participation. (2B.P4)
- Describe the physiological and immediate and long-term psychological responses to injury in sport. (2C.P5)
- Describe how to manage physiological and immediate and long-term psychological responses to injury in sport. (2C.P6)

- Using sports specific examples, discuss the relationship between the causes of injury and basic and complex types of injury. (2B.M1)
- For a selected sports injury, explain the responses and process of physiological and psychological management. (2C.M2)

- For a selected injury or illness give a detailed account of how it might occur, analysing the associated types and signs of injury or illness. (2B.D1)
- Justify selected methods used to manage physiological and psychological responses to a selected injury in a sporting context. (2D.D2)

Tackling the assignment

The best way to approach this assignment is to create a PowerPoint® presentation that tackles each of the criteria step by step, thereby making it clear that each of the criteria has been met. You could include links to video footage of various injuries that support the commentary, or you could simply provide pictures. However, the presentation needs to be visually engaging so that people at the event are interested and want to see it.

Meeting the Level 2 Pass criteria

Basic injuries in sport

Michael Aliss

These are simple injuries that are relatively easy to deal with, and that do not generally have any long-term, lasting effects. Examples include sprains, strains, and blisters.

Blisters

These are sore spots on the skin, with fluid trapped underneath. They are caused by items of clothing or equipment rubbing, and are most common on the heel where ill-fitting footwear has been rubbing. As such, they are very common in sports that require specialized footwear, such as football, rugby, and ice skating. They are very painful and often leave the player unable to take part until the injury has healed.

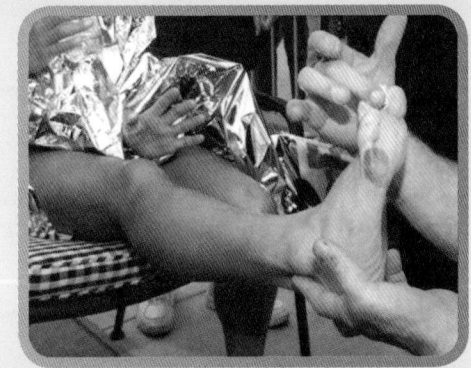

Complex injuries in sport

These are more serious injuries that tend to take longer to heal, and require specialist management from a medical professional. Examples include fractures, dislocations, and concussion.

Fractures

These are sometimes called 'breaks' as they relate to damage to a bone, though this can be confusing as they do not always relate to a bone that has actually snapped. They occur most often in contact sports, such as rugby and karate, but can also be the result of collision with equipment, when trampolining for example.

Fractures require specialist treatment from a hospital doctor, and are usually covered with a 'pot' or 'plaster cast' until the injury has healed.

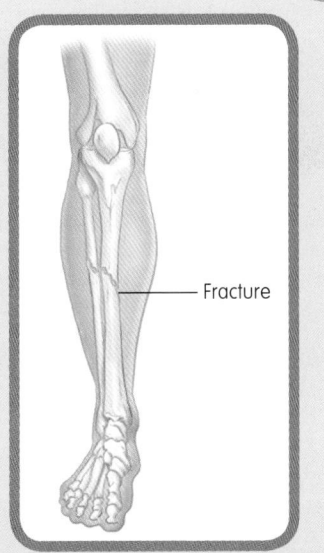

— Fracture

Michael's PowerPoint® slides are very basic. He has mentioned what the injuries are, how they occur, and given a basic insight into their treatment. However, I would have liked to see a little more information on the injuries themselves, such as how the fluid gets trapped and why it gets trapped in such a way as to form blisters. This extra information, as well as a description of a second basic injury and a second complex injury, would be necessary for Michael to meet the criteria for 2B.P3. I would say that this is a work in progress, rather than a complete answer.

Meeting the Level 2 Merit criteria

BTEC Level 2 Unit 10

Ali Al Hamza

Causes of injury in sport

There are two main types of injury that can be sustained while playing sport: basic injuries and complex injuries. Very often, the cause of the injury has a significant effect upon the severity of the injury, and subsequently on the treatment needed and the time spent recovering.

Collision injuries

One of the most common causes of all injuries is collision with another player, either an opponent or a team-mate. This is most prevalent in contact sports, such as football and rugby, and can be caused either through deliberate contact (such as a tackle in rugby) or though accidental contact (such as a clash of heads when jumping for the ball at a corner in football). The force of the contact will usually determine the severity of the ensuing injury.

Force of contact = severity of injury

In general, the greater the force of impact, the more severe the ensuing injury. For example, contact with an opponent in a controlled scrum in rugby is much less likely to cause injury than a full tackle with both players moving at speed, though obviously this can be complicated by the part of the body involved and the 'angle of attack' from the tackle.

Minimal force of contact is likely to leave little or no injury, but if the force is increased slightly, then the likelihood of a **basic injury**, such as **bruising** (discoloration of the skin due to damage caused to cells underneath), is the most likely injury to occur. If the force of impact is greatly increased, then a much more serious **complex injury**, such as a **dislocated joint** or **a fractured bone**, will often occur.

There are several other factors that can contribute to the severity of an injury and even minimal force, if applied at the wrong location and the wrong time, can cause a major complex injury. However, in general the link between force of contact and severity of injury is pretty strong.

Ali has made an excellent start to this presentation, though he has not yet covered the different causes of injury in enough depth to be awarded 2B.M1. He needs to extend his presentation further, and include at least two or three more examples of the sport-specific injuries before he fully meets the Merit criteria.

Having said this, Ali's slide on the link between the force of contact and the severity of injury is very good. It clearly explains the link between the force of contact and the likely resulting injury that a participant can sustain, and does so in a way that shows how the causes of an injury and the actual injury are very closely related. If Ali was to replicate this approach in covering two or three further causes of injury, then I would have no hesitation in awarding him 2B.M1.

Dislocated joints in sport

Sean Walters

What is a dislocation?

A dislocation occurs when the bones that form a joint are forced out of position, so that they no longer meet in a way that allows the joint to move in the way that it should. A dislocation is extremely painful for the injured player, and if not treated effectively can result in long-term weakness of the joint.

What causes a dislocation?

A dislocation is caused by the application of force to a joint, in such a way that the ligaments that hold the joint in place are either snapped or stretched and the bones slip out of position. One of the most common dislocations in sport is a dislocated finger, which is particularly prevalent in basketball players, netball players, and football goalkeepers. In almost all of these cases the player is guilty of mistiming the contact with the ball, such that the velocity of the ball forces the finger out of position. Other common dislocations involve the knee and elbow joints in contact sports, caused by a tackle in rugby or a throw in judo for example.

What are the signs of a dislocation?

The most commons signs of a dislocation are:

- Severe pain.
- A lack of feeling in the areas beyond the dislocation, such as a lack of feeling in the hand after a dislocated elbow.
- A very obvious lack of alignment in the joint, so that it appears to be bent at a very unnatural angle.
- Immediate and quite severe swelling around the joint.
- Discoloration of the joint.
- Possible breakage of the skin surface at the joint.

The problem is that the signs and symptoms of a dislocation are very similar to the signs and symptoms of many other injuries, in particular closed fractures (where a bone has been broken but has not pierced the skin).

Sean's work centres on dislocated joints, and it is pleasing to see that he has focused on the injury in general rather than on one particular example of it, such as a dislocated knee.

What are missing from Sean's work are diagrams or pictures that would support his explanations. In addition, I'm not convinced that Sean has given a 'detailed' account of how the injury can occur, which prevents me confidently awarding him 2B.D1. I would like to see Sean add a scenario that leads the reader through the cause of a dislocation step by step, especially if this was supported by a series of pictures or diagrams to show the application of force step by step.

Unit 11: Running a Sports Event
Types of sports event

Sports events take on many guises, from inter-school competitions to regional and international events. Sports events can also be run for fun or to raise money for charity; a good example of this are Cancer Research UK's Race for Life events that take place every year. In order to successfully plan and run a sports event, many different factors should be considered as part of the planning and delivery process.

Will it be a school or college sports day?

The first step when organizing an event is to decide what type of event it will be.

Whichever type of event is chosen, there is always one burning question: should it take place indoors or outdoors? The advantages of an indoor event are largely weather related because the event can go ahead even in torrential rain. But there are disadvantages to running an indoor event. The main problem with an indoor facility is lack of space for a large number of participants and spectators, something that is rarely a problem for an outdoor event. There is also the cost of hiring an indoor venue, which is often significantly more expensive than hiring an outdoor venue, because there is a higher demand for indoor facilities. If you are planning an outdoor event, consideration must be given to areas to shelter from both the rain and the sun (sunstroke is the most common problem requiring first aid at an outdoor event). Suitable consideration should also be given to a contingency plan in case the weather prevents the event going ahead outdoors.

Will it be a sports activity day run by the local leisure centre to encourage members of the public to try new activities to promote their facilities?

BRONZE

1. Choose three national or international sporting events and list five things they have in common that make them successful events.

2. Research a major event, such as the London Marathon, the Great North Run, or Cancer Research UK's Race for Life, and find out:

- What the event aims to do.
- The target audience for the event.
- How the organizers of the event measure their success.

Bobby Moore captained the World Cup-winning England team in 1966. Here, members from the charity set up in his honour arrange a fund-raising dinner.

Will it be a community-based event to raise awareness about an issue or raise money for a charit

Planning and organizing a sports event

Sports events don't just happen. There is a considerable amount of planning and organization required, even for small-scale events, and if the planning stage isn't approached methodically many problems can emerge during the event itself.

Once it has been decided what type of event you will run, the planning can begin. You will need to consider the following:

Aims and objectives

All events need an overall aim and a series of objectives. A school activity day could aim to get more pupils taking part in a particular sport and to develop their understanding of a healthy lifestyle. Or the aim of your event could be to raise money for charity, develop participants' skills in a particular sport, or just to ensure that participants have a great time!

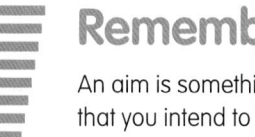

Remember:

An aim is something that you intend to achieve by the end of the event. An example of an aim is: 'To raise awareness of the new facilities at an existing sports centre'. An objective is a small step that helps you achieve your aim. An example of an objective is: 'To carry out a poster campaign to showcase the new facilities'.

The nature of the event

Events come in all shapes and sizes, so you need to decide if you're going to run a large event, with large numbers of participants and spectators, or a smaller-scale event, which focuses on a few selected participants. Whichever you choose, the size of your event will dictate the location. For example, a large regional event may need a large central venue while a smaller event could take place in the school sports hall.

The target audience

All events have a target audience, which means they are aimed at a particular group of people, such as young children under seven years old, Key Stage 4 students, or senior citizens. An event can also be targeted at members of one or more local sports clubs or at a group with specific needs, such as a local disability group. It is important to make sure that the planned event is suitable for the target audience and that you meet the needs of the participants you are aiming your event at.

The needs of each target audience are going to vary, but some of the things you should consider include:

- Do the participants have any particular access needs? Will they require wheelchair access to the venue or seating because they cannot stand for a long time? Will you need to provide parking because young children will be dropped off and collected by their parents?
- Do the participants have any particular language needs? Can you provide participants with all the information they require; for example, in another language if English is their second language, or written at the right level if they are younger children?
- Do the participants need to be able to perform to a certain standard in order to participate? Can you clearly describe that standard?
- Do participants have any special requirements that need to be taken into consideration? These could include medical conditions and dietary requirements.

Resources

A key part of planning and organizing an event is making sure that you have all the resources you need to run the event efficiently. Resources can include equipment, uniforms for staff, refreshments, a public announcement system, and contact information for staff and/or participants. Make a list of everything you think you will need and note down the place where you might be able to source it.

Will you have to pay for it? All events need a budget to pay for things, including hiring the venue, purchasing or hiring equipment, producing and distributing promotional material, and ensuring that adequate first-aid equipment is available. The budget can be the biggest constraint on the size, nature, and success of an event. It is therefore crucial that, before any decisions are made about the nature of the event, all the requirements are fully costed so that you can work out if you can afford to run the event as envisaged. You should then consider all the options and choose whichever is the most cost-effective.

Promotion

Events are only successful if they are well advertised, so you should plan all promotional activities carefully. Leaflets, posters, and adverts on local radio are some of the most effective ways of publicizing an event.

The roles and responsibilities of staff

Successful events will require a range of people to be involved, all with different roles. Each member of the team needs to be clear about their role and the responsibilities it involves. You may need some or all of the following roles:

- Coordinator
- Chairperson
- Secretary
- Finance officer
- Publicity officer
- Marketing officer
- Steward
- Specialist coach or trainer
- Referee
- Caterer

The planning process needs to be managed effectively, and this is normally a role conducted by the event coordinator. Key issues should be discussed and actions allocated to team members at event meetings, which need to take place on a regular basis. During meetings, minutes (which are a record of the issues discussed, decisions taken, and actions allocated to people) should be taken and all information should be circulated to team members soon after the meeting has finished.

During the planning and organizing phase of the event the importance of teamwork cannot be over-stated, as everyone will need to pull together to ensure all aspects of the plan are addressed. It is also important that everyone communicates effectively and regularly because failing to communicate well – before, during, and after the event – is often one of the main reasons why an event doesn't go as well as it could.

Timings

For an event to run smoothly accurate timings must be incorporated into the plan. The length of time allocated to each component of the event – the introduction, warm-up, skill development, main activity, cool-down, and the prize giving for example – needs to be considered so that there is enough time to do everything and participants are not kept hanging around.

Obtaining feedback

Although it may seem like a long way off at the moment, it is always good practice to get feedback from participants both during and after the event. This will help you improve the event next time you run it and will help you develop your event-planning skills. Feedback can be obtained via questionnaires, comments cards, and interviews, and it is important to consider how and when you will gather your feedback while you are planning your event so that you don't forget about it. Feedback should also be sought from participants' parents, teachers, and other observers, if appropriate.

Health and safety

Health and safety is an essential component of any event, and it is important that the health and safety of participants, staff, and spectators is considered. Some of the key questions that should be asked during the planning phase include:

- **Has a person or a team been given responsibility for health and safety?**
- **Has a risk assessment been completed and have potential hazards been identified?**
- **Has a first aider been arranged? Is one employed by the venue or does one need to be organized?**
- **Has the location of a first-aid point been considered?**
- **Is a first-aid kit available or does one need to be borrowed or purchased?**
- **Are disclaimer and informed consent documents for volunteers and participants in place?** An informed consent document states that anyone taking part in the event is aware of the risks and potential dangers involved and asks them to agree that they will take all reasonable precautions to ensure that neither they nor anyone else is injured. It may also ask for details of a participant's medical history and sporting experience. A disclaimer document states, for example, that the organizers have no responsibility for participants' valuables during the event.

Contingency plans

All events should have a contingency plan, just in case things change during the build up to the event or on the day itself. Contingency plans need to be in place:

- For poor weather, such as rain or snow, which means that an outside event needs to relocate or some participants can't get to the venue.
- In case there is an accident.
- In case the number, age, or ability of participants changes.
- In case staff are ill or cannot attend due to unforeseen circumstances.
- In case equipment has been damaged, lost, or is not delivered on time.
- In case the venue has been double-booked.

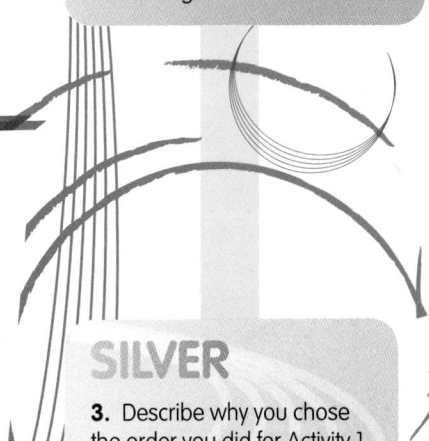

BRONZE

1. Imagine you are producing an outline plan for an inter-form or inter-department competition. Make a list of the things you would need to consider and place them in the order that you would do them.

2. Even though minutes of all meetings will be taken, it is important to keep your own records. To help you do this, produce a document that you could use to record what happens at planning meetings. It will need to record the discussions that take place, the decisions made, and the actions agreed.

SILVER

3. Describe why you chose the order you did for Activity 1.

Unit 11 assignment, part one

Background

Your local community sports centre has been threatened with closure because it isn't being used very much and its income has dropped. You have been tasked with helping to keep the facility open and the manager has suggested four options for raising the centre's profile:

- A charity dinner for local business people, with a special guest speaker from the world of sport.
- A sports holiday camp for children from local primary schools.
- A sports award ceremony with awards for members of local sports clubs, voted for by the local community.
- A multi-sports competition, with teams from the local community entering to try and win a grand prize.

Task

Working in a small group of three to five people, choose one of the four options that have been suggested by the sports centre manager and contribute to the planning and organizing of the event. Or, come up with your own idea for an event. You will need to think carefully about the option you select, because you will have to run the event later on in the assignment. You will need to:

Grading criteria to be assessed
1A.1, 1B.2
2A.P1, 2B.P2
2A.M1
2A.D1

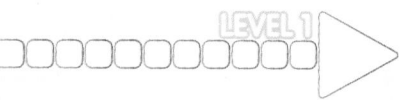 **LEVEL 1**

- Produce, with guidance, a plan for running a given sports event. (1A.1)
- Contribute, with guidance, to the organisation of a given sports event. (1B.2)

 **LEVEL 2 PASS**

- Produce a plan for a selected sports event, outlining the planning process to meet event aims and objectives. (2A.P1)
- Contribute to the organisation of a selected sports event. (2B.P2)

LEVEL 2 MERIT

- Produce a plan for a selected sports event, describing the planning process to meet event aims and objectives. (2A.M1)

LEVEL 2 DISTINCTION

- Justify the plan for a selected sports event, explaining the planning process. (2A.D1)

Tackling the assignment

The first thing to do when tackling this assignment is to make sure you work to your strengths and use the facilities that are most readily available. For example, if you have easy access to a running track and have links with school students, then a sports day event is likely to be the easiest option for you. Alternatively, your school or college may organize a charity event on an annual basis, so helping to organize the event might be a good choice. In essence, the secret to this assignment is to keep it simple, because the simpler you make it the more likely you are to succeed.

Once you have decided on your event, you need to set up an initial planning meeting where you'll make most of the major decisions. You will also need to hold a series of meetings throughout the time you plan and organize the event, checking things out step by step before making any final decisions. Be sure to keep detailed records of everything that is discussed and any agreements that are made because these can count as evidence towards meeting the assignment criteria.

Ultimately, to be successful in this assignment you need to be disciplined, contribute to the best of your ability, play an active role as part of your team, and record your contribution at every opportunity. Your team might produce minutes for your meetings, but you will also need to keep your own record of discussions and decisions, and the things you do.

Meeting the Level 2 Pass and Merit criteria

James Taylor

I have decided to keep a diary of our discussions, decisions, and actions as the planning process progresses. I will use this information to help me outline and then describe the planning process, and to support my plan.

First meeting   **19 May 2012**

1. Deciding on the type of event and its aims and objectives: We propose to run a sports camp for local primary school children with the aim of encouraging them to use the sports centre more often.

2. Deciding on dates and timings: The provisional dates we have identified are during the half-term holiday (24–27 May 2013). Exact timings and activities have yet to be decided.

3. Having the correct staff roles: Due to the nature of the event we have decided we will need a coordinator, a secretary, a finance officer, a marketing officer, a first-aid officer, and an activity officer.

4. Identifying resource requirements: The exact resources we need have yet to be decided, but we will need such things as a first-aid kit, sports equipment, refreshments for the participants, etc.

Items to be discussed at the next meeting, which will be on 26 May 2012:

- Decide on the frequency of meetings: where and when and for how long will we meet?

- Decide on the nature of the event, such as when, where, what, etc.

- Discuss the costs associated with the event and plan a budget to make sure it is financially viable.

- Allocate roles within the group so that everyone knows what they are doing and what their roles and responsibilities are.

- Discuss what resources will be needed.

Action: All group members to consider the items for discussion at the next meeting and bring their ideas to the next meeting.

James has made a good start. He needs to make reference to all aspects of the planning process, including producing contingency plans, conducting risk assessments, and health and safety but this looks promising and I am sure that the other items will be covered as the planning and organization progresses.

James needs to make reference to the aims and objectives of the event, which should emerge at the group's second meeting, to meet the criteria for 2A.P1. If he then goes on to describe how the planning helped his group meet the aims and objectives then he will also meet the criteria for 2A.M1.

Activity camp plan   James Taylor

Area	Task	Responsibility	Due by	Complete ✔	Notes
Volunteers	• Send out invitation to invite volunteers to participate in sports day. Invitation should include reply form. • Letters should include: ❑ times ❑ what the day will include (types of activity) ❑ who's been invited ❑ contacts ❑ benefits of being involved ❑ reply form ❑ venue ❑ parking facilities ❑ aim of sports day ❑ expectations of volunteers ❑ cost (buses)	Event coordinator	Eight weeks prior		Reply date should be approximately three weeks from the date the invitation is sent.
	Follow up with phone call to confirm attendance.	Event coordinator	Four weeks prior		A phone call is required to double check their attendance and to make sure their circumstances haven't changed.
	Collate replies to confirm how many volunteers will be attending and who they are.	Event coordinator	Three weeks prior		Having a list is important to present back to the group meeting and to have a written record of the volunteers who will be helping (names, ages, etc.)
	Follow-up phone call to confirm attendance.	Event coordinator	One week prior		
	Organize for back-up volunteers, in case of illness, etc.	Event coordinator	One week prior		Make sure the back-up volunteers are still available and we have their contact details.

> James has clearly spent a lot of time planning this aspect of the event. The planning sheet provided as evidence is clearly aimed at meeting the Pass criteria. He could add to his evidence by also including an example of the letter sent out to volunteers.

> Because James has added details in the 'Notes' column, he has also started to address the Merit criteria by describing the planning process. If James continues to provide this level of detail throughout the planning phase he will meet the criteria for 2A.M1.

Kieran Kilcoyne

Week 1

Task	My contribution	Evidence	Where located
First team meeting where roles were confirmed and the schedule set.	My contribution (as finance officer) was to confirm I understood my role and to outline the costs I thought would be associated with the event. I was asked to produce a detailed spreadsheet for the next meeting. I was also asked to agree to the schedule, which I did.	Team minutes Event schedule	Event file Event file
Produce finance spreadsheet.	I produced the financial spreadsheet on the next day so it was done. I circulated it to everyone via email so they had time to look at it and make comments before the next meeting.	Finance spreadsheet	Copy in my finance file and event file

Week 2

Task	My contribution	Evidence	Where located
Present my ideas at the team meeting.	I presented the spreadsheet, which had been slightly changed in light of team comments. I was asked by the event coordinator to expand on certain areas, such as: • Would there be additional costs if we had to use a different indoor venue if the weather was bad? • How will participants' payments be recorded and how will we store the money securely?	Minutes of meeting Teacher observation record	Event file Teacher evidence file
Get confirmatory letter from sport centre manager regarding cost of sports hall (if needed).	I sent an email to the sport centre manager asking for confirmation (in writing) that we wouldn't have to pay any extra for the venue if bad weather forced us indoors. She sent a reply (via email), which I circulated to the group and printed off.	Email Email reply	Event file Event file

> The method Kieran has used to show his contribution to the organization of the event is excellent. It is easy to follow, concise and, most importantly, he has identified where the evidence can be located. This, coupled with the teacher's observation of Kieran's performance, is clear evidence that if he continues in this way he will meet the criteria for 2B.P2.

Meeting the Level 2 Distinction criteria

Janine Burton

Element of the planning process	Explanation	Justification
Holding regular meetings.	We will need to hold regular meetings so that progress can be monitored, actions can be allocated within the team, and any issues can be identified and addressed. A well-structured meeting schedule will help communication within the team (and with the centre manager) and keep us on track.	There are 12 weeks between now and the event, so we have decided to hold a meeting every two weeks. This will ensure we can monitor progress and put contingency actions in place if needed. If problems do arise we could hold a meeting every week if needed, although as we are in the same group at school we could meet informally if required, i.e. during a lunch break.
Develop contingency plan(s).	Contingency plans are needed in case anything changes during the planning process, i.e. one of us is ill, if volunteers can't help, or if equipment is not available. If we have contingency plans in place it will allow us to quickly make changes without too much interruption or inconvenience.	We have built contingencies into all aspects of our plan, such as identifying an alternative venue, putting extra volunteers on standby, making sure all group members have a 'second' role, etc. This means that every angle is covered – just in case!

Although many aspects of Janine's explanation and justification will be delivered verbally and recorded by the teacher, this table is an excellent example of support material. Janine has clearly explained and justified two examples of the planning process and, if she replicates this detail for all the planning considerations, she will be able to meet the 2A.D1 criteria.

Running a sports event

Once you have planned and organized the event, the next step is to actually run it. It is at this stage that you will find out how successful your planning and organization has been. The old saying 'fail to prepare and be prepared to fail' will certainly be tested during the event. However, it is important to remember that things rarely run as precisely as they were planned, and the real skill is coping with last-minute changes.

Running an event can be broken down into three stages: setting up before the event, the event itself, and setting down after the event. The complexity of the event will determine how meticulous the planning for each stage needs to be. Every event will be different, and although the following ideas cover the most common aspects of running a sports event, the list is not exhaustive. You will need to remember this when attempting part two of the assignment.

Setting up before the event

Signs
Participants and spectators will need to know lots of things, and the use of well-written, clear, and informative signs is the easiest way to get information across. Signs will be needed to show people the locations of facilities such as car parking, toilets, first-aid points, and refreshments. Signs may also be needed to inform competitors and spectators of the timing of events or the order of play.

Other equipment
This includes practically everything else, from seating areas to shelter and transport. As with all aspects of setting up an event, it is important to follow the plan that has been put in place but be prepared to make adjustments on the day if necessary.

Sports equipment
Sports equipment needs to be organized well in advance of the event in case any repairs or replacements are needed. On the day, the sports equipment will need to be readily available, but not left out so that it could cause a hazard, be broken, or, worse still, stolen. The sports equipment will also need to be suitable for the ages and abilities of the participants.

Food and drink
Food and drink can be provided by outside caterers or prepared in-house by the event organizers. As with the entertainment, someone should be allocated the responsibility of ensuring that the outside caterers have everything they need to set up properly. If you decide to prepare the refreshments yourselves, at least one person should be given the responsibility of doing this. A preparation and service area needs to be set up and you may require an electric socket if you are going to be using a fridge or a cooker. There may also be food hygiene regulations to consider. It could, however, be that none of the above is necessary because the participants bring their own refreshments.

Entertainment
Any entertainment needs to be booked well in advance and, on the day of the event, one person should be allocated the responsibility of ensuring that the entertainment is set up correctly. This is a relatively easy task in the case of a music player and speakers, but if a live band or sports personality has been arranged, then the person responsible for meeting them and helping them set up will need to know exactly what they require in terms of equipment and space.

During the event

During the event, all members of the team will need to work together to ensure its success. It is unlikely that everything will go smoothly and so any difficulties should be dealt with quickly and with the minimum of fuss. Event organizers will need to be available to deal with requests from the participants and the spectators and, for this reason, should not be directly responsible for officiating or instructing. Instead, these tasks should be delegated to willing volunteers or paid personnel. However, event organizers should be responsible for monitoring the overall event and supervising all other employees, regardless of whether they are paid employees or volunteers.

Setting down after the event

Waste disposal
All litter should be collected and disposed of safely, with as much as possible recycled. If you have food and drink left over, perishable items, such as fruit, should be shared out among the organizers and helpers or thrown away and non-perishable items, such as wrapped cereal bars or unopened isotonic drinks, should be carefully stored ready for the next event.

Sports equipment
All the sports equipment used will need to be collected, checked for damage, and returned to storage. Any broken items should be kept separate and a list prepared so that they can be repaired or replaced.

Signs and posters
Signs, posters, and similar items should be taken down at the end of the event and stored for future events or disposed of, recycling wherever possible.

BRONZE

1. Refer back to your outline plan of a sports event that you produced for Activity 1 on page 225. Take on the role of event organizer and allocate roles and responsibilities to yourself and four other people on the day of the event. Remember that people can have more than one job to do but, if they do, you will need to list their responsibilities in the order that they should approach them.

Leading a sports event

Whether you are directly leading one of the activities that forms part of a sports event or are responsible for members of the team who are leading activities, it is important that you understand the leadership skills required and the responsibilities of a leader and demonstrate them during your event.

Leadership skills

The skills a leader should display while running a sports event include:

Being able to demonstrate a range of personal qualities, including humour, enthusiasm, confidence, and the ability to motivate people.

Evaluating your performance afterwards to make sure any improvements you identify are rectified for future events.

Being able to maintain control over a group by setting clear boundaries and enforcing them if necessary.

Being able to improvise or adapt activities if required, if, for example, they are proving too difficult for some of the participants.

Being able to demonstrate a technique, skill, or tactic to a participant so they can clearly understand what is required.

Being able to communicate effectively with a range of different people, and with the target audience in particular.

Responsibilities

Responsibilities accompany leadership; one cannot come without the other. The responsibilities someone leading a sports event needs to be aware of include:

- Acting in a professional manner, in a way that reflects well on themselves and the organization they are representing. This includes making sure your appearance is professional.
- Ensuring that spectators, staff, volunteers, and participants are kept safe and secure during the event. This involves everything from making sure there is an up-to-date risk assessment for the venue and the event, to ensuring that there is appropriate first-aid provision, the equipment is safe to use, and that the activities match the abilities of those taking part.
- Treating everyone equally and being aware of individual differences that may exist between participants, such as any access or language requirements they may have.
- Enforcing rules and regulations so that everyone is kept safe and poor behaviour does not spoil everyone else's enjoyment of the event.

Indicators of success

As with most things, your leadership skills will develop with confidence and experience. It is therefore important to assess how successful you were in your leadership role so that you can work on becoming a better leader in the future. Typical indicators of success include:

- **Participant enjoyment:** Participants may make favourable comments when feeding back at the end of the event or may just show, through their behaviour, that they are enjoying the activities or event.
- **Meeting aims and objectives:** If the aims and objectives of the event have been met, then this again is a good indication that it was a success.
- **Good organization:** If everything runs to plan, if all the different aspects of the day start and finish on time, and everyone is where they need to be, when they need to be there, with the right equipment, then the organizational side of your event could be viewed as a success. However, well-organized events don't always meet their overall aims and objectives, and participant enjoyment levels can still be low. This can often be down to other factors, such as a poor choice of activities or ineffective leadership skills.
- **Lack of injuries:** If the event runs without any injuries or safety scares then it could be down to good leadership.

This young leader has the full attention of the participants, who all seem to be having a great time!

BRONZE

1. a) Identify which leadership skills you think you already possess and which you need to develop or improve.

b) Discuss your list with your teacher and, together, identify opportunities where you can practise those skills you feel you need to develop or improve.

Reviewing a sports event

It is important for event organizers to evaluate the events that they have run to provide themselves with feedback on their performance. If an event is unsuccessful for any reason, the organizers can work on improving things for the next time that they run an event. Equally, if something worked really well, they may want to use this method in the future.

Gathering feedback

There are three things to think about when gathering feedback: who you ask, what you ask, and how you ask it.

Who you ask

When evaluating an event it is important to gather information from everyone involved, including the organizing team, the volunteer helpers, the participants, and the spectators, to build an accurate picture of how it went. You should also question yourself about how you think the event went.

What you ask

You might want to ask people about:

- **Planning:** How well was the event planned? Were the contingency plans that were in place appropriate?
- **Content:** How suitable was the content of the event for the participants? Was there enough/ too much going on?
- **Organization:** How organized were the leader(s) before the event and on the day? Did they respond to changes from the original plan calmly and efficiently?
- **Health and safety:** Were the participants safe? Were there any incidents? If anyone was injured or ill, were they treated efficiently?
- **Achievements:** Did the organizers achieve the aims and objectives set out for the event? Did the event keep to the budget?
- **Areas for improvement and recommendations for future events:** What could have been done better? What should the organizers do next time to make the event run more smoothly?

How you ask it

There are two types of feedback: qualitative feedback and quantitative feedback. How you ask a question determines which type of feedback you receive. Qualitative feedback describes feelings and behaviour. It will tell you why someone enjoyed something. Quantitative feedback measures things. It will tell you how many of the participants enjoyed themselves. Gathering both qualitative and quantitative feedback will allow you to build a fully rounded picture of your event. It will tell you how many people enjoyed the event and why they enjoyed it. This is useful because you can measure the success of the event by how many people enjoyed it, and you can use the information about why they enjoyed it to inform future event planning because they may not have enjoyed it for the reasons you think they did.

Reviewing an event is easiest if everyone involved is asked the same questions in the same way, which allows responses to be compared more effectively.

When gathering qualitative feedback it is important to ask open-ended questions, because this allows participants to express their opinions more effectively. You can do this by conducting face-to-face interviews during and after the event, asking people to complete a questionnaire, or asking an observer to record what happens during the event using a video camera or by taking notes.

When gathering quantitative feedback you should ask closed questions, which have precise answers that can later be measured. You can do this by asking people to complete a survey or fill in a comments card.

Analysing and presenting your feedback

When you analyse your feedback, try to step back from each individual answer and view the feedback as a whole. What is the big picture? What are the big messages coming from the feedback?

When you have established what it is the feedback is trying to tell you, it is time to present your findings.

Qualitative data is best presented using direct quotes from your feedback to illustrate the narrative (the story) the data is telling you. You could also include photographs or clips from a longer video with explanatory captions.

A review of a sports event requires the organizers to get together after the event has taken place.

> The aim of the event was to encourage more people to use the sports centre. I think the event was successful, because many of the participants told us that they will be coming back.

> I really enjoyed the event. It was great fun. The staff were very friendly and helped me improve my skills in a range of different sports. I definitely want to carry on using the sports centre.
>
> Samantha (aged eight)

> My son, Reilly, had a great time. He didn't shut up about it all night! The event has made me realize how important the facility is to the community and all the family will now start to use it more often, especially Reilly, who has already told me he wants to join the Judo and table tennis clubs!
>
> Mrs Dodson, mother of Reilly (aged seven)

Quantitative, on the other hand, is best presented using graphs and tables.

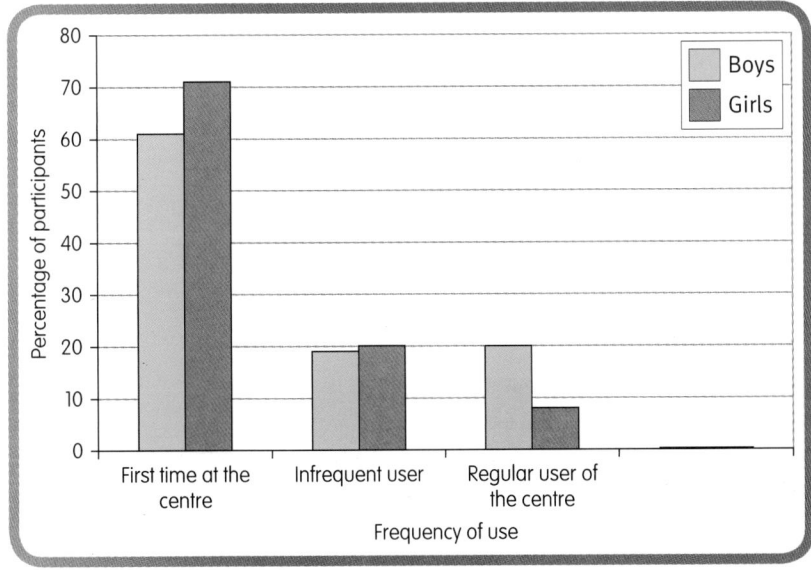

This data shows that for over 60 per cent of boys and 70 per cent of girls this was their first visit to the sports centre. This is a real success. Hopefully many of them will return.

BRONZE

1. You should already have thought about suitable methods for collecting feedback on your event. Take another look at your plan now that you know more about gathering, analysing, and presenting feedback. Do you want to change the way you plan to collect your feedback? You will need to use at least four methods, so now is as good a time as any to get them all in place.

Identifying strengths and areas for improvement

Once you have analysed and presented your feedback, you should compare it against your original plan and the log showing how you executed that plan to identify strengths and areas for improvement.

Remember:

Reviewing your event doesn't have to be a negative experience. There is every chance that you will have exceeded expectations.

What about the event went well? Were the aims and objectives of the event met? Did the event come in on budget? How effective was the planning and organization? How effective was the contingency planning? For example:

- There were no incidents during the event, because of the excellent health and safety management.
- 98% of all participants said they would like to come back to a similar event if one was run in the future.
- 76% of participants said they would use the centre more often. In fact, 32% have already joined clubs that operate out of the sports centre.

Why did these things go well?

What evidence do you have from the feedback provided that these things went well?

What about the event didn't go so well? Are there examples of the outcomes of the event not meeting the planned aims and objectives? Were there problems with the planning that caused issues with the event itself? For example:

- There wasn't enough space in the car park for parents dropping off and picking up their children. This caused congestion, some late arrivals, and was a potential safety hazard.
- There was a very uneven gender split. Although there were 87 participants (our target was 90), 72% were boys and only 28% girls. We were aiming for a 50/50 split.
- Only 6 of the 15 clubs sent a representative to the event, so the aim of getting participants to join clubs wasn't as effective as we had hoped.

Why didn't these things go well?

What evidence do you have from the feedback provided that these things didn't go well?

Making recommendations for the future

The final stage in reviewing your event is to set targets for improvement and make recommendations on how they can be achieved. This is best achieved using the SMARTER target-setting technique. For example:

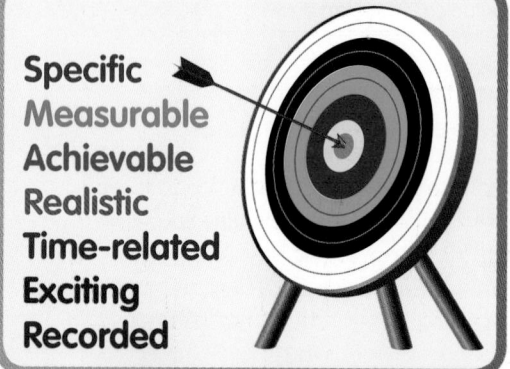

Specific
Measurable
Achievable
Realistic
Time-related
Exciting
Recorded

Targets for improvement should be SMARTER. More information on SMARTER targets can be found on page 55.

SMARTER target for improvement	Recommendation	Barriers to meeting the target
Increase the percentage of girls by 10 per cent at the next event, which is to be run in ten weeks' time.	Target girls more actively in local primary schools by ensuring that the activities planned are those that are enjoyed by girls.	The fact that limited coaches are available in sports enjoyed by girls, such as netball, hockey, and gymnastics, is a possible barrier.\n\nThis could be overcome if members of the team were trained to coach these sports or if we recruited qualified volunteers.
Get five more clubs to attend the next event, which is to be run in three months' time.	Phone the clubs that didn't attend to find out why. Find out what we can do to ensure they can attend the next event.\n\nIf they can't attend, we could display promotional material for them.	As the event is held during the day, club representatives may be at work. If this is the case we could ask them for leaflets that we could display at the centre or give to parents when they come to pick up their children.

Unit 11 assignment, part two

Background

All the planning and organizing for the event has taken place and the day of the event is here. Everybody is clear about their role and keen to put on a good show.

There is a post-event feedback meeting planned so, as well as doing a great job during the event, you should also be prepared to contribute to the debrief session.

Grading criteria to be assessed
1C.3, 1D.4, 1D.5
2C.P3, 2D.P4, 2D.P5
2C.M2, 2D.M3
2D.D2

Task

Working in the same group as you did for part one of the assignment, it is time to run your chosen event. In addition, you will need to collect feedback that can then be used to evaluate the success of the event. You need to:

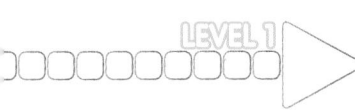

- Contribute, with guidance, to the running and leading of a given sports event. (1C.3)
- Collect qualitative or quantitative feedback from participants using two different methods. (1D.4)
- Review feedback obtained, identifying strengths of the event and areas for improvement. (1D.5)

- Contribute to the running and leading of a selected sports event, demonstrating the application of leadership attributes. (2C.P3)
- Collect qualitative and quantitative feedback from participants using four different methods. (2D.P4)
- Review feedback obtained, describing strengths of the event and areas for Improvement. (2D.P5)

- Contribute to the running and leading of a successful sports event, demonstrating the application of leadership attributes. (2C.M2)
- Assess feedback, evaluating strengths of the event and areas for improvement, providing recommendations for future events. (2D.M3)

- Analyse strengths of the event and areas for improvement, justifying recommendations for future events. (2D.D2)

Tackling the assignment

There are various points to consider when approaching this assignment. Looking at the criteria as a whole, you need to perform your duties at the event to the best of your ability and show that you can apply leadership skills effectively when situations arise. You also need to collect both qualitative and quantitative feedback, using the methods you will have decided upon before the event gets underway.

During the evaluative phase you need to use the feedback you have collated to identify what went well and where you need to improve. For the higher grades you will need to expand upon your ideas by adding more detail, such as how important certain aspects of the feedback were, and use this to make sound recommendations for improvement.

Meeting the Level 2 Pass criteria

Quantitative feedback

Anna Boon

All participants were issued with a form at the end of the session and asked to circle which 'face' reflected their feelings about the session. 80 forms were issued and 78 were returned. I have indicted how many circled each option.

How much did you enjoy the activities?	71	7	0
Would you like to do the activity again at the centre?	66	10	2
Would you like to attend a similar event during the next school holidays?	69	7	2

Qualitative feedback

All parents were interviewed as they left the event, and asked 'What did you think of the event?', 'What was good about the event?', and 'What wasn't so good about the event?'.

Q) What did you think of the event?

The event was great. My twin boys really enjoyed it. They both want to come to the next one if you decide to run another. It was a great idea and should help the sports centre as well as giving my boys something to do!

Q) What was good about the event?

The times of the sessions were good, as I could drop them off before work and collect them after work. The staff were very good as well.

Q) What wasn't so good about the event?

My only slight complaint was the cost. If I only had one child the cost would have been fine, but to pay for two was expensive. It would be good if there was a discount for a second child next time please!

Q) Any other comments?

Overall I thought it was fantastic. Well done!

Mrs Billingham, mother of Tom and Ben

Anna has used a really innovative way to collect quantitative feedback. The questionnaire is quick and easy to complete and presented in a style that children will enjoy completing. She has also indicated how each child responded. Her method for collecting qualitative feedback is more traditional, but again she is getting some good feedback from parents as they leave. Anna needs to summarize all the responses though to give a clear picture of the feedback received.

If Anna can provide examples of feedback gathered using two more methods she will meet the criteria for 2D.P4.

Meeting the Level 2 Merit and Distinction criteria

Activity camp feedback sheet   Jocelyn Brown

Your name (optional):_____

Please circle your opinion of each aspect of the event noted below.

Activities:	Excellent	Good	Satisfactory	Unsatisfactory
Maps/letters:	Excellent	Good	Satisfactory	Unsatisfactory
Catering:	Excellent	Good	Satisfactory	Unsatisfactory
Facilities:	Excellent	Good	Satisfactory	Unsatisfactory
Staffing:	Excellent	Good	Satisfactory	Unsatisfactory
Prizes:	Excellent	Good	Satisfactory	Unsatisfactory
Overall:	Excellent	Good	Satisfactory	Unsatisfactory

I handed out my feedback sheet to the parents of all participants. I did not hand out sheets to the children because I got their feedback verbally (see taped evidence). With hindsight, I believe I should have designed a different feedback form that participants could have used to give their perspective about the event. I would definitely do this next time as the feedback would probably be more detailed.

In total I received 67 out of 80 potential replies (in other words, only 13 parents did not return their feedback sheets). This is a response rate of over 80 per cent, which I am quite happy with. Perhaps next time I would ask people to hand their form to someone, rather than placing it in a box, because this would make it more explicit that a response is expected.

As for the event itself, over 90 per cent of the responses rated all components of the event as 'Good' or 'Excellent', and there were only a handful of 'Unsatisfactory' ratings. Of these, the majority related to staffing, and were due to poor refereeing in some cases. I have learned from this that next time I would try to use fully-qualified officials.

Some of the responses received stated that the catering was good, but not excellent. This was because we had opted to serve cold drinks and snacks, but the weather was cold on the day and some people said they would have appreciated a hot drink of tea or coffee. Again, this is something I would look to improve on next time.

Maps, letters and facilities were rated as 'Good' overall. Next time I would use the same format again.

Overall, I am happy with the feedback I received, and I would look to change very little if I was to run the event again.

In places, Jocelyn's analysis shows an attempt to meet the Distinction criteria. This is evidenced through her comments, which justify her decisions, such as: 'Perhaps next time I would ask people to hand their form to someone, rather than placing it in a box, because this would make it more explicit that a response is expected.'

To fully achieve the criteria for 2D.D2, Jocelyn needs to justify her statements in more detail. For example, her statement, 'Maps, letters and facilities were rated as 'Good' overall. Next time I would use the same format again', is not a Distinction-level answer. If the maps, letters, and facilities were only rated as good, what could she do to make them excellent? She has made a positive start though and with more depth to her analysis and greater justification she is more than capable of achieving the Distinction criteria.

The feedback form Jocelyn used has enabled her to make accurate judgements about the success of her event, and is evidence to support those judgements. By evaluating each component of the event and by providing recommendations for the future, she is well on the way to meeting the criteria for 2D.M3.

Unit 12: The Sport and Active Leisure Industry

Organizations in the sport and active leisure industry

The sport and active leisure industry has grown more than any other over the past two decades. It employs over 600,000 people across the public, private, and voluntary sectors, who work in a variety of diverse and interesting jobs.

Providers of sports opportunities

Most people who participate in sport do so at a local level, at a local sports centre, or by playing for a team near to where they live for example. These local sporting opportunities are provided by three different types of provider: the voluntary sector, the public sector, and the private sector.

The voluntary sector

Voluntary sports clubs provide many, many people with the opportunity to take part in their favourite sport, thanks to the dedication and hard work of the coaches, leaders, and administrators. They all help the clubs to function effectively and many carry out their roles on a voluntary, unpaid basis.

Two benefits of the voluntary sector are:

- It provides opportunities at an affordable cost, which means that sport and active leisure activities are accessible to a lot of people.
- The clubs and organizations within the voluntary sector generally concentrate on one particular sport, such as swimming or gymnastics. This means that the expertise is focused, which benefits the club, the coaches, and the participants.

Voluntary sector · **Private sector**

Local sporting provision

Public sector

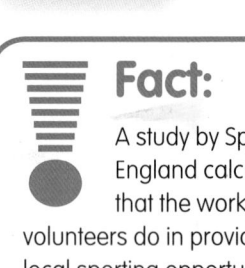

Fact:

A study by Sport England calculated that the work volunteers do in providing local sporting opportunities is worth £14 billion per year!

Spondon Cricket Club was established in 1883. It is home to five senior teams, who compete in varying divisions within the Derbyshire Cricket League. It also has a thriving junior cricket section, with up to 150 young players (both boys and girls) playing at all levels; from kwik cricket up to under-17s.

Spondon Cricket Club is a designated English Cricket Board Focus Club and has achieved Club Mark status. Club Mark is a national cross-sports quality accreditation scheme for clubs with junior sections. Clubs that achieve Club Mark status operate to a set of consistent and safe standards.

English Cricket Board Focus Clubs are selected by the local County Cricket Board. They are clubs that support the County Cricket Board's strategic development plan and are committed to delivering junior development programmes and/or development activities with specific target groups, such as disabled people, women and girls, and ethnic minorities. Clubs that are designated as Focus Clubs are able to access and utilize resources run by the English Cricket Board and the County Cricket Board, as well as local development resources, to support the delivery of their development plan.

Spondon Cricket Club generates income from a variety of sources including:

- Players' fees
- Sale of food and drinks at the bar
- Local sponsorship deals
- Fund-raising events, such as bingo evenings and race nights.

The club is run by a committed team of helpers and club officials, including:

- Coaches
- Groundspeople
- Welfare officer
- Social secretary
- Treasurer
- Fixture secretary
- Club chairperson.

Although Spondon Cricket Club is fortunate to own its own facilities – most voluntary sporting organizations use council facilities – the club's organizational structure is similar to many other clubs in the voluntary sector.

Remember:

Most voluntary clubs survive on the fees their members pay to play. Some are fortunate enough to secure sponsorship or obtain grants from their local authority or their national governing body, but for the majority it is a constant struggle to make ends meet.

BRONZE

1. Think of a voluntary club that you have been (or still are) a member of and make a list of the different roles people have within the club. For example, is there a head coach?

2. Read about Spondon Cricket Club and think about the local voluntary clubs in your area. What similarities can you identify between the way they are structured and the way they are funded?

The public sector

The public sector also plays an important role in providing sporting and physical activity opportunities at a local level. The level of provision varies from local authority to local authority, but as a general rule the facilities provided by the public sector include:

- Playing fields
- Sports centres
- Swimming pools
- Athletics tracks
- Tennis courts.

Public-sector facilities are funded at a local level by local authorities, who receive income from central government grants, council tax (which is collected at a local level), redistributed business rate revenue, and money generated by visitors to sports centres.

Local authority provision is often easily accessible and is reasonably priced. Admission fees to local authority

An aerobics class at a local authority leisure facility.

facilities are usually kept at a level that allows as many local people to participate in sport as possible. Often, discounted rates are available for senior citizens, people with disabilities, and those who are out of work and receiving benefits.

The private sector

Over the past few years there has been a tremendous increase in private-sector sports facilities, as more and more people become aware of the importance of having a healthy lifestyle. Private-sector facilities range from small businesses, such as dance studios owned and run by individuals, through to multinational chains of health clubs, such as David Lloyd and Virgin Active.

The money to run private-sector facilities comes predominantly from membership fees, sales of goods and services, personal or company savings, and financing initiatives, such as bank loans. In recent years, in an effort to increase investment and improve efficiency at public-sector facilities, many local authorities have been getting private companies to run their facilities for them, in return for an agreed management fee.

Although membership of a private-sector tennis club or health club is often expensive, they usually provide state-of-the-art equipment in a high-quality environment.

BRONZE

3. Which public-sector facilities do you use in your local area? How could they be improved and what would the implications of making the improvements be?

Some state-of-the-art equipment at a private-sector facility.

Remember:

As a rule, membership fees and the price of activities at private-sector facilities are higher than at public-sector facilities.

Fact:

There are over 330 private-sector companies currently operating public-sector sport and leisure centres; this is an investment of over £30 million a year.

Joint and dual-use facilities

The number of joint or dual-use facilities is on the increase. A joint or dual-use facility has more than one 'owner' and the two owners share the costs of the facility, including staffing and maintenance. For example, a sports centre built on a school site and used by the school during the day and the public in the evenings and at weekends is a dual-use facility.

Joint and dual-use facilities are often more heavily used than single-use facilities; the costs are shared between at least two organizations and links are created between the different groups of people who use the facilities at different times.

BRONZE

4. Design a private-sector facility that your local area would benefit from. Money is no object!

5. Use the internet to find out about the sports provision provided by each of the three sectors – the voluntary sector, the public sector, and the private sector – in your local area. If you live in an area with limited facilities, think about your nearest town or city.

Occupations in the sport and active leisure industry

The sport and active leisure industry is varied and diverse, so it's not surprising that there are a range of job opportunities open to you. You may already have a good idea of the type of opportunities that exist, but if not there are plenty of sources of information you can access for help, such as professional sport bodies, for example The Chartered Institute for the Management of Sport and Physical Activity (CIMSPA) and specialist publications, such as *Leisure Opportunities*.

Occupations within the sport and active leisure industry include:

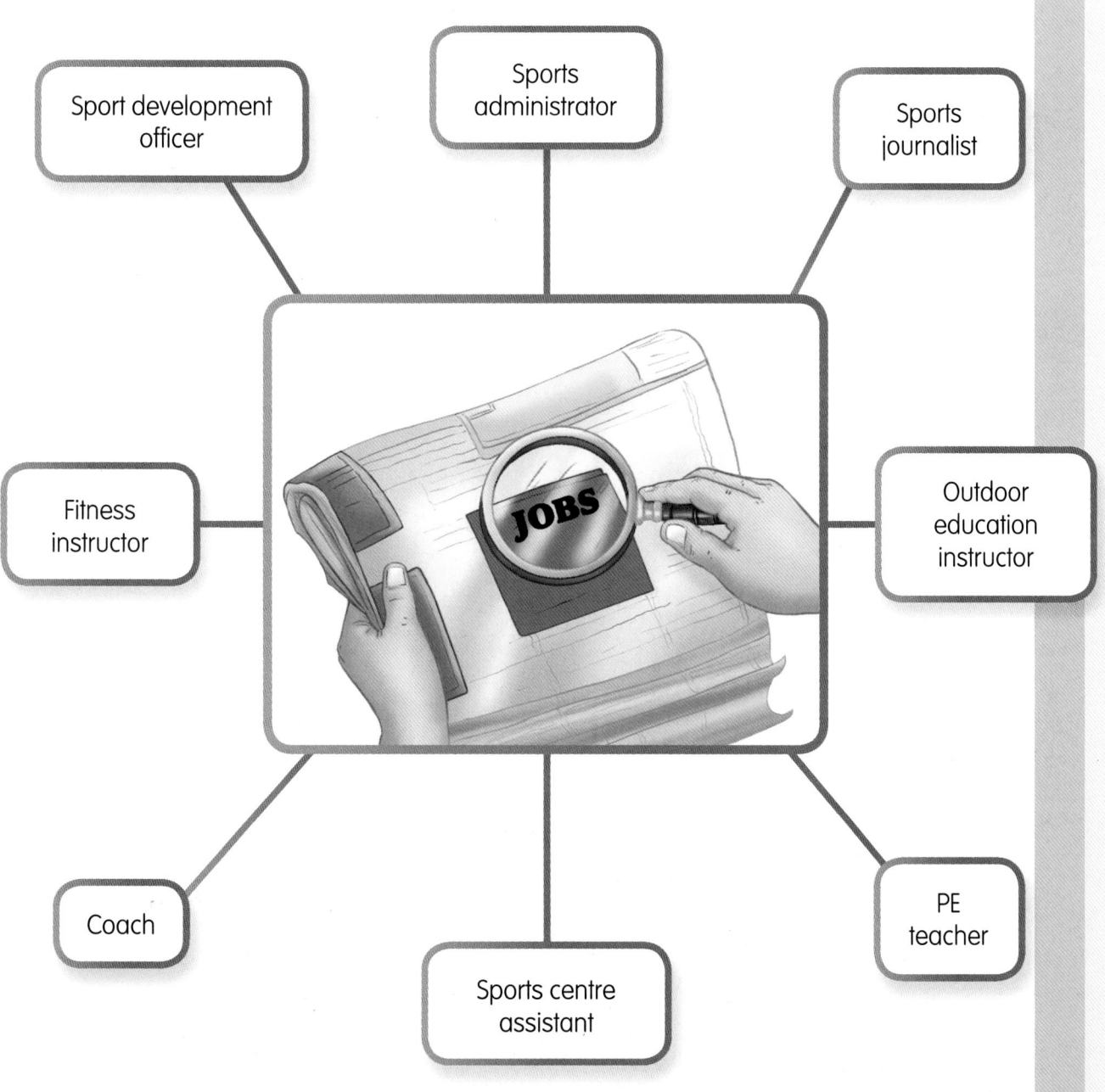

- Sport development officer
- Sports administrator
- Sports journalist
- Fitness instructor
- Outdoor education instructor
- Coach
- Sports centre assistant
- PE teacher

Skills, responsibilities, and requirements

Although there are a wide variety of occupations within the sport and active leisure industry, many roles require similar skills and have similar responsibilities and requirements.

Skills
- Communication skills, including both verbal and non-verbal communication skills and using technology to communicate effectively.
- Organizational skills, including project-management skills, creative-thinking skills, numerical and statistical skills.
- Time-management skills.
- Leadership skills.
- Motivational skills.

Responsibilities
- Ensuring excellent customer care.
- Ensuring the health and safety of staff and customers.
- Ensuring all child protection requirements are fully met.

Requirements
- Possess relevant qualifications for the role, such as the National Pool Lifeguard Qualification (NPLQ) or a coaching award like the STA Certificate in Teaching Swimming.
- Pass the Criminal Records Bureau (CRB) check.
- Possess an appropriate first-aid qualification.
- Be motivated and have a positive attitude.
- Be able to demonstrate previous experience appropriate to the role.

A case study: Outdoor education instructor

Steve is an experienced outdoor education instructor.

Steve has a range of skills. He is well organized and makes sure all the equipment he needs is in place and checked for safety. He also has to organize first-aid provision, transport to the facilities where the activities are taking place, and organize participants into suitable groups.

One of Steve's main responsibilities is ensuring that all health and safety regulations are adhered to. He needs to make sure that all activities are safe and appropriate for participants of different levels. He also needs to have rescue plans in place, just in case they are needed, and be able to deal with injuries if they occur.

As part of his role, Steve needs to have a current Criminal Records Bureau (CRB) check in place before being allowed to take young people out on activities. This means he has no criminal convictions that could possibly put the participants he is working with in danger.

BRONZE

1. Compile a list of five occupations within the sport and active leisure industry that would appeal to you. Try and make them as diverse as possible and record where you found the information about them.

2. a) Read the case study about the outdoor education instructor. Then select two of the occupations you identified for Activity 1 and list the skills, responsibilities, and requirements you would need for each of them.

b) Describe each skill, responsibility, and requirement you have listed.

Advantages and disadvantages of different occupations

All careers, in all industries, will have some good points about them and some things that aren't so good. Although they will differ slightly between different occupations and different employers, advantages and disadvantages of jobs in the sport and active leisure industry include:

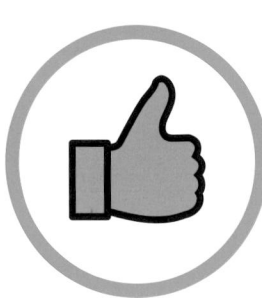

- Flexible working patterns, to fit in with your own training needs.
- Working with talented sports people, helping them achieve excellence.
- Working with disadvantaged groups, developing their ability to integrate into society.
- Variety: each day is potentially very different and no two days are ever the same.

- Working outdoors, especially when it's cold and wet.
- Working unsociable hours, especially at weekends.
- Poor rates of pay in some roles.

Football development manager: Advantages and disadvantages

BACK TO HOME PAGE | CAREERS: JUMP TO... | LATEST CAREERS IN SPORT NEWS

PROFESSION:
FOOTBALL DEVELOPMENT MANAGER

NAME:
George Carney

DEGREE:
BA Hons, PGCE, QTS

EMPLOYER:
BUCS

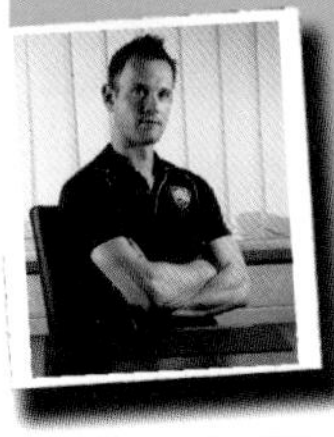

TYPICAL DAY | ADVANTAGES | QUALIFICATIONS | RESOURCES

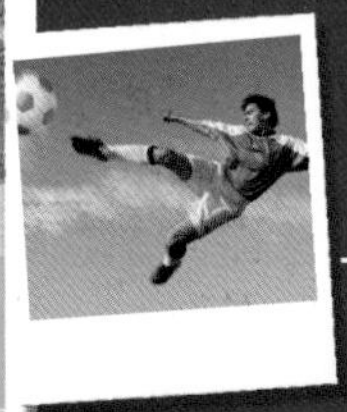

3 great things about being a football development manager

1. Being responsible for delivering good sporting events
2. Working with some excellent students and staff
3. Being part of the bigger sporting network in the Higher Education sector

3 not so great things about being a Football Development Manager

1. Having to compile numerous spreadsheets
2. Scepticism from members
3. Chasing up people all the time e.g. those who do not enter futsal teams

SILVER

3. There are lots of different places where you can find out about jobs in the sport and leisure industry, including:

- www.cimspa.co.uk CIMSPA
- www.u-xplore.com/online/dsl/skillsactive-2.5/ue.asp SkillsActive, the Sector Skills Council for the sport and active leisure industry.
- Local and national press, specialist publications, and periodicals.
- Recruitments agencies and job adverts.

Explore these sources of information, choose three occupations and identify as many advantages and disadvantages of each as you can find during your research.

GOLD

4. Compare and contrast the advantages and disadvantages of two of the occupations you researched for Activity 3.

Unit 12 assignment, part one

Background

Imagine you are a sport development officer employed by your local authority. You are often asked to go into schools to talk to their Year 11 students about career options in the sport and active leisure industry and the different organizations they might like to work for.

Grading criteria to be assessed
1A.1, 1A.2
2A.P1, 2A.P2
2A.M1, 2A.M2
2A.D1, 2A.D2

Task

Prepare a presentation for students, giving them an insight into the sport and active leisure industry and the range of occupations within it. Bearing in mind the target audience, your presentation should be engaging and varied.

 **LEVEL 1**

- Outline the different types of organisations in sport and active leisure. (1A.1)
- Using information from given sources, outline the responsibilities of, and skills required by, two occupations in sport and active leisure. (1A.2)

 **LEVEL 2 PASS**

- Describe the different types of organisations in sport and active leisure, and the benefits of each. (2A.P1)
- Using information from selected sources, describe the requirements for, responsibilities of, and skills required by two occupations in sport and active leisure. (2A.P2)

 **LEVEL 2 MERIT**

- Explain, using relevant examples, the benefits of each of the different types of organisations in sport and active leisure. (2A.M1)
- Summarise selected information about occupations in sport and active leisure, describing the advantages and disadvantages of each. (2A.M2)

 **LEVEL 2 DISTINCTION**

- Compare and contrast the benefits of each different type of organisation in sport and active leisure. (2A.D1)
- Explain the advantages and disadvantages of occupations in sport and active leisure. (2A.D2)

Tackling the assignment

You need to make sure you cover the public, private, and voluntary sectors and joint and dual-use provision when you address the organization section of the task; followed by an in-depth examination of at least two different occupations within the sport and active leisure industry.

You could create your presentation in PowerPoint® and prepare a series of factsheets to support it. It would be great to add graphics to your presentation, as this may help you get the information across more effectively.

 ## Remember:

- When you **describe** something you need to paint a picture in words, making sure you include sufficient detail so that someone else can see the picture you are painting.
- An **explanation** requires you to gives reasons why something is as it is, so the word 'because' should appear prominently in your answer.
- A **summary** is a shortened version of something, so when you summarize something you need to present only the key points.
- When you **compare and contrast** something you identify the similarities and differences between two or more things.

Meeting the Level 2 Pass criteria

The sport and active leisure industry
Bobby Brown

The public sector

The public sector, which is the sector that is funded by local authorities and central government, provides numerous sport and active leisure facilities. These include facilities such as:

☑ Sports centres, which may contain a swimming pool, an indoor sports hall, squash courts, a health suite, outdoor tennis courts, etc.

☑ A local park, which may have a trim track, a cycle route, and football and cricket pitches, etc.

The benefits of the public sector are that the fees charged for people to participate in sport are usually kept at a level that allows as many people to participate in sport as possible. For example, the cost of swimming at public-sector pools in Langbridge is £3.10, which is discounted to £2.25 for juniors under 16 years of age.

Another benefit is that discounted rates are often available for certain groups such as senior citizens or those who are out of work and receiving benefits. An example of this is the price of swimming. If local people have a Passport to Leisure Pass – which allows them cheaper access – the price drops to £2.50 for a swim. Swimming is free during off peak times (9am–4pm) for members of the public who are unemployed.

Having spoken to the head of sport and leisure at Langbridge District Council it became clear that there are many possible occupations within the public sector. The large sports centre in the middle of town employs ten full-time and eight part-time leisure attendants, who need a range of skills and have a variety of responsibilities. There are also certain requirements placed upon them, all of which are described below.

Skills	Responsibilities	Requirements
☑ A leisure centre attendant will need good communication skills for giving safety instructions to swimmers or going through membership options with someone wanting to join.	☑ One of the most important responsibilities an attendant has is to make sure the centre is clean and tidy. This will include making sure the changing rooms are free from dirt, etc., because bacteria can spread quickly in a warm and wet environment.	☑ An attendant will need to have the right qualifications, especially if they are working on the poolside. This will include such qualifications as the National Pool Lifeguard Qualification (NPLQ), which is the standard qualification needed to become a lifeguard in England.

Bobby has started well. His factsheet includes a brief description of the public sector and the types of organizations within it, and he has expanded on this by adding detail about the type of benefits the sector and organizations bring. If he replicates this level of detail for the private and voluntary sectors, and covers joint and dual-use facilities, he should meet the criteria for 2A.P1.

This is an effective way for Bobby to present his work, and he clearly understands what to include in a description. He has used a good source of information (the head of sport and leisure at Langbridge District Council) and has started to describe the types of skills required by an attendant. He has also started to describe the responsibilities and requirements associated with the role; all he needs to do now is to provide some more examples.

Bobby has made a great start and, if he continues like this and adds a second occupation, he will achieve the criteria for 2A.P2.

Meeting the Level 2 Merit criteria

Leah Benton

Explanation of benefits: Public sector

- Being affordable means that all sections of the community will be able to participate because the entry costs are low. This will not only benefit the people taking part, because they can exercise regularly, but could also mean that the people will rely less on health services (saving money), will hopefully have less time off work, and generally enjoy a more healthy lifestyle.

Well done Leah! These PowerPoint® slides are a sound base from which Leah can explain the benefits of the different sectors in the speech she is giving to accompany them. As long as she provides details of further benefits of the public and voluntary sectors, and mentions the private sector and joint and dual-use facilities in similar detail, she will meet the criteria for 2A.M1.

Explanation of benefits: Voluntary sector

- The extensive range of opportunities provided by the voluntary sector is a real benefit because it means that nearly everybody can take part in some form of sport, from a netball club through to an archery club. Many voluntary clubs also cater for disabled people, which means they can play an active role in leisure pursuits, which in turn will help raise their self-esteem and allow them to take part in healthy activities.

The advantages and disadvantages of different occupations in sport

There are a variety of advantages of working in sport. They are:
- ☑ Good working conditions.
- ☑ Healthy environment in which to work.
- ☑ Good pay for some jobs.

However, there are some disadvantages, such as:
- ☑ Working unsociable hours.
- ☑ Some jobs don't pay well.
- ☑ Working outdoors.

Leah is well off the mark here. To start with she has not specified what types of occupations she is referring to and has only produced a list, not a description.

To rectify the situation, and meet the criteria for 2A.M2, she needs to be more specific about exactly which occupations she is describing. She needs to summarize two or three occupations and then expand on her descriptions of their advantages and disadvantages. She needs to add a lot more detail to the advantages and disadvantages, stating pay rates, outlining working hours for a sport development officer, or describing the weather conditions outdoor adventure staff may need to work in from time-to-time for example.

Amir Shafqat

Organizations in sport and active leisure: The benefits

Do the sectors provide similar benefits?

They certainly do! All of them provide sport and leisure activities that benefit the people taking part. Increased activity levels result in a fitter population, which in turn reduces health problems and increases energy levels for people, which in turn helps them with normal day-to-day and workplace tasks.

Other similar benefits are

Are there any contrasting benefits?

Of course there are! Private-sector sports organizations generate income and potentially wealth for the owners, as well as providing state-of-the-art facilities that many elite performers can benefit from. Voluntary clubs, on the other hand, provide opportunities for volunteers to get involved in coaching or administration. This is a benefit because it allows people to do something worthwhile with their leisure time and also lets younger volunteers develop skills and qualities that they may need when entering the workplace.

Other differences include

> Amir is well on the way to achieving the criteria for 2A.D1. This snapshot of his poster shows that he understands how to compare and contrast and support this information with an explanation. Good stuff!

Occupations in sport and active leisure: Let's explore the advantages and disadvantages

Gym instructors

> Again, Amir is on the right track. As long as he maintains this level of detail for the other occupations he explains he will meet the criteria for 2A.D2. Well done Amir, your posters will certainly help Year 11 pupils understand the advantages and disadvantages of various sports-related occupations.

Advantages

☑ There are opportunities in both the private and public sectors

This is an advantage because it increases the number of jobs open to people and allows them to choose which sector they work for. It also gives staff the opportunity to learn about the different sectors, which in turn helps broaden their future career opportunities.

☑ Work environment

The work environment is an advantage because staff are shielded from the weather elements and gyms are usually clean and warm. Working in an environment where people are enjoying themselves should also make going to work a real pleasure.

Disadvantages

☒ Working unsocial hours

Due to the nature of the job many instructors are required to work evenings and weekends, when the customers are not working. This means that they may miss out on their own leisure time because they are working when their friends are out enjoying themselves!

☒ Low pay

Some instructors have to supplement their income by working as personal trainers, because pay rates can be low. This means that they may be working long hours, which can be tiring and, again, has an impact on their social life.

Why people participate in sport

It is estimated that approximately 75 per cent of people in the UK aged between 16 and 24 take part in some form of physical activity, and although this percentage decreases with age, sport is still a major pastime for over-55s. In fact, statistics indicate that over 40 per cent of the UK population exercises to some degree. So, why are sports and physical activities so popular and why has there been a growth in participation over the years?

It is important to keep exercising as you get older.

Health and fitness benefits

For lots of people, sport is great way to help them stay fit and healthy. Regular participation in physical activity:

- Benefits every part of your body, including the mind. This in turn helps your body stay in good working order so that you can cope with everyday tasks that involve physical exertion.
- Helps you look better and feel more positive about yourself.
- Helps you lose weight and lowers the risk of some diseases, including high blood pressure and heart disease.
- Helps you age well, keeping your bones strong and your joints mobile as you grow older.

Social benefits

Participating in sport is not only good for the body. It also has social benefits.

Personal development

Sport is a great way to develop many of the personal qualities and skills required for life. Sport can help an individual:

- Build character and develop resilience if things aren't going well.
- Develop their ability to think strategically.
- Think analytically.
- Set goals and targets.
- Learn and use leadership skills.
- Take calculated risks.
- Develop the motor skills needed to perform many day-to-day tasks.

Growth in participation

The steady increase in participation can be attributed to many things, such as:

- Greater publicity about the health benefits of physical activity, including information and advice from health organizations and government departments.
- A general increase in leisure time as the working week decreases and people start to retire at an earlier age.
- An increase in disposable income (the money left after essential bills have been paid) means that people have money to spend on sport and active leisure activities, although this is affected during times of recession.
- An increase in new and exciting activities, including extreme sports.
- Sport is now seen as fashionable and becoming a professional performer or a high-profile coach is seen as a way to earn a good income. Many sportswear manufacturers, such as Nike® and Adidas®, also spend millions of pounds securing top sports stars to promote their products.

Social benefits of sport

- Taking part in sport develops your self-confidence and increases your self-esteem.
- Taking part in sport offers you opportunities for making new friends or developing existing friendships.
- Taking part in sport helps to develop your team-working skills and helps you to become more disciplined.
- Taking part in sport can help to divert you from being involved with anti-social behaviour.

Factors that affect participation in sport

Although many people may want to participate in sport, whether they do or not is often influenced by many factors.

Barriers to participation

Disability
The opportunities for people with a disability to take part in sport have increased over the years, but having a disability can still be problematic for some participants. It can still be difficult to find facilities that are modified for disabled use, with easy access, user-friendly changing, and suitable equipment. It can also be difficult to find coaches or leaders with the correct training and sufficient confidence to help participants with disabilities.

Provision
Access to a wide range of facilities varies greatly across the UK, and depends on the investment made in sport by the local authority and the willingness of the private sector to build and run facilities in that particular area. Also, many public-sector facilities were built during the 1970s, so although an area may appear to be well served with sports provision, it is often in poor repair or is suffering from a lack of investment.

Cost
The cost of taking part in sport can have an impact on someone's level of participation, especially if the cost of participation is high and their income is relatively low. Many local authorities have concessionary schemes in place at public-sector facilities, offering discounts to people with low incomes to address this problem. Similarly, many voluntary sports clubs try to keep their membership costs low to encourage participation, often with the support of grants from local authorities and governing bodies. Generally, the private sector only caters for those in the community who can afford their prices.

Location
Facilities may exist, but can you get to them? Location is critical and can often have a significant impact on the opportunity a person has to participate in sport. For example, are the facilities accessible via public transport? If participants do have a car, is parking provision adequate? Do people living in rural communities have to travel great distances to participate? Do elite performers have to travel to access the appropriate facilities or coaching?

Age
Although many people over 55 do take part in sport and physical activity, age can affect participation. Participation rates generally decrease as people get older for a variety of reasons, including:

- Reduced mobility and other health problems.
- Less money to spend on physical activity after retirement.
- Problems accessing facilities using public transport.

Ethnicity
There are many people from ethnic minority communities in the UK who want to participate in sport but have to overcome significant barriers in order to do so. Reasons put forward for not participating include limited access to facilities and racist incidents. One initiative that hopes to address this is Sporting Equals.

Gender
Gender has often been a barrier, particularly for women due to their traditional involvement in childcare at home and the image portrayed by many sports that they are for males only. This has often resulted in fewer sporting opportunities for women, although this is now changing at schools and in sport in general.

Sporting Equals

Promoting ethnic diversity across sport & physical activity

Sporting Equals was set up in 1998 by Sport England in partnership with the Commission for Racial Equality. It is now an independent body that aims to create an environment in which:

- People from black and minority ethnic (BME) communities can influence and participate in all aspects of sport and physical activity.
- National governing bodies and providers of sport and physical activity recognize and value a fully integrated and inclusive society.
- Ethnic diversity is recognized and celebrated.

Sporting Equals has three objectives:

- To raise awareness and understanding of the needs of BME communities within the sports and health sector in order to change attitudes and increase participation in sport and physical activity.
- To empower individuals and communities to play a part in this change, and achieve their full potential through playing sport and being active.
- To advise and support policy-makers and delivery bodies to be inclusive.

Sport in the community events held by organizations such as 't.a.a.rget' aim to reduce barriers to participation and make sport more accessible for everyone.

BRONZE

1. Choose a sports facility in your local area and investigate its provision for participants with disabilities.

SILVER

2. Look at the three scenarios below and identify the factors that are affecting participation. Once you have done this, explain why the factors you have identified are affecting participation:

- A large family with children who all like different sports.
- An aging couple who have always been active but no longer drive.
- A talented gymnast who cannot access the level of training she needs due to a lack of elite facilities and coaches where she lives.

Trends in participation

There are numerous trends in the sport and active leisure industry that influence participation levels, some of which have a positive impact and others which have a negative impact.

Sports with increasing participation levels

Some sports are becoming more popular and showing increasing levels of participation among different age groups. Sport England monitors trends in participation and their Active People Survey published in December 2010 showed that certain sports were benefiting from increased numbers. Examples include athletics, which saw a 4.5 per cent increase in 2009 and cycling, which saw a 4.45 per cent increase in 2009. Schemes such as Go-Ride, British Cycling's development programme for young people, have helped increase the popularity of cycling.

Sports with decreasing participation levels

Unfortunately, not all sports are showing increasing participation levels. Research by Sport England has also revealed that some major sports, such as swimming, tennis, and football, are experiencing a drop in the number of people participating, especially among young people. Influences such as the higher cost of living and work pressures have been cited as possible reasons why participation levels in some sports have dropped.

New and emerging sports

There are many new sports emerging for people to take part in, including cyclo-cross, inline skating, open water swimming, kite surfing, and triathlon. They are very different to more established sports, such as hockey, volleyball, and golf, and therefore appeal to a different group of people; people who are looking for something adrenalin fuelled and out of the ordinary.

A triathlon combines three sports – running, swimming, and cycling – in one event. Triathletes therefore have to excel in three different disciplines, and although they all require good levels of aerobic endurance, the skills and techniques required for success are very different.

These trainers look pretty trendy, and will be attractive to those who like to keep up-to-date with the latest fashion.

Fashion

Many major sportswear companies now produce items of clothing and footwear that are seen as fashionable must-have accessories. Although this doesn't directly affect participation levels, the advertising and publicity connected with the clothing and footwear brands does raise awareness of the sporting industry and the opportunities to get involved that are on offer.

The commercial benefits are also huge. Many fans, especially football fans, like to wear their favourite team's replica kit. The crowd at many Premier League games is often populated by fans in their team's colours with the name of their favourite player emblazoned across their back.

The sweet smell of success and the stink of failure

Watching sport continues to be very popular, with more and more people attending sporting events. The 2011 Grand National drew a crowd of 79,291 and many Premier League Football grounds regularly have crowds of over 40,000 when the top teams are playing.

When a team is on top, the number of spectators increases, but a team on a losing streak can see its fan base dwindle to only the most loyal; especially if it is relegated to a lower league or doesn't take part in a major competition for a while. Having said that, there are some exceptions to this trend; Wimbledon continues to generate huge crowds despite the long wait for a home-grown winner.

When England won the Rugby World Cup in November 2003 there was an influx of more than 50,000 new players in the following two years. The Rugby Football Union reported an increase of 18,000 extra players during 2005, on top of the extra 33,098 that started playing in the first year after England became world champions.

Technological developments

The sport and active leisure industry has benefited enormously from technological developments over the past few years. New jobs have been created and some of the developments – such as the video referee in rugby league or the use of Hawk-Eye in test cricket – have increased the interest in sports by adding to the excitement.

For example, many test matches now use Hawk-Eye technology to give both teams the opportunity to have decisions reviewed by the third umpire in the stands. Six cameras record the action at different angles and these images are turned into a 3D picture that can be used to review the original decision to see if it was in fact accurate. Each team is allowed to make two unsuccessful review requests per innings during a match, so they have to use them wisely. The decision is then shown on the big screen, with tremendous tension and excitement generated while the crowd waits for the decision!

Sports equipment and clothing has also benefited from technological advancements. Manufacturers invest time and money into the research phase and then often employ extra staff to help production, ready to sell it to the industry and the waiting athletes. Bicycles are now significantly lighter and more aerodynamic than they were in the past; some of those used in track cycling look almost space-aged compared to those being used a few years ago. The design of competitive swimming costumes has also changed dramatically in recent years. The suits, or 'fast skins' as they called, are made from a material that absorbs less water and makes the swimmer far more streamlined, mainly by restraining the muscles and so decreasing the swimmer's resistance through the water.

Technological developments, such as Hawk-Eye, help umpires make the correct decision and add more excitement for the crowd as they await the third umpire's decision/ruling.

Unit 12 assignment, part two

Background

You are spending a week on work experience with a sport development officer, and are working with a range of partners on a local regeneration project that is actively trying to increase participation levels in sport and physical activity with many of the families that are part of the scheme.

Grading criteria to be assessed
1B.3, 1B.4, 1B.5
2B.P3, 2B.P4, 2B.P5
2B.M3, 2B.M4
2B.D3

Task

Prepare a presentation about why people take part in sport, the factors that affect participation, and trends in participation. Your presentation should:

 **LEVEL 1**

- Outline reasons for participation in sport and active leisure. (1B.3)
- Describe four factors that can affect participation in sport and active leisure. (1B.4)
- Describe two different trends that can affect participation in sport and active leisure. (1B.5)

 **LEVEL 2 PASS**

- Using relevant information, describe reasons for, and growth in, participation in sport and active leisure. (2B.P3)
- Describe six factors that can affect participation in sport and active leisure. (2B.P4)
- Describe six different trends that can affect participation in sport and active leisure. (2B.P5)

 **LEVEL 2 MERIT**

- Explain, using relevant examples, how different factors can affect participation in sport and active leisure. (2B.M3)
- Explain trends in participation in sport and active leisure. (2B.M4)

 **LEVEL 2 DISTINCTION**

- Compare and contrast trends in participation in sport and active leisure. (2B.D3)

Tackling the assignment

You need to plan your presentation with the target audience in mind, which in this case is likely to be a combination of young people, adults, and older adults. Engaging everyone will require a variety of methods, including handouts, a PowerPoint® presentation, and perhaps even a flipchart presentation. Also, as you will be delivering a fair amount of your presentation verbally, a series of crib cards to prompt you while you are speaking would come in very handy.

Meeting the Level 2 Pass criteria

Samantha Stevenson

Information based on research conducted by Sport England, UK Sport, and some research I did at the local authority sport centre.

People participate in sport for many reasons, including:

- Health benefits – to keep them fit, active, and to help keep them stay mentally sound. (1)
- Social benefits – to develop self-confidence, increase self-esteem, or as an opportunity to make new friends. (2)

Factors that can affect participation in sport include:

- Cost – the price of participating in sport can affect how many people actually take part. (3)

Trends that affect participants in sport

- New sports and facilities, such as the BMX track in Cliff Park. (4)

(1) Give examples of the over-60s swimming session at the local pool. All the swimmers still live independently and enjoy quite active lifestyles. There are about 20 who swim regularly, with four of them over the age of 85!

(2) I can use me as an example. Since I joined the athletics club my confidence has improved (such as talking to groups like this) and I have a whole set of new friends that I have made at the club.

(3) The figures I've got from the local pool show that since the free swimming sessions finished, attendance by under-16s has dropped by 7 per cent and by 11 per cent for over-60s. This could show that cost is important.

(4) Since the track was built a few months ago, attendance has risen steadily. There was a regional competition there last week that attracted over 500 spectators and included a 'come and try it' session that attracted 11 new junior members!

Although we can only see a small part of Samantha's work, it's pretty clear that she is covering the right areas and has plenty of support material to back up her descriptions. She obviously has to cover all the requirements of the criteria but the standard of her work meets the 2B.P3, 2B.P4, and 2B.P5 criteria.

Meeting the Level 2 Merit and Distinction criteria

James Woodruff

One factor that can affect participation is disability. People with disabilities often find it more difficult to participate because:

- There may be access issues, such as a lack of parking spaces close to the facility or stairs they need to go up with no lift or ramp in place.

- They may need specialist equipment to take part in certain activities, such as a modified or strengthened wheelchair, which could be very expensive.

- They may need specialist coaches/leaders/carers to help them participate, who may not be available locally.

One trend that can affect participation is success. A great example of this is women's and girls' participation in cricket, which saw an 11 per cent increase among women and a 27 per cent increase among girls in 2009. This has been attributed to two things:

1. The increasing success of the England women's team, who are the best team in the world and have won the Ashes against the Australians on a regular basis.

2. The successful Get into Cricket campaign run by the England Cricket Board and the increase in coaches supported by the Sky Sports Coach Education Programme.

Although we can only see a small amount of James' work we can see that he is clearly explaining trends in participation and how factors affect participation. He has included some reasons to support his ideas and has added details by including some statistics and details of initiatives that promote participation. If James continues in this way, he will meet the criteria for 2B.M3 and 2B.M4.

It is interesting to see that some of the trends we have looked at are very similar, whereas others are very different.

An example of this is the increase in participation in some sports, such as athletics, and a decrease in others, such as squash, which is predicted by Sport England to decrease by 36 per cent between 2005 and 2013.

Other sports have shown similar increases and decreases down to a variety of reasons, such as lack of funding, more active governing bodies, and an increase in funding for coaches.

So, when you are choosing a sport

This extract from James' leaflet does not meet the Distinction criteria. The information is too superficial, and although James has started to compare and contrast trends in participation and has included some statistics, there is no depth to his work.

To improve, and to reach the necessary standard, James needs to explain why these differences are occurring, supported with some facts and figures. For example, he could make reference to the fact that squash is declining in popularity because many local authority sports centres, and some private ones, have converted their squash courts into health suites, reducing the amount of court space available.

Issues and their impact on the sport and active leisure industry

If there is one thing that can be said about the sports industry, it is that it is never dull! There is always something happening, whether it is a drugs scandal, a famous England win, poor behaviour by a footballer, or a fantastic performance by an athlete at the Olympic Games. And all these events have impacts on the sports and active leisure industry, some of which are positive and some of which are, unfortunately, not!

Sky Sports: A television revolution!

British Sky Broadcasting has had a significant impact on sport in the UK since the early 1990s, most notably encouraging the Premier League to break away from the Football League in 1992. It has recently won the rights to show test match cricket and F1 motor racing, so its influence is growing even more.

As a result of British Sky Broadcasting's influence, football in England has changed beyond recognition, sometimes for the better and sometimes for the worse.

Positive impacts	Negative impacts
Huge influx of income into the English game.	Many lower league teams are in financial difficulties because bigger clubs now buy more players from abroad instead of from football league clubs.
Helped top clubs buy the best European and world players.	Matches have been moved away from the traditional 3pm Saturday kickoff so that they can cater for larger television audiences, thereby maximizing advertising revenues.
Helped clubs build bigger and safer stadiums.	The BBC and ITV cannot compete financially with Sky Sports, so many matches are not on terrestrial television and people have to pay to watch them.
Helped The Football Association (FA) redevelop Wembley Stadium.	Top players' wages are now 'sky' high, and many people think of them as overpaid prima donnas.
Helped the FA develop many grass-roots initiatives.	If Sky Sports pulled out of their current deal with the Premier League, the FA and the Premier League clubs would be in serious financial difficulties.

Making a costly mistake: Dwain Chambers

In 2003 Dwain Chambers tested positive for tetrahydrogestrinone or THG, a banned anabolic steroid. Dwain was subsequently found guilty of taking performance-enhancing drugs and banned from athletics for two years. This created a considerable amount of negative publicity for athletics and many people openly stated that they wouldn't want their children going into a sport where drug taking was rife.

Since his return to the sport, Dwain has taken a strong anti-drug stance, regularly mentoring young athletes and warning them against the dangers of using drugs to enhance their performance. He is now seen, in some quarters, as a force for possible good.

Dwain Chambers competing after his ban ended.

The impact of Dwain's behaviour	
On Dwain • He was not able to compete while serving his ban. • Any funding he received prior to the ban will have stopped. • It may affect his popularity among other athletes. • The British Olympic Association had a policy of banning athletes who had been caught taking drugs from Team GB for life. Dwain Chambers spent a great deal of time and money getting his lifetime ban overturned.	**On athletics** • The image of athletics has been affected. • The spotlight moves away from athletics as a whole and focuses on just one athlete for a while. • Dwain has taken responsibility for his mistakes and has now taken a strong anti-drug stance, which perhaps goes some way to repairing the damage caused to athletics by his actions.
On future athletes • Fewer young people may take up athletics, deciding that other sports have a better image. • They may see Dwain's behaviour as acceptable and consider taking performance-enhancing drugs themselves. • Young athletes who listen to Dwain's warnings may be persuaded not to take performance-enhancing drugs.	**Other impacts** • All the good work Dwain has done in raising the profile of athletics, especially within the black community, may be undone. Although some may see his strong anti-drugs stance as a positive outcome of the scandal.

The growing obesity problem

It is a well researched fact that there is a growing obesity problem in the UK, which is regularly featured in television, radio, and newspaper reports. Here are some key facts from the latest NHS report published in 2010:

Many schemes are now in place to help young people develop more healthy lifestyles.

- In 2008, almost a quarter of adults (24 per cent of men and 25 per cent of women aged 16 or over) in England were classified as obese.
- A greater proportion of men than women (42 per cent compared with 32 per cent) in England were classified as overweight in 2008.
- 39 per cent of adults had a raised waist circumference in 2008 compared to 23 per cent in 1993. Women were more likely than men (44 per cent and 34 per cent respectively) to have a raised waist circumference (over 88cm for women and over 102cm for men).
- In 2008, 16.8 per cent of boys and 15.2 per cent of girls aged 2 to 15 were classed as obese, an increase from 11.1 per cent and 12.2 per cent respectively in 1995.

(Source: *Statistics on obesity, physical activity and diet: England 2010*, a report prepared for the NHS by The Health and Social Care Information Centre, 2010)

So, what impact is this growth in obesity having? Perhaps surprisingly, there are some positives:

- Levels of physical activity in schools are increasing steadily due to greater focus on school sport.
- School dinners are now more in line with the requirements of a healthy diet.
- Junk food adverts are banned from some of the most popular children's television programmes.
- Some sports are starting to include healthy-eating advice in their coach education programmes.

BRONZE

1. What are the negative impacts of the growth in levels of obesity?

2. What were the positive and negative impacts of Great Britain hosting the 2012 Olympic and Paralympic Games? Record your ideas in a table.

More sporting issues and an overview of their impacts

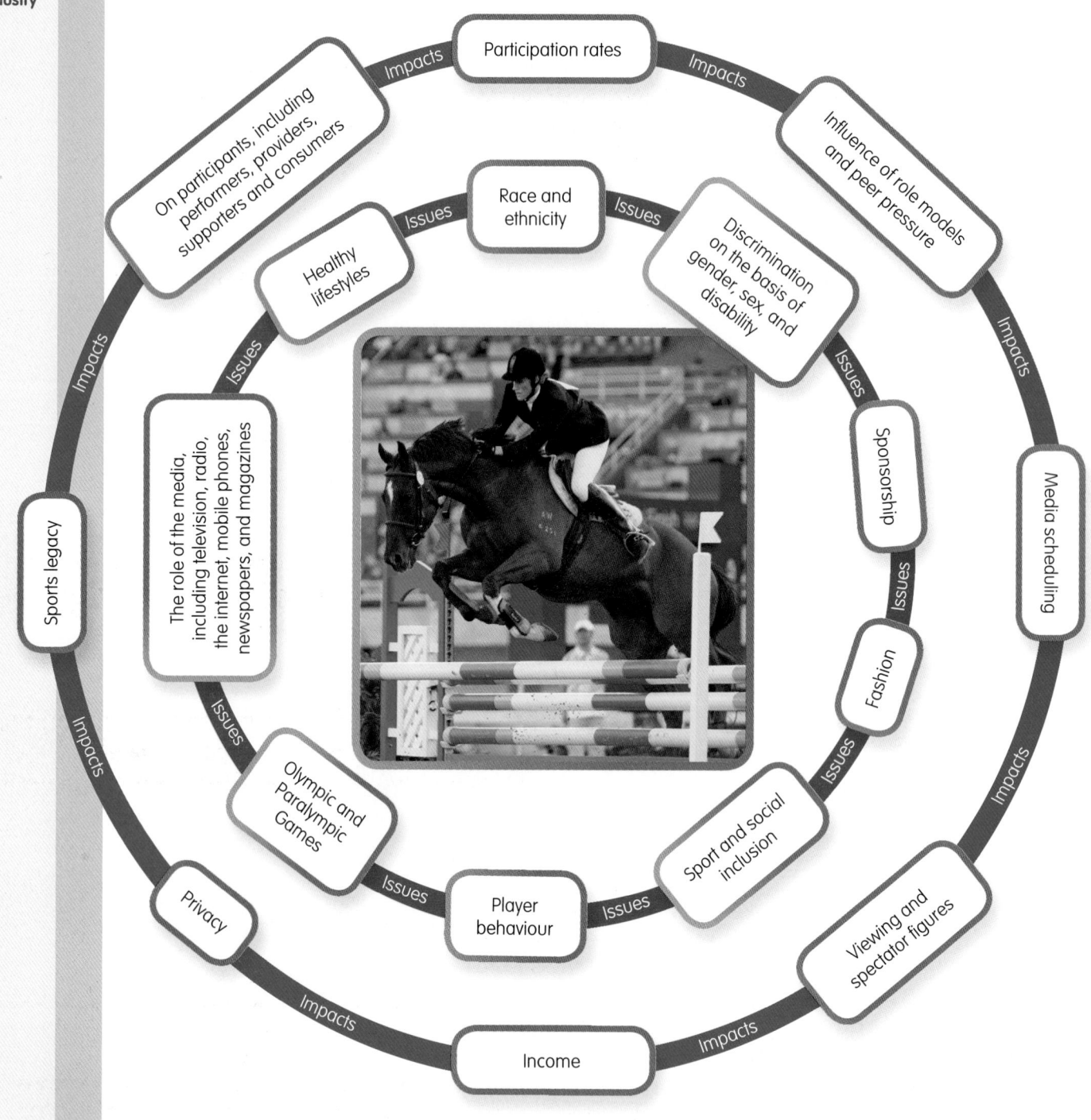

Impacts — Participation rates — Impacts

On participants, including performers, providers, supporters and consumers

Influence of role models and peer pressure

Issues — Race and ethnicity — Issues

Discrimination on the basis of gender, sex, and disability

Healthy lifestyles

The role of the media, including television, radio, the internet, mobile phones, newspapers, and magazines

Sports legacy

Impacts

Issues

Sponsorship

Media scheduling

Fashion

Issues

Olympic and Paralympic Games

Sport and social inclusion

Privacy

Issues — Player behaviour — Issues

Viewing and spectator figures

Impacts — Income — Impacts

BRONZE

3. Choose one issue relating to the sports industry that you would like to investigate in more detail and collect a range of reference material, including newspaper cuttings and information from websites, to help you develop your understanding.

SILVER

4. Having completed Activity 3 you should be much more familiar with the issue you have chosen, so it is time to explain the impact it has had on sport. Think carefully about the positive and negative impacts and, most importantly, the reasons **why** you think the impacts are as you describe them.

GOLD

5. Analyse the significance of the impacts you explained for Activity 4. Do the impacts, individually or collectively, make the issue a serious one? Remember to support your conclusion with facts and figures to explain why you have drawn the conclusion you have drawn.

Unit 12 assignment, part three

Background

The sport development officer you are working with is very pro-active and always keen to find out what sporting issues are affecting local people employed in the sports and active leisure industry. To keep up-to-date she has organized regular forums where various people from the sport and active leisure industry, including gym instructors, inclusion officers, leisure centre managers, and so on get together to discuss key issues in sport and the impacts they are having.

Grading criteria to be assessed
1C.6
2C.P6
2C.M5
2C.D4

Task

Prepare an article for the sport development unit's monthly newsletter that is titled 'Sport: The impact of key issues'. Your article should:

 **LEVEL 1**

- Describe four different key issues and their impact on sport and active leisure. (1C.6)

 **LEVEL 2 PASS**

- Describe six different key issues and their impact on sport and active leisure. (2C.P6)

 **LEVEL 2 MERIT**

- Explain, using relevant examples, the impact of key issues on sport and active leisure. (2C.M5)

 **LEVEL 2 DISTINCTION**

- Analyse the impact of key issues on a selected sport and active leisure activity or business. (2C.D4)

Tackling the assignment

There is so much happening in the world of sport it might seem hard to decide which issues to choose, but try to focus on six current issues because there will almost certainly be more information easily available about these. It would also be advantageous to actually speak to people employed within the industry to get your information first hand.

You need to imagine that the readership of your article have a little knowledge of the issues you are going to address, so your **description** needs to include enough detail to keep them interested, give them a really good insight into the issue, and make sure that they learn something new. Make sure you look at both the positives and negatives, but don't worry if there is an imbalance. Some issues will have far more positives than negatives (and vice versa).

Your **explanation** of the impacts needs to be just that – an explanation. So don't forget to build on your description with some clear reasons why. Remember, a reason often includes the word 'because', so make sure you use it, supporting your work with examples to help get your message across.

Finally, when **analysing** each issue you should explain its significance and draw some conclusions based on your findings.

Meeting the Level 2 Pass criteria

Issue 1: Healthy lifestyles

<u>Courtney Roberts</u>

Almost all of the professions represented at the last forum had experienced mainly positive impacts from the public's increased awareness of healthy lifestyles and diet.

The sports centre manager reported increased visitor numbers over the past six months, especially in family-based activities, such as swimming and badminton, while the gym instructor had experienced a large increase in the number of clients she has produced exercise plans for.

The inclusion officer has received funding from the local authority to run activity days in many of the inner-city suburbs and reported that attendance figures were high, with extra staff having to be employed to deal with demand.

The school sport coordinator had probably noticed the greatest impact though, with schools now allocating more time to physical activity during curriculum time and running more out-of-hours sports clubs. They also said that many schools were now including healthy options at lunchtimes and that they were proving popular with many pupils.

Courtney has the foundation from which to meet the criteria for 2C.P6 criteria but needs to go into more depth with her descriptions of both the issues *and* impacts.

For example, when describing the issues, she needs to describe the healthy lifestyle initiatives in her local area. What form do the activity days being organized take? Where are they held? Who attends them?

She also needs to provide more detail when she describes the impacts. For example she could include the following information:

- How many more after-hours clubs have been started at schools?
- Has pupil attendance at after-hours clubs increased and, if yes, by how much?
- Is there any indication that the children attending the after-hours clubs are healthier? Have they had fewer days off school for example?

More detail please Courtney!

Meeting the Level 2 Merit criteria

Poor behaviour rubs off

Craig Constantine

I am a junior referee at my local under-11s community football league and I have noticed that players are more likely to challenge the referee's decisions than they were in the past. I think this is mainly because they see professional footballers challenging the referee on television and think it is OK to do the same.

I disallowed a goal last week (for offside) and one of the players, who was only eight, told me I was wrong and actually swore! When I booked him for using bad language he said 'Wayne Rooney swore at the ref last week when I was watching the match on TV and wasn't booked – so why am I?'

This shows a negative impact of poor player behaviour by national players on young players.

I have also noticed that there has been an increase in parents shouting at their children if they do things wrong during the match. Last week, one parent shouted, 'Get your act together. There is a scout here from DRFC and if you play like that there is no way you will be selected for their academy programme.' I could see the player was upset and it definitely affected his performance.

This is happening because many parents now see the huge wages top footballers earn and want their children to have the same opportunities. There is nothing wrong with that, but the pressure they are placing on their children at such a young age is sometimes too much and in some cases it is actually putting children off playing. I know that three players from one team have dropped out of the game this season due to pressure placed on them by the team manager.

> This is excellent work from Craig. He has clearly explained why the impact is occurring and has given some examples to support his views. He will need to replicate this level of detail for all the other issues he is looking at, but this clearly demonstrates that he is working at the level needed to achieve 2C.M5.

Meeting the Level 2 Distinction criteria

Palminder Chohan

Positive aspects of the new velodrome:	Negative aspects of the new velodrome:
It is a brand new facility in the city, which has generated a lot of publicity and is going to be used as the venue for the next GB national championships.	The money used to build and run the facility has meant that other facilities and schemes in the city have suffered.
The significance of this is that our city is now seen as somewhere that is serious about sport. The local council thinks this will encourage other sports to build elite facilities here, which will in turn create additional jobs.	This is significant because many of the facilities in the city are old and need money spending on them to repair them. One of the swimming pools was shut for two weeks recently because the roof was leaking and it was unsafe to use. The impact was that all swimming lessons, club sessions, and casual swimming sessions had to be cancelled. The council said that the repairs budget had been cut and redistributed to the velodrome project due to a shortfall in funding.
A facility such as this should also encourage local talent. The GB head coach has already stated that he expects future champions to come from our city! This is really positive. When we had a swimmer from the city win a medal at the last Commonwealth Games the clubs in the area reported a 15 per cent increase in membership numbers. This makes them more sustainable because they are getting more income and possibly more volunteer helpers.	There has also been an article in the press about plans to stop, or cut in size, the local netball league, which is part funded by the council. This has created a lot of negative publicity in the city and the feeling that the only focus is on cycling and that all other sports are being neglected.

In conclusion, the building of the new velodrome will be a good thing as long as other sports don't suffer. The local authority and national governing bodies need to look at a development plan for other sports and facilities in the city so that they too can benefit from better facilities and new initiatives in the future. There will be a need for more partnership work between the private, voluntary, and public sectors to make sure this happens.

> Although we can only see a small amount of Palminder's work it's clear that she has the ability to analyse. She has explained the possible significance and impacts of the velodrome project, has included both positives and negatives, and has brought her ideas together in a brief conclusion that is based on her findings.
>
> There may still be more for Palminder to add to this issue (such as the possible uptake of cycling as a hobby in the city, the increase in cycle-to-school schemes, and the increase in traffic around the velodrome) but this is a really positive start.
>
> Well done Palminder, this is good stuff!

Unit 13: Profiling Sports Performance

Performance profiling

A whole new role has emerged in sport during the past few years, that of the sports pundit; the expert on TV, radio, or in the print media who analyses every facet of an individual's or a team's performance. This is in addition to the role of the coach, who works directly with athletes, to improve all aspects of their performance.

One of the techniques used by pundits and coaches is peformance profiling, the process of assessing the attributes, traits, and qualities needed to be successful. Profiling establishes a performer's current strengths and areas for improvement and, in the hands of a coach, can form the basis of a structured development programme.

The diver Tom Daley will often have his performance profiled so that he is in the best possible position to dive to his full potential.

There are two distinct aspects to a performance profile: a subjective assessment and an objective assessment.

Subjective assessment

A subjective assessment is based on personal opinions or beliefs. For example, a football commentator makes a subjective assessment of a player when they watch a match and summarize what they thought of the footballer's performance afterwards, without any tangible data on the number of passes made, tackles won, or possession retained.

Objective assessment

An objective assessment is based on tangible information, such as statistical data, and is a much more reliable method of assessing a performance. Methods used for objective assessments within sport include:

Notational analysis

Notational analysis is a system used to record information while observing a performance. To record information quickly, a range of strokes and symbols are used that are specific to an individual sport. For example, a hyphen with a letter above it may be used to indicate offside in football, whereas it may symbolize a double fault in tennis.

Key

-	Possession lost
+	Possession gained
⬇\	Pass backwards complete
⬇/	Pass backwards incomplete
⬆\	Pass forwards complete
⬆/	Pass forwards incomplete
©	Shot on goal
©✓	Shot scored

Attacks in match

+ ⬇\ ⬇\ ⬆\ ⬆\ ⬆\ ©

(Unsuccessful shot after five passes, two backwards and three forwards.)

+ ⬆/ - + ⬆\ ⬆\ ©✓

(First pass incomplete, followed by regained possession. Then two forward passes resulting in a goal.)

Notational analysis of two attacks in a football match.

Statistical data

Many sports, especially those with a high profile on television, are accompanied by statistical data to support a player's or a team's performance. For example, in tennis, information on the number of aces served, the percentage of points won on the first serve, or the amount of break points converted may be provided.

Player	David Ferrer	Andy Murray
Country	Spain	Great Britain
Statistics on service		
Ist Serve %	64% (90 of 141)	53% (84 of 158)
Aces	3	3
Double faults	5	1
Ist serve points won	68% (61 of 90)	60% (50 0f 84)
2nd serve points won	39% (20 of 51)	39% (29 of 74)
Fastest serve	196kph	220kph
Avg Ist serve speed	179kph	183kph
Avg 2nd serve speed	140kph	140kph
Statistics on return		
Break points conversion	53% (10 of 19)	33% (5 of 15)
Return points won	50% (79 of 158)	43% (60 of 141)
Statistics on points		
Total points won	160	139
Winners	32	49
Unforced errors	32	59

The statistics of a game between Andy Murray and David Ferrer at the French Open in June 2012.

Psychological profile

It is recognized that, at the top level in sport, a performer's mental strength is often as important as their technical ability or physical attributes. Producing a psychological profile is therefore important. It measures aspects such as a performer's confidence, concentration, commitment, and ability to re-focus. More information on how to develop a psychological profile can be found on pages 46 and 47.

BRONZE

1. Choose a sport of your choice and identify the five most important psychological skills a performer needs in that sport if they are to succeed.

The qualities, traits, and attributes required for success

Sports performers, whether they are taking part in an individual sport, such as tennis, or a team sport, such as netball, need a combination of various qualities, traits, and attributes to be successful. For example, an elite netball player will need qualities such as high levels of physical fitness, traits such as a strong desire to win, and attributes such as excellent passing skills to be a good all-round player.

These qualities, traits, and attributes can be broken down into five groups of requirements, all of which can be analysed in a performance profile. These are: technical requirements, tactical requirements, fitness requirements, psychological requirements, and attitudinal requirements.

Technical requirements

Success in sport is underpinned by the performer being able to carry out the essential skills required by that sport; by a rugby player being able to execute an effective tackle or a golfer being able to drive the ball straight off the tee, for example.

Some sports rely heavily on discrete skills where there is a definite beginning and end to the action (such as a golf swing), while others rely on continuous skills (think of a swimmer, who repeats the same stroke action repeatedly during a race), and others on serial skills, where various discrete skills are linked together in a sequence (the triple jump is a great example, where the discrete hop, skip, and jump phases form the overall jump).

Once a performer understands the skills required for success in their sport they can work on developing their technique, on the way in which they perform the skills. It is important that all performers, at whatever level, develop a good technique. Otherwise, their ability to perform well in competitive situations will be affected.

The technical requirements of skills, such as shooting, differ from sport to sport:

- Bend your knees before taking the shot, so that the power comes from the floor.
- Concentrate, staying focused on the ring.
- Keep your back straight and your head up.
- Just before you release the ball, drop your hands behind your head. Do not start the shot with the ball in front of your body.

- Take a quick, early look at the goal and the position of the goalkeeper.
- Aim for the most exposed part of the goal or the part of the goal you think the goalkeeper will struggle to reach.
- Shoot quickly so that the goalkeeper has as little time as possible to prepare and anticipate the direction of the shot.
- Concentrate on power and accuracy. Accuracy is most important.
- Focus on the ball at all times.
- Place your non-kicking foot firmly next to the ball.
- Flex the knee of your kicking leg to increase power.
- Strike the ball at the middle or the top, keeping your head over the ball.
- After you have made contact, ensure a strong follow through.

'The more I practise the luckier I get.'

Attributed to Gary Player, Golfer

BRONZE

1. Pick one team sport and one individual sport and produce a list of the technical requirements associated with each of them. Make sure you include the essential techniques for each sport, those that are fundamental to success.

Tactical requirements

Tactics are the strategies a player or a team devises and uses to outwit their opponent(s). Tactics are often developed before a game or competition based on the player or team's strengths and their opponent's weaknesses, but successful athletes need to be able to alter their tactics during a game if circumstances change.

Appropriate tactics will, of course, differ from sport to sport and will vary according to the opponent or the competition, but all tactics involve developing:

- **Decision-making:** A player will make numerous tactical decisions during a game. For example, when serving, a tennis player must decide whether to go for power, use slice, play a wide serve, or put top spin on the ball.
- **Defensive and attacking strategies:** A team or player will usually set out with a defensive or an attacking strategy based on the opponent(s) they are facing, but a team that planned a defensive approach may need to change mid-way through the match if they fall behind. The tactics used by Chelsea in the latter stages of their 2011/2012 Champions League campaign were based on a sound defensive strategy, with energetic midfield play, combined with quick counter-attacking strikes.
- **Variation:** All teams and individuals need variety in their game, otherwise their play becomes predictable and easier to counteract. For example, a swimmer in the 400-metre freestyle might go out fast in the heats but change tactics in the final, reserving their energy for a strong finish.
- **Conditions:** Playing conditions vary, especially when it comes to outdoor sports where the weather can have a considerable impact. A successful team or player needs to be able to change tactics if the conditions are going to have a significant effect on their game play. For example, a rugby team whose backs play a quick passing game may need to change to a more methodical approach, playing through their forwards, if pitch conditions are heavy and the ball is wet and slippery.
- **Positioning:** A player needs to understand where to position themselves during different phases of play. For example, a rugby player will need to know where to best position themselves when a ruck is formed, so that they are available to receive the ball if they are attacking or defend their line if they are defending.
- **Use of space:** Good players always seem to have plenty of time on the ball or are in position early to play the correct shot. They are reading the game, predicting what is about to happen, and using the space that exists to the maximum tactical effect.

Tactics are often agreed with the coach or manager before a game starts, but it's important for all performers to have the confidence and ability to adapt or change tactics during a game if needed.

BRONZE

2. List five tactics a team or individual player might use when defending and five tactics they might use when attacking in a sport of your choice.

3. a) Select two examples from the tactics identified in Activity 2 and, for each, describe a situation that could occur and which would require a change of tactics.

b) What new tactics could be used to overcome the problem or change in circumstances identified in Activity 3a)?

Fitness requirements

As you know from Unit 1 (see pages 4–7), the components of fitness can be divided into physical fitness and skill-related fitness and, while a good level of both physical fitness and skill-related fitness is required for most sports, the relative importance of each component is dependent upon the sport chosen. The fitness requirements of a shot-putter will vary greatly to those of a jockey or distance cyclist, for example.

Although most golfers pride themselves on their physical fitness, there are exceptions, as John Daly demonstrates in this pose!

Component of physical fitness	Why the component of fitness is needed for football	Why the component of fitness is needed for golf
Aerobic endurance	Footballers rely heavily on aerobic endurance because they have to keep up a high level of activity for a prolonged period of time.	Golfers rely less on aerobic endurance, although walking around 18 holes (maybe for four days) will require some level of aerobic endurance.
Muscular endurance	Footballers need muscular endurance to repeatedly strike the ball when passing or shooting. It is also required by a defender making repeated tackles.	Golfers need muscular endurance when they have to strike the ball off the tee and during approaches to the green.
Flexibility	All footballers need elements of flexibility, although goalkeepers will need it most of all when saving the ball, reaching high, low, and into the goal corners.	Golfers need to be flexible because, when they strike the ball, their bodies go through a wide range of motions during the backswing, impact, and follow through.
Speed	Speed is a vital component for most footballers, as they have to cover the ground quickly to get past an opponent, lose their marker, or mark an opponent before they receive the ball.	Speed is less important for golfers, although they will need speed to get the club through quickly during a drive to ensure maximum impact on the ball.
Strength	Footballers need strength to withstand a tackle or to hold their position in a crowded penalty area.	Strength is less important for a golfer, but strength is required to drive the ball over long distances. An amateur male can drive the ball 200–260 metres!
Body composition	Footballers have a greater distribution of muscle in the body than fat because they train regularly and need to be fit to compete.	Golfers generally have more muscle than fat, although there have been examples of successful golfers, such as John Daly, who carry too much weight.

Serena Williams generates plenty of power on the tennis court, as well as utilizing all the other elements of skill-related fitness.

GOLD

4. Pick your favourite sport and justify the three most important physical fitness requirements of the sport and the three most important skill-related fitness requirements of the sport.

Component of skill-related fitness	Why the component of fitness is needed for cricket	Why the component of fitness is needed for tennis
Agility	Cricketers need agility, especially when fielding. Wicketkeepers in particular need to be nimble and move quickly when keeping to fast and spin bowlers.	Tennis players need agility in order to get around the court quickly and remain in control at the same time.
Balance	Balance is vitally important for cricketers, especially when batting. They need a solid stance in order to play the range of shots required on both sides of the wicket.	Tennis players will need excellent balance when playing a shot such as a volley, backhand drive, serve, etc.
Coordination	Both batters and bowlers need coordination. A bowler has to coordinate their whole body when approaching the wicket and a batter needs to coordinate their foot movement and body position before playing a successful shot.	Tennis players rely heavily on coordination when serving (ball toss, backswing, contact point, and follow through) as well as when playing all other shots.
Power	Batters need power when striking the ball for a four or a six, while a bowler needs power to generate the pace required to bowl up to 90mph.	Tennis players need power to generate speed on the ball when serving or powering the ball to the baseline during a rally.
Reaction time	Reaction time is the key to success for a cricketer. For example, batters need to think quickly. When facing a fast bowler they have only 0.5 seconds to pick up the trajectory of the ball, decide which shot to play, and then execute it.	Tennis players definitely need to react quickly. For example, when returning a serve sent at 135–155 mph.

Psychological requirements

It is a widely held view that the difference between success and failure at the elite level of sports performance is often determined by the performer's psychological approach, by their personality, which can sometimes be more important than their technical abilities and their fitness levels, which are often very similar. According to trait theory we have a set of personality traits which largely fix our personality. However, it is possible to develop the psychological skills required to succeed in sport with training, which is often conducted by a sport psychologist.

Motivated to succeed. Motivation can be intrinsic (come from within) or extrinsic (come from outside, in the form of rewards or accolades). A motivated performer will be able to maintain high levels of performance during periods of strenuous training or a run of poor results. More information on motivation can be found on pages 52–55.

Able to control anxiety. And, although all sports performers need an element of arousal to make sure they are ready for competition, the ability to control their level of **arousal** is also imperative. See pages 61–63 for more information on the relationship between arousal and anxiety.

Able to remain **attentive** for the duration of a game or match, and this is a key requirement for all sports performers. Considering a rugby game lasts for 80 minutes, a cricket match can last for five days, and the Tour de France often lasts for 20 days; maintaining a high level of **concentration** for this amount of time is no mean feat!

Self-confident, which means they have faith in their own ability to meet their goals. This allows them to build on their successes and approach training and competition with a positive attitude. It also helps them to overcome setbacks. More information about self-confidence and sport can be found on page 56.

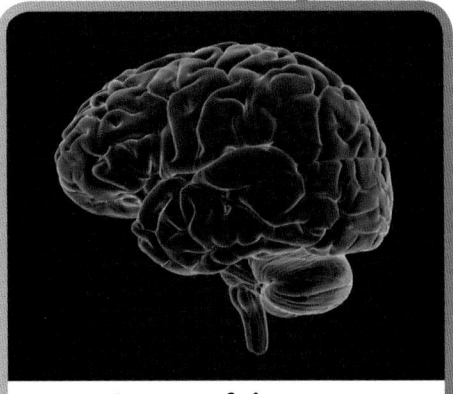

Successful sports performers need to be…

Enthusiastic. Enthusiastic performers are not always successful performers because enthusiasm can only take a performer so far, but it is an important component of a successful athlete's personality, especially when linked to motivation. Getting up at 4.30am to train in the pool or row on the river in the middle of winter requires a great deal of enthusiasm, no matter what the eventual rewards.

BRONZE

5. Identify a sports performer who you think has strong psychological skills, and describe these skills using examples to support your view.

Joe Hart may be called upon to make a match-winning save in the 90th minute of a game, so needs to be attentive and maintain high levels of concentration throughout the whole game.

Attitudinal requirements

A performer's attitude or mindset – the way they think about things – stems from their personality and their psychological approach to their sport. And, as with psychological requirements, the key attitudinal requirements are similar throughout all sports.

Discipline and dedication: Discipline comes in different forms. For example, a performer needs to have both the discipline to train hard and regularly and the discipline to remain calm under provocation. Dedication to following a healthy lifestyle is also vital if a performer is to succeed.

A desire to win: All successful performers need that magic ingredient: the desire and commitment to win.

Aggression: All performers need an element of aggression if they want to be successful, because this provides them with the drive they need to fight hard to win. Too much aggression can, however, have a negative effect on results if it leads a performer to hurt their opponent or abuse fellow players, referees, or officials.

Successful sports performers need to have…

Competitiveness and determination: Top performers are renowned for their ability to compete under pressure. The tougher the competition the more they raise their game and the strength of mind to do this comes from a determination to win. A willingness to 'take on anyone' is often seen as part of a performer's competitiveness.

Positivity: Successful performers have the ability to stay positive, even in the aftermath of a poor performance or a disappointing result. A positive mental attitude is essential if a performer is to refocus and prevent negative thoughts from getting in the way of future performances.

'Champions aren't made in the gym. Champions are made from something they have deep inside them – a desire, a dream, a vision.'

Muhammad Ali

The tennis player Novak Djokovic enjoyed considerable success in 2011, winning ten tournaments, setting a new record for the most prize money won in a single season, and becoming world number one. Although technically good and incredibly fit, Djokovic attributed much of his success to his improved mental approach and a strong belief in his ability to win tight matches.

BRONZE

6. a) Identify two examples where performers have succeeded because of their attitude and two examples where performers have lost or been defeated because of their attitude.

b) Describe what happened on each occasion.

SILVER

7. Compare and contrast the attitudes of the performers identified in Activity 6.

Unit 13 assignment, part one

Background

As an active and enthusiastic volunteer at your local sports club, which is home to a number of different sports, you enjoy working with the senior coaches to develop talent in the junior sections of the club. The under-14s in two particular sports are starting to show some real potential, so much so that their coach thinks the time is right to introduce performance profiling to enhance their development, and has asked you to play an instrumental role in the process.

Grading criteria to be assessed
1A.1
2A.P1
2A.M1
2A.D1

Task

Choose two different sports. Prepare a short presentation that outlines what performance profiling is and details what the technical, tactical, fitness, psychological, and attitudinal requirements of each sport are.

 LEVEL 1

- Identify the technical, tactical, and fitness profiles required to successfully participate in a selected sport. (1A.1)

 LEVEL 2 PASS

- Describe the technical, tactical, fitness, psychological, and attitudinal profiles required to successfully participate in two selected sports. (2A.P1)

 LEVEL 2 MERIT

- Compare and contrast the technical, tactical, fitness, psychological, and attitudinal profiles required to successfully participate in two selected sports. (2A.M1)

 LEVEL 2 DISTINCTION

- Justify the technical, tactical, fitness, psychological, and attitudinal profiles required to successfully participate in two selected sports. (2A.D1)

Tackling the assignment

It is important that you choose two sports that you understand and enjoy watching and/or playing. This will personalize your work, make producing it more enjoyable, and will ultimately lead to a better presentation. However, it is also important that you choose two very different sports if you are aiming for a Distinction, so that you are able to identify similarities and differences relatively easily.

Remember, when **describing** the technical, tactical, fitness, psychological, and attitudinal requirements needed for success you need to be concise but provide enough detail to paint a clear picture in words for the audience. To **compare and contrast** the two sports you have chosen, show where the technical, tactical, fitness, psychological, and attitudinal requirements are similar and where they are different. Some text on why there are differences is also needed to show you have an in-depth understanding of the qualities, traits, and attributes required to successfully participate in two different sports.

Finally, for a Distinction, you should **justify** why the requirements are so important for success, and provide examples that support and reinforce your key messages.

Meeting the Level 2 Pass criteria

Performance profiling:
swimming

Charlotte Carew

A performance profile is an assessment made by a coach that looks at the performance of a team or individual. It is based on their subjective views combined with a more objective assessment, such as a notational analysis, a statistical review, or a psychological profile of a performer.

Success in sport depends on the following being met:

- Technical requirements
- Tactical requirements
- Fitness requirements
- Psychological requirements
- Attitudinal requirements

A performance profile must therefore analyse each of these requirements in turn.

In swimming, each stroke has its own technical requirements.

Front crawl
Throughout the stroke, the swimmer should maintain the correct body position (head in the water looking forward and down) as well as good body streamlining. This means keeping the head steady when breathing, with a slight body roll coming from the hips when a breath is taken. The legs should be kept close together with a long shallow kick.

During the propulsion phase, the underwater hand should push the water back towards the feet, making sure

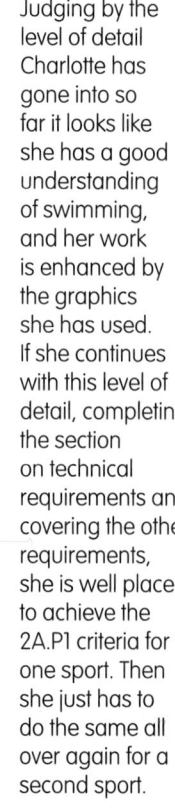

Judging by the level of detail Charlotte has gone into so far it looks like she has a good understanding of swimming, and her work is enhanced by the graphics she has used. If she continues with this level of detail, completing the section on technical requirements and covering the other requirements, she is well placed to achieve the 2A.P1 criteria for one sport. Then she just has to do the same all over again for a second sport.

Meeting the Level 2 Merit criteria

SKIING VERSUS BADMINTON

Lindy Harrison

There are many similarities between the traits, attributes, and qualities required to be successful at skiing and badminton, but there are also many differences.

Similarities	Skiing	Badminton
Motivation (a psychological requirement)	Skiers need to be motivated as they may well be training in very cold conditions that could be unpleasant. They may also have to travel extensively to follow the snow around the world. Skiers also need to be highly motivated as the sport can be dangerous and they may have to battle back after injury.	Badminton players need to be motivated because they have to train for long hours to get to the standard required. This is the same for a skier, or any elite performer, but neither badminton nor skiing are highly paid sports and so both may rely more on the performer being intrinsically motivated than extrinsically motivated.

	Skiing	Badminton
Aggression (an attitudinal requirement)	Neither sport may appear to need aggression, but they do. A skier needs to be aggressive when attacking the gates during a slalom race or knowing when to put in extra effort on the approach into a tricky bend. The aggression will need to be well controlled, as an over-aggressive approach could easily result in a fall and injury.	Badminton may not seem aggressive at all, but aggression is needed when attacking the shuttle and powering it over the net using a smash. Many players aim the shuttle at their opponent's body as well, which is an aggressive move but makes it almost impossible to return.

Differences	Skiing	Badminton
Defending (a tactical requirement)	Skiers don't really defend. They are always on the attack, trying to get down the slope as quickly as possible. They may need to show caution on certain sections, but this can't be classed as defending.	A successful badminton player needs to defend as well as attack. They have to be able to block return shots and force the shuttle high and long when trying to get time to recover to a central position. Defence is also very important in doubles. The formation players take in defence (side-by-side) is very different from the position they take when attacking (front and back).
Fitness	Although both sports require high levels of fitness, a skier will rely mainly on muscular strength (especially in the legs) and agility (being able to change direction quickly and under control).	A badminton player also needs muscular strength and agility, but these aren't the most important fitness requirements for success. The key fitness requirements for a badminton player are power (driving the shuttle downwards when smashing) and speed (covering all four corners of the court quickly).

> Lindy has chosen a good method to present her information but, although the framework of a good answer is visible, she needs to go into more depth with the answers she has provided (for example, she needs to explain why a skier needs muscular strength in their legs).
>
> Lindy also needs to include additional examples for the four requirements covered so far and include information on the similarities and differences in the technical requirements between the two sports in order to meet the criteria for 2A.M1.

Meeting the Level 2 Distinction criteria

Success in cricket
Joost Van Steyn

Cricket is a sport that needs players who have a varied and comprehensive range of qualities, traits, and attributes. Different positions have different requirements, although many requirements apply to all positions.

The examples below show why a player like Mark Boucher (the ex-South African wicketkeeper) needs a range of technical, tactical, fitness, psychological, and attitudinal profiles to be successful.

Fitness requirements

A top-class wicketkeeper like Mark Boucher will need to be fit to perform to a high level throughout a five-day test match. The key physical and skill-related requirements he needs are:

- Flexibility: This is because he needs to field the ball in a variety of positions, low down one minute and high up the next. He also needs to be flexible to get to balls that may be bowled wide down both sides of the wicket.
- Reaction time: The ball will be reaching the keeper at very high speeds, so he needs to react very quickly. If a batsman 'nicks' the ball off a fast bowler, the direction of the ball will also change and the keeper will need to react quickly to field the ball or make the catch. Dale Steyn, one of Boucher's team-mates, is one of the quickest bowlers in the world so the ball will be reaching the keeper approximately one second after leaving the bowler's hand, which means the keeper will need to react very quickly.

> Joost appears to have chosen a sport he is interested in. In this snapshot of his work, he is clearly justifying why certain traits, attributes, and qualities are needed because he is giving clear reasons why they are required. He does, though, need to give additional examples of the fitness requirements needed by a wicketkeeper and tackle the other traits, attributes, and qualities to the same level of detail to demonstrate a full understanding and achieve the criteria for 2A.D1, as well as produce work to a similar level of detail for another sport.

Creating a performance profile

Now you have an understanding of the qualities, traits, and attributes covered by a performance profile and the subjective and objective methods used to analyse them, it is time to look at exactly how a performance profile is compiled.

1. Defining the list of qualities, traits, and attributes that will be profiled

A definitive list of the technical, tactical, fitness, attitudinal, and psychological requirements that will be profiled should be agreed. As we have already established, the mix of requirements will vary from sport to sport. It is essential that the performer who is being profiled works together with the coach to define the list of requirements, so that they don't feel as if the results are coming out of the blue and they are motivated to engage with the development plan that results from the performance profiling.

2. Conducting an initial perception audit with the performer

An initial perception audit should be conducted. Both the coach and the performer should look at each of the requirements identified and state how well they think the performer meets those requirements, to see where views are similar or vary greatly. This initial perception audit may shape the focus of future observations.

For example, the initial perception audit below was completed first by the player and then by the coach. It shows that the coach and player agree on most aspects of the player's technical skills, but that there is some disagreement about the player's ability to control the ball with the lower body and pass accurately over a short distance. These two technical requirements could therefore become the focal point for the notational analysis.

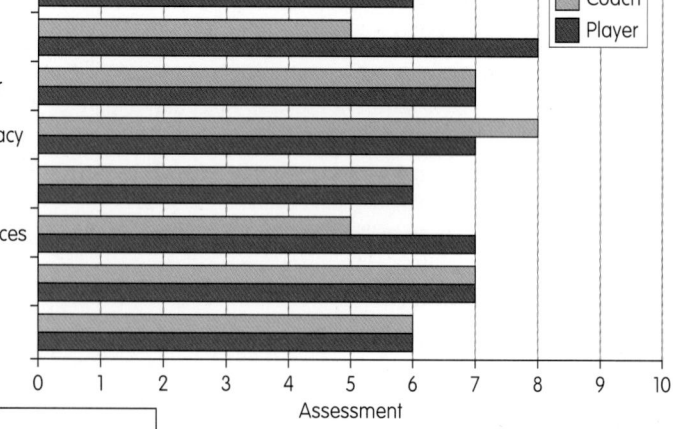

1. Controlling ball on chest
2. Controlling ball with lower body
3. Striking the ball on goal with power
4. Striking the ball on goal with accuracy
5. Shielding the ball/holding up play
6. Passing accuracy over short distances
7. Heading the ball with accuracy
8. Heading the ball with power

Assessment — 0 1 2 3 4 5 6 7 8 9 10

Legend: Coach / Player

Scale:
1 = very poor, considerable improvement needed
5 = satisfactory, with room for improvement
10 = excellent, virtually no improvement needed

BRONZE

1. a) Identify a performer, in a sport you know well, with whom you can work to create and complete a performance profile.

b) Create a definitive list of the qualities, traits, and attributes required by the performer to be successful in their chosen sport.

c) Create and complete an initial perception audit covering the technical, tactical, fitness, psychological, and attitudinal requirements needed by the performer, as identified in Activity 1b).

d) Choose one aspect of the performer's profile and decide the method you will use to assess their performance and the best opportunity for carrying out that assessment.

e) Complete the assessment.

2. Armed with the results of the assessment you carried out in Activity 1, complete the performance profile by describing the results.

③ Deciding on the methods of assessment that will be used

Once you know which technical, tactical, fitness, attitudinal, and psychological requirements you are profiling, you must decide which assessment method you will use to collect the information. For example:

- If you want to profile one or more components of the performer's fitness, you could use fitness tests to collect data that you compare to data previously collected about the performer or to normative data.
- If you want to profile the technical aspects of the performance you could prepare a subjective commentary, use notational analysis, or create tally charts to count the frequency of certain skills being performed with a good technique. For example, you could create notational analysis to show how many backhands are performed and a tally showing how many points were won on the backhand return, which would help you determine the frequency with which the backhand is performed successfully.
- If you want to profile the tactical aspects, a subjective commentary could again be used. Observing a number of performances against different opponents and under different conditions would give an overview of the performer's tactical abilities.
- If you want to gather information about aspects of the performer's psychology or attitude, you could perform a personality test or complete observational analysis.

④ Identifying the opportunities available for carrying out the assessment

The opportunities that are available to carry out the assessment could include:

- Live performances the performer has scheduled. These need to be competitive situations so that the profile accurately records the performer's response to the pressurized conditions of competition.
- Video recordings of past performances. Again, these need to be recordings of competitive situations.
- Interviews between the coach and the performer. These interviews should be allocated quality time and should not be shoehorned into convenient windows during training or post performance, when emotions may be running high.

⑤ Collecting the data and completing the performance profile

When the data has been collected, it is time to return to the list of qualities, traits, and attributes identified as important and complete a second version of the audit.

For example, this notational analysis monitors the two areas where the coach and player disagreed during the initial perception audit in Box 2.

Player: Ryan Rooney
Match: Rovers versus Villa 3rd March
Conditions: Firm pitch and windy

Period \ Technical skills	Successful control with lower body	Unsuccessful control with lower body	Accurate short pass	Inaccurate short pass
0–22.5 minutes	//////// 8	/// 3	//////// 8	/////////// 11
22.5–45 minutes	////// 6	//// 4	///// 5	/////// 7
45–67.5 minutes	/// 3	// 2	//// 4	//// 4
67.5–90 minutes	/ 1	///// 5	/ 1	///// 5

As we can see, the player was more accurate with his initial assessment of his ability to control the ball with his lower body, while the coach's initial assessment was more accurate when it came to passing accurately over short distances. Although fitness wasn't being measured, the notational analysis also indicates that fitness could be an issue because the player's performance deteriorates as the game progresses, especially during the last quarter.

SILVER

3. Look carefully at your assessment of the qualities, traits, and attributes of the performer and evaluate your findings, giving clear reasons why you have given them the results you have, backed up by evidence.

GOLD

4. Justify your completed performance profile, providing sufficient detail about the results you gave the performer, to show that there is absolutely no doubt that your profile is valid.

Reviewing the performance

Once the profile has been completed, it is time to use it to review the findings and establish the performer's strengths, so they can be consolidated, and areas for improvement, so they can be developed.

When you are doing this, remember to focus on the qualities, traits, and attributes that you have already identified as important for success in the performer's sport and to take into account the level at which the performer is playing, or aspires to play. A hockey player competing at county level will not require the same level of fitness and technical expertise as someone playing at international level.

	Player: Lesley Moore	Match: versus Maria Ward (county finals)							
Technical skills \ Game	Result	Forehand winners	Errors on forehand	Backhand winners	Errors on backhand	Successful boasts	Unsuccessful boasts	Successful drop shots	Unsuccessful drop shots
1	Lesley 11, Maria 6	//////// 8	// 2	/// 3	/////// 7	//// 4	/ 1	/ 1	/// 3
2	Lesley 11 Maria 5	/////// 7	//// 4	//// 4	/////// 7	// 2	0	/ 1	/ 1
3	Lesley 11 Maria 8	//////// 8	// 2	/// 3	///////// 9	// 2	/ 1	0	/// 3
Totals		23	8	10	23	8	2	2	7

- **Lesley has a strong forehand, which produces the majority of her winning shots. This is a consistent shot for Lesley.**
- **Lesley makes considerably more errors on her backhand. This is an area for improvement.**
- **Lesley's boasts are consistent and an apparent strength. Far more are successful than are unsuccessful.**
- **Lesley plays only a few drop shots and when she does the success rate is low. Again, this is an area that needs to be improved.**

Creating a development plan

Once a performer's strengths and areas for improvement have been established, it is time to create a development plan. A development plan should consist of:

Aims and objectives
An aim is what you want to achieve by the end of the development plan and an objective is a small step that helps you achieve the aim. For example, an aim for a netballer could be to improve their movement and ability to find space during a game. The objectives to support this aim could be:
- Improve overall aerobic endurance levels via a series of fitness-training sessions.
- Practise movement drills during isolated practices.
- Integrate movement drills into conditioned practices and short-sided games.
- Monitor performance during different quarters in a competitive game.

Goals
Setting goals gives a performer something tangible to work towards, which helps keep them motivated. They should focus on the specific qualities, traits, and attributes – the technical, tactical, fitness, psychological, and attitudinal requirements – that have been previously identified as areas for improvement.

Goals can be short term or long term.

- A short-term goal should normally be achievable within three to six months, although the performer may achieve the necessary improvement more quickly, depending on their motivation, the time they spend training, and the support they receive from their coach.
- A long-term goal can be based around a season or a competition, although long-term goals can take many years to achieve if they are about achieving the highest accolades in a sport.

Regardless of whether a goal is short-term or long-term, it should be SMARTER.

 Specific: Goals should be specific, so the performer knows exactly what they are aiming for.

 Measurable: Goals should be measurable so you know if you have achieved them or not. If your goals are measurable then they automatically become specific.

 Achievable: Targets should be appropriate to the fitness and skill levels of the performer. They should be close enough for the performer to see but not so far away that he or she gets demotivated.

 Realistic: All goals need to be challenging so that the performer has to work hard to achieve them, but they must also be realistic in order for them to serve their purpose and be motivating.

 Time-related: Goals should be linked to a point in time by when they should have been achieved or it becomes too easy to put them off.

 Exciting: An exciting goal will act as a spur for the performer.

 Recorded: It is important to record targets in order to identify whether or not progress is being made.

Actions to be taken to achieve goals

Once the goals have been established it is necessary to identify what actions should be taken in order for the performer to achieve those goals. Opportunities could include:

- Focusing existing training sessions on the areas identified for development.
- Adding additional training sessions to focus on the areas identified for improvement.
- Attending workshops or specialized training camps.
- Attending higher-level training sessions if, for example, selected to represent a regional team or become part of a national development squad.
- Taking a recognized qualification, such as attending a course on sport psychology.

Alongside the opportunities, it is also important to identify any potential barriers the performer may have or may experience that prevent them from meeting their goals and, if possible, contingency plans should be put in place to minimize the disruption these barriers might cause. Barriers can include:

- Cost: For example, the cost of additional training and coaching or additional travel costs.
- Lack of time: For example, conflicts with work, study, or family commitments.
- Injury.

As with the initial stages of the process, it is important that the performer is involved in establishing their development plan to ensure they buy into it and are motivated to follow it.

The development plan also needs to be monitored regularly and adapted if necessary. A rigid plan will be ineffective if circumstances change, injury strikes, or progress is made more quickly or more slowly than anticipated.

BRONZE

5. Using the performance profile you created and completed in Activities 1 and 2 on page 274, summarize the performer's strengths and areas for improvement.

BRONZE/SILVER

6. Working with the areas for improvement you identified in Activity 5, create a development plan for the performer.

GOLD

7. Discuss the development plan with the performer you are working with, justifying why you have chosen the activities you have specified to help them improve.

Unit 13 assignment, part two

Background

As an active and enthusiastic volunteer at your local sports club who understands performance profiling, you have been asked by the senior coach to complete performance profiles of several members of the club.

Task

Design and complete two performance profiles for a team or individual in two different sports. Then, use your performance profiles to help you describe their qualities, traits, and attributes, before moving on to set goals for them as part of a development plan. You must:

Grading criteria to be assessed
1B.2, 1B.3, 1C.4
2B.P2, 2B.P3, 2C.P4
2B.M2, 2C.M3
2B.D2, 2C.D3

 **LEVEL 1**

- Design and complete a performance profile to assess performance of a team or individual in a selected sport, with guidance. (1B.2)
- Use the completed performance profile to describe the qualities, traits, and attributes for a team or individual in a selected sport. (1B.3)
- Review the performance profile for a team or individual, outlining goals and recommendations for future performance. (1C.4)

 **LEVEL 2 PASS**

- Independently design and complete performance profiles to assess performance of a team or individual in two different selected sports. (2B.P2)
- Use the completed performance profiles to describe the qualities, traits, and attributes for a team or individual in two different selected sports. (2B.P3)
- Review the performance profiles for a team or individual in two different selected sports, summarising goals for future performance and development planning. (2C.P4)

 **LEVEL 2 MERIT**

- Evaluate the qualities, traits, and attributes for a team or individual in two different selected sports. (2B.M2)
- Explain set goals for future performance and development for a team or individual in each selected sport, describing the development plans. (2C.M3)

 **LEVEL 2 DISTINCTION**

- Justify the completed performance profiles for a team or individual in two different selected sports. (2B.D2)
- Justify the selection of activities within the development plans for the performers in each selected sport. (2C.D3)

Tackling the assignment

This is a big assignment, so start by breaking it down into manageable chunks:

- First, you need to design performance profiles for two different sports. This is covered by Boxes 1–4 on pages 274–275. Your profiles can be of a whole team, an individual in a team, or an individual taking part in an individual sport. It would make sense to use the sports you used in the first part of the assignment, although it is important that you have access to performers you can profile, because it will be difficult to compile attitudinal and psychological data if you're relying solely on video evidence. When designing the performance profile, it is important to work independently or you will not be able to meet the criteria for 2B.P2.

- Next you need to collect the data and complete the performance review. This is covered by Box 5 on page 275.
- Then, to meet the criteria for 2B.P3, 2B.M2, and 2B.D2, you must describe and evaluate the qualities, traits, and attributes for both sports and, if appropriate, go on to justify your findings. This is covered by Box 6 on page 276.
- Finally, you must review the performance profile and draw up a development plan, focusing in on the goals if you are aiming for a Pass and creating a more detailed development plan if you are aiming for a Merit or a Distinction. This is covered by Box 7 on pages 276–277.

Meeting the Level 2 Pass criteria

Louise's performance profile
Frankie Coutts

The first stage I undertook with Louise, a school tennis player, was to establish what psychological and attitudinal requirements we thought were important for tennis. We agreed on the list below.

Psychological and attitudinal requirements	Importance (1-10, with 1 = low importance and 10 = essential)	Athlete's self-assessment (1-10, with 1 = low demonstration of requirement and 10 = high demonstration of requirement)	My assessment after watching Louise play in a school match (1-10, with 1 = low demonstration of requirement and 10 = high demonstration of requirement)
Concentration	9	5	5
Desire to win	10	9	9
Aggression	8	8	8
Control over emotion	9	6	4
Confidence	8	7	7
Positivity	7	6	4

Commentary completed during the game

Result: Louise lost the game two sets to nil.

- Concentration was poor. At numerous important stages of the game, such as break points, Louise made errors that were more down to lack of concentration than to poor technique. Louise was also too easily distracted by her opponent arguing with the umpire. She mainly lost the points that immediately followed.
- Her desire to win was strong. For example, coming back from 5–2 down in the second set to take the game to a tie break. The opponent was ranked five places higher in the county standings but this didn't faze Louise.
- Aggression generally good. Louise attacked the ball, took up strong positions at the net, and served well with her second serve (good pace).
- Emotional control poor. Borderline decisions unsettled Louise and resulted in an outburst of temper and annoyance. Her opponent played on this

Frankie's approach is a good one. He embraces the player's views from the off. The profile format he has used is similar to recognized models, but he has adapted it to meet his and Louise's needs. However, although the table is a good starting point to achieve 2B.P2, Frankie needs to expand the performance profile to gather similar information about Louise's technical, fitness, and tactical abilities in order to be awarded the criteria, as well as repeating this for another sport.

Frankie's commentary performs two roles. It demonstrates the method he used to collect data during the game, and is therefore evidence for 2B.P2, as well as serving to describe Louise's qualities, traits, and attributes for 2B.P3. I would have preferred to see the notes Frankie took during the game supported separately by a description.

However, Frankie's commentary does support his initial assessment of Louise's psychological and attitudinal profile and his descriptions are good. If he had explicitly made the link back to the initial profile, his comments could have been even better, but Frankie has made a good start. If he continues to describe all the qualities, traits, and attributes and repeat the process for a second sport, Frankie should be able to achieve the criteria for 2B.P3.

To finish this part of the assignment, Frankie still needs to review Louise's performance profile and summarize her development goals in order to meet the criteria for 2C.P4. For example, he could set Louise the short-term goal of getting through her next match without losing her temper with herself or with the umpire.

Finally, Frankie then needs to produce similar work for a second sport.

Meeting the Level 2 Merit criteria

Development plan for Lucy, a talented 14-year-old gymnast

Sara Summers

Development in fitness for asymmetric bars

Goal 1: Improve overall flexibility and range of movement around the shoulder.

Goal 2: Improve muscular endurance in arms.

Goal 3: Improve power, especially at dismount.

Actions to improve fitness for asymmetric bars

- Dedicated stretching routine planned, working on upper body to improve shoulder flexibility and range of movement.
- Weight training programme to improve upper body strength and muscular endurance.
- Plyometrics sessions (medicine ball catch) to develop upper body power.

Sara has attempted to meet the criteria for 2C.M3 by producing a presentation that builds on her evaluation of Lucy's qualities, traits, and attributes (which we can't see here). Unfortunately, Sara hasn't applied the assessment criteria accurately. She needs to provide a lot more detail. She needs to explain the aims and objectives of the development plan, before going on to include information on *why* each individual goal has been set. For example:

Goal 1: Improve overall flexibility and range of movement around the shoulder. This is needed because your fitness profile, specifically the static shoulder flexibility test, indicated only average readings and as routines on the asymmetric bars require extensive movement around the shoulder area this needs to be improved.

Sara also needs to explain the actions for development in more detail, making sure that all tasks are SMARTER. What exercises does she expect Lucy to do? How often should she do them? What improvement is required in what timescale, and how will it be measured? And all of this needs to be tied into Sara's evaluation of Lucy's qualities, traits, and attributes.

All this has to be done for two sports too, so a big effort is required from Sara if she is going to meet the criteria for 2B.M2 and 2C.M3!

Hello Richard,

I'm glad you like the look of your development plan and I'm also pleased you're asking questions about it.

As we discussed at the face-to-face meeting, there are certain technical aspects of your squash game that need to improve, especially as you will be playing in a higher league next season where the competition will be much tougher.

As your technical performance profile identified, your defensive boast is the area where improvements are most needed. The 20 per cent success rate during matches is low and will be targeted by better players. The development activities will help improve your technique and ultimately your ability to compete at the higher level. The three-month target is realistic as you have the basic racket skills but need to work on executing them under pressure.

The practice drills we have identified will progressively develop the skill levels needed, and integrating them into each training session will help improve the reliability of the shot so it becomes an automatic response during a game. The scheduled training matches with Toby will help replicate the standard you will be faced with in the higher league. Toby is experienced at this level and is particularly strong at forcing opponents to the back of the court. These matches will be played at a level of intensity that will require you to play at the top of your game, and, although you will want to win, the main focus will be on your defensive boast. The games will be videoed so we can analyse your performance afterwards.

Alfie has certainly justified why certain activities have been included in Richard's development plan, linking them to the completed performance profile and the level at which Richard wants to compete in the future. There also appears to be a clear rationale for choosing specific drills, which we can't see here but which will have been developed to meet the criteria for 2C.M3.

This level of detail indicates that Alfie is more than capable of meeting the criteria for 2C.D3 as long as he continues in this way.

Glossary

A

Abduction the name given the movement at a joint when a part of the body is taken away from the centre line of the body is a sideways motion. It is the opposite of adduction

Accelerative speed the speed with which you start moving faster

Acute injuries these are injuries that reach a crisis quickly

Adduction the name given to the movement at a joint when a part of the body is moved towards the centre line of the body in a sideways motion. It is the opposite of abduction

Adhere when you adhere to something you stick to it, so adherence factors are the things that keep you committed to a course of action and barriers to adherence are the things that get in the way of this

Aerobic endurance a measure of how efficiently you are able to keep your muscles supplied with nutrients and oxygen

Aerobic energy system when the energy you are using is created with oxygen present you are using the aerobic energy system

Agility the ability to move and change direction quickly and under control

Agonist when a muscle pulls to create movement it is called the agonist or prime mover

Aim the purpose or intention of an event or action

Anaerobic endurance a measure of your muscles' ability to work for an extended period of time without burning oxygen

Anaerobic energy system when the energy you are using is created without enough oxygen present you are using the anaerobic energy system. There are two parts to the anaerobic energy system: the ATP-CP/alactic acid energy system and the glycolysis/lactic acid energy system

Antagonist muscles work in pairs to bring about movement because they can only pull and not push. When the agonist pulls to create movement, the partner muscle is called the antagonist

Autocractic (command) leadership a style of leadership where the leader gives out instructions that the group follows

B

Balance the ability to keep the body stable, when still or moving, by keeping the centre of gravity over the base of support

Balanced diet a diet that consists of the right balance of the six components of a healthy diet (carbohydrates, fat, protein, water, vitamins, and minerals)

Body composition a measure of how much of your body is made up of fat-free mass, of vital organs, and how much is made up of fat

Borg Rating of Perceived Exertion Scale (Borg RPE) a scale used to measure exercise intensity by asking a performer to rate their perceived level of exertion

C

Cardiovascular system the name given to the body system that comprises the blood, the heart, and the blood vessels. The main role of the cardiovascular system is to transport oxygen and nutrients to all the tissues in the body and to remove waste products, such as carbon dioxide from them

Circumduction the name given to the movement at a joint when the bone or bones rotate fully around an axis to complete a full circle of movement

Concentric contraction the name given to a muscular contraction when the muscle shortens

Contingency plan an alternative plan that can be put into action, if necessary, to ensure that an event takes place safely if something unexpected happens

Coordination the ability to move two or more parts of the body at the same time efficiently and accurately, while ensuring a smooth flow of movement

D

Democratic leadership a style of leadership where the leader involved the group in the decision-making

Depression the name given to the movement at a joint when a part of the body moves downwards. It is the opposite of elevation

Diastolic pressure the pressure measured when the heart is relaxed

Dorsiflexion the name given to the movement at the ankle joint when the angle between the top of the foot and the tibia is decreased. It is the opposite of plantarflexion

Dynamic strength a measure of the amount of force that can be exerted repeatedly by a muscle

E

Eccentric contraction the name given to a muscular contraction when the muscle lengthens

Elevation the name given to the movement at a joint when a part of the body moves upwards. It is the opposite of depression

Ethics principles of moral conduct

Expiration the name used to describe what happens when we breathe out

Extension the name given to the movement at a joint when the joint is fully stretched out or straightened when it is extended. It is the opposite of flexion

Extrinsic the name given to external things that come from outside you

F

Flexibility a measure of the range of movement possible at a joint

Flexion the name given to the movement at a joint when a joint is bent and the two bones either side come towards each other. It is the opposite of extension

G

Gaseous exchange the name given to the process that ensures we get the oxygen that feeds our working muscles and organs into our blood, and the carbon dioxide and other waste products produced by the working muscles and organs out of our blood

Goal a clear idea of what you want to achieve. A goal can be short-term, medium-term, or long-term. Long-term goals can be outcome goals or performance goals

H

Hazard anything that could cause danger or harm, from a simple pool of water on the floor to a faulty light switch

Heart rate the number of times the heart contracts (or beats) per minute

Hypertrophy muscles adapt to training by increasing in size

I

Inspiration the name used to describe what happens when we breathe in

Intrinsic the name given to things that come from within you

Isometric contraction occurs when a muscle that is working stays the same length

Isotonic contraction occurs when a muscle changes length as it works

J

Joint and dual-use facilities a joint or dual-use facility has more than one 'owner' and the two owners share the costs of the facility, including staffing and maintenance

L

Laissez-faire leadership a style of leadership where the responsibility for decision-making is largely given to the group

Legislation the name given to rules and regulations that have been made into law by the government of a country

Ligaments the fibres that connect bone to bone

M

Maximum Heart Rate (MHR) the maximum number of times the heart can contract in one minute

Metabolic rate the rate at which the body burns calories

Muscular endurance a measure of how long your muscles can continue to exert force

Muscular strength a measure of the amount of force that can be generated by a muscle when it is contracting. It is measured in kilograms (kg) or Newtons (N)

Muscular system the name given to the body system that is made up of all the muscles in the body. There are three types of muscle: voluntary muscle, heart muscle, and involuntary muscle

O

Objective a small step that helps to achieve the overall aim

Objective assessment an assessment based on tangible information, such as statistical data

One Repetition Maximum (1RM) the maximum weight a person can lift in a single repetition of an exercise

Outcome what has actually been achieved at the end of an event or action. An intended or expected outcome is something that you hope to achieve at the end of an event or action

Overuse injuries these often occur when a sports performer pushes themselves hard over long periods of time and continuously puts the same muscles, bones, and joints under pressure

P

Physical Activity Readiness Questionnaire (PAR-Q) a questionnaire used to assess a client's current level of activity and their lifestyle to find out if they are fit enough to begin an exercise programme

Physiological injuries these are injuries that occur to the body

Plantarflexion the name given to the movement at the ankle joint when the angle between the top of the foot and the tibia is increased. It is the opposite of dorsiflexion

Power the ability to combine strength with speed to perform a strong muscular contraction very quickly. It is expressed as the time it takes to perform a task

Prime mover when a muscle pulls to create movement it is called the prime mover or agonist

Private sector this consists of all organizations that exist to make a profit

Psychological injuries these are injuries that occur to the mind

Public sector this consists of all organizations funded by the government

Pure speed your maximum speed

Q

Qualitative feedback describes feelings and behaviour. It will tell you why someone enjoyed something

Quantitative feedback measures things. It will tell you how many people enjoyed something

R

Reaction time the time it takes to respond to a stimulus

Regulations these control how a sport will be played or conducted, including what surface it will be played on and what safety standards need to be met in order to help prevent injuries. There are also regulations that cover how sport and leisure facilities should be run to ensure the health and safety of employees and visitors

Respiratory system the name given to the body system responsible for bringing about actions in the body that we call 'breathing'. Breathing is the means by which oxygen from the air is brought into the body

Risk   the combination of the likelihood of a hazard causing harm and the severity of the potential injury. The more likely it is to happen and the more severe the consequences, the greater the risk

Rotation   the name given to a spinning or turning movement at a joint, where part of the body rotates around an imaginary axis

Rules   these ensure a sport is played fairly by all competitors

S

Skeletal system   the name given to the body system that is made of bones and joints. The skeletal system performs five functions: protection, movement, shape, support, and blood production

Skill   something that often requires practice in order for something to be able to carry it out consistently, again and again. Skills can be discrete, continuous, or serial

Speed   a measure of how long it takes for an individual or an object to travel a certain distance

Speed endurance   being able to maintain your maximum speed or near your maximum speed for a period of time

Stroke volume   the amount of blood ejected with each contraction of the heart

Subjective assessment   an assessment based on personal opinions or beliefs

Systolic pressure   the pressure measured when the heart beats

T

Tactic   the plan of action used to outwit your opponent and gain an advantage

Technique   the way in which you perform a skill

Tendons   the fibres that attach muscles to bone

Thermoregularion   the name given to the process by which the cardiovascular system regulates the body's temperature by regulating the flow of blood to certain blood vessels. See *vasoconstriction* and *vasodilation*

Tidal Volume (TV)   the amount of air inhaled and exhaled with each breath

V

Vasoconstriction   blood vessels narrow (constrict) to restrict the amount of blood passing through them to stop the body's temperature falling too low

Vasodilation   blood vessels widen (dilate) to increase the amount of blood passing through them to stop the body's temperature rising too high

Vital capacity (VC)   the amount of air that can be forcibly exhaled after breathing in as deeply as possible

VO$_2$ max   a person's maximum oxygen uptake

Voluntary sector   this consists of all not-for-profit non-governmental organizations

Index